TEACHING WITH TECHNOLOGY

TEACHING WITH TECHNOLOGY

Seventy-Five Professors from Eight Universities
Tell Their Stories

DAVID G. BROWN
Editor

International Center for Computer-Enhanced Learning
Wake Forest University

Assisted by:
Diane J. Davis, University of Pittsburgh
Janet R. de Vry, University of Delaware
Susan J. Foster, University of Delaware
J. Thomas Head, Virginia Polytechnic Institute & State University
William K. Jackson, University of Georgia
Thomas Laughner, University of Notre Dame
Sue M. Legg, University of Florida
Leila C. Lyons, University of Delaware
Walter B. McRae, University of Georgia
Robert F. Pack, University of Pittsburgh
Larry Rapagnani, University of Notre Dame
Elizabeth Rubens, Indiana University (IUPUI)
Tom Wilkinson, Virginia Polytechnic Institute & State University
Gary E. Wittlich, Indiana University

ANKER PUBLISHING COMPANY, INC.
BOLTON, MASSACHUSETTS

Teaching with Technology
Seventy-five Professors from Eight Universities Tell Their Stories

ISBN 1-882982-34-7

Composition by Lyn Rodger, Deerfoot Studios
Cover design by Boynton Hue Studio

Anker Publishing Company, Inc.
176 Ballville Road
P. O. Box 249
Bolton, MA 01740-0249

www.ankerpub.com

ABOUT THE EDITOR

DAVID G. BROWN, a vice president at Wake Forest University, is a professor of economics and dean of the International Center for Computer-Enhanced Learning. He has served as president of Transylvania University, chancellor of the University of North Carolina, Asheville, and has chaired several national groups, including the American Association for Higher Education and the Higher Education Colloquium. While serving as Wake Forest's provost (1990-98), he chaired the committee that brought ubiquitous computing to Wake Forest University, founded the Annual Conference of Ubiquitous Computing Colleges and Universities, and founded the Journal of Computer-Enhanced Learning.

Since leaving the position of provost in 1998, he has authored and edited *Always in Touch, Electronically Enhanced Education,* and *Interactive Learning: Vignettes from America's Most Wired Campuses.* Editor of the *Journal of Computer-Enhanced Learning* and a member of the editorial board of *Multiversity,* he regularly leads workshops and has given more than 50 speeches to professional meetings. He currently serves on the EDUCAUSE Current Issues Committee and was chair of the Teaching and Learning Subcommittee of the Program Committee for the 1999 EDUCAUSE Annual Meeting.

Dr. Brown regularly teaches. An active user of technology in his own classroom, he has been recognized as an "inspirational teacher of undergraduates" by the University of North Carolina, Chapel Hill.

ABOUT THE
LEARNING TECHNOLOGY CONSORTIUM

Founded in 1997, the Learning Technology Consortium (LTC) is comprised of nine universities with common interests and facing common challenges in the area of teaching and learning with technology: Indiana University, University of Delaware, University of Florida, University of Georgia, University of Notre Dame, University of Pittsburgh, University of North Carolina, Chapel Hill, Virginia Polytechnic Institute and State University, and Wake Forest University.

The member institutions have similar instructional goals, and each has developed strong technology and faculty support programs. LTC representatives meet twice each year at a member campus to exchange ideas and experiences, to discuss issues related to instructional technology, and to identify areas for collaboration.

Faculty from many of the LTC universities have contributed to this book in an effort to share their instructional experiences with colleagues.

TABLE OF CONTENTS

PART III: VIGNETTES
COURSES TAUGHT WITH TECHNOLOGY

Physical Sciences, Mathematics, and Engineering

Biological and Health Sciences

Languages, Literature, and the Humanities

Art and Music

Business, Education, and Social Sciences

PREFACE

The intent of this book is to provide a gold mine of specific ways in which technology may be used to enhance teaching and learning. This is a practical guide to current and effective practice. Our target readers are all those who are involved—or would like to be involved—in redesigning courses, both face-to-face and online.

ORGANIZATION OF
TEACHING WITH TECHNOLOGY

Part I of *Teaching with Technology* consists of four chapters that provide an introduction to the concept and practice of teaching with technology. Chapter 4, "A Framework for Redesigning a Course" includes a worksheet that may be especially helpful in transforming a traditional course to one that integrates technology.

Part II describes the computing environments at each of the eight universities featured in *Teaching with Technology*. These eight chapters provide information on each university's computer infrastructure and faculty development efforts and set a helpful contextual framework for the courses taught with technology that are presented in Part III.

Part III is the heart of the volume, containing 52 vignettes by teaching faculty from the eight universities comprising the Learning Technology Consortium. (The University of North Carolina, Chapel Hill reactivated its participation in the LTC too late to join this project.) Each brief vignette describes a specific course, the technology tools used, the educational notions behind course design, course outcomes, and lessons learned. At the end of each essay, contact information is provided for those who wish more information on a specific course.

The vignettes in Part III are grouped by discipline: physical sciences, mathematics, and engineering; biological and health sciences; languages, literatures, and the humanities; art and music; and business, education, and social sciences. Vignettes common to a particular university can be located through the University Index at the back of the volume.

Since the use of computers tends to be specific to discipline and to educational philosophy, separate indexes are provided so all the vignettes written by, for example, chemists or from a desire to emphasize, say, immediate feedback, may be quickly identified. Introductory chapters and a concluding chapter provide an overview and summary.

ACKNOWLEDGMENTS

As was the case with our book *Interactive Learning*, we have many people to thank for their various contributions. When vignettes are compiled from so many people and places, the volume's editor accumulates many debts. Most of all, thanks go to the individual professors who have taken time from their normal teaching and research responsibilities to share their experiences with others. These authors were chosen by a corps of assistant editors, whose hard work has provided quality control and coherence to this project. A special thanks is due Julie Edelson and Janice Schuyler, both of Wake Forest, who edited and nurtured the volume to publication. The financial responsibility for the volume was assumed by Wake Forest's International Center for Computer-Enhanced Learning under the leadership of Craig Runde and John Anderson.

Together, we hope that each reader will gain insight from the ideas and experiences of others. If questions remain, or if you wish to share one of your own insights, please email me at brown@wfu.edu.

David G. Brown
Wake Forest University

PART I
INTRODUCTION

CHAPTER 1

AN OVERVIEW

David G. Brown, Wake Forest University

Seizing opportunity requires thought, creativity, and time. Suddenly, with computers, today's professors have a bafflement of alternatives. Hard choices must be made.

The beauty of this new, multitooled environment is that each choice can be evaluated against teaching objectives, educational philosophy, student constituency, aspirations, experience, disciplinary distinctions, instructor predilections and capacities, and the unique teaching environment.

Together, the essays in this volume display both the multiplicity of options and the diversity among choices made. Our authors were selected by the teaching-with-technology centers at eight of the nation's most technologically advanced universities. They are the proud exemplars and early adopting professors from the exemplar and early adopting campuses! The courses they chronicle are the accumulated result of years of experimentation. Mid and late adopters should not expect to replicate instantly what has taken our authors years to achieve.

These vignettes are to be mined for educational notions that resonate with our own and for creative ideas. Usually, it is best to limit the ambitions and complexities of first efforts with technology. Redesign efforts seem always to take more time than anticipated. Two guidelines may be helpful here:

- Go first for the "low hanging fruit," the computer-supported enhancements that yield high benefit for modest effort.

- Undertake a project that can, within available budgets and time, impact an entire course. Don't spend a week redesigning the first three class sessions and leave untouched the thirty-two remaining. Leave the multimedia CD for later.

The most important insight from these vignettes is not to be found in computer usage that pushes against the limits of our knowledge. The key message is in the redundancies. There is a core strategy, common to most computer enhanced-learning initiatives:

- Virtually all authors are pursuing more interactivity and collaboration.

- Virtually all authors are using email, URL citations, and posting course materials to the web.

- Virtually all authors report high scores on end-of-course student evaluations and their own sense that computers are making a positive learning difference.

First steps toward computer enhancements should wisely focus on the core. The embellishments can be added later. Big payoffs come from adopting the core, especially when balanced against short learning curves, low risks, and modest investment requirements.

CHAPTER 2

THE JURY IS IN!

David G. Brown, Wake Forest University

More computers equal more learning. This rule is broken by occasional neglect, misuse, or mismatch, but overall, there is a positive relationship between the availability/use of computers and the amount of learning that occurs. Students using computers as one tool in the learning process tend to learn more subject matter and, at the same time, acquire the lifetime skill of information fluency.

Such bold statements call for evidence. In *Interactive Learning* (Brown, 2000), where 143 essayists from 36 universities were asked to cite their evidence that the technology used in their teaching increased learning, the answers could be placed in three categories:

- matched pair outcomes on examinations

- the perceptions and opinions of students and faculty

- metadata regarding the time spent on various tasks

Essayists in this volume provide similar answers. Among the matched pair answers are the 40% decreases in failure rates cited in beginning calculus by Virginia Tech and in beginning physics by IUPUI. Citing both local and national tests, several universities noted higher grades. Many essayists have received higher student evaluations than they did before using the computer and higher evaluations than sections of the same course without computer enhancements that are taught by other professors.

Using metadata automatically generated by the computer, Francis Doyle at the University of Delaware interprets the frequent use of the "muddiest point forum," especially immediately prior to an examination, as evidence of its usefulness. Others, for example,

Wake Forest University's Gordon McCray, cite the frequent use of practice questions and the correlation of using practice questions with final course grades as evidence that the computer is proving useful in learning.

When asked for measured results, almost three-fourths of our essayists cite high scores on student evaluations of teaching, high rates of student satisfaction with the computer-enhanced portions of their courses, and their own observations about the positive impact of computers.

However, the most compelling evidence is in the logic. First, more choice leads to more learning. The teacher has a larger, more diverse box of tools to deploy. No one tool fits all situations. Just as carpenters can be more productive when their tool kits are not restricted to a hammer, so also can teachers be more productive when new computer-enhanced tools are added to their alternatives. The computer is one more option. Among the challenges in delivering diverse material from diverse teachers to diverse learners in diverse circumstances, there are some situations where the computer is the most effective tool. In a particular situation—for example, a parent teaching a child one-on-one—the computer should not and will not be chosen if it is not viewed as the most effective choice. In other circumstances—for example, a single teacher of 400 students living in diverse geographies—the computer's interactive and individualizing capacities will lead to its use. The point here is that the computer adds a rich array of options.

Second, the computer is a proven means of pursuing proven educational strategies. The computer supports repetition, for example, replaying the videotape of a lecture over and over until the points are understood. The computer is useful in supporting dialog (question-

and-answer, point and counterpoint), a primary way in which we all learn. The computer supports individual attention, even in large classes. It supports collaborative learning and continuous communication. The computer assists professors in their delivery of the picture that is worth a thousand words, of sound accompanying text, of attention-grabbing animation. Computer simulation supports practicing new concepts. The computer's worth is proven not by studies of computerized learning but by studies of the worth of repetition, simulation, visualization. If the computer supports these activities, it enhances learning.

Third, we already know that time and effort invested in rethinking usually results in improved outcomes. The sudden appearance of a rich array of new teaching tools that are enabled by the computer has forced the entire profession to rethink what it is doing and why. At the very least, the yellowed lecture notes must now be compared and contrasted with the new alternatives. This refocusing is likely to be with us for a long time, because new teaching tools are being delivered daily by the software professions around the world. The constant flow of new alternatives is likely to keep warm the debates about best methods.

Fourth, both students and faculty consistently testify that they can observe the positive difference in learning. Students choose computer-enhanced courses over traditional courses, and faculty continue to use computer enhancements after experiencing their results. Very few faculty who have gone to the trouble of adding computer enhancements to their teaching methods have later abandoned them.

The case for computers rests on scant amounts of hard evidence, and their undeniable logical advantages for specific learning methods, diverse learning environments and subject matters and learning styles, for time on task, collaborative learning, and more options available to both professor and student.

REFERENCE

Brown, D. G. (Ed.). (2000). *Interactive learning: Vignettes from America's most wired campuses.* Bolton, MA: Anker.

CHAPTER 3

CENTERS FOR TEACHING WITH TECHNOLOGY

David G. Brown, Wake Forest University

Each of the eight universities represented in this volume has, in its own way, made major commitments to assure that faculty are in a position to consider the use of new technologies in their teaching. University-by-university details are provided in chapters 5 through 12.

PREREQUISITES TO ENCOURAGE TEACHING WITH TECHNOLOGY

Individual faculty members bring experience and special knowledge to each decision about course organization, individual nurturing, and what to do in class tomorrow. Course objectives, instructor capacities and preferences, student capacities and preferences, time and resource constraints, subject matter structure, institutional policy, pedagogical alternatives, and distractions of the moment must also be accounted for. It is simply not practical to expect course designers, often unfamiliar with the subject matter of a particular discipline or the distinctive circumstances of individual students, to acquire the necessary breadth to work on thousands of university courses. Universities must rely on the proven strategy of investing virtually all authority for classroom strategy in individual professors.

This model presumes that professors are well informed about their alternatives. Faculty must be enabled and motivated to keep up with the developments in their field and to judge their efficacy for various teaching assignments.

BARRIERS TO TEACHING WITH TECHNOLOGY

Three barriers face faculty who attempt to keep up-to-date on teaching with technology.

Infrastructure

Faculty will not and should not take time away from student interaction and scholarship to learn techniques that cannot be applied in their own teaching setting. Before faculty will explore teaching with technology, they must have powerful computers. Before faculty will explore the web and email, they must have reliable network access. Before faculty will require computer-dependent assignments, they must have confidence that all students have fair and appropriate access. Without appropriate hardware, networks, and student access, faculty development programs never get off the ground. Fortunately, the universities represented in this volume have decisively overcome this first barrier.

Motivation

What is the payoff for faculty exploration of new computer-enhanced learning methods? Rarely is it pay bonuses and cash awards. Faculty are driven by curiosity, by a sense of obligation to their students, and by the norms of the profession. Fortunately, all three of the key motivators are pushing today's faculty to consider new methods. Email has become the established standard for communicating and collaborating. American scientists must now submit funding proposals to most government agencies electronically. Most search committees explore prospective faculty recruits' capabilities in the use of technology. The teaching professions, as a whole, believe that the computer provides a useful alternative, and they expect fully qualified members of the profession to be knowledgeable about these methods. At this point, all faculty have a high motivation to explore the possibilities of computer-enhanced teaching.

Understandably, faculty do not wish blindly to implement new methods only later to find them inferior to proven older methods and to have misdirected an entire cohort of learners. Faculty are appropriately cautious. They are also unwilling to "dumb down" their courses because computers and the knowledge to use them wisely are not available. Faculty at the eight universities represented in this volume and throughout the country are highly motivated—without special cash awards—to figure out what is best for their students and to maintain the respect of their colleagues. Motivation is not a problem.

Time

At Wake Forest University, we once renovated the chemistry building while maintaining all classes in the same building. We taught in the labs while they were under construction. It was tough. Analogously, faculty members are challenged to assure that current students are taught with the same success as in the past, largely by traditional methods, while simultaneously learning and testing new methods. During the times of rapid change, time must somehow be found to maintain the old and to explore the new. The eight universities featured in *Teaching with Technology* have devised a number of programs to minimize learning time, to lower the learning curve. All of them have sponsored learning sessions outside normal teaching times. Many provide special grants that often involve release time.

With the three barriers in mind, we now examine the computer infrastructures of our eight universities, focusing on their faculty development programs.

PRACTICES THAT FACILITATE TEACHING WITH TECHNOLOGY

From Chapters 5 through 12 emerge common practices that seem important for successful faculty development programs:

- **Start from course objectives, not technology.** The impetus for course redesign is often the availability of new technology. Faculty members typically come to the center asking for technology training, typically not educational theory. However, after a brief exposure to the types of technology tools that might be made available (for example, listservs, PowerPoint, web pages), redesigning a course requires an understanding of educational convictions, teaching style, and course circumstances.

- **Consider nontechnological solutions.** Centers must be valued for their support of effective teaching and not thought of as blind advocates for technology. Once teaching objectives are newly highlighted, the consideration of nontechnological as well as technological strategies adds credibility and value.

- **Offer just-in-time instruction.** Instruction in how to use PowerPoint, how to manipulate an Excel chart, or how to post course materials to the web must be fast and frequently available. Both faculty and students are reluctant to learn quickly forgotten skills until just prior to their need to apply those skills to a specific course. Education must be specifically timed to match a need. General classes are generally poorly enrolled.

- **Recognize disciplinary and student-constituency differences.** It is wise to have available specialists who are familiar with the distinctive challenges in various disciplines. Scientists tend to use the computer very differently than artists or social scientists. Techniques appropriate for hybrid courses with both face-to-face and online elements are often not appropriate or even possible for virtual courses.

- **Recognize the lowest common denominator of student access.** Web pages with slow-loading graphics should be avoided if some students may be accessing through slow modems. If students are using several browsers, materials that require a specific Internet browser should be avoided. Java applets and other specialized programming must be limited to those circumstances where the expected readers can access the materials.

- **Use development teams and encourage collaboration.** Rare is the individual who knows the subject matter, pedagogy, and technology and has the time to maintain a teaching and research schedule, while single-handedly creating a totally new version of a course. Teaming is desirable and essential.

- **Support both online and face-to-face courses.** Many of the new strategies ultimately used in on-line courses are first tested in face-to-face settings.

- **Identify a preferred course management system.** Several universities use WebCT. Several use CourseInfo. Several have their own course management system or course shell. From all perspectives—faculty effort, student effort, support staff needs, overall costs—the advantages of a standard course shell are immense. When using the same course shell, faculty members learn from each other, and students learn from roommates and friends. Fewer support staff and less training are needed, and when needs arise, the advice can be more knowledgeable, and the training more frequent.

- **Provide computer labs and studio classrooms for high-end users.** Expensive equipment can be better justified when it is available to a broad spectrum of faculty.

- **Gain advice and/or direction from faculty users.** Policy and advisory committees are the most common way to gain such input.

- **Assure individual, when-needed access to five talents.** The five talents are faculty mentors (colleagues willing to share their prior experiences); hook-up specialists and help desk advisors (technologists capable of establishing and maintaining basic systems); learning tool specialists (trainers and mentors willing to teach software programs); instructional designers (specialists to design and program some of the more complex uses of the computer); and grunt workers (people to enter new data and implement routine postings to the web).

PROGRAMS AND STRATEGIES FOR FACULTY DEVELOPMENT

All of the universities in this book offer help for faculty who are implementing and using technology-centered courses. They include a wide range of support.

- **Help desks.** Professionally staffed help desks with student consultants assisting in the staffing. Most are open seven days a week, 24 hours a day.

- **A wide variety of courses, classes, and seminars.** There are two-hour programs to teach a particular software, day-long programs to introduce course management systems, multiple-session courses to teach html and other hard-to-learn applications, and (in seven of the eight universities) summer institutes where faculty gain practice in applying available technologies to specific courses and projects. Most universities maintain public listings of upcoming learning opportunities, which are freely accessible from the web. Only a few universities rely on online modules for a substantial portion of their training.

- **Individual consultation.** Following up courses, classes, and seminars are opportunities for individual consultation, often in a central computer laboratory. Some are central to colleges, and some to the entire university. These are the same centers that house one-of-a-kind equipment, such as an extra-large color printer, for general campus access. Even the campuses with ubiquitous computer ownership among all students (three of the eight) maintain high-end laboratories for specific departmental and college use.

- **Faculty grant programs.** All of the universities operate faculty grant programs, most of which provide release time to incorporate technology into teaching. Some of the programs place special emphasis upon the largest classes that impact the most students. Most of these grant programs have been seeded by a foundation grant but are now at least partially hard funded from university budgets.

- **Standardization.** At most universities, training and consultation are greatly simplified by the specification of a preferred course management system, preferred Internet browser, preferred email system, other preferred software, and, in the case of two universities, preferred hardware. Such standardization means that relevant training sessions can be offered more frequently, that help desk workers can be more familiar with the issues likely to be raised, and, most of all, that students and faculty can find friends and associates to help them with their problems.

- **Student assistance.** Most of the universities have formal programs to hire students, both to supplement staff in IS departments and to aid individual professors.

- **Course designers.** Most universities hire course designers and focus their availability upon the development of distance-learning courses.

ORGANIZATION AND FURTHER EXPLORATION

The organizational charts for teaching-with-technology centers understandably reflect the unique history of each university. No two centers carry the same name. The only general trend is toward consolidation. Several universities have recently merged units, such as multimedia, teaching and learning, distance-learning support, and course designing. An impressive listing of the URLs for well over one hundred online university teaching centers is maintained by the University of Kansas at http://eagle.cc.ukans.edu/~cte/Educational Sites.html.

CHAPTER 4

A Framework for Redesigning a Course

Janet R. de Vry, University of Delaware
David G. Brown, Wake Forest University

Technology by itself neither improves learning nor saves money. Used improperly, technology can cause learning roadblocks and cost a great deal. New technology offers new choices. To make wise choices, the exciting search for new learning strategies had best start by focusing on what we want our students to learn. In conversations with faculty members who are interested in using technology, curriculum redesign facilitators from teaching-with-technology centers usually ask them what they want their students to learn. If coverage of material is the simple objective, putting a syllabus online and adding links to Internet resources can make more information available more of the time, and it is easy to update. If avoiding hours of mundane course administration is the objective, an electronic grading book may be a response.

The real promise of technology in learning, however, is using it to do something that we could not currently do as well using traditional methods. A conceptual framework is needed to assess the promise of the various technologies; something not laden with pedagogical jargon, backed by research, and easy to understand.

Choosing a Rubric of Objectives for the Course Redesign Process

To provide context for course redesign, many conceptual frameworks are useful. Many disciplinarians construct unique frameworks based on common sense derived from experience. Bloom's six levels of complexity (knowledge, comprehension, application, analysis, synthesis, and evaluation), especially his suggestions of verbs for each level, often guide course designers, who start from detailed statements of objectives for each course unit. Howard Gardner's (1999) ten types of intelligence (linguistic, logical-mathematical, spatial, bodily-kinesthetic, musical, interpersonal, intrapersonal, naturalist, spiritual, and existential) are another guide. No single framework will be best for all individuals in all circumstances.

To illustrate the type of "thinking system" that is often helpful, we have chosen the "Seven Principles for Good Practice in Undergraduate Education" developed by Arthur Chickering and Zelda Gamson (1987). Because of their broad acceptance by faculty from many disciplines and types of colleges, the seven principles offer an easy-to-understand framework for categorizing the educational notions that inform the essays that follow.

The Seven Principles for Good Practice in Undergraduate Education

1) **Good practice encourages student/faculty contact.** Contact with faculty can encourage students during difficult times in their college experience. Faculty are invigorated with fresh perspectives and can share their love of learning and problem solving skills with students.

2) **Good practice encourages cooperation among students.** Sharing ideas and responding to the suggestions of others can improve thinking skills. Learning to cooperate prepares students for the workplace.

3) **Good practice encourages active learning.** We must provide opportunities for students to gather, organize, analyze, present, and challenge information and assumptions. In so doing, we give them skills for a world where the answer is not in the book. We give them skills to ask questions we have not yet imagined.

4) **Good practice gives prompt feedback.** Students benefit from knowing early in a course how they are doing and what they must do to improve. Professors are more effective when they are adjusting assignments and approaches on the basis of student feedback. The dialogue between a professor and a student enables each to help the other.

5) **Good practice emphasizes time on task.** Learning is difficult. There is simply no substitute for the amount of time and concentration it requires. Students must be enticed to, and engaged in, the learning process. By providing more action, more interactivity, greater scheduling flexibility, and a broader spectrum of learning materials, technology can increase the amount of time and effort students devote to their studies.

6) **Good practice communicates high expectations.** We must set high standards and communicate how students can achieve them. We need to make our grading rubrics available. We should showcase excellent student work.

7) **Good practice respects diverse talents and ways of learning.** Our world is multicultural, and all humans, regardless of culture and gender differences, have preferred ways of learning. Traditionally, higher education has relied heavily on abstract conceptualizations of theories and formulas. Using a variety of teaching and learning strategies helps those students who need more concrete experience to master subjects. Also, students learn at different rates: repetition is more important for some students than for others.

A New Set of Tools

Faculty come to workshops on teaching with technology to learn enough about a set of new tools to enable them to determine if its use will increase teaching effectiveness and learning.

Worldwide, the teaching profession has been provoked to reexamine teaching methods by the sudden appearance of many new possibilities enabled by the computer. Ultimately, the reexamination catalyzed by computer tools may or may not result in the actual deployment of technology. It is almost certain, however, that the process of teaching will be improved by the very act of reexamination.

A Framework for Matching Principles with Technology Tools

From the essays that follow, the following matrix has been devised. It is offered as a framework that may be helpful when redesigning a course or curriculum. The left-most column lists some of the most common tools and activities used in college courses, both technological and nontechnological. Many other tools and activities could be added as additional rows in the matrix. The remaining columns are headed by different Chickering-Gamson principles that an instructor might wish to augment in the redesign process. The columns might instead be Bloom's six levels of complexity, Gardner's ten types of intelligence, or another rubric. (See Greg Kearsley at http://www.gwu.edu/~tip for a survey of 50 different theories.)

A professor considering course redesign might, for example, decide to increase student/faculty contact, hypothesize which tools or activities could best be deployed, and then plan the course in detail. Less desirably, a professor might start with a tool or activity and query its likely usefulness in achieving more/better student/faculty contact.

Figure 4.1 Principles and Tools/Activities Matrix*

(For Hypothetical Course with 10%–90% of the Activity Face-to-Face)

TOOLS AND ACTIVITIES**	1. Student/ faculty contact	2. Cooperation among students	3. Active learning	4. Prompt feedback	5. Time on task	6. High expectations of learning	7. Respect for diverse ways
1. Use library materials & electronic databases							
2. Communicate via email & listservs	*	*	*	*	*	*	
3. Use practice quizzes & exercises			*	*	*	*	
4. Establish a web page for course with course management system	*			*		*	
5. Lecture in class or chat session	*						*
6. Present PowerPoint slides					*	*	
7. Handle course mechanics outside class	*		*		*		
8. Use subgroup projects & discussions		*	*				
9. Use multimedia presentations					*		*
10. Discuss with entire class, face-to face or online	*		*				

* Asterisks appear when a tool is frequently and effectively used to support the goal identified.

** Tools and activities are listed from those used more frequently and effectively to support the goals of the course at the top to those used less frequently and effectively.

Used properly, all tools and activities support, to some extent, each of the seven principles. However, the average faculty member tends to have more success with some of the tools than with others. Our assistant editors, who have consulted with hundreds of faculty members on their respective campuses, were asked to rate each of the tools and activities by how frequently redesigning faculty effectively incorporate them into their hybrid (that is, 10%–90% face-to-face) courses. The winner was the use of library materials and electronic databases. Email and listservs were close behind.

A careful reading of the essays, coupled with a further polling of our assistant editors, provides more specific insight about which tools and activities tend to be most frequently and successfully used to support each principle. When reading down a column (for example, more student/faculty contact is desired), an asterisk at email means that many are using email effectively to support more contact between students and faculty.

The matrix is presented as a compact and easy device that encourages redesigners to consider the full spectrum of tools and relate them to the full spectrum of principles. The asterisks are an additional aid to suggest where it might be most fruitful to start. The matrix may also be used when designing all face-to-face courses and courses that are 100% online, but this ordering of the tools and asterisks is less relevant.

An individual may easily add tools and/or change principles. The idea behind the matrix is to provide a framework for thinking and to summarize best practice as represented by our vignettes.

One way to use this matrix is to identify one or two principles to be enhanced and then to check several boxes that would seem to offer the greatest promise. But principles and tools alone do not a course make. The tools are used to support specific activities and assignments. By listing the activities that might be incorporated into the course, one is well down the road to redesign.

In selecting tools, there is a delicate balance between ease of learning and ease of use on the one hand and effectiveness on the other. It's good fortune when a tool like email is one of the easiest and most universal technologies and also one of the most effective. Posting course materials to the web falls in this same category. More controversial are presentation tools, such as PowerPoint, which are effective in more limited circumstances. When assessing ease of use, it is important to account for both setting up the activity (normally, a cost in faculty time) and implementing the activity (a cost of both faculty and student time). For example, synchronous "bull sessions" are often not worth the cost, because modest benefits easily offset modest set-up costs but rarely justify the high time costs of participating in the actual sessions.

It may be helpful to cite a few specific examples of how tools, activities, and principles can be related from the essays and experiences at Learning Technology Consortium universities.

Principle 1: Student/faculty contact. No doubt about it—many of our essays emphasize that email is dramatically increasing student-faculty contact. When George Watson (Vignette 5) sent a "welcome email survey," he received responses from almost half of his students before the first class even met! Also successful with large classes are bulletin boards.

Threaded discussions and chat rooms can be successful if carefully structured to focus discussion on a narrow topic, actively monitored by the instructor, and even graded. One of the best uses of chat rooms is for focused question and answer prior to an exam. Setting up a student electronic communication group with no structure or requirements is like reserving a classroom and simply inviting students to attend and talk.

To provide close contact in large classes, trained student liaisons facilitate group discussions at the University of Delaware (Vignette 22) and the University of Florida (Vignette 7). David Allbritton (Vignette 48) is successfully using a Frequently Asked Questions web space and other online archives.

Principle 2: Cooperation among students. When faculty promote the use of bulletin boards, group mailing lists and the web, students start assisting each other. Anne Boyle (Vignette 32) sets up collaborative writing groups who work together toward a final written product. After initial email exchanges, preliminary papers are posted to the web and peer reviewed. Taking student collaboration a step further, she has set up a collaborative relationship with a writing class at Acadia University. Groups at both colleges peer review group written work from the other university.

At the University of Georgia (Vignette 39) students actively collaborate to produce a multimedia project thus gaining valuable technical skills, but they do so in the context of a classroom that is an informal live "studio" designed to foster professional and social interactions among students of differing levels of expertise.

Principle 3: Active learning. Active learning (i.e., engaging students as active participants in their own learning) resonates throughout these essays. Christine Pistella (Vignette 20) requires students to select a relevant web site and provide a critique of its usefulness, accuracy, and value for public health professionals or consumers.

In a totally online course in educational psychology at Indiana University (Vignette 46), computer conferencing and collaborative writing tools are used to extend class discussions, to promote small group projects, and to provide preparation for exams. What makes this truly exciting is they are using these same tools to do things previously done only in the classroom or in person, such as to structure role playing, to link students to preservice teachers as mentors, and to provide interaction with guest expert teachers.

At Virginia Tech's Math Emporium (Vignette 1) students can actively choose activities best suited to their learning style. They can meet with individual mentors, work through online courses, meet with a focus group, attend lectures, and take quizzes mostly at their own time and at their own choosing. This makes them take charge of their own learning rather than being passive recipients of what someone has already digested for them.

Principle 4: Prompt feedback. Online self-quizzing and surveys provide feedback about learning and are becoming increasingly popular as course management systems make them easier to implement and grade. Structuring the use of these tools for maximum result is the challenge.

Physics students at both Wake Forest (Vignette 2) and Indiana University (Vignette 4) use "Just-in-Time-Teaching." Student "warm up exercises" are posted to the web. Students complete and submit answers electronically just before class. Faculty can adjust their lecture based on student responses. At Wake Forest students receive automatic email feedback immediately on their multiple-choice responses.

Gordon McCray (Vignette 42) takes prompt feedback even further in his business class at Wake Forest University. Students take an online true/false type quiz and then automatically receive a probing response based on their initial answer. This immediate feedback

encourages them to think more deeply about the questions before submitting their final answer.

Katrien Christie's Italian students (Vignette 29) have a web-based personal tutor or reading assistant that provides immediate assistance. The students are guided through the text with various comprehension checks. Based on their answers, they receive a rich variety of tools including glosses, visualizations, and links that help students gain a sense of the cultural context of the words and phrases.

Principle 5: Time on task. Posting tests from previous semesters and solutions to in-class quizzes entice students to do more problems and spend more time on task (Vignette 13). Beyond providing rich links, having students hunt for answers, critique web-based information, or find their own links, all require that students spend more focused time than mere web surfing would require. Updating the site frequently or releasing information incrementally are other techniques mentioned in the vignettes that draw students to their web site.

Kern R. Trembath (Vignette 35) posts complete lecture notes to the web before each class and holds the class responsible for the information. He is shortening his lecture time and using the class time more and more to engage in meaningful dialogue.

Principle 6: High expectations of learning. Just as email is no longer a topic of debate, the online syllabus is becoming well accepted. Those syllabi and web sites that include clearly spelled out expectations, samples of exemplary student work, and grading rubrics are the most useful for setting high expectations.

Ellen Cohn (Vignette 21) uses the web to clearly communicate computing competency requirements to her future healthcare professionals. She links the competency requirement to specific activities that the student can use to obtain mastery.

Bernadine Barnes (Vignette 38) has students publish their work to the web. "Students write better when they have a purpose and an audience."

Marguerite Koepke (Vignette 39) has students use multimedia materials for their portfolio development and uses a class web site to make project progress available to all participants. Setting high standards, making new technological ways of achieving those standards available, and constantly evaluating student progress raises student expectations and performance.

Principle 7: Diverse ways of learning. The rich resources that most faculty are providing on the web, combined with the varieties of interaction allow for diverse learning styles that the printed word and lecture alone do not provide.

Donald Hall (Vignette 16) includes digitized photographs, video clips, sound and animations to illustrate insect behavior in an introductory science class.

Jeanne Sept (Vignette 18) provides a rich dataset that simulates authentic data from a wide range of archaeological sites. Students gain a simulated hands-on experience as archeologists.

The ultimate experiment in providing diverse ways of learning is the Math Emporium at Virginia Tech (Vignette 1) where students have the choice of computer-based learning modules, individual mentors, and lectures.

THE REDESIGN CHALLENGE

The seven principles are not the only framework currently available, but it has been widely accepted. There are certainly other worthy frameworks for thinking about enhancing learning. Many of these seem to include in one way or another the basic concepts specified in the seven principles. Some may add principles, such as community building and critical thinking. Some schools of thought focus more on one specific type of teaching technique, such as problem-based learning, which is an extension of active learning.

In this rapidly changing technological world, we need proven guideposts to help us know where we are going. Just as forming learning objectives is critical in determining what students will learn in the class, forming objectives about the purpose and function of technology is critical to whether or not the promise of technology to transform education will ever be realized. Without guidelines, we are adrift. We do not have time to drift. We have students to educate for a world far more technologically complex than we can imagine. They need to be well equipped.

REFERENCES

Chickering, A. W., & Gamson, Z. F. (1987, March). Seven principles for good practice in undergraduate education. *AAHE Bulletin, 39* (7), 3-7.

Gardner, H. (1999). *Intelligence reframed: Multiple intelligences for the 21st century.* New York, NY: Basic Books.

CONTACT INFORMATION

Janet R. de Vry
Manager, Instructional Services
IT/User Services
User Services, Smith Hall
University of Delaware
Newark, DE 19716
Email: janet@udel.edu
Phone: (302) 831-6714
Fax: (302) 831-4205

David G. Brown
Vice President and Dean of International Center for Computer-Enhanced Learning
Professor of Economics
Wake Forest University
P. O. Box 7328, Reynolda Station
Winston-Salem, NC 27109
Email: brown@wfu.edu
Phone: (336) 758-4878
Fax: (336) 758-4875

PART II
COMPUTING ENVIRONMENTS
AT EIGHT UNIVERSITIES

CHAPTER 5

COMPUTING ENVIRONMENT AT THE UNIVERSITY OF DELAWARE

Leila C. Lyons and Susan J. Foster

INTRODUCTION

The University of Delaware is a land-grant, space-grant, sea-grant, and urban-grant university of seven colleges, 38 research centers, and more than 21,000 matriculated students, including 3,250 graduate students. It is a private university with public support, recognized as a national leader in the use of information technologies and for its success in embedding technology-based information resources into the campus culture. The university employs exemplary campus-wide network planning, management, and accessibility practices and makes effective use of the network, the Internet, and Internet2 to enhance teaching, learning, and research, and to support administration and community service (see http://www.udel.edu).

The university promotes active and problem-based learning in introductory-level courses to develop students' critical learning habits early in their academic careers. University president David Roselle has made undergraduate education the centerpiece of his administration and created an ideal climate for educational transformation and innovation. Faculty training and development are essential to implement and to sustain outstanding student-centered teaching and learning.

DESCRIPTION OF THE COMPUTING ENVIRONMENT

The university's gigabit-switched, fiberoptic backbone reaches every research laboratory, office, classroom, and residence hall and provides links to the commodity Internet through two Internet service providers and through data services from the local telephone company to assure sufficient capacity and redundant access. The university is a charter member of Internet2 and uses an OC3 (155Mb/s) connection to the Abilene Internet2 network. All residence hall rooms, occupied by about half of the undergraduate student body, are wired for voice, video, and data. The university provides high-speed modem services for dial-up access to those living off campus, though increasing numbers are taking advantage of low-cost, full-service Internet service providers. All faculty and staff offices as well as classrooms, dining halls, and meeting spaces are connected to the campus network. Many classrooms have network connections at student seats, and many others are equipped with computers and network connections. Network connections are also available in library carrels, study areas, and general purpose computing facilities throughout the campus.

A centrally operated server cluster provides campus-wide email, web, and computation services. The university has centrally managed computing sites for general-purpose student computing and network access as well as extensive facilities within departments and colleges to support their academic programs. The university funds an information technology refreshment program for classrooms, faculty and administrative desktops, and general purpose computing facilities. The classroom technology program provides ongoing upgrades of analog and digital projection and display equipment. The program is designed to accommodate the four major types of campus classrooms and provides projection and display technology that faculty can readily connect to laptop computers for classroom presentations.

PROGRAMS THAT SUPPORT COMPUTER-ENHANCED LEARNING

Early in the 1990s, a cadre of university faculty leaders began to examine student learning styles and outcomes in their courses and to explore various ways to improve delivery of undergraduate education. Within a short time, this focused, faculty-driven project led to the creation of the Institute for Transforming Undergraduate Education (ITUE). The institute's faculty train and mentor their colleagues to implement active and problem-based learning in their respective courses. Now, at the end of the decade, nearly 30% of the faculty have participated in the institute and workshops for active learning strategies and effective use of technology in their courses. This has resulted in more than 150 courses revised or identified for transformation.

Incorporation of active inquiry based instruction has helped to refine the instructional mission and resources of the University of Delaware. Since 1994, the university has received and matched over three million dollars in competitive grant awards for course restructuring for active learning and for related faculty development. These include a 1998 grant from Pew Charitable Trusts to apply active and problem-based learning to high-enrollment courses in the social sciences, education and mathematics. In 1997, the University of Delaware was among only ten institutions to receive the National Science Foundation's Recognition Award for the Integration of Research and Education (RAIRE). At Delaware, more than 60% of all faculty and 90% of the sciences faculty participate in an undergraduate research program in which students conduct research with their faculty advisers.

FACULTY AND STUDENT ACCESS TO COMPUTERS

The university funds replacement of faculty desktop and laptop computers. Increasingly, faculty members are encouraged to use this program to acquire a laptop for the classroom and office. Computer ownership by students is strongly encouraged but not mandated. Undergraduate student ownership is currently at 86% and will continue to rise. Combining student-owned machines with those available in computing labs and classrooms, students have access to more than 14,000 computer workstations—a ratio approaching one-to-one.

All enrolled students have access to university network services, such as email, the resources of the university's intranet, the Internet, and the web. The university is nationally recognized for fostering responsible computing on campus and educating future citizens of the electronic community through the Electronic Community Citizenship Exam (ECCE). Each new student is required to pass ECCE with a perfect score before gaining access to university computing and network resources. In a 1999 survey, 98% of upperclass students reported that they regularly use electronic mail to correspond with professors; 86% reported that their professors use information technologies in the classroom, and approaching 100% use the intranet, Internet, computational services, and the web to complete assignments.

SYSTEMS FOR SUPPORTING FACULTY USE OF COMPUTERS

The Office of Information Technologies (IT) provides integrated services for teaching, learning, research, service, and administration. The technological maturity of the campus has enabled many campus collaborations. IT's collaboration with the continuing education department is transforming delivery of distance-learning courses from a solely videotape-based model to one that uses the web and streaming video. IT partners with several campus units to provide comprehensive services to faculty: pedagogy, scholarly resources, course design, and the technology to support delivery. A Teaching, Learning and Technology Institute (TLTI), offered twice a year to faculty, is a highly visible example of this collaboration. The institute's curriculum covers a wide range of topics, such as pedagogical issues of active learning and best use of classroom time, technology in teacher education, and technology workshops. These workshops include the use of computing productivity software in the classroom and web skills that range from putting a syllabus on the web using templates through advanced html skills. Also included are teaching a course on the web using streaming video and a web-based instructional development and management environment, and the use of digital cameras and digital video production.

Critical to the university's support of faculty is a teaching, learning, and technology center, called the PRESENT, and a suite of web-based resources that are a virtual equivalent. At this center, the first question to faculty is always, "What are your teaching goals?" not, "What technology do you want to use?" Most of the University of Delaware faculty whose vignettes appear in this book are ITUE and TLTI graduates who have also worked closely with the PRESENT to develop and to prototype their ideas.

Numerous faculty develop their own course web pages. Many more use central servers (called scholar servers) or microcomputers to incorporate discipline-specific software into their courses. Use of automatically generated electronic mailing lists for class communication and newsgroups for class discussions is almost universal. An increasing number of faculty work with IT to stream their courses to the web, enabling students to attend them live or at any other time. A growing number of faculty have developed online courses using an instructional management system developed at the university. The university is also moving distance-learning courses that are currently videotape-based only to online courses developed with an instructional management system.

SUMMARY

The robust and ubiquitous information technology infrastructure at the University of Delaware, coupled with its institutional goals to implement and to sustain outstanding student-centered education, provides an environment in which computer-enhanced teaching and learning thrive.

CONTACT INFORMATION

Leila C. Lyons
Director
013 Smith Hall
University of Delaware
Newark, DE 19716
Email: leila@udel.edu
Phone: (302) 831-1983
Fax: (302) 831-4205

Susan J. Foster
Vice President for Information Technologies
University of Delaware
Newark, DE 19716
Email: sfoster@udel.edu
Phone: (302) 831-6068
Fax: (302 831-3283

CHAPTER 6

COMPUTING ENVIRONMENT AT THE UNIVERSITY OF FLORIDA

Sue M. Legg

Rapid changes in technology cause computing environments to be in a constant state of flux. What used to be impossible or impractical now becomes an urgent priority, and that seems to be a never-ending scenario. There is no question that upgrading our infrastructure is a top priority for the University of Florida (UF). This overview of our computing environment will describe the on-campus infrastructure and its expansion into the state of Florida and beyond. Changes in administrative computer services and policies will be described as well. Access to, and academic support for, computing and multimedia have infused technology into the curriculum.

INFRASTRUCTURE

The infrastructure for multimedia computing on campus includes networking, mainframe computing, computing laboratories, and associated computer support units. The UF environment is a complex, distributed system with some centralized functions.

The Northeast Regional Data Center (NERDC) is located on campus and provides mainframe support for public institutions in this region of the state. It operates an ATM campus core network to campus buildings, supports the Internet2 protocol, has IBM System 390 processors, and an RS/6000 SP that provides the connection to the TCP/IP-based Internet network. The Florida Center for Library Automation uses NERDC to support the statewide LUIS system, which serves as an online reference system, and it works with the center to support the statewide digital library services project.

The Center for Instructional and Research Computing Activities (CIRCA) is the academic computing support service. It manages the help desk, software support, open computer laboratories, and computer classrooms. CIRCA is a unit within the Office of Instructional Resources (OIR). OIR is also responsible for the support of classrooms, technology training, media, instructional design, and other academic support functions such as the Language Learning Center, Teaching Center (tutoring), Reading and Writing Center, Media Library, and the Testing and Evaluation unit. This consolidation of support units creates a synergy that is cost-effective and productive. (See the OIR web page at: http://www.oir.ufl.edu.)

Networking on campus includes the campus core network; CIRCA classroom network; access to Internet2; DHNet (network taps to the pillow in the residence halls); HealthNet (the Health Sciences state wide T1, ISDN, and data network); IFAS network (supporting the agricultural research and extension units in the 67 counties of Florida with T1, ISDN, and data communication), and VideoNet (the campus broadband for video and satellite transmission). Colleges also support internal networks. While most networking is wired, UF has several wireless applications.

ACCESS

Access to computing resources is provided by NERDC, CIRCA, and the academic departments. Many of the access policies are driven by the computer access requirement for students. All entering students are required to have their own computer. The specific requirement varies by college; for example, some colleges, such as the Colleges of Business and Architecture, require laptops. Students are given free GatorLink accounts for email and web pages, but access to the open laboratories is fee-based except for the use of software required by instructors. Limited dial-up services are provided by NERDC, and cable modem and ADSL access is available locally.

ADMINISTRATIVE APPLICATIONS

The use of computing and the Internet is driven not only by the computer access requirement, but also by the plan to put administrative computing on the Internet. Faculty and staff are now required to have a GatorLink account to access administrative functions such as purchasing and travel. By 2000, faculty will submit course grades online. Even the system for updating the campus directory is online, as is the system for ordering textbooks and required class software. To facilitate this transition to the Internet, the university has developed an interface called EAGLE that provides straightforward development and display of web pages from databases developed with CICS software.

STUDENT APPLICATIONS

Students use the Internet for administrative functions as well. ISIS, the student information system, is online. Students apply for admission and register for classes online. The course tracking system helps students monitor their academic progress toward their degree requirements. A statewide advising system, FACTS, is coming online that will enable students to match their transcripts against degree requirements in the state universities and community colleges.

ACADEMIC PROGRAMS

The impact of the computing requirement on instruction can be characterized as both gradual and explosive. Some projects have been in place for several years, but the growth of projects has been exponential in the last two years.

There have been several longstanding Internet-based and/or video courses offered both on campus and at satellite campuses. On campus, the English department has had Internet-based writing courses for several years. The networked writing environment was originally funded by a grant and has grown to serve several thousand students each year. Courses range from introductory composition and rhetoric to graduate-level theory courses. Interactive online classes are taught in computer laboratories. The College of Business has delivered courses taped live each morning through the campus television station. For 1999, the College of Business has encoded these courses and streams them live over the Internet.

The College of Engineering has spearheaded the Florida Educational Engineering Delivery System (FEEDS) consortium that has offered videotape and satellite courses for many years. The Institute for Food and Agriculture Sciences (IFAS) and the College of Agriculture have been offering interactive video courses through the nine IFAS research stations throughout the state. The College of Nursing uses interactive video to deliver courses to hospitals located in major Florida cities. The College of Medicine has T1 and ISDN connectivity to its many hospitals and clinics throughout the state. The Brain Institute at the College of Medicine provides high-quality, interactive video used for teaching, research, and telemedicine.

Laptops in the College of Architecture have been used in computer-based design courses for several years. More recently, the College of Business instituted a laptop requirement that is enhanced by providing specialized software in the business labs and open study areas. The resulting collaborative learning environment is evident as one walks through the college buildings. The College of Law has just completed a renovation of a large lecture hall to provide laptop ports to each seat.

While the use of computers at the graduate level is not new, the graduate school is phasing in a system of online transmission of theses and dissertations. CIRCA provides an electronic thesis and dissertation computing laboratory to facilitate this project. Training programs and technical assistance are offered.

Off-campus distance education programs are exploding at UF. At the graduate level, the university offers the FlexMBA, the PharmD, masters degrees in engineering, international construction, health administration, and nursing and agriculture; Phd in audiology; as well as an undergraduate degree program in electrical engineering and fire and emergency services. All of these programs are offered primarily through the Internet. Several individual undergraduate courses are also offered completely online, and an additional 130 courses have web-based components using WebCT.

The most recent academic project undertaken at UF is called Pacific Global Learning and is the result of a grant from the Lucent Foundation and the Lucent Technologies Corporation. This project will provide three universities in Brazil and one in Mexico with ISDN connectivity to the University of Florida and Bell Laboratories in New Jersey. Once Internet2 connectivity is available, streaming video will supplement the ISDN connectivity. A number of academic research and instructional projects will use this infrastructure.

INSTRUCTIONAL SUPPORT

Support for the development of instruction using technology comes in several forms. The OIR Center for Instructional Training and Technology (CITT) offers training in the use of productivity and course development tools in both a hands-on and a demonstration format. The CITT will tailor programs for individual departments or colleges that can be delivered on-site or in the CITT classroom. A current experiment is to use the Real G2 and IBM video charger servers to stream training from the CITT classroom to faculty and staff through the Internet. Alternative training is available online and by videotape from the Gartner Group and NetG courses licensed by the university.

CITT also provides technical support for the development of web-based and multimedia instruction. Instructional designers and technical assistants on staff offer a fee-based service. High-end equipment is available for faculty who choose to do their own course development. The Technical Assistants Program (TAP) provides an alternative form of technical support. This program, run by CIRCA, trains undergraduate students to assist faculty in the areas of desktop support, network support, and web page development. OIR offers minigrants, matched by departments, to support the development of multimedia modules and courses.

Facilities that support multimedia also include studios that are used for videoconferencing and interactive video for distance education. Regular production studio classrooms are managed by the Health Science Center's Brain Institute, the College of Engineering, and the College of Agriculture's Institute for Food and Agricultural Sciences. OIR has a studio connected to the campus video broadband network that allows faculty to experiment on campus with video-based instruction.

CLASSROOM SUPPORT

Part of the explosion of technology on campus is due to the university's commitment of over six million dollars in 1998-2000 to upgrade campus classrooms. Plans are to provide network access to all classrooms. In addition, classroom technology will be provided by levels. Level four classrooms will have full multimedia; level three classrooms will have network ports and video projectors; level two classrooms will have network ports, TVs, and VCRs; and level one classrooms will have network ports. All classrooms have overhead projectors. Moveable media carts are distributed to classrooms as needed. It should be noted that the classroom upgrade project is not limited to media enhancement. The intention is to provide a good learning environment that considers furniture, chalkboards, lighting, window coverage, and media.

The University of Florida is making a concerted effort to universalize data and video interconnectivity on campus and to improve access off campus. At the same time, we are pushing the envelope. We are encouraging the use of new and innovative techniques to solve old instructional problems. Technology does not replace traditional instruction at the University of Florida but provides exciting opportunities to enhance and to extend it beyond our campus.

CONTACT INFORMATION

Sue M. Legg
Director, Office of Instructional Resources
1012 Turlington Hall
P. O. Box 117345
University of Florida
Gainesville, FL 32611
Email: Smlegg@ufl.edu

CHAPTER 7

COMPUTING ENVIRONMENT AT INDIANA UNIVERSITY

Gary E. Wittlich and Elizabeth Rubens

THE IU SYSTEM

Indiana University comprises two core campuses and six regional campuses, with nearly 93,000 students and 5,000 faculty and staff. The core campus at Bloomington (IUB) was established in 1820 and enrolls some 36,000, mostly residential students, about 80% of whom are undergraduates. The Indianapolis core campus (IUPUI) offers programs from both IU and Purdue, with fiscal management by IU. IUPUI enrolls some 28,000 nonresidential, undergraduate students, about 50% of whom are full-time. IUPUI is also the site of the IU School of Medicine, one of the largest in the nation. The regional campuses are located at Gary, Ft. Wayne, Kokomo, South Bend, Richmond, and New Albany.

THE IU BUDGET MODEL: RESPONSIBILITY CENTER MANAGEMENT (RCM)

Initiated at IUPUI in 1989 and IUB in 1990, RCM is a decentralized budgeting model based on the following principles:

- All costs and income attributable to each school or other academic unit should be assigned to that unit.

- Appropriate incentives should spur each academic unit to increase income and reduce costs to further a clear set of academic priorities.

- All costs of other (nonacademic) units should be allocated to the academic units. Examples are the main library, space, and the University Information Technology Services (UITS). Such units are taxed according to an algorithm.

RCM brings certain challenges to information technology support and development, among them maintaining campus computing standards within a distributed environment. Currently, each campus funds technology in slightly different ways, although the recent IT strategic plan (see below) has done a great deal to boost computing across the campuses.

INFORMATION TECHNOLOGY ORGANIZATION AND PLANNING AT IU (http://www.indiana.edu/~itiu/)

To address rapidly growing IT needs and complexities, in 1997, University Information Technology Services (UITS) was created by joining the IT organizations on the two core campuses into a single organization. The merger resulted in five divisions: 1) Teaching and Learning Information Technology, 2) Distributed Education, 3) Research and Academic Computing, 4) Telecommunications, and 5) Information Systems (http:/www.indiana.edu/~uits/).

At about the same time, IT strategic planning was initiated across the university. By late 1998, the IT strategic plan was adopted and is being implemented on all campuses (http://www.indiana.edu/~ovpit/strategic/itplan/). Among the key recommendations for teaching and learning IT are:

- Support for faculty, student, and administrative computing resources to permit a seamless computing environment

- Substantial improvements in classroom technology development and deployment
- Lifecycle funding for technology resources

The seamless environment is a long-term goal. Lifecycle funding for technology resources for faculty and students in classrooms and offices throughout IU is now a reality.

To assist IT development on the regional campuses, each hired a chief information officer (CIO) funded jointly by them and the office of the vice president for information technology. Implementation of the plan has been greatly assisted by additional technology funding from the state.

THE IT ENVIRONMENT AT IU

Some key features of the IT environment at IU are the following.

Student Technology Fee

All campuses levy a student technology fee (STF) that provides student computing facilities. STF funding and support differ across the campuses. At IUB, for example, the STF fee is administered centrally to provide more than 40 student technology centers, including hardware, software, and consultants (http://www.indiana.edu/~uits/stc/). At IUPUI the funds are distributed to individual units (schools and departments), each of which creates and maintains their STCs in cooperation with UITS.

Classroom Technology

A ten-year plan created in 1997 has elevated support for technology in the classroom (http://www.indiana.edu/~ctcdoc/ctc.html).

Local Support Providers (LSPs)

On the core campuses, a well-developed cadre of LSPs provides for local support, with training provided in various ways by UITS. Centrally located help desks also provide a large measure of call-in, walk-in, or email support. Requests for support are logged into databases that prioritize responses and provide a history of reported problems and their solutions.

Computing Education Classes

UITS has developed an extensive and well-received catalog of classes for faculty, staff, and students on a wide variety of computing topics, called STEPS and PROSTEPS (http://www.indiana.edu/~iuep/).

Awards for IT Development

Since 1996–1997, IT developments at IU have won a variety of awards, including national recognition from several organizations for its extensive frequently asked questions (FAQ) site, "Knowledge Base" (http://www.indiana.edu/~uits/cpo/kbedu/), and as a "best wired campus" from Yahoo (http://www.indiana.edu/~uits/cpo/press/). In addition, IU has been chosen as the network operations center for the national high-speed research and academic computing project, Abiline, (http://www.indiana.edu/~uitsnews/times/1998/t346/index.html) and has also been chosen by NSF to lead in developing TransPAC, a high-speed international network connection between the NSF's high-performance Backbone Network Service (BNS) and the Asian Pacific Advanced Network (http://www.indiana.edu/~uitsnews/times/1998/t353/index.html).

Two recent grants for IT support and development. Eli Lilly has recently awarded IU thirty million dollars to establish the Indiana Pervasive Computing Research (IPCRES) Initiative. IPCRES will be devoted to research in one of the most important new areas for information technology in the next century, pervasive computing. Under this initiative, six world-class research laboratories will be established at IU in key areas that underpin the pervasive computing environment of the future. IU will recruit distinguished scientists of the highest international standing to lead the IPCRES Laboratories (http://www.indiana.edu/~uits/cpo/ipcres/).

Ameritech has awarded IU one million dollars to support faculty innovation in teaching and learning with IT. The award will create as many as 65 faculty fellows on IU campuses over the next five years. In addition to the fellows, a unique feature of the program will be to develop a database of information about best practices and a knowledge management system (for information on the Ameritech award, see http://www.indiana.edu/~uits/cpo/ameritech/).

The Oncourse Initiative at IU

IU has a long history of experimenting with online education, beginning with VaxNotes. More recently, faculty have used First Class, Lotus Notes, Alta Vista Forum, Ceilidh, COW, and WebCT as well as their own customized packages. For a long time, there was no serious move to integrate what faculty were doing individually into a coordinated university system, but as interest in the World Wide Web expanded, demands for unity have grown. Students took different courses from different professors on different software packages with different interface designs. The university needed a coherent plan for the delivery of distributed learning.

In 1996, the IUPUI WebLab, under the direction of Dr. Ali Jafari, began work on a new web-based environment called Oncourse. Unlike other course delivery tools, Oncourse was designed as a campus "umbrella environment" with which faculty and students could link not only to their courses but to all of the university's web-based resources. It would be an online environment accommodating all of the students' campus transactions. Students could locate their course materials, engage in an online conference, send and receive mail and assignments, participate in a chat session, and check their grades. Student data would be automatically uploaded from the registrar's office, and students would easily link to IU's electronic library resources as well as the vast resources of the web. Because IU would own the code, the environment could be customized and adapted to the changing needs of faculty, staff, and students.

The environment was beta-tested at IUPUI in 1997 and 1998. The beta-test received immense faculty interest, and approximately 400 course spaces were set up to accommodate those who wished to try out the system. Based on that large response, UITS began to consider implementing the environment for all eight campuses of Indiana University. The environment was intended for use as either a stand-alone product or a common student gateway to other tools, such as WebCT or Lotus Notes.

In February 1999, an implementation team was commissioned to move Oncourse from beta to production status. In fall 1999, IU was able to offer an online course environment for every faculty member and student who wished to participate. Oncourse version 1.0 provided a new file management capability and improved performance, using version 4.0 or higher of both Netscape and Internet Explorer.

However, a great deal of work remains on automatic data uploading on the regional campuses, where it has not yet been implemented because of the variety of user-ID generation and authentication methods employed. Conferencing, chat, and mail features of Oncourse are not yet as sophisticated as some of the competitive products. Testing software has not yet been integrated with Oncourse, although faculty can link to an online testing system as an interim strategy. Group project space and student tracking are two other high priorities identified for future development. Developers would also like to integrate the testing package with the online gradebook and ultimately with the university registrar's student records.

If the development team can realize these improvements in a relatively short time, IU will be well on its way to accomplishing a common interface for the university community's online environment.

The Center for Teaching and Learning at IUPUI

The Center for Teaching and Learning on the Indianapolis campus combines the resources of the office of professional development, University Information Technology Services, and the university library to provide faculty with an integrated approach to meeting their professional and instructional support needs. Consultants with a range of expertise representing professional development, instructional design, informatics, web development, audio and video production, copyright management, and grant writing are all housed together. Plans are underway to hire specialists in assessment and problem-based learning. Center consultation services are provided free of charge to faculty and instructional support staff. The center also sponsors a variety of demonstrations, workshops, presentations, and conferences and serves as a focal point for coordinating new initiatives on behalf of the IUPUI learning community.

THE TEACHING AND LEARNING TECHNOLOGIES LABORATORY AT IUB

The Teaching and Learning Technologies Laboratory at IUB is a joint effort of Instructional Support Services and UITS. The TLTL provides assistance to faculty who want to integrate technology effectively into their courses. Staffed by consultants with expertise in instructional technology, video and audio production, photography, and graphic design, the TLTL offers one-on-one consultation services to assist in creating course web sites, multimedia presentations, image databases, interactive textbooks, electronic communications, and innovative instructional strategies. There are also satellite centers in key locations in the School of Education, Kelley School of Business, and the College of Arts and Sciences.

REGIONAL CAMPUSES

Finally, as part of IU's strategic directions initiative, centers of teaching excellence are being either expanded or newly formed on the six regional campuses as part of a concerted effort to develop an exemplary learning environment, enhanced by electronic technologies, across all campuses of Indiana University.

CONTACT INFORMATION

Gary E. Wittlich
Distinguished Consulting Technologist
University Information Technology Services
Wrubel Computing Center
Indiana University
Bloomington, IN 47408
Email: wittlich@indiana.edu
Phone: (812) 855-4837

Elizabeth Rubens
Instructional Systems Project Manager
Center for Teaching and Learning
755 W. Michigan UL1125
Indiana University-Purdue University Indianapolis
Indianapolis, IN 46202
Email: erubens@iupui.edu
Phone: (317) 274-4590
Fax: (317) 278-0241

CHAPTER 8

COMPUTING ENVIRONMENT AT THE UNIVERSITY OF GEORGIA

William K. Jackson and Walter B. McRae

The responsibility for supporting computer-enhanced learning at the University of Georgia (UGA) is shared by University Computing and Networking Services (UCNS) and the Office of Instructional Support and Development (OISD). The larger campus community informs the work of these units through representatives on the institution's information technology forum and instructional advisory committee. In addition, the university instructional technology advisory committee (ITAC), a 14-member committee including faculty members and senior administrators appointed by the chief academic officer, is responsible for the development and implementation of institutional initiatives in support of instructional technologies. The director of OISD chairs ITAC, and the director of UCNS is a permanent member.

Recently, efforts to support the use of computers and other instructional technologies to enhance learning at UGA have focused on both faculty and students. Support for faculty includes the ITAC-administered learning technologies grants program, a major effort by UCNS and OISD to support campus-wide deployment of WebCT, and the development of technology-enhanced classroom facilities. Student use of instructional technologies is supported through investments in public access and departmental computing facilities, extension of high-speed network access to the residence halls, and establishment of information literacy training. The university is also currently engaged in its decennial self-study for the Southern Association of Colleges and Schools and elected to use an alternate model for this activity. This forward-looking model focuses on the undergraduate experience at UGA, and one of the four major self-study committees is the Committee on Information Technology and the Undergraduate Experience. Guided by the academic goals of the colleges and schools and by ongoing institutional IT assessment and planning efforts, this committee will prepare a blueprint for the coming years to ensure that information technology is incorporated in the classroom in a meaningful, instructive way.

SUPPORT FOR FACULTY

Learning Technologies Grants

The learning technologies grants (LTG) program at UGA supports both innovative explorations and thoughtful implementation of proven applications. Funded at approximately $500,000 annually, it is administered by ITAC and provides up to $75,000 for projects designed to enhance teaching and learning through the effective use of media and information technology. Funding can be requested for equipment, software, materials, facilities renovation, faculty release time, technical support, external consulting, travel, and design and production services. Proposals are reviewed by ITAC using weighted criteria with the highest weights assigned to 1) purpose and quality of the project, including relevance to priorities of the unit and the university, 2) quality of the project's instructional development plan, and 3) the extent to which students will interact directly with the proposed learning technologies.

The UGA WebCT Initiative

During 1997, a group of approximately 50 UGA faculty members evaluated a number of web-based course development tools. That evaluation lead to the adoption of

Web Course Tools (WebCT) as the institutional standard for delivery of web-based instruction. Following this adoption, a collaboration was formed between UCNS and OISD to support WebCT deployment at UGA. A joint WebCT support team provides faculty consultation and training. UCNS team members provide applications support, and the OSID team members provide instructional design support. This collaboration draws upon the strengths of both support units and eliminates the potential for duplication or competition. During the first two years of this initiative, approximately 1,000 UGA faculty members received training in the use of WebCT, which is now being used to enhance more than 1,300 course sections at UGA. Three important factors contributed to the success of this effort: 1) The decision to adopt WebCT as the institutional standard was made with substantial faculty participation. 2) The collaboration between UCNS and OISD combined the strengths of both units in support of this initiative and produced a level of success that nether unit could have achieved on its own. 3) Student access to computing resources on campus was adequate to meet the increasing demand caused by extensive use of WebCT in the curriculum.

Classroom Enhancements

WebCT and other applications of learning technologies have provided substantial opportunities to extend learning beyond the classrooms; however, our students continue to spend approximately 45 hours in the classroom for each course they take. Recognizing that technological enhancements can create more effective in-class learning environments, the university has been aggressive in the installation and support of classroom technologies. Data projection systems and network connections have been installed in most classrooms with more than 150 seats. A wireless student feedback system that includes immediate data analysis and classroom display is available for use in classes of up to 75 students. Recent construction and plans for new facilities include network connections to all classrooms and to student desktops in selected rooms. As the amount of technology in the classroom increases, additional support for the faculty using these rooms is needed. To meet this need, the university has installed phones in technology-enhanced classrooms and hired classroom support specialists, assigned to various campus zones, to provide rapid response to classroom problems. To re-

duce the potential for problems, a common control panel is being installed in all classrooms and a model classroom facility provides faculty members with training in typical technological enhancements.

SUPPORT FOR STUDENTS

Public Access and Departmental Computer Clusters

The university's goal is to provide every student reasonable on-campus access to information technology resources. This access is required in order for UGA students to take advantage of online registration, electronic library resources, electronic mail, personal web pages, and web-based instruction delivered by WebCT. Public access microcomputer clusters have been placed throughout the campus and support development of discipline-specific computer laboratories and learning centers within departments, colleges, and schools. To date, approximately 2,200 student-access workstation seats have been deployed in both of these environments. Institutional financial support for this strategy was originally provided through a tariff on campus PABX voice services. This source of funding has recently been discontinued because of federal audit requirements for indirect costs. The university is currently seeking to implement a technology fee to offset, in part, this loss of investment capital.

The public access-microcomputer clusters are located throughout campus in major academic buildings and a number of residence halls. Student workstations are also located in learning centers and other specialized facilities, and an additional 500 student workstations will be located in the information commons of the university's new Student Learning Center, scheduled for completion in 2002. Off-campus access is available to students through their own private Internet service provider or through a low-cost dial-in service available through the University System of Georgia.

Cable Modems in Residence Halls

High-speed data access will become the norm for all new residence halls and older facilities undergoing major renovation at UGA. However, most of the student housing at UGA was built in the 1960s and 1970s and, therefore, is too old to have a network infrastructure and too new to be scheduled for renovation. As the faculty increasingly rely on WebCT for delivery of learning resources, the student desktops in the residence halls require high-speed access to these resources. Fortunately, OISD supplies cable television service to all residence halls, with cable drops in each bedroom. During the spring of 1999, the university committed to the installation of cable modems in the university's three largest residence halls. This initiative, another joint effort of UCNS and OISD, will make high-speed data access available through cable modem to approximately one-third of students residing on campus by spring 2000. As funding becomes available, this access will be extended to all campus residents.

Information Literacy for Students

The number of classes using instructional technology is increasing rapidly at UGA. Students enrolled in introductory chemistry are required to take all of their tests and perform a number of their laboratories on microcomputers. Freshman composition requires word-processing and web-searching skills. In recognition of this new technology-rich learning environment, the University Instructional Technology Advisory Committee recently developed a plan for a one-credit information literacy course available to entering students. The purpose of this course is to introduce students to the networked computer environment at UGA and the basic software that they will use. Sections are taught using UCNS Computer Services sites located in the freshman residence halls. Although entering freshmen are encouraged to take this course, the course is not required, and the grading is pass/fail.

SUMMARY

The University of Georgia is committed to the development and support of technology-enhanced learning environments, and two robust support units, UCNS and OISD, have developed productive collaborations to assist in this effort. The university provides substantial funding to faculty members who are developing innovative applications of instructional technology or who are seeking to implement proven concepts. The university was one of the earliest adopters of WebCT, which is now used by hundreds of UGA faculty members and thousands of their students. The university has created numerous technology-enhanced classrooms and provides support required for faculty's effective use of them. Students' access to learning resources is facilitated by a high density of public access and departmental student workstations and by high-speed data access for students living in residence halls. Finally, to ensure that every UGA student develops the skills to take advantage of these learning resources, the institution has developed an information literacy course for entering students. The university's decennial self-study will assure that the initiatives currently under way are thoroughly examined and modified, as required, to address the future needs of UGA undergraduates.

CONTACT INFORMATION

William K. Jackson, Director
Office of Instructional Support and Development
Instructional Plaza
University of Georgia
Athens, GA 30602
Email: bjackson@arches.uga.edu
WWW: www.isd.uga.edu
Phone: (706) 542-1355
Fax: (706) 542-6587

CHAPTER 9

COMPUTING ENVIRONMENT AT THE UNIVERSITY OF NOTRE DAME

Tom Laughner and Kevin Barry

PHILOSOPHY

The Educational Technology Services team collaborates with faculty and teaching assistants to select and to implement technology that will help them meet identified learning goals.

A typical collaboration between Educational Technology Services and an instructor begins with the development of a mutual understanding of the goals for the course. When the goals have been clearly identified, tools or methods that may assist in achieving them are considered. They may or may not be based on computer technology. They are evaluated to determine whether they fit with the instructor's style within time pressures and other external constraints.

At this point, if there are tools that meet these criteria, the best are selected, and implementation plans are developed. If these criteria cannot be met, ETS does not encourage the pursuit of a technology solution. Instructors feel at ease while discussing possibilities, without the concern that technology will be forced on them. The model also results in increased efficiency, because no time is spent attempting to implement solutions that are not likely to succeed.

STAFF

The Educational Technology Services team has a strong understanding of technology but is grounded in pedagogy. Each team member also teaches an accredited course at the university. In addition to providing a forum in which to sharpen our teaching skills, teaching lets us try out various technology tools to discover their strengths and weaknesses.

The students we hire work primarily in our faculty lab, providing assistance when instructors stop by. They also frequently work one-on-one with faculty to create educational materials for a course. The students must possess strong communication skills and interact easily with others. We also look for students who can demonstrate an interest in discovering and learning new things. Knowledge of technology is lowest on the list of skills that we seek. We have learned that it is far easier to teach the technology components than to teach the interpersonal skills.

FACILITIES AND RESOURCES

Educational Technology Services maintains a Faculty Educational Technology Development Center, located in the primary classroom building. This lab contains high-end equipment that is not easily accessible from faculty offices. The lab has six computers with flatbed scanners and transparency adapters, a CD burner, a high-resolution 35mm slide scanner, and video capture equipment. An Avid system is also available for digital video editing. This lab is staffed by ETS student consultants and available to any instructor creating materials for a Notre Dame accredited course.

COLLABORATION

While Educational Technology Services is structurally within the Office of Information Technologies, a strong relationship exists with Notre Dame's Kaneb Center for Teaching and Learning. When the Kaneb Center was created and staffed in 1997, both groups immediately foresaw the benefits of working together. The collaboration also includes conducting a "Teaching Well Using Technology" workshop at Notre Dame and colleges and universities across the country and collaborating on applications for external funding.

GRANTS AND OTHER FUNDING OPPORTUNITIES

Realizing that many academic departments did not have the financial resources to assist faculty who wished to incorporate technology into their courses, the Office of Information Technologies instituted the Jump Start grant program. The purpose of this grant is to help faculty overcome the financial burdens associated with implementing technology into a class.

The grants, usually between $1,000 and $2,000, can pay for most anything to help implement technology. They most often pay for student assistance to scan materials or set up PowerPoint presentations or WebCT courses. They have also paid for software to be used at home. Notre Dame provides a suite of applications from centrally located servers, which meets most needs when faculty are on campus. Costs associated with obtaining copyright permissions are also covered. The grants cannot be used to subsidize the instructor's time, nor to pay for the purchase of hardware. Notre Dame has a separate program to pay for hardware maintenance, upgrade, and replacement. The grants are not competitive and offered throughout the year.

In addition to the internally funded Jump Start program, ETS collaborates with faculty and departments to obtain grants from external resources. Sources of grants have included AT&T and the Rockefeller Foundation.

SERVICES

The Educational Technology Services team offers the following services:

- **Instructional design and materials development.** We help content experts develop or identify materials to meet learning objectives. These materials may be developed in any combination of media.

Assistance may include consulting, exploring, teaching, and assisting with the use of technology.

- **Facilities design.** We help design computer clusters and technology classrooms to enhance teaching and learning.

- **Research and study.** We provide data on the use of technology in education, with or without analysis. This research may be a literature review or a formalized process of collecting and synthesizing data.

- **Needs analysis.** We diagnose and analyze instructional needs in order to define requirements for educational materials. We identify an instructional goal, learning objectives, subordinate skills, entry-level behaviors, time constraints, learner analysis, and delivery methods.

- **Evaluation.** We collect and analyze data to determine the educational effectiveness of materials or instruction.

FUTURE

Recent efforts by the Office of Information Technologies and the Kaneb Center for Teaching and Learning will solidify Notre Dame's model, emphasizing learning goals before identifying technology tools. In July 2000, two of the current Educational Technology Services faculty will become assistant directors of the Kaneb Center for Teaching and Learning. With this move, the Kaneb Center will be in a better position to work with Notre Dame instructors on a wide range of tools to improve teaching and learning, including technology. The Kaneb Center and the Office of Information Technologies will collaborate on those projects that require the creation of a technology solution. Collaborative efforts will also be initiated with the library and the Institute for Educational Initiatives to further integrate faculty development efforts.

CONTACT INFORMATION

Tom Laughner, Assistant Director
Kaneb Center for Teaching and Learning
University of Notre Dame
353 DeBartolo Hall
Notre Dame, IN 46556
Email: laughner@nd.edu
Phone: (219) 631-8270

Kevin Barry, Assistant Director
Kaneb Center for Teaching and Learning
University of Notre Dame
353 DeBartolo Hall
Notre Dame, IN 46556
Email: kbarry2@nd.edu
Phone: (219) 631-4443

CHAPTER 10

COMPUTING ENVIRONMENT AT THE UNIVERSITY OF PITTSBURGH

Robert F. Pack and Diane J. Davis

THE UNIVERSITY

The University of Pittsburgh is one of the nation's top public research universities and a member of the Association of American Universities (AAU). Founded in 1787, Pitt became state-related in 1966. The university offers graduate, undergraduate, professional, and continuing education programs through 19 schools and four campuses, located between 30 and 170 miles from the fifth, main campus in Oakland, Pittsburgh's cultural and medical center. It typically serves about 28,000 FTE and employs nearly 4,000 full- and part-time faculty members. For more information on the university of Pittsburgh, see the university's web site at http://www.pitt.edu/.

TECHNOLOGY AND SERVICE ENVIRONMENT

The University of Pittsburgh has a rich technology environment. An active member of the Internet2 Project, Pitt is working with industry and government leaders to develop the new networking capabilities and advanced applications that will enable research and education into the next century. The university's computing network, PittNet, provides local and global network connectivity for students, faculty, and staff. It operates over an FDDI/FastEthernet backbone that joins hundreds of local ethernets into a large, geographically distributed network. We currently are using ATM technology to develop a video distribution system and planning is underway to evolve the campus network to Gigabit Ethernet.

The five-campus system has about 22,000 network ports. Eight hundred dial-up lines handle more than 6,000 remote connections per day. The university jointly owns and operates an Internet connection with the Pittsburgh Supercomputing Center, the Pennsylvania State University and Carnegie-Mellon University.

In addition to its computing infrastructure, Pitt provides academic centers with state-of-the-art video-conferencing capabilities through its Interactive Television (ITV) network, enabling two-way audio and video connectivity throughout the global ITV community. Each campus has at least one fully equipped ITV classroom. Satellite downlink capabilities enable program distribution at ten different locations. Since 1992, the university has invested $1.5 million annually to renovate campus classrooms, installing an array of instructional technologies. Each media-enhanced classroom has been equipped with at least a VHS videotape player, a large TV monitor or video projector, a data port, and a campus telephone. To date, more than 70 classrooms have been renovated to provide faculty and students with a learning environment that can effectively accommodate new technologies and modes of instruction. Instructional technology has been a high priority at Pitt. Through an annual program initiated five years ago, faculty have been allocated approximately 1,350 desktop computers. In addition to hardware and software, comprehensive technology support services for teaching and learning are available. The primary central support units for instructional technology include the following.

The University Library System

Fourteen libraries are located on the Pittsburgh campus in addition to Allegheny Observatory Library, the Barco Law Library, the Health Sciences Library System, and the four regional campus libraries. A member of the Association of Research Libraries, the university library system (ULS) is committed to the use of technology to support the university's research, teaching, and service missions. Voyager, a new library management system for the public catalog, offers author, title, subject, and keyword access to materials in all university libraries. PITTCAT contains bibliographic holdings and circulation information for more than three million titles, representing most of the university's book and periodical collections. In addition, ULS provides access to many remote resources for faculty, students, and staff, including the Encyclopedia Britannica, EBSCOhost, IAC SearchBank, CIS Compass, MUSE, JSTOR, and numerous other electronic journals. PITTCAT and the other databases are available through the ULS web site at http://www.library.pitt.edu.

Computing Services and Systems Development (CSSD)

CSSD provides an array of computing support services for the university community, including public computing labs, computer accounts, a seven-day, 24-hour help desk, and technical assistance for the selection and maintenance of computing equipment. CSSD also provides centralized software licensing and distribution services. Through an agreement with Microsoft Corporation, all active university students receive the following software free of charge:

- Office 2000 for Windows including Word, Excel, PowerPoint, Access, Outlook, and Publisher

- Office 98 for Macintosh including Word, Excel, and PowerPoint

- FrontPage 2000 for Windows

- Windows 98 Upgrade

- Windows NT Workstation 4.0 Upgrade

- Visual Studio 6.0 including Visual Basic, C++, FoxPro, J++ and InterDev

- Office Starts Here Step-by-Step Interactive

A variety of training classes are offered through CSSD, and the university is one of a few worldwide designated an Authorized Academic Java™ Campus by Sun Microsystems. For additional information about CSSD, see http://technology.pitt.edu/index.html/.

Center for Instructional Development and Distance Education (CIDDE)

In 1995, the University of Pittsburgh consolidated existing resources to strengthen the instructional support available to faculty through CIDDE. CIDDE works directly with schools, departments, and individual faculty members to facilitate the academic goals of the university. Within this broad mission, CIDDE provides support services for course design and development, faculty development, and instructional technology. Staff offer expertise in instructional design, instructional computing, electronic graphics and design, video production, media services, classroom engineering, development of print materials, and student support services for distance and distributed learning. For additional information about CIDDE, see http://www.pitt.edu/~ciddeweb/.

Support for Online Courses

In spring 1998, the university adopted CourseInfo to facilitate the development and use of online instruction. The software was selected on the basis of the review and recommendation of a faculty and staff committee (see http://www.pitt.edu/~washburn/ccs.htm). It is easy to use and adheres to standard query language (SQL) and emerging standards such as Instructional Management System metadata model (EDUCAUSE'S IMS Project). CourseInfo was the only package previewed that enabled inexperienced faculty to create effective materials with no knowledge of html, and still allowed more advanced users to leverage their knowledge of html and web-based authoring tools to produce sophisticated results.

A primary goal in our pilot use of CourseInfo and throughout its dissemination has been to provide strong support services. CIDDE worked closely with CSSD, ULS, and the university's Systems and Network group, to develop the following.

- A faculty program focuses on instructional development and training in CourseInfo and related software, such as MS Word and PowerPoint. Training is required to use CourseInfo for a number of reasons. First, we wanted to optimize its use as an opportunity for faculty to rethink established teaching methods. Second, we recognized that even technically sophisticated faculty would make better use of the software if they were more familiar with its capabilities and limitations. Finally, we viewed training as a means to minimize the demand for technical assistance, enabling us to better meet that demand.

- The director of the university library system trains faculty on copyright issues related to the use of CourseInfo and the Internet.

- The server environment is stable, secure, and efficient. The university acquired multiple licenses of the CourseInfo package to implement three levels of servers. A test server (Apache on a low-end Pentium processor running Linux) experiments with new releases and patches of the software. Faculty use a development server to create web pages in a secure, confidential environment. The production server (high-end Sun processor also running Solaris/Apache) is constantly maintained by a central computing staff and supports online courses, faculty, and students.

- CIDDE instructional designers designed a Pitt CourseInfo to encourage logical course structure and format consistency across courses, allowing students familiar with one CourseInfo section to easily adapt to a second.

- CSSD staff developed and delivered a student orientation to CourseInfo in the classroom at the request of instructors.

- Systems and network staff developed a program to automatically load students into courses from ISIS, our student information system, particularly important for the large, introductory courses that were the target of our pilot term.

- CSSD help desk staff supports students and faculty using CourseInfo.

- CIDDE and the university's Office of Measurement and Evaluation of Teaching developed student and faculty evaluation instruments for use with CourseInfo.

In the university's first summer Instructional Development Institute (SIDI) in 1998, 12 faculty from five science disciplines developed online instructional materials as part of a strategic effort to enhance large, introductory science courses. In response to growing faculty demand, a second SIDI was offered that summer serving an additional 12 faculty. Twenty-three courses used CourseInfo in the fall of 1998, affecting more than 1,800 students. Since that time, we have conducted dozens of shorter training sessions, typically one day, and three more summer institute sessions and trained about 400 university faculty. In fall 1999, one and one-half years after its initial adoption, CourseInfo was used in nearly 350 courses, a few of which are fully online. The vignettes in this book written by University of Pittsburgh faculty exemplify the enthusiasm with which our faculty have embraced the web as an instructional tool.

CONTACT INFORMATION

Robert F. Pack
Vice Provost for Academic Planning and Resources
    Management
University of Pittsburgh
826 Cathedral of Learning
Pittsburgh, PA 15260
Email: robert.pack@pitt.edu
Phone: (412) 624-4228
Fax: (412) 624-4618

Diane J. Davis
Director, Center for Instructional Development
University of Pittsburgh
4227 Fifth Avenue, Suite 820
Pittsburgh, PA 15260
Email: djdavis+@pitt.edu
Phone: (412) 624-3335
Fax: (412) 624-7213

CHAPTER 11

COMPUTING ENVIRONMENT AT VIRGINIA POLYTECHNIC INSTITUTE AND STATE UNIVERSITY

J. Thomas Head and John Moore

Virginia Tech's computing-intensive and high bandwidth communications environment for both students and faculty is an integral component in fulfilling its tripartite mission of instruction, research, and outreach. All entering students are required to purchase a computing system, and all faculty participate in instructional technology workshops on a continuing four-year cycle. The state-of-the-art campus network environment received an award from CAUSE for excellence in networking, and the Blacksburg Electronic Village and Net.Work.Virginia provide connectivity for off-campus students.

The Instructional Development Initiative (IDI) at Virginia Tech has created the opportunity for significant holistic changes in teaching and learning throughout the university. The initiative goals are structured into three components.

FACULTY DEVELOPMENT

- Allow all university faculty to participate in the development program. The overarching goal is to motivate faculty to investigate, create, and use alternative instructional strategies.

- Provide participants who complete the program with access to state-of-the-art instructional technology, the knowledge to use it, and the motivation to collaborate with their colleagues in leveraging instructional technology in their courses.

STUDENT ACCESS

- Advise all students on their investment in computer technology to maximize its usefulness during their college careers.

- Provide access to computer labs and computer-integrated classrooms that run specialized software unique to disciplinary areas, such as Perseus, Mathematica, and Daedalus.

- Provide orientation and hands-on training sessions for new students to ensure that they have a foundation in the use of computing and instructional technology resources.

COURSE DEVELOPMENT

- Support faculty in the development of network-accessible courseware and instruction.

- Facilitate the development of electronic libraries of scholarly materials supporting designated courses.

- Improve classroom and presentation facilities to support faculty efforts in introducing new technologies into core curriculum courses.

One component, the Faculty Development Initiative (FDI), began with three pilot faculty workshops during the summer of 1993 and has continued with additional workshops through August 1999. The FDI is a large-scale effort to invest in our faculty by providing them recurring, scheduled opportunities to rethink their teaching and to explore technology's potential for improving the effectiveness of the teaching/learning process. A total of 120 customized workshops have been conducted. During the first four-year cycle, faculty development workshops were conducted for 1,425 participants from all academic departments. In the second four-year cycle, currently underway, approximately 400 faculty participate each summer in track-oriented workshops. Recurring replacement of workstations is coupled with the scheduled workshops.

As part of the IDI initiative, approximately 55 classrooms have been upgraded with computers and projection systems, and ten centrally scheduled distance learning classrooms equipped with two-way interactive video have gone online. More than 1,000 computing stations have been installed for use by students in computer labs, the Math Emporium was created, and the New Media Center was established in Newman Library.

Faculty attendees continue to evaluate the IDI positively. Faculty clearly value the opportunity to explore instructional issues with their colleagues and to discover technology's potential for enhancing their teaching. They have indicated that these resources are critical if they are to adapt to their students' needs.

The content of the workshops has radically changed since the 1993 pilot workshops. As the effects of IDI have spread across the campus and awareness of the Internet has increased, appropriate changes in foci have been implemented. The core skill set has become more advanced, reflecting the more sophisticated computer skills and computer awareness of the participating faculty. Principles used in designing the 1999 IDI workshops were developed from the feedback received from previous workshop sessions.

Faculty selected a workshop from nine tracks:

Track A: New Faculty

Track B: Basic Computing Skills

Track C: Enhancing Your Course with the Web

Track D: Distance & Distributed Learning: Web-Based Instruction

Track E: Using Geographic Information Systems: Spatial Data

Track F: Distance & Distributed Learning: Two-Way Interactive Video

Track G: Instructional Design Strategies

Track H: Creating Digital Video, Audio, and Multimedia

Track I: Advanced Topics in Course Transformation

Most workshop instructors and facilitators have been from Educational Technologies, the Computing Center, and the university libraries. However, the expertise of faculty and staff from geography, forestry, English, entomology, mathematics, computer science, veterinary medicine, engineering, architecture, theater arts, art, music, and humanities have been included where appropriate. A very effective feature of IDI includes presentations by faculty who have previously attended. Faculty demonstrate how they changed their courses and answer questions about effects on student learning, productivity, development time, and similar issues.

Beyond the core skills, many workshops have focused on discipline-specific software over the past several years. For example, the department of mathematics is engaged in large-scale experimentation in the Math Emporium. The emporium is a student-centered, advanced learning center that provides an active learning environment for over seven thousand undergraduates using interactive, self-paced courseware, diagnostic quizzes, small-group work, and faculty/student tutoring. This new approach allows more realistic problems to be brought up even in elementary courses, speeding the transition to professional-level work.

Surveys of students and faculty involved in classes that have been restructured as a result of this initiative show strong support for the new approaches. Active learning has been facilitated both in the classroom and out, and constructive collaboration among students encouraged. Technology is promoting communication outside the classroom by electronic mail, threaded discussions, and chats. There is evidence that these efforts have had a positive impact on students' understanding of, and interest in, the course material, while promoting better class attendance. In addition, students believe they are being provided more opportunities to develop skills that transcend the subject matter, including problem solving and critical thinking.

Ongoing Course Development

Over the past three years, 77 course transformation projects for more than 100 faculty across every college have been funded by the Center for Innovation in Learning. Established by the provost in 1996, the center aims to develop online courses and provide related infrastructure, technical support, and assessment of results in targeted curricular areas. The center also serves as an umbrella for coordinating communications and developing partnerships focused on integrating technology in learning. The early focus of these grants was on high-enrollment, core curriculum courses. The goal has been expanded to include upper-division courses and distance-learning programs. These grants have supported courses enrolling over 10,000 students.

The center also assists in coordinating assessment and the technical support and equipment needs of successful grantees. By strategically targeting areas of the curriculum for development, the university can realize more effective use of human, physical, and financial resources. Communities of scholars and instructional development faculty and staff can develop, assess, and communicate the results of their activities. Opportunities exist for cost sharing across parts of the university on strategic activities. Research on teaching and learning can accompany online course development more systematically. New uses of space and technology for experimentation and development of new approaches to teaching and learning can emerge.

For additional information, see the following web sites:

Instructional Development Initiative at
    http://www.edtech.vt.edu/idi

Faculty Development Institute at
    http://www.fdi.vt.edu

Blacksburg Electronic Village at http://www.bev.net

Net.Work.Virginia at http://www.networkvirginia.net

Student Computer Requirement at
    http://www.compreq.vt.edu

Math Emporium at http://www.emporium.vt.edu

New Media Center at http://www.nmc.vt.edu

University Libraries at http://www.lib.vt.edu

Center for Innovation in Learning at
    http://www.edtech.vt.edu/cil

Contact Information

J. Thomas Head, Director
Instructional Services
Virginia Polytechnic Institute and State University
102 Old Security Building
Blacksburg, VA 24061
Email: tom.head@vt.edu
WWW: edtech.vt.edu/idi.html
Phone: (540) 231-6822
Fax: (540) 231-5922

John Moore, Director
Educational Technologies
Virginia Polytechnic Institute and State University
102 Old Security Building
Blacksburg, VA 24061
Email: john.moore@vt.edu
WWW: edtech.vt.edu/idi.html
Phone: (540) 231-8991
Fax: (540) 231-5922

CHAPTER 12

COMPUTING ENVIRONMENT AT WAKE FOREST UNIVERSITY

David G. Brown

The leap in technology at Wake Forest was part of a 1995 comprehensive plan that added faculty, staff, scholarships, books, and research support to arts and sciences programs.

Today, all students and faculty have their own laptop computers and inkjet printers. Freshmen get their first computer at fall registration. At junior registration, they trade up to a new computer, which they take with them upon graduation. Faculty and staff are on the same two-year cycle, so that at any one time, everyone on campus has one of two computers. The freshman/junior computer for fall 1999 is the IBM390 with 128 RAM, 333 MHz, 6 GB, 56 modem, and CD-ROM.

The fall 1999 software for all computers includes Netscape 4.5, Dreamweaver 2, SPSS9, Maple V 5.1, Windows 98, MS Office Pro 97, and CourseInfo. Certain departments, for example art and physics, add other programs. Specialized needs beyond the capacity of the laptops are met by computer laboratories in several departments.

On Yahoo's most-wired campuses list, Wake Forest is ranked number three among all universities and number one among liberal arts colleges. Internet connectivity is available in all classrooms and laboratories, 60% of the classroom seats, all residence hall rooms, throughout the library, and at many other public locations. Virtually all administrative services and financial systems are computer accessible. For more information, see http://www.wfu.edu/WIN/winLauch Page.html. Faculty may access the Internet from local phones in over 6,000 worldwide locations.

Most of our 3,700 undergraduates and 400 arts and sciences faculty are full-time. Over 80% of the students graduate in four years. Nearly 100% regularly use email. Over 80% rate the computer as useful in enhancing learning and use some aspect of the computer in their classes. Surveys indicate that the biggest gains in learning are achieved by better communication between professors and their students, more interactive assignments, and greater team-learning among students. More complete descriptions of our program are available at http://www.wfu.edu/technology/index.html and in a 1999 book entitled *Electronically Enhanced Education* available through http://iccel.wfu.edu/publications/index.html.

Comprehensive computer programs similar to the undergraduate program also exist in our schools of management, medicine, and divinity.

STRATEGIES FOR ENCOURAGING THE USE OF TECHNOLOGY IN TEACHING

Faculty development strategies are more fully discussed in a *Multiversity* article at http://www.hied.ibm.com/multiversity/Win99/bestpractice.html. Intentionally, there is no "dean-level" pressure upon Wake Forest faculty to teach with technology. The computer infrastructure, much like the library, is there for faculty who want to use it. Increasing pressures from international communities of scholars and from students are, without any special push from the administration, leading almost all faculty toward the use of computers in their teaching and research.

Most learning about computers in our community occurs among roommates, office colleagues, and friends. Colleague learning is greatly facilitated by our common computers and our standardized software.

In academic departments, more specialized assistance is available from a full-time academic computer specialist, who is typically dually trained in the discipline and in computers and who reports to the department's chair. For a fuller explanation of this program, see http://www.wfu.edu/wfuacs/.

Each member of a corps of very well-trained students, most of them selected and trained in their freshman year, is assigned for up to 18 hours per week for an entire semester to help individual faculty members incorporate technology in their teaching, research, or advising. For a fuller explanation of this program, see http://www.wfu.edu/Computer-information/STARS/index.html. Another student corps is on duty throughout our residence hall system to provide special assistance to students, especially in the evening. For a fuller explanation of this program, see http://www.wfu.edu/Computer-information/RTA/. Our 120-hour per week help desk is staffed by seven full-time professionals plus a corps of students.

Computer skill classes for students and faculty, including new student orientation, are taught by professional librarians. For more information on training, see http://www.wfu.edu/Library/ITC/training/tramat.htm. Computer skills classes for the professional staff are taught by the International Center for Computer-Enhanced Learning (ICCEL). For more information, see http://iccel.wfu.edu. Special seminars, customized classes, computer-based training tapes, and an array of on-campus conferences sponsored by ICCEL are also available.

POLICY, ADMINISTRATION, AND INSTRUMENTATION

Strategic policy (for example, the choice of a course management system, an email system, and the standard load) is set by an elected faculty committee. Decisions regarding back office networks, servers, and support systems are the purview of the IS department, which now numbers over 60 members and occupies a new building.

The strategy for faculty exposure to computer-enhanced teaching is implemented by full-time faculty under the aegis of the Computer-Enhanced Learning Initiative (CELI). For more information, see http://www.wfu.edu/CELI/. Each year, this group cosponsors a Learning Technology Fair where roughly 50 faculty and their student consultants, in a very well-attended two-hour poster session, share how they are using technology in their own teaching. CELI also allocates a relatively small number of release-time grants and summer stipends for faculty who wish to redevelop their courses.

A modest multimedia laboratory is located in the library. For more information, see http://www.wfu.edu/Library/ITC/mmlab/mmlab.htm. Virtually all departments now have scanners. Unlike many other universities, Wake Forest has not invested in a corps of professional course designers.

PHILOSOPHY

Wake Forest strives to provide up-to-date technology and appropriate training to support its liberal arts mission. Whenever possible, specific and unique needs of individual faculty members, for example, a larger monitor or a special software program, are supported without hassle. The intent is to provide the computer facility that is felt to be needed.

The initiative in adopting computer methodologies should be faculty-centered. Students will push. The administration should facilitate. The extent and manner of adoption is a decision best made by individual faculty.

As the speed of dissemination of scholarship accelerates, and as communication among similarly trained scholars around the world becomes commonplace, the computer will play an ever-increasing role in the individualization and customization of all learning.

REFERENCE

Brown, D. G., & Elson, F. S. (1999, Winter). Faculty development. *Multiversity*, 17-20.

CONTACT INFORMATION

David G. Brown
Vice President and Dean of International
    Center for Computer-Enhanced Learning
Professor of Economics
Wake Forest University
P. O. Box 7328, Reynolda Station
Winston-Salem, NC 27109
Email: brown@wfu.edu
Phone: (336) 758-4878
Fax: (336) 758-4875

PART III
VIGNETTES
COURSES TAUGHT
WITH TECHNOLOGY

PHYSICAL SCIENCES, MATHEMATICS, AND ENGINEERING

Vignette 1 The Math Emporium

Monte Boisen, Virginia Polytechnic Institute and State University

Math 1015, a freshman precalculus course, has always been one of our most difficult to teach because of the demographics of its student body. These students are not engineers, mathematicians, physicists. They are everything else. They come from over 50 different majors. Consequently, providing focus for each individual in this environment is a significant challenge. This course must serve a wide variety of learning styles. The challenges in addressing student preparation are even greater. Most of the students have seen most of the material in high school. Some of them have had all of the topics. Unfortunately, many of them have experienced "mathematical abuse" in the past and have significant negative attitudes attached to the subject and their ability to be successful in learning it. They are victims of twin evil thoughts: 1) Math is hard to learn; and 2) Math is of no value. Many of these students have selected their majors based, at least in part, on a perception that they will not have to take a lot of mathematics.

For all of the above reasons, Math 1015 was a disaster when taught in a one-size-fits-all lecture format. Students who basically understood the material from the beginning became very angry with the students who asked elementary questions, and the students who really needed help were made to feel stupid. All of the self-defeating attitudes of the past were reinforced in the students for whom the course was designed.

This course aims to empower our students in several ways. First, we want them to master a certain set of mathematical skills that they will need to be successful in their future course work and in their careers. Second, we want them to become active learners who can take some level of responsibility for their own development. Third, related to active learning, we want our students to feel comfortable as lifelong learners. We want them to leave the course believing that they are capable of learning mathematics, that mathematics is of value to them, and that if they need to learn mathematical topics in the future, they will come to the task with confidence.

The creation of the Math Emporium, a 500-computer learning center, enabled us to completely reinvent the Math 1015 course. The design and implementation of this course are described below.

COURSE DESIGN

It would be a great mistake to expect students to come to technology with glad hearts. They must see a human face to the course, expression of a concern for their success. The technology should be used to redeploy our human resources to address individual learning needs.

The Focus Group

The design element most responsible for addressing the attitudinal and adjustment issues is the focus group. Each student is assigned to a 40-student focus group that meets once a week in a classroom setting. The focus group has three basic responsibilities. First, it must make sure that each student is fully aware of all of the learning activities and how each addresses specific learning styles. During the first half of the course, students are continually encouraged to try a variety of learning activities so that for the remainder of the course, they can make wise choices. The group's second responsibility is to summarize the material covered in the course. Strategies for tackling the toughest of the topics are discussed. The third responsibility is to provide context for student learning through the presentation of applications that are as up-to-date as possible and as close to the students' areas of interest as possible. The mathematics in the application should be no more advanced than that being learned in the course.

Textbook

A good textbook is also part of this design. One of the minor goals of the course is to help students learn how to read a math textbook. We use *College Algebra and Trigonometry* by Lial, Hornsby, & Schneider (1997).

Computer Tutorial

Created by Addison-Wesley, the computer tutorial is matched exactly to the book in terms of notation and organization. Every computer in the Math Emporium has this software loaded, and all students get a CD bundled with their book that contains the tutorial for use in their dorm rooms.

Lectures on CDs

We have recorded thirty-four 15- to 20-minute lectures on topics that typically give students difficulty. These play on the computers in the emporium and on any MPEG-ready machine. The students were given a pack of ten CDs that they can use anywhere they wish. This feature of the course is particularly attractive to students who are auditory learners (the computer tutorial has no audio) and who wish to experience a very careful, slow-paced discussion of each topic. Since approximately 80% of our students perceive themselves as auditory learners, this is an important element of the course design.

Work with Math Staff in the Emporium

In the Emporium, math helpers are available whenever a student gets stuck on a mathematical or computer-related problem. Because the helpers cover many different courses, their approach centers on helping students develop as learners with the immediate problem as the tool. Such an interaction usually begins with the helper asking the student to describe the process he or she has been using to attack the problem and to show the helper where in the book or tutorial or web site the material about the problem is located. Then they work together from that perspective. In this way, students become more aware of how they should go about dealing with difficult problems on their own in the future. Math staff teachers are available in the emporium for about 80 hours per week.

Tutoring Lab

From 6:00 to 9:00 p.m. each evening, Sunday through Thursday, the tutoring lab is available to students in the emporium. Students can sit down with a tutor to work through the details of some of the math problems and to have their individual questions answered. Students highly value the tutoring lab.

Lecture Series

All of the topics in the course are covered in lectures that are given at several different times convenient to the students. In the original design of the course, we tried to convince students that lectures were not the way to learn this material. Despite all of the evidence we had to support that contention, a large percentage felt strongly that they needed them. We came to realize that this issue was causing students to create mental blocks against coming freely to the learning activities that we felt were more appropriate for them, so we decided to provide them with the lecture series. About 5% to 10% of the students attend the lectures and really enjoy them. The students who attend all want to be there, so the antisocial behavior we used to experience in our classes is absent. The best thing about the lecture series is that 90% to 95% of our students choose not to go to lectures and, consequently, participate in our other activities with a very positive attitude.

Testing

Of all of the elements of a math course, the one that generates the most anxiety is testing. Through the use of technology, we have been able to modify the testing procedure so that it makes a major contribution to student learning and is conducted in a way that minimizes anxiety. We offer three different versions of each computer test for the students to take. Their grade on each test is the best grade they obtain on the three versions. Because we want them to have sufficient time to learn from their mistakes, we require that they cannot take more than one version on any particular day. To support their efforts to learn from their mistakes, we offer a Coaches' Corner, at which a math coach goes over each student's test and suggests specific, immediate learning goals that students can pursue to improve their performance. Also, the coach will suggest which of the many learning activities would be particularly helpful in accomplishing these goals. The technological features that allow us to provide for testing include the computer programs' capability to deliver a virtually unlimited number of different but closely related tests and the existence of database management tools able to control the flow of such tests. Therefore, students can take the tests asynchronously. Of course, we had to develop methods to maintain the integrity of the testing procedure, making it at least very difficult to cheat. The students really like this approach to testing, and it allows us an opportunity to remind them that when there is an annoying glitch in technology, that same technology enables us to test them in this positive manner.

The computer test accounts for 80% of the grade on each test. A written portion of each test is given in the focus group accounting for 20%. The written test assures that we actually see students' work and that our evaluation of student performance is comparable to past expectations.

Coaches' Corner

Each student is given an opportunity to take up to three versions of each computer test. Between versions, students may elect to meet with a math coach who will go over the problems that were missed in the previous version and suggest study strategies that might be used to prepare for the next version.

A LITTLE PHILOSOPHY

Giving students a large number of choices in learning activities is not very effective unless the students have sufficient knowledge and experience to make wise choices. I have seen a number of course designs in which this principle is badly violated. For example, sometimes making choices is used as a way to blame the students for an inappropriate educational environment ("Well, you made the choice, so if you didn't learn it, it's your fault, and you have no right to complain"). The appropriate balance between creating structure and providing freedom of choice is difficult to determine. It depends on the type of course and the motivation and maturity of the students. In this course, we know a lot about the attitudinal and academic challenges that our students face, and we developed the course with these factors in mind.

One design element aimed at the creation of structure for student learning is the requirement that each student must spend three hours in the emporium each week. In my department, this aspect of the course design is controversial. In my opinion, this would be an inappropriate requirement for a math class for such students as engineering students, who know their futures are strongly related to their computer and mathematical skills. But I feel that it is essential when working with Math 1015 students. When my students get up in the morning, they can commit to spending an hour in the emporium. They know what that means; they know what that task will require of them. If, instead, I told them they were required to go to the emporium and learn Cramer's rule, they would be unsure what that would entail and whether they would be able to accomplish it. A computer-based philosophy course pulling students from a similar pool as Math 1015 tried using task-oriented goals instead of time on task and flunked a high percentage of students. It is important that, when the students show up in the emporium, we have ways to engage them in stimulating learning activities. Only after students are fully engaged in the learning environment is it reasonable to expect that they will be prepared to make good choices.

THE FUTURE

The current organization of our universities enforces a compartmentalization of learning based on departmentally defined disciplines. Nationally, much effort has been expended to moderate the negative effects of this through bundling courses. At Virginia Tech, our partnership program deals with this issue in a way that does not require the university to make major changes.

The Partnership Program
(with courses in other majors)

Over the years, the mathematics department has been aware of some common concerns about students' preparation. Faculty have been frustrated that many of their juniors and seniors have forgotten much of the mathematics that they were suppose to have learned as freshmen or sophomores. Faculty are then faced with the choice of either taking valuable time reteaching the specific mathematical topics needed or watering their courses down to avoid the mathematics. Studies have shown that the average student will have forgotten about 40% of the material learned in a class during the first year after finishing the class. While a significant amount of material is forgotten, it can be relearned relatively quickly if the student's learning is adequately supported. However, many students required to review mathematical material no longer have their textbooks, and most find trying to learn material using only a mathematics textbook futile. Our experience also has shown that when mathematical topics are expressed in terminology that differs from the language presented in their mathematics course, students tend not to recognize them. Because the Math Emporium is a dynamic learning center, we can provide sustained support for student learning throughout their careers at Tech, and hence, we can finally effectively address this difficult issue.

One of the main products of a partnership is to establish a web page with three basic components:

- **A diagnostic test** will enable students in the partner course to determine which specific mathematical topics they may need to restudy. Specific suggestions will be made as to which software packages or other instructional tools, available in the emporium, could be used to relearn this material. The chance for success in this relearning process is very high because math teachers are available in the emporium to help the students approximately 80 hours per week. Because the material was originally learned in this educational environment, the amount of time required for a student to reacquire the necessary mathematical skills should be minimal.

- **A dictionary** compares terminology that is used to express mathematical concepts in the partner course with the way those same concepts appeared in the mathematics course.

- **A collection of applications** of the mathematical concepts that appear in the partner course is designed to convince students that reviewing the mathematics is going to pay off. The applications also help to motivate students who are currently taking the mathematics course and looking forward to taking the partner course to learn the mathematics well.

The main goal in creating these partnerships, of course, is to enhance student success and to reinforce the notion that students can be successful as independent, active learners of mathematics. However, there are some other worthy goals that we expect will also be accomplished. Through the dialog that occurs during the creation of the web page, the mathematics faculty will become better aware of exactly what the students in the mathematics course will need when they take the partner course. This dialog may result in the development of more robust mathematical techniques being applied in the partner course, resulting in enrichment in that course as well.

SUMMARY

Using the Math Emporium, we have redesigned this course in exciting ways. The assessment of student learning in the course has indicated that we have significantly improved student success. We have fewer students failing the course now than before, and each year as we get more adept at this teaching/learning environment, we see student success continuing to improve. To learn more about the details of the course and the emporium, please visit our web pages. The web page for the emporium is http://www.emporium.vt.edu/ and for the Math 1015 course, http://www.math.vt.edu/math1015/.

REFERENCE

Lial, M. L., Hornsby, E. J., & Schneider, D. I. (1997). *College algebra and trigonometry.* Reading, MA: Addison-Wesley.

CONTACT INFORMATION

Monte B. Boisen, Jr., Professor
Virginia Polytechnic Institute and State University
Mathematics Department
Blacksburg, VA 24061-0123
Email: boisen@math.vt.edu
Phone: (540) 231-7252
Fax: (540) 231-5960

Just-in-Time Teaching for Introductory Physics

D. B. Kim-Shapiro, C. W. Yip, W. C. Kerr, and T. Concannon,
Wake Forest University

Just-in-Time Teaching (JiTT) is a pedagogical technique developed by Gregor Novak, Evelyn Patterson, Andrew Garvin, and Wolfgang Christian (1999). We recount here our experiences using this technique in our introductory physics classes at Wake Forest University. In particular, we address our use of warmup exercises on the web, since we did not implement all the aspects of JiTT elaborated by Novak et al.

MOTIVATION

The classical lecture style of teaching has been described as a situation where information goes from the professor's notes to the students' notes without passing through the minds of either. Too often, the students become unthinking note-taking machines, concentrating on getting the lecture onto paper during class rather than thinking about its content.

It is much more desirable to foster active learning. One excellent example of active learning is *Peer Instruction* developed by Eric Mazur (1997). The goal of peer instruction is to motivate the students to think more about the material while in the classroom and to discuss it there. In this method, the professor poses a conceptual (i.e., nonquantitative), multiple-choice question and gives the students one minute to think about the answer. The students communicate their answers to the professor by holding up a card with an "A," "B," or "C," etc., on it. At this point, the professor has already obtained some information on each student's understanding of the material. Next, unless the class has nearly unanimously given the correct answer, the students are asked to discuss their answers with their neighbors for one to two minutes. Then they are asked to show their answers again, and if there is still no consensus, the class as a whole discusses the problem. Finally, the professor gives the correct answer and the explanation.

We have found that using peer instruction in our introductory classes improves the students' understanding of physics. Dr. Kerr gave the Force Concept Inventory (FCI) to his section as a pretest at the first class meeting and as a posttest as part of the final examination. The FCI is a multiple-choice conceptual evaluation and has been used nationwide for about seven years to measure student achievement in beginning physics courses. The students averaged 42.6% on the pretest and 75% on the posttest. The correlation between the pretest score and the improvement in the posttest score is in nearly perfect agreement with results from other universities that utilize active learning methods. (The data can be seen at this web site: http://www.physics.umn.edu/groups/physed/Research/MNModel/FCI.html.)

One problem with using peer instruction or any other technique that promotes active learning in the classroom is that it can be very time consuming; the technique takes about five minutes per question. In courses where external pressures require that a certain amount of material must be covered (for example the MCATS for introductory physics courses), the time that is consumed in active learning must be recovered in some way. One method for doing this is to ensure both that the students read assignments before class and that the professor obtains feedback before class on their comprehension of the reading. This way, less time can be spent lecturing on factual information that the students have learned from reading, and professors can adjust their lectures "just-in-time" for class based on students' demonstrated comprehension of what they have read.

GOALS

1) Encourage the students to read ahead. As described above, this is done so that time is class can be used to maximize active learning.

2) Enhance communication between professor and students. The use of the web is intended to enhance communication on the reading assignment and on class material in general.

METHODS

After each class meeting, an assignment for the next meeting is posted on the web. This warm-up assignment is written in html and linked to a CGI script (Dr. Kim-Shapiro is willing to share the CGI script with anyone who wants it). An example of such an assignment is shown in Figure 2.1. The heading includes the reading assignment and a reminder of the time the warm-up is due, although students already knew they were due one hour before class. The CGI script is written so that the form cannot be submitted if nothing is entered in the name and student ID fields. Often other announcements will be put in the header, such as reminders about review sessions or hints on a certain homework problem. The questions in the warm-up are based on the reading assignment. There is always one text question and at least one multiple-choice question. As discussed below, the comment box can be used to make observations about the reading, the lecture, or anything at all.

When the student submits his warm-up answers, s/he receives a notice that the professor received it and a grade. During the first semester that Dr. Kim-Shapiro's class used the warm-ups, they were graded only on a completed/uncompleted basis. In the second semester, the CGI script was modified to grade the multiple-choice questions. The warm-ups were graded by awarding two points just for submitting and one additional point for each correct multiple-choice answer. The students were also given an email hot link to the professor at that point if they wanted to discuss their grades.

The students' answers are emailed to the professor. In addition, their student ID number, grade, and time of submission are written into an ASCII file. The ASCII file can be read by an Excel macro that uses a pivot table to keep a spreadsheet of the grades. The professor reads the warm-up answers and the students' comments before class, responds to some queries by email, and modifies the day's lesson just-in-time for class. To obtain the maximum benefit from this active learning technique, it is important to go over the day's warm-up as part of the day's activities in class.

RESULTS

Reading Ahead

At the end of the 1998 spring semester, the students in Dr. Kim-Shapiro's class were asked to evaluate the use of warm-ups. During this same semester, Dr. Kerr had been asking his students to submit short reading summaries before each class to encourage them to read ahead. A comparison of the students' evaluations is shown in Table 2.1. A larger proportion of the students evaluated the warm-ups in a positive way when compared to the reading summaries.

TABLE 2.1

SUMMARY OF EVALUATIONS
FROM SPRING 1998 SEMESTER

	Warm-ups		Reading Summaries	
A	12	28%	5	18%
B	22	51%	12	42%
C	2	5%	5	18%
D	3	7%	3	11%
E	4	9%	3	11%

A = Very good, B = good, C = Average,
D = Fair and E = Poor.
The students were asked: How would you rate the use of warm-up (reading summaries) exercises for class?

Enhancement of Communication

Instead of having the text field for comments, Dr. Kerr just had a hot email link on his form. After the first day of class, Dr. Kim-Shapiro found that 21 out of 50 students had added comments in the text field. For the warm-up due the day before spring break, a day when students are especially apathetic, six out of 50 students added comments in the text box. The first day of class, only two of Dr. Kerr's students sent him email. In teaching the same class in a previous year, before trying JiTT, Dr. Kim-Shapiro invited his students to email him with their questions, but only a few ever did so.

Below are a few excerpts from comments sent to Dr. Kim-Shapiro.

- I don't know if other people feel the same way, but problem 30-41 from our homework due next Monday just seems very difficult. I've read my notes on displacement current, read section 30-8 twice, and looked at the example problem in it and I just can't figure it out. Could we maybe do 30-41 in class?

FIGURE 2.1

AN EXAMPLE OF A WARM-UP EXERCISE

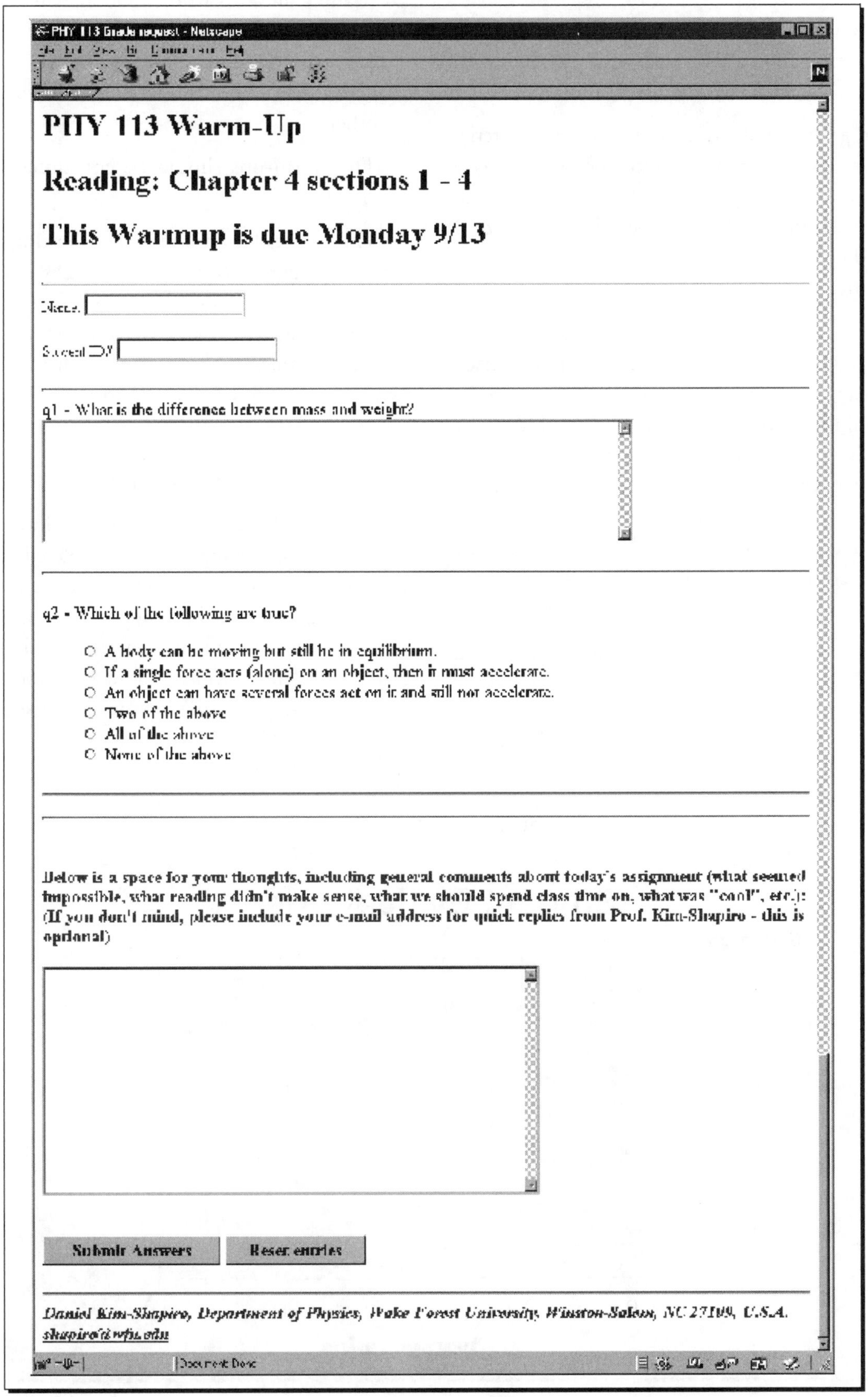

PHY 113 Warm-Up

Reading: Chapter 4 sections 1 - 4

This Warmup is due Monday 9/13

Name: [   ]

Student ID: [   ]

q1 - What is the difference between mass and weight?

[   ]

q2 - Which of the following are true?

- ○ A body can be moving but still be in equilibrium.
- ○ If a single force acts (alone) on an object, then it must accelerate.
- ○ An object can have several forces act on it and still not accelerate.
- ○ Two of the above
- ○ All of the above
- ○ None of the above

Below is a space for your thoughts, including general comments about today's assignment (what seemed impossible, what reading didn't make sense, what we should spend class time on, what was "cool", etc.): (If you don't mind, please include your e-mail address for quick replies from Prof. Kim-Shapiro - this is optional)

[   ]

[Submit Answers]   [Reset entries]

Daniel Kim-Shapiro, Department of Physics, Wake Forest University, Winston-Salem, NC 27109, U.S.A.
shapiro@wfu.edu

- I have had difficulty conceptualizing what a 'closed surface' is, and the connection between Gauss' Law and such surfaces.

- Would you be willing to do some sample electrical force problems in class? I am having problems with the homework, more than I feel I should...

- I find great trouble in understanding the material on the electric flux and electric field lines. I have difficulty in conceptualizing the field lines. What exactly are they? What do they help us visualize? I hope I will understand these points better after class tomorrow.

In the case of the student asking for a homework problem to be done in class, Dr. Kim-Shapiro realized that he had forgotten to cover the relevant material and so adjusted his lecture to include it. Often, he would solve some particular problems in class at the students' request.

At the end of the semester, a survey was sent to the students in three sections of introductory physics. The students were asked to respond to the following statements:

1) The use of the warm-ups encouraged you to read ahead.

2) The use of the warm-ups enhanced communication between you and your professor.

3) Reading ahead is worthwhile, making it easier to understand the lecture, making it so the professor can spend more time on applications and less on derivations or reiterating facts from the book, or other.

4) The warm-ups should be continued in future classes.

They selected from among the following responses: 1) Strongly Agree, 2) Agree, 3) Do Not Disagree or Agree, 4) Disagree, or 5) Strongly Disagree. Figure 2.2 tabulates the results of this survey where each response was assigned a numeric value equal to that in parentheses above (e.g., Strongly Agree = 1, Strongly Disagree = 5).

DISCUSSION

The first time that Dr. Kim-Shapiro used warm-ups, he graded them on a completed/uncompleted basis. Most students said that it encouraged them to read ahead, but one student said that none of the students read; they just guess. This singular comment indicates that at least one student didn't read ahead a large percentage of the time. The professor's review of the students' re-

FIGURE 2.2

RESULTS FROM JiTT SURVEY

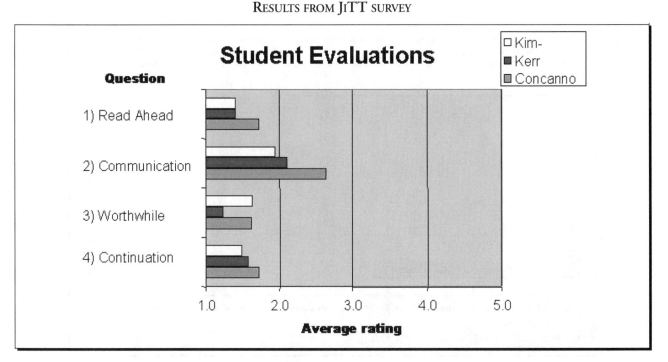

sponses to the text question should indicate their level of reading comprehension, and thus, students who just guess should be noticed. However, Dr. Kim-Shapiro decided to grade the multiple-choice questions to more strongly encourage reading ahead and discourage guessing. Incorporating some kind of grading is likely to encourage reading more than if no grading is done. Figure 2.2 clearly shows that the students mostly strongly agreed or agreed that the warm-ups encouraged them to read ahead. The authors also feel that the warm-ups encourage the students to read ahead.

Interestingly, the students generally agreed that the warm-ups enhanced communication between professor and students, but not overwhelmingly. One student commented that computer communication made it less likely he would come to office hours, where he would have otherwise spent more time communicating face-to-face. Overall, the students and authors felt that using warm-ups enhanced communication.

As also indicated by Figure 2.2, the students felt strongly overall that the warm-ups were worthwhile and that they should be used again in other classes.

REFERENCES

Mazur, E. (1987). *Peer instruction.* Upper Saddle River, NJ: Prentice Hall.

Novak, G. M., Patterson, E. T., Garvin, A. D., & Christian, W. (1999). *Just-in-time teaching: Blending active learning with web technology.* Upper Saddle River, NJ: Prentice Hall.

CONTACT INFORMATION

Daniel Kim-Shapiro, Assistant Professor of Physics
Wake Forest University
Winston-Salem, NC 27109-7507
Email: shapiro@wfu.edu
WWW: http://www.wfu.edu/~shapiro/warmdes.html
Phone: (336) 758-4993
Fax: (336) 758-6142

Vignettes 3 Circuit Simulation Software in Electronics Courses

G. Eric Matthews, Wake Forest University

INTRODUCTION

"I hate CircuitMaker. It tells me when I'm wrong." Peter smiled as he told me what he thought of the circuit simulation software.

I teach electronics, a course taken principally by science majors and designed to equip them to build and to troubleshoot laboratory equipment. I introduced CircuitMaker into the course three years ago. CircuitMaker is a program for drafting electronic circuits. More importantly, it simulates the operation of circuits. Virtual voltmeters and oscilloscopes probe signals anywhere in the circuit. Since introducing CircuitMaker, my assignments and tests have become more challenging, while student success on these projects has improved.

EDUCATIONAL THEORIES

My electronics course involves only a few difficult concepts. However, students must master many simple ideas, and they must weave these together in complex and creative ways. I want students to be able to design novel circuits to meet the unusual needs that they encounter in research. They must synthesize what they learn of the behavior of many electronic devices so that they can create circuits that can do the things they want.

Students can only learn to design circuits by designing circuits. The structure of my assignments has changed little in the past 15 years: I ask students to design a circuit that fulfills a specific function. For example, I may ask students to design an audio amplifier with specific characteristics.

Prior to introducing CircuitMaker, the most obvious shortcoming I saw in my course was that the students rarely got anything but the simplest assignments correct. A student's work might be pretty good, but usually a design error or two would keep the circuit from working. I caught many of these errors (and surely missed many more), corrected the homework, and returned it to the student. The student was happy to have a good grade, I was happy to have finished grading, but nowhere in the process was there a circuit that worked. Outside academe, there is little use for circuits that do not work!

Unlike my other physics courses, students rarely collaborated on circuit designs. They completed their assignments quickly and therefore saw little need to work with others. There was little value in my assigning more problems, as students would generally make the same mistake on each circuit.

Lab provides an opportunity for students to find their own errors. A few quick measurements determine whether the circuit is doing what it should. If not, probing signals throughout the circuit yields clues that are helpful in identifying the problems with the circuit. Unfortunately, lab meets only a few hours each week, and students can troubleshoot only one or two circuits in that time.

Active learning, interactive engagement, immediate feedback, discussions with other students and/or faculty have been demonstrated to improve learning in physics classes (Hake, 1998). Computer applications serve as vehicles to stimulate such activities (Novak et al., 1999; Christian & Titus, 1998). I wanted students to work harder. I wanted them to work together and learn from each other. I wanted them to know when they had completed an assignment successfully and when they had not.

COMPUTER-ENHANCED TECHNIQUES USED

In spring of 1997, I introduced CircuitMaker, a circuit simulation package from Microcode Engineering. CircuitMaker is one of many such packages based on SPICE (Simulation Program [with] Integrated Circuit Emphasis), developed at the University of California, Berkeley, or XSPICE, developed by Fred Cox of the Georgia Tech Research Institute.

SPICE and its variants allow one to model the behavior of electronic circuits. The user calls upon component definitions from a library and describes how these are connected to form a circuit. The libraries of components and the interconnections define a set of mathematical relationships. The SPICE software solves these equations numerically to determine how voltages and currents will behave throughout the circuit as a function of time. SPICE and its variants have long been the industry standard, and models of many or most electronic devices are available from manufacturers.

Until recently, such simulation packages were difficult to use. However, programs like CircuitMaker use a graphical interface to simplify the process, making design easier and more intuitive.

At first glance, CircuitMaker looks much like common drawing or drafting software. A pop-down menu presents lists of electronic devices. More than 4,000 devices are available in the standard library, and the library can be supplemented with devices downloaded from the web sites of device manufacturers. The user selects devices, arranges them on the screen, and connects them with wires by dragging the mouse. Circuits go together quickly, yielding a schematic diagram of the circuit.

Now the fun begins: The user clicks *Run* and a simulation is performed. CircuitMaker includes several virtual test instruments that behave much like the physical instruments that students use in lab. The oscilloscope tool can be placed anywhere in the circuit, resulting in a graph of voltage versus time. Using such tools, students determine whether the circuit they designed works as intended. A screen shot of the circuit and the virtual oscilloscope are shown in Figure 3.1.

ASSESSED OUTCOMES

The change in student learning was immediate and obvious only a week after introducing CircuitMaker. Alan Tackett, my graduate teaching assistant, had assisted with the lab portion of the electronics course for two years. In lab, following introduction of the simulation software, he asked me, "What's going on?"

"What do you mean?" I replied.

"We're talking."

"So?"

"We've never had time to talk in here before. Our help has always been the bottleneck. Why aren't the students asking for our help?"

In the past, students did not confront their misunderstandings until lab. Corrected homework assignments never seemed to communicate that they did not know enough about the current topic. My corrections often seemed obvious and they would not realize that they still did not understand, or could not do, something in the topic until confronted with their failures in lab.

With the introduction of CircuitMaker, I no longer grade homework. More accurately, the only grades I assign are 0 or 100. I expect students to turn in circuits that work. With the software, they can check for themselves. Initial designs rarely work, as these circuits are complex. The student must have a thorough understanding of the concepts involved, synthesize them, and carry out the calculations without error. This rarely happens on the first try.

In previous years, upon completion of a design, a student would look it over for obvious mistakes and turn it in. Now, having designed the circuit in CircuitMaker, the student clicks on the *Run* button and observes the output with the virtual oscilloscope. More often than not, the output is incorrect.

Learning begins at precisely the point where, without CircuitMaker, the student would have finished the assignment. He will merely have rendered a representation of what he *thinks* will accomplish the task. Now he realizes his understanding is incomplete. He reexamines his assumptions, looks through notes and text. He probes several points throughout the circuit to determine just where the signal is bad. He shows his design to other students, and they argue about the appropriateness of different design approaches. He visits me in my office.

This explains Peter's assessment of CircuitMaker quoted at the beginning of this article. Peter and the other students spend much more time on their homework than they would were it not for this software. However, the time is very productive, spent not on the original design, but in confronting their misunderstandings. CircuitMaker gives students feedback at the best possible time—the moment when they think they understand and have accomplished the assignment. Prompt feedback stimulates many students to go beyond the assignment to explore more sophisticated problems. Their explorations are rewarded with immediate feedback; they know if they have been successful.

FIGURE 3.1

SCREEN SHOT OF CIRCUIT AND VIRTUAL OSCILLOSCOPE

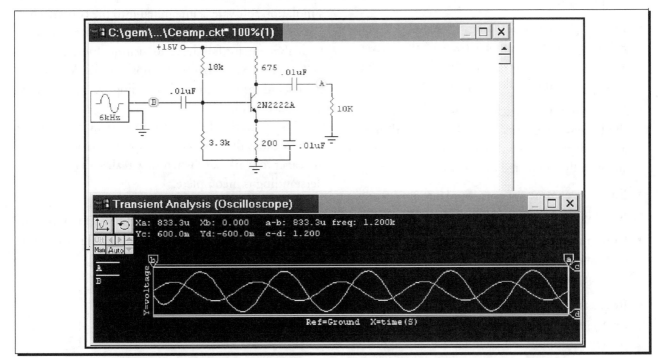

An unexpected consequence is much improved diagnostic skills. When their virtual circuits do not work, they probe with the oscilloscope tool to find symptoms of the problem. The techniques they use are transferable to real circuits.

As I have seen students learn more rapidly and thoroughly, I have become more demanding. My assignments are harder, and my tests are tougher. In spite of my increased expectations, grades in the course have improved slightly.

I did not expect CircuitMaker to bring so many improvements to my course. All I expected it to do was to provide prompt feedback so that students would put more work into homework. Students are not lazy; however, they are often overly optimistic in their assessment of how well they have completed assignments. Accurate and prompt feedback stimulates them to work harder.

I have been pleasantly surprised to see that CircuitMaker effectively addresses all of the "seven principles for good practice in undergraduate education" (Chickering & Gamson, 1991). The use of simulation software:

- **Encourages student/faculty contact.** I get many more office visits now that students know when they need help.

- **Encourages cooperation among students.** Students must work together to successfully complete assignments.

- **Encourages active learning.** Homework is more engaging due to the interactivity of the software, and students are now much more likely to push beyond the required task to explore their own ideas.

- **Gives prompt feedback.** This is the key to most of the benefits. Students are willing to work harder and study more when they know that they have not successfully completed their work.

- **Emphasizes time on task.** Students are spending much more time on their homework than before.

- **Communicates high expectations.** I no longer accept homework that is not perfect! My assignments and tests are more demanding.

- **Respects diverse talents and ways of learning.** The highly interactive nature of simulation software presents an important complement to the mathe-matical analysis that is the core of the original circuit design. Students are able to bring different talents to bear in the original design and subsequent diagnostics.

LESSONS LEARNED

Students have become accustomed to designing with CircuitMaker, and I now allow them to use the software during tests. CircuitMaker reveals their minor mathematical errors so that they can correct them. This lets me focus on assessing understanding rather than grading the accuracy of their arithmetic. However, letting students use CircuitMaker on tests presents new challenges in assessment. My old circuit design problems seem trivial now. Students complete some of the old problems, not through understanding the mathematical relationships, but by choosing components experimentally. Finding more challenging problems that reveal differing levels of understanding requires more care when students can use such software.

I was forced to rethink my exams even before I allowed students to use CircuitMaker on tests. Students in my course know more electronics now, and the old exams poorly test their new understanding.

SUMMARY

Students of electronics learn more rapidly when circuit simulation software is integrated into the course. They put more effort into their assignments, work together to analyze circuit failures, and visit me more often for help. They develop better diagnostic skills. My assignments and tests are more demanding, yet students are more successful.

The remarkable transformation in this course demonstrates the power of prompt feedback. Students are eager to work hard when they realize that their understanding is incomplete.

For further information, see http://www.wfu.edu/~matthews/cel/Electronics-cel.html for more on my use of CircuitMaker and for links to circuit simulation software and SPICE models.

REFERENCES

Chickering, A. W., & Gamson, Z. F. (1991). *Applying the seven principles for good practice in undergraduate education.* San Francisco, CA: Jossey-Bass.

Christian, W., & Titus, A. (1998). Developing web-based curricula using Java Applets. *Computers in Physics, 12,* 227-232.

Hake, R. R. (1998). Interactive-engagement versus traditional methods: A six-thousand-student survey of mechanics test data for introductory physics courses. *American Journal of Physics, 66* (1) 64-74.

Novak, G. M., Patterson, E. T., Garvin, A. D., & Christian, W. (1999). *Just-in-time teaching: Blending active learning with web technology.* Upper Saddle River, NJ: Prentice Hall.

CONTACT INFORMATION

G. Eric Matthews, Professor and Chair
Department of Physics
Wake Forest University
Winston-Salem, NC 27109-7507
Email: matthews@wfu.edu
WWW: http://www.wfu.edu/~matthews
Phone: (336) 758-5340
Fax: (336) 758-6142

Vignette 4 Just-in-Time Teaching: Blending Active Learning with Web Technology

Gregor M. Novak, Indiana University-Purdue University Indianapolis

This vignette describes the teaching strategy we developed at IUPUI and dubbed Just-in-Time Teaching. For more details, please visit our web site at http://web-physics.iupui.edu/jitt.html and/or examine our book (Novak et al., 1999).

INTRODUCTION AND BACKGROUND

Today's introductory physics classrooms are populated with a mix of traditional and nontraditional students. We feel both a desire and an obligation to meet the students where they are, to help them to learn from our courses. Over the past four years, Professors Gregor Novak and Andy Garvin, in collaboration with faculty at the United States Air Force Academy, have been developing a teaching strategy to attain the list of goals identified by physics education researchers over the last two decades (Arons, 1997; Redish, 1994; Tobias, 1990). Students should control their learning processes, be motivated to learn physics, and be able to make connections between physics in the classroom and the real world. We strive for both physics content mastery and the acquisition and honing of more general skills. Students must improve their critical thinking skills, estimation skills, and problem-solving skills. We also strive to emphasize teamwork, collaborative learning, and effective communication.

At IUPUI, we face additional challenges due to the characteristics of our urban institution and our student population. IUPUI students are older and more mature than those at many colleges and universities, but they often have poor study habits. They are under severe time constraints due to job and family obligations. These constraints lead to inefficient use of out-of-class time. We strive to help them manage their study time effectively and encourage frequent, short study sessions.

Our students have widely varying backgrounds and study skills. It is not uncommon to find both technically underprepared and technically advanced honors students in the same course. Many have mathematical skills that have grown rusty since their last educational experience. In response, we try to help the entire spectrum advance rather than target the phantom average student.

Retention is also a major problem. Commuting students, who are often part-time, have particular difficulty staying in the course. These problems are not unique to IUPUI or to science and engineering: high attrition rates are common among students returning to higher education nationwide (Cope & Hannah, 1975). JiTT strategies represent a deliberate, coordinated attempt to address these challenges.

Our collaboration with the United States Air Force Academy has been very fruitful because, despite the fact that IUPUI and the USAFA appear to be very different institutions with very different students, we find that we share many of the same goals and challenges. At the Air Force Academy, the breadth of student backgrounds and interests is especially significant. All students, regardless of their major, take calculus-based physics. The Just-in-Time Teaching strategies are designed to work well with extremes of student capability, as they provide remediation and encouragement to the weaker students, and they provide enrichment to and pique the curiosity of the stronger students. At both institutions, we expect our students to demonstrate mastery of fundamental physics, connect the classroom physics to the real world, develop cooperative work habits and communication skills, and control their own learning processes. We want the students to develop their critical thinking ability, estimation skills, and ability to frame and solve ill-defined problems.

There is no longer any doubt in the physics teaching community that learning environments emphasizing student engagement enhance learning (Hake, 1998). The Just-in-Time Teaching approach blends an active-learner classroom with the around-the-clock communication capability of the World Wide Web. Students interact with one another, human instructors, and technology in ways that optimize effectiveness. While no technology can match the benefits of an expert human mentor who observes the learning activity and intervenes as needed, there are aspects of learning where technology can have an edge over a human instructor.

THE JiTT CLASSROOM

The heart of the JiTT method is a collaborative recitation/discussion session. Students meet in a common room with at least two faculty instructors, one or two graduate students, and several undergraduate student mentors.

Sessions start with a short review of homework, with special emphasis on systematic problem solving techniques. Teams of two to four students are given a set of unfamiliar problems. The teams first discuss the approach they will take. With the help of the facilitators, they reach a consensus. Then they systematically solve the problem. Students practice problem solving, teamwork, and communication. Faculty and teaching associates get to know the students. This approach builds a sense of class community that leads to more engaged attendance and eliminates some of the causes of attrition.

Lectures are built around student answers to warm-ups, which are short quizzes that have an electronic due date just hours before class. They are constructed so that the student must preview the upcoming material in the textbook. The instructor collects the students' electronic submissions, reads them, and presents a selected subset of them to the class, weaving them into the discussion as appropriate. Discreet in-class critique of these submissions helps improve writing skills and the construction of physics knowledge.

THE JiTT WEB PAGES
(http://webphysics.iupui.edu/introphysics)

JiTT web material is designed to blend human and technological resources effectively. The web assignments encourage students to prepare for the classroom activity, where the instructors will provide intellectual mentoring. We require that their exposition be in plain English, with supporting arguments referring to the underlying physics and mathematics but without the use of equations. This is how an engineer or a scientist communicates with the nontechnical members of a project team.

The web assignments have different educational goals as detailed below, but they also work together in several important respects. By scattering the credit over several pages, we encourage students to work on physics frequently and in short sessions and to be in constant electronic communication with the instructors and with one another.

JiTT Web Parts

By providing a map to the wealth of information available on the web, our web pages encourage the students to think beyond the limits of the course material. From a sidebar menu students can branch out to the various web parts.

This Week in Physics

Keeping up the drumbeat is the weekly "This Week in Physics." This newsletter-style page keeps the students informed of the class news and often calls attention to physics-related news events. Often there is a midweek edition of the page; e.g., after a major test or an important news event.

The Warm-Up

The warm-up affords the students some ownership of the lecture session. These conceptual exercises are the heart of the just-in-time instruction system. Each morning before class, the instructor reads the student responses and then adjusts the lecture material to respond to the students' demonstrated knowledge, while the issues are still fresh in their minds. By doing this, the instructor individualizes the lecture. Conceptual questions are particularly valuable JiTT items. It is easy to forget the misconceptions that many students bring to their first contact with various physics concepts (Peters, 1982). For example, consider the words *force*, *power*, and *energy*. In everyday English, these are generally considered synonymous. However, in physics, these words all have special meanings and cannot be equated. Students, pressed for time, often miss this fact on a first reading of the book. A warm-up question asking the students to write about these concepts motivates many to reread a few sections. Students in the classroom recognize their own wording, both correct and incorrect, and thus become engaged as part of the feedback loop. It is quite common for the classroom

discussion to continue via email. Paradoxically, technology used this way encourages a more personal and intimate bond between instructors and students. It is clear from course evaluations that students feel part of a team working on a common project.

The Puzzle

The puzzle is a weekly assignment, consisting of a single question that typically involves several concepts. After the student responses have been collected electronically, a classroom discussion closes the topic and integrates it with the rest of the course material.

What's Physics Good For?

The What's Physics Good For? page brings the students a weekly essay on some related topic not central to the course material. These essays differ from the application essays in physics textbooks in important ways. First, they contain numerous links to external web sites containing a wealth of related material. Second, they always end with extra-credit assignments, which induce the students to follow the web links and thus relate the course material to the real world. We noticed that students would not visit the JiTT site unless there was a direct academic incentive. We did not wish to reduce the amount of traditional homework, nor did we wish to require extra work without a concomitant increase in the number of credit hours earned. Offering extra credit answers both of these concerns, while simultaneously improving student morale.

Lastly, the information and the communication pages contain electronic versions of traditional handout material, such as the syllabus, the course calendar, and the electronic version of the course bulletin board.

Assessment

The introduction of the JiTT strategy has led to improved retention, better learning outcomes, and more positive student attitudes. Since JiTT was introduced in 1995, attrition in the introductory calculus-based sequence has dropped by approximately 40% in each of two courses. In addition, enrollment in both courses has increased.

To gauge the students' cognitive gains, we have adopted the Force Concept Inventory (FCI) test (Halloun, 1985), a national standard for first-semester introductory physics. Students take a 30-item test in the first week of classes before any instruction has taken place. At the end of the semester, they take the identical test again. The results are given in terms of normalized gain, defined as (posttest percentile/pretest percentile)/(100 percentile/pretest percentile). FCI is a respected instrument in physics education research. Richard Hake has compiled data on 62 introductory physics courses taught at a variety of high schools and universities. He finds that normalized gain hovers around 0.23 for traditionally taught courses and averages about 0.48 for interactive engagement courses (Hake, 1998). At IUPUI, the results for the combined day sections of Physics 152 were 0.40 for fall 1998 and 0.35 for spring 1999. The 35% to 40% gain at IUPUI places the Just-in-Time Teaching strategy into Hake's category of interactive engagement teaching.

REFERENCES

Arons, A. B. (1997). *Teaching introductory physics.* New York, NY: John Wiley.

Cope, R., & Hannah, W. (1975). *Revolving college door: The causes and consequences of dropping out and transferring.* New York, NY: John Wiley.

Hake, R. R. (1998). Interactive-engagement versus traditional methods: A six-thousand-student survey of mechanics test data for introductory physics courses. *American Journal of Physics, 66* (1), 64-74.

Halloun, H. (1985). Force Concept Inventory (FCI). *American Journal of Physics, 53,* 1043-1055.

Novak, G. M., Patterson, E. T., Garvin, A. D., & Christian, W. (1999). *Just-in-time-teaching: Blending active learning with web technology.* Upper Saddle River, NJ: Prentice Hall.

Peters, P. C. (1982). Even honors students have conceptual difficulties with physics. *American Journal of Physics, 50* (6), 501-508.

Redish, E. F. (1994). Implications of cognitive studies for teaching physics. *American Journal of Physics, 62* (9), 796-803.

Tobias, S. (1990*). They're not dumb, they're different: Stalking the second tier.* Tucson, AZ: Research Corporation.

CONTACT INFORMATION

Gregor M. Novak, Professor of Physics
Indiana University Purdue University Indianapolis
402 N. Blackford Street
Indianapolis, IN 46202
Email: gnovak@iupui.edu
WWW: http://webphysics.iupui.edu/introphysics
Phone: (317) 274-6911
Fax: (317) 274-2393

PHYS345 Electricity and Electronics for Engineers

George Watson, University of Delaware

In the fall of 1998, the department of physics and astronomy at the University of Delaware offered a new course designed specifically for sophomore mechanical engineering majors. Its content was to be a subset of the material from the traditional second semester course in electricity and magnetism merged with material from a second course on electronics taught to seniors by the department of electrical engineering. The goal of the department of mechanical engineering was to streamline its curriculum and provide its students with better working knowledge of electricity and electronics early in their studies, with the hope that they would be better prepared to incorporate that experience into their later design projects. Having taught both the electricity and magnetism course to engineering majors and the electronics course to physics majors, I was tapped to design and to deliver the new course.

EDUCATIONAL THEORIES

Problem-based learning has been widely adopted across the University of Delaware as a method for promoting cooperative learning among students. Our Institute of Transforming Undergraduate Education has been working with about 100 faculty members each year to employ such active learning strategies along with effective use of technology in their courses. As a founding coleader of the institute, I have been active in promoting the use of the Internet and online resources to leverage active learning and to implement best practice. In the design of this new course, I was eager to incorporate the best practices that I had adopted in earlier courses; for reference, my first web-enhanced course was offered in fall 1995.

My philosophy on the use of web resources to enhance student learning emphasizes multiple learning channels: The more channels engaged in learning, the better. In addition, among T. A. Angelo's 14 principles for improved higher learning (Angelo, 1993), I believe my use of the web emphasizes the following three:

1) To be most effective, teachers need to balance levels of intellectual challenge and instructional support.

2) Motivation to learn is alterable; it can be affected positively and negatively by the task, the learning environment, the teacher, and the learner.

3) Interaction between teachers and learners is one of the most powerful factors in promoting learning.

These points are mirrored in the well-known "seven principles for good practice in undergraduate education," first published by AAHE in 1987 (Chickering & Gamson, 1987).

WEB-ENHANCED FEATURES USED

Course Email List

UD automatically provides a mailing list for each section of a course. One powerful use of that list is to contact students even before the course officially starts. About 24 hours before our first class meeting, I broadcast a welcome message to the class and direct them to our web site. Thus, they learn a bit about both the course and me before we ever meet.

Online Forms

The students receive their first assignment in the welcome message. They are asked to go to the assignment's page and participate in a quick survey. Two questions are posed to each student: "How often do you check your email?" and "How often do you use the World Wide Web?" The possible answers are displayed as radio buttons on the form: "several times per day," "at least once per day," or "every few days." Their choices are emailed anonymously to me via the form processor, along with information about the type of connection and web browser used to submit the form. At the beginning of each course, I establish a profile of student computer and Internet habits. Remarkably, I received responses in fall 1999 from almost half of my students within 24 hours, before our first class even assembled!

I also use online forms to process queries about student preferences and attitudes regarding class formats and possible dates for rescheduling exams. The students are pleased to have the opportunity to participate in guiding the course's organization. Each student gets one vote; no one speaks louder or more persuasively than another on an emailed form.

Online Anonymous Suggestion Box

This web feature is simply a modernized approach to the student suggestion in/official response out paper cycle that I had witnessed for many years on a remote wall of our library. I make available a very simple online form—just one textbox area—where a student can enter a suggestion and click to email it to me anonymously. For the students' protection, I password-protect the access to the suggestion submission box; after all, if you receive a troubling suggestion, you want to ensure that it comes from one of your students and not some meddling imposter!

Rather than posting suggestions automatically, I give each one some thought, perhaps holding onto it for a day or two if some action is warranted. I then provide a response along with the suggestion, maintaining as much of the original wording as is prudent. This opens a powerful communication channel for some students. It allows me to defuse difficult issues, to air my views as well as the students', and to justify my actions publicly. The availability of this online forum saves me time, as I can avoid repetitious queries and private responses.

PRESENT, a faculty technology resource center run by user services at UD, now provides a template so that instructors who wish to incorporate such a feature on their course web sites may do so. This feature has been popular with my students—they have been very respectful for the most part. One caution: If you are easily disturbed by criticism, an anonymous suggestion box may not be for you.

Out-of-Class Announcements

An announcements page can free you from spending time at the beginning or end of each class on organizational details. I especially like to use it to avoid making unneeded references to upcoming exams, such as location of review session and availability of previous exams. I once heard that instructors typically make reference to an upcoming or past exam in about 80% of their classes. I conscientiously avoid organizational announcements in class now, particularly regarding exams; instead, I rely on the announcements page and the class mailing list as often as possible.

Exam Archives and Quiz Solutions

These two features are great for increasing the time that students spend out of class. In a typical engineering course I assign about 100 end-of-chapter problems. While the students are generally diligent in working out solutions to the assigned homework, they are often far more interested in seeing how problems on previous exams are solved. Thus, I actually increase the students' workload dramatically by making all copies of prior exams available to them —and they thank me for it! I did not provide online solutions, since I have had bad experiences in the past with students who try to memorize the written solutions rather than use the problems as a learning opportunity to test their understanding. I do provide a special evening review session several days before the exam; otherwise, the anxiety levels of some students might escalate dangerously.

Another aspect of web publishing that I rely on is the prompt posting of solutions to in-class quizzes. I customarily present a quiz in the last ten to 15 minutes of the last class of the week; this helps to offset any attendance problems associated with some students' desires for an early start to the weekend. After the class ends, I promptly post to our web site a detailed solution to the quiz. It is remarkable how many students check in to the solution page over the weekend, regardless of the hour.

Student Directories

I make a special effort to learn students' names; this is essential for making a large class seem smaller and friendlier. I begin to learn many of their names through the use of the weekly quiz described above. When students hand in their quizzes at the end of class, I glance at the name on the paper as well as the face and begin to build the mental database. I use web-based directories to reinforce the names. Early in the semester, I attend each laboratory section (about 20 students in each) with a digital camera that I borrow from PRESENT. A photo of each group of three or four students becomes a central feature of a student directory that includes name, email address, and personal URL, when available. The process of looking up each email address and checking on the availability of a personal homepage helps impress at least their usernames in my mental database. With this approach to learning student names, I generally command about 80% within the first four weeks and all of them by the end of the term.

Measured Results

I am interested in the various roles that technology can play in enhancing learning. When surveyed the first time that I relied on the web for course material delivery in fall 1995, the majority of my students felt that a course web site was "extremely beneficial" to their learning. They also ranked the use of computer-based demonstrations in class and in labs as beneficial. Of course, I do not believe that the use of technology by itself guarantees increased student learning. When used in conjunction with clearly defined learning objectives and active learning strategies, students have generally found incorporation of technology in the classroom to be effective.

Lessons Learned

In addition to the web-enhanced features listed above, I present the usual array of course materials on the course web site. These include class notes, laboratory notes and exercises, hints and selected answers for homework assignments, textbook errata, and relevant online resources. Over the past four years, I have learned the following about using course web sites:

- Avoid spending too much class time presenting web pages that you have created. After all, you would not stand in front of the class and read from a textbook. If your students have ready access to the online material, they can study it on their own. Show the students how to use the online course material, then communicate your expectations for its use during their out-of-class time.

- As I refine a course web site, I try to dream up ways to build a dynamic site, one where the student enthusiastically checks in at the end of each class. I sprinkle in relevant animations, sound files, and hidden text boxes that appear when the mouse cursor rolls over a graphical element. I try to make the course fun by including motivational quotes, Letterman top-ten lists, and call-backs to earlier demos and stunts from class. When organizational announcements and assignment updates are not the only reason to visit the web site, the out-of-class

FIGURE 5.1

MEASURING EFFECTIVENESS

http://www.physics.udel.edu/wwwusers/watson/scen103/eval95b.gif

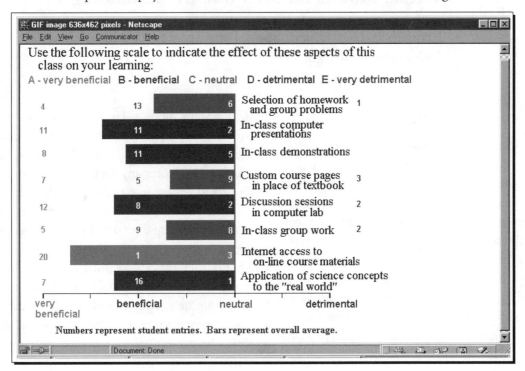

time students spend on your web site grows. The opportunity for students to learn from the material you have created and made available online grows proportionately.

CONCLUSION

Course web sites are a powerful aid to student learning. Appropriately designed interactions can enhance communication between you and your students; web-enhanced communication is especially important in large classes. Online course materials can help you make the most of class time and increase the time students spend outside of class engaged with the course material.

REFERENCES

Angelo, T. A. (1993, April 1). A teacher's dozen. *AAHE Bulletin*, 3-13.

Chickering, A. W., & Gamson, Z. F. (1987, March). Seven principles for good practice in undergraduate education. *AAHE Bulletin, 39* (7), 3-7.

CONTACT INFORMATION

George Watson, Professor
Department of Physics and Astronomy
University of Delaware
Newark, DE 19716
Email: ghw@udel.edu
WWW: http://www.physics.udel.edu/~watson/,
http://www.udel.edu/present/best_practices/
Course: http://www.physics.udel.edu/~watson/phys345/
Phone: (302) 831-6677
Fax: (302) 831-1637

Vignette 6 **The Virtual Solar System Project: Students Building Virtual Models for Scientific Understanding**

**Kenneth E. Hay, J. Scott Shaw, Peter H. Hauschildt,
University of Georgia**

INTRODUCTION

The Virtual Solar System Project has two general goals. The first is to bring students up to date on emergent and vital activities of authentic scientific practice. The second is to transform a traditional, lecture-based course, Introduction to Astronomy, into a learner-centered, collaborative, project-based course where learners interact with distant peers and experts to vastly deepen their understanding of both the concepts and practices of science. Specifically, this course puts learners into small project teams where they address basic astronomy questions through the construction of virtual solar system models. Using new software developed with the support of the University of Georgia Learning Technology Grants Program and a strategic partnership with a private company, Cybernet, students create 3-D models to answer questions about the solar system.

This course is based on our belief that learning environments using digital technology function less like books or films and more like studios and laboratories. That is, they provide a setting where students can immerse themselves in problematical situations. These situations are enriched through peer interaction, electronic information, and the guidance of the professors. The project brings together professors from the physics and astronomy department and the Learning and Performance Support Laboratory in the College of Education.

NEEDS AND RATIONALE

"Learners come to all formal learning situations with a set of alternative conceptions of many scientific phenomena based on their previous experience and prior instruction. The study of students' alternative conceptions of fundamental domain concepts has led to the identification of an abundance of alternative conceptions that cut across all areas of science" (Pfundt & Duit, 1991). The film, *A Private Universe* (Pyramid Film & Video, 1988), presents a dramatic example of university students' misconceptions about the earth, moon, and sun. In the film, 21 of 23 of the graduating seniors interviewed during a Harvard University commencement ceremony were unable to provide an accurate scientific explanation for the seasons. The film also shows that these misconceptions are resistant to change, especially if the students are being taught by traditional, "chalk-and-talk" instruction.

This project also meets institutional needs as identified in the university's strategic plan by taking "advantage of new technologies to improve the quality and reach of its academic, research, and service programs." More specifically, this project meets the objective to "create learning environments designed to stimulate active learning and critical thinking" by transforming the lecture class where dispensing knowledge is the goal into a scientific environment where critical and active inquiry through modeling and visualization is the goal. Furthermore, this learning environment can be taken out of official labs and into the dorms and homes of students anywhere. Thus, the project meets several other institutional needs:

- Creating instructional programs "with fewer constraints of time and place"

- Expanding the university's distance learning capacity

- Supporting activities on and off campus

INSTRUCTIONAL METHODOLOGY

Our methodology is based on constructivist learning theory. Groups of students address a set of questions which require them to construct solar system models. Each group negotiates plans to answer the questions, identify resources (textbook, web, and scientists), design their models, build them, evaluate them, use them to demonstrate answers to the initial questions, and share them with other groups. The entire course is held in the computer lab, where students use special equipment and software to construct their virtual reality models of the solar system. The course professor conducts just-in-time lectures in the context of students' struggle to address the questions and to build their models. Thus, the lectures are structured to meet the direct needs of the students, not an official syllabus. The information presented in the lecture is easily incorporated into the students' evolving understanding of astronomy and the practices of science.

The final stage of each of three projects has two parts. The first part is a group presentation of its model and how it addresses, answers, and demonstrates answers to the initial questions. The second part is an independent reflection paper that compares and contrasts the students' model with other groups' models and the solar system. In the final paper, students are forced to integrate their knowledge into a broader scientific framework. Students also take graded comprehensive midterm and final exams patterned after traditional astronomy courses.

Celestial Construction Kit

The Celestial Construction Kit is a virtual, 3-D modeling environment where learners can construct models of the solar systems. The modeling requires learners to use a variety of resources, such as NASA data, textbooks, and web resources. Learners construct models through a direct manipulation interface and explore fundamental science concepts. The Celestial Construction Kit represents an exciting learning environment that uses the power of cyberspace to learn about outer space.

Web-Based Collaborative Environment

The online collaborative support system was designed to help students and faculty learn. It increases student/student and student/faculty communication and organizes those communications to meet the needs of learning and constructing a virtual world. Collaborative support magnifies the power of instruction from the professor as well as from peers.

LEARNING OUTCOMES FOR STUDENTS

We are currently analyzing data from the summer prototype course. Although a number of bumps in the road affected the learning in the prototype, we expect that the thinking will continue. For example, in a pretest, we learned that Jason was significantly confused about the cause of lunar eclipses.

Interviewer: When do we get a lunar eclipse?

Jason: I think it has something to do with the day-night sequence.

I guess that when the earth is turning, we see different sides of the moon.

Through the building of virtual models, his understanding was transformed as was evidenced in his posttest interview.

Interviewer: So when do we get an eclipse?

Jason: The moon is going around the earth, and the moon is behind the earth, and the earth is going around the sun. The ecliptic and the rotational path intercept at the line of nodes, and due to the five-degree tilt, they cross at certain points. If it is a total eclipse—that is, it is an umbral eclipse—it is beet-red. If it is penumbral eclipse, then it is a partial eclipse. It depends on when the moon is on the line of nodes.

LESSONS LEARNED

There was an important transformation in the course when we used the new software, Celestial Construction Kit, based on previous work by the lead author at Indiana University, rather than off-the-shelf vrml (virtual reality modeling language) toolkits. The Celestial Construction Kit created new and exciting opportunities to explore the elliptical orbits and the physics underlying them, which were never possible with the vrml toolkits. However, because of the software design, more basic understandings about sizes and distances were more difficult to compare. These problems are being addressed in updates of the software.

CONCLUSION

This project represents a unique opportunity to develop powerful, active learning in an introductory university course. Through the use of advanced technologies and innovative thinking about learning and instruction, the project immerses students in the new science practices of modeling and visualization. Students work in teams to inquire into the fundamental workings of the solar system and, in doing so, develop deep understandings of astronomy, science, and the general skills that will make them valuable team members, critical thinkers, and online collaborators in the economy of the future. The technology that once seemed spectacular to us is now available with a $1,500 home computer.

REFERENCES

Pfundt, H., & Duit, R. (1991). *Students' alternative frameworks and science education.* Kiel, Germany: Institut fur die Paedagogik der Naturwissenschaften.

Pyramid Film & Video. *A private universe: An insightful lesson on how we learn.* (1988). Santa Monica, CA: Pyramid Film & Video.

CONTACT INFORMATION

Kenneth E. Hay
Learning and Performance Support Laboratory
College of Education
University of Georgia
611 Aderhold
Athens, GA 30602
Email: khay@coe.uga.edu
WWW: http://lpsl.coe.uga/LIVE/
Phone: (706) 542-3157

J. Scott Shaw
Department of Physics and Astronomy
College of Arts and Sciences
University of Georgia
235 Physics
Athens GA, 30602
Email: jss@juno.physast.uga.edu
Phone: (706) 542-2870

Vignette 7 — Data Warehousing and Decision Support: Tales from a Virtual Classroom

Joachim Hammer, University of Florida

In this graduate-level seminar, we examine the problems, principles, techniques, and mechanisms to support information management using the data warehousing approach. We explore the current state of the art in both data warehousing and decision support by studying the relevant literature and surveying selected products from industry. For most students, this course is their first opportunity to get hands-on experience with data warehouse software and related tools.

The decision to offer this seminar as part of the university's distance education program was influenced by several factors:

- Given the heightened interest in data warehousing and industry's insatiable demand for data warehousing specialists, we wanted an alternative delivery mechanism to provide training to a much broader audience than to traditional, on-campus students alone. For example, we are targeting computer professionals in related fields who cannot attend classes due to their daily job schedules or location but who are interested in learning more about this exciting new area. By opening our classroom, traditional students can benefit from professionals' working experience and knowledge of real-world problems. The computer professionals, on the other hand, learn a new technology, which can help them advance in their careers.

- A large portion of the course is dedicated to researching and learning about state-of-the-art warehousing technology in both academia and industry. Given the wealth of information on the World Wide Web, this task is best accomplished by guiding students to relevant online resources and letting them share their newfound knowledge and experience with the rest of the class. In fact, the material is still so new and changing so rapidly that there are no good textbooks available. Thus, a virtual classroom, which provides not only the tools for conducting web explorations but also encourages their seamless integration into the daily learning process and allows students to communicate and to share their results whenever the need arises for as long as necessary, seemed an ideal setting.

- About a year ago, when we told our chair the plan for a new course on data warehousing, he encouraged us to develop it for use in the distance education program. At the time the department of computer and information science and engineering was still evaluating the best possible long-term strategies for entering distance education and in need of a case study. Rather than experiment with one of the existing, high-enrollment core courses, it made sense to start with a new, smaller course that could be designed from the ground up to fit into the new program.

Recently, the transformation of the Internet from a network supporting data exchange among scientists to a high-speed, high-bandwidth delivery medium for general-purpose information has revolutionized the way we conduct many interactive tasks, including distance education (Vouk, Bitzer, & Klevans, 1999). However, this new Internet-mediated, collaborative learning involves significant changes in the way we teach students. In the next sections, we describe how these changes are reflected in the design of our course and what our experience has been now that we have reached the halfway point of the semester.

IDEAS BEHIND THE COURSE

The design of our virtual classroom was driven by the following requirements:

- Asynchronous, place-independent delivery of the core material, using an electronic, multimedia-enriched format

- Use of the web as a valuable source of information to enhance the material presented in the lectures

- Collaboration among students as an important form of learning; for example, team projects, students helping each other

- Multiple forms of communication, with support for easy integration of multimedia information; for example, private communication among students and instructor, real-time question-and-answer sessions, long-running, asynchronous discussion threads

- The ability to present different perspectives on class topics to reinforce the learning process

- Student assessment and grading

Generic network tools, such as email, newsgroups, computer and video conferencing, do not satisfy all of the above requirements and impose significant user overhead, because they were not specifically designed to support educational activities. Based on advice from the Office of Instructional Resources (OIR), we chose WebCT as the platform on which to develop the course. WebCT is a web-based, integrated, course-management system that features:

- A closed classroom community with private user logins to limit access to enrolled students only

- A virtual classroom space, with links to all of the available tools and resources

- A variety of shared and private file spaces for storing lecture materials, group projects, home pages

- Bulletin boards

- Online (typed) chat with automatic recording

- Class email

- Grading and student assessment tools, such as a gradebook, quiz generation and administration, student progress tracking

- A variety of system administration and file management tools; for example, to create and to manage accounts, to upload documents, to backup course

To participate in the course, students need a computer with a soundcard, a web browser, and a 28.8kb or better modem plus the appropriate connection to the Internet. The virtual classroom is represented as an in-terconnected set of web pages that can only be accessed by registered students (ID and password necessary).

Lecture material is provided in the form of voice-annotated slide presentations that can be downloaded to the local computer and viewed in a multimedia player that is freely available for installation. In the presentations, sound and pictures are synchronized, allowing easy searching as well as random access to desired slides. We decided against digitizing videotaped lectures, which would increase bandwidth requirements for download connections and require us to find alternative dissemination methods. Furthermore, after viewing videotaped lectures from other courses in a web browser, we realized that not enough value is added by, for example, low picture quality, jerky movements, to justify the significant increase in bandwidth. The same is true for our online chat sessions in which the communication is typed rather than spoken.

COURSE ACTIVITIES

Among the new approaches used in our seminar are the following:

Viewing of Lecture Material
The lecture material is divided into seven course modules that correspond to the different topic areas that this course covers. Each module contains a number of units, which contain the technical content of the module. Each unit is a voice-annotated slide presentation, which takes approximately 15 to 30 minutes to view. We have designed a viewing schedule that specifies for each week which units are to be viewed. However, it is up to the students to decide the exact time and day when they want to view the lectures.

Biweekly Chat Sessions
The purpose of the chat sessions is to provide students with a real-time question-and-answer session for lecture related material. Each chat lasts 60 minutes and is moderated by a team of students to keep the discussions focused. Given the relatively short period of time, we encourage students to post follow-up questions or issues and concerns not directly related to the lectures on the bulletin board. Chat sessions are coordinated with the lecture schedule and typically focus on no more then one or two units. Before each chat session,

the moderators post the discussion topic on the bulletin board (see below) so that students can prepare in advance. Chat sessions are automatically recorded, and the transcripts are posted on the bulletin board.

Bulletin Board Discussions

The bulletin board and, to some extent, email serve as the glue that holds together our virtual classroom community whenever students are not actively engaged in real-time discussions like the chat room. It is meant to provide a forum for long-running discussion threads on all class-related topics. We have divided the bulletin board space into the following topic areas: MAIN (general discussions and class announcements), HELP (questions regarding the usage of WebCT tools and computers), HOMEWORK (questions regarding homework), PROJECT (project-related questions), MODULE1 to MODULE7 (questions specifically related to the content in any of the modules as well as the relevant chat sessions), and ARCHIVE (storage for terminated discussion threads that are not frequently used).

Homework and Exams

Both serve as important measures for student progress and are completed by each student individually. There are four homework assignments and two written exams. For each homework, the best two or three submissions are published on the bulletin board and serve as useful references. In addition, they provide an added incentive for students to provide quality work. Exams are take-home. The questions are posted on the bulletin board at a predefined time; answers are submitted to the instructor via course email. The format of written work is flexible: html is encouraged, but we accept regular text documents as well as documents formatted using various word processing systems.

Team Project

The team project is another attempt to stimulate collaborative learning. In the beginning of the semester, students form teams of two or three and pick from a list of predefined topic areas. The project progresses along a set of milestones that represent due dates for the individual deliverables: first, exact specification of the topic; second, a project plan that outlines the final deliverable as well as concrete ideas of how to complete the project; finally, the project deliverable, which is presented to the rest of the class on a set of web pages

that are posted in the project space for each team. Projects are judged by other teams as well as the instructor. Although contents and correctness are important, teams must also pay attention to presentation and are encouraged to be as creative as the tools in WebCT allow them to be.

Online Bibliography

This is an ordered index of web resources (for example, white papers, reports, project and product home pages) that we have put together to supplement the lecture material. The bibliography serves students as a jumping board into the web, while at the same time providing some guidance as to where to start the investigation of a specific topic. Without this guidance, the web is too unstructured and confusing to be used as an electronic library by our students. Resources on the online bibliography are referenced in the electronic reading list that accompanies the course modules.

Communication Via Email

Class email enables private communication between class members. It is also very effective for notifying students of last-minute changes in the course schedule and for targeting specific subgroups of students. On the other hand, given its private nature, email limits the audience of the message unless it is sent to whole class, and we discourage its use for discussing technical questions.

MEASURED RESULTS

One of the side-effects of constantly stressing the importance of communication among class members is the fact that students quickly become much more comfortable in expressing their opinions about technical material as well as about the course itself. So far, the feedback we have received from students is very positive. Most importantly, students commented on the fact that being able to read other students' questions and the corresponding answers, for example, on the bulletin board or in the transcripts of chat sessions, helped them understand and master the material better and faster. Students also commented that they have a much stronger feeling of belonging to a team with the same goals since there is a clearly defined class space with room to express opinions and to receive help. Finally, students also like the fact that they can decide when and where to listen to the lectures, assuming proper computer access, and that the course is more fun than many others they have taken, probably because of its novel approach to learning. On the negative side, students regretted that face-to-face meetings are limited and that they spend relatively more time and effort on this course relative to other classes, since written communication is much more labor-intensive and slower than spoken word.

In addition to the explicit feedback that we received, we also noticed the following positive side-effects. Due to the increased practice, some students improved their written communication skills significantly during the course of the semester. Furthermore, students were a lot more willing to share their opinions and knowledge with the rest of the class than in traditional classrooms, where the physical presence of the other students is sometimes intimidating.

LESSONS LEARNED

Overall, our experience with the class has been very positive and showed that our initial course design put us on the right track. However, as with everything untried, some mistakes were made. Here is short list of things that we would do differently next time or had to change during the course of the semester.

Provide More Structure in Chat Sessions

After the first several chat sessions, we noticed that attendance was dropping, and some students were getting frustrated with the increasingly unfocused discussions. As a result, we implemented a set of guidelines and procedures that govern how students can request the chat floor and make themselves heard, what the role of the moderator is, how to prepare for a chat session, and what the expected outcomes are. In addition, to increase the students' stake in the chat, we selected different teams of two students who moderate each discussion rather than the instructor, as we initially planned. We expect that this approach will work better, since it is an excellent chance for students to take an active leadership role in class. Moderators are also required to post the topics to be discussed in advance on the bulletin board. After each chat session, the moderators will summarize the outcome and continue to moderate any follow-up discussions on the bulletin board.

Establish a Download Center for Different Course Materials

In the beginning, lecture material was available for download exclusively in the form of voice-annotated presentations. Both the audio part and the presentation were encoded as one inseparable presentation file. This worked well for viewing lectures but was inconvenient when trying to reference individual presentation slides without audio; for example, during a chat session. Thus, we created a download center where lecture material is available for downloading in a variety of different formats, including notes, notes and graphics with no audio, etc.

Reward Participation in Conversations

When setting up the course assessment policies in the beginning of the semester, student participation counted for 10% of the total grade. However, we have since realized that the effort that many students are putting into the discussion sessions, the bulletin board communication, as well as email far exceeds 10% of their total invested effort. Thus, an allocation of 20% for course participation is probably fairer. On the other hand, as a positive side-effect to relying on written word and transcripts, we realized that measuring course participation is a lot easier than in a traditional course where most of the communication is transient.

Complete Lecture Material before the Start of the Course

Most of the course design, including layout, course schedule, reading list, and lecture presentations was completed before the beginning of the course. The only thing left to do was to record our narration for the individual lectures. This is being done as the course is progressing. The drawback of this approach is that we cannot release all of the lecture slides to the students in advance, preventing them from working ahead if they so desire. Furthermore, it prevented us from releasing all of the course materials on CD-ROM to the students at the beginning of the semester, which would have reduced the students' dependency on a relatively high-speed download connection.

Obviously, designing and teaching a course is work in progress. After completing the first semester of the

WebCT version of data warehousing and decision support, we plan to make another assessment of the course. We will report our findings to our department and other communities in the hope that many more educators will discover this new form of teaching that we and many others continue to explore (Harasim, 1999).

REFERENCES

Harasim, L. (1999). A framework for online learning: The virtual-U. *IEEE Computer, 32,* 44-49.

Vouk, M. A., Bitzer, D. L., & Klevans, R. L. (1999). Workflow and end-user quality of service issues in web-based education. *IEEE Transactions on Knowledge and Data Engineering, 11* (4), 673-687.

CONTACT INFORMATION

Joachim Hammer, Assistant Professor
Department of Computer and Information Science and Engineering
University of Florida
Gainesville, FL 32611-6120
E-mail: jhammer@cise.ufl.edu
Instructor Home Page: http://www.cise.ufl.edu/~jhammer
Course Home Page: http://grove.ufl.edu/~cis6930
(Send mail to instructor for guest login and password.)

 **Computer Communications Using a Lectures-on-Demand-in ALN Approach**

Haniph A. Latchman, University of Florida

INTRODUCTION

Technology is rapidly revolutionizing our society, and our approach to education must adapt. Instead of producing citizens who memorize facts and mimic skills, the rapid advancement and implementation of technology has dictated that we produce individuals with high-level thinking skills. Students of today must learn how to actively seek knowledge in a lifelong learning mode and to apply such newfound knowledge creatively in solving increasingly complex problems. Because of these needs, education is no longer associated exclusively with a classroom or a particular phase of life.

Today, cyberage technologies permit both real-time and asynchronous interaction between students and instructor. We have experimented with such technologies, focusing on the exciting possibilities of asynchronous learning that might prove viable in academia by utilizing emerging Internet standards. We will describe the successes and challenges that we have experienced in developing and offering online courses using a lectures-on-demand approach. A graduate level course in computer communications will be featured as an example of this effort.

With the model implemented at the University of Florida, on-campus lectures are encoded digitally for live broadcasting and simultaneously the audio and video streams are archived so that students can access the material from anywhere at any time. Asynchronous student to student and student to instructor interaction is facilitated via mailing lists, bulletin boards, and WWW pages. In addition, the asynchronous experience is enhanced by synchronizing the lecture notes with the streaming video and audio so that the browser automatically displays appropriate lecture material in separate windows (or frames) as the class progresses.

EDUCATIONAL THEORIES

The fundamental philosophy on which the efforts at the University of Florida are based is to allow the students to participate actively in online courses that combine the best aspects of effective traditional teaching and interactive Internet-based multimedia services. To realize these objectives, the system developed should be capable of providing a low-cost, multimedia resource that encourages the students to explore new avenues of learning.

Figure 8.1 shows the various mechanisms used to convey information and facilitate interaction among the students and with the instructor. The key components include an audio/video window, a textual/graphic window and links to chat rooms and mailing lists. In Figure 8.1, the PowerPoint lecture notes are synchronized with the activities in the video window so that the slides change automatically as the lecture progresses. The student maintains control of the lecture and can fast forward or reverse the video stream as well as scan the PowerPoint slides backward and forward at will. In addition, the lecture is also classified into major topical areas (as shown in the MENU window in Figure 8.1) so that the student can go to a specific topic of interest.

In the *lectures on demand in ALN* approach that we adopted for delivering online courses, we aim to provide a low-latency, low-bit-rate video and audio stream of the instructor lecturing live in the classroom with an on-campus contingent of students. The audio quality using four to eight kbps of bandwidth is typically better than telephone quality and video quality at twelve kbps or above is intended to be of sufficient quality for the written material on the board to be easily read by remote students. The dynamic development of equations or other technical material is thus assimilated by the online students who also have sharp images of the same material in the form of PowerPoint slides synchronized with the streaming video and audio.

COMPUTER-ENHANCED TECHNIQUES USED

Synchronized Streaming Media
When we refer to streaming media, we are referring to RealMedia (Progressive Network) clips, which are continuous video and audio presentations created by RealProducer. The video and audio components are also known separately as RealVideo and RealAudio, respectively. Before the advent of RealMedia, a media file had to be completely downloaded to a temporary or

FIGURE. 8.1

WEB-BASED ASYNCHRONOUS LECTURES (FALL 1998)

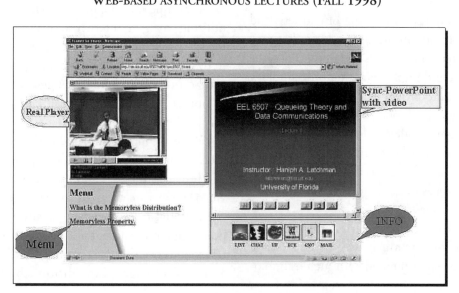

permanent local storage location before it could be played. With streaming content such as that provided by the RealNetworks systems, the Internet user can play the multimedia content almost instantly, with only a few seconds of buffering delay. Furthermore, live media can be streamed so that content is sent directly to the audience in almost real-time—our experience shows that on typical connections, the latency is of the order of 15 milliseconds.

Whereas the *lectures on demand in ALN* system relies on most asynchronous interactions, our experience is that some real-time communication is also beneficial, such as by a telephone or conference call. Real-time interaction or feedback from the remote students is achieved using electronic conferencing software such as web-based Bulletin Board System (BBS) software and WebCT Java-based chat systems. Using these forums, the instructor as well as the students can logon to the same chat room for synchronous interactions at a pre-arranged time. The option to list all participants in a chat session is desirable so as to mimic virtual presence in the chat room. Alternatively, as a student follows the archived online lectures, spontaneous interaction is facilitated by being able to pause the lecture and submit a question to the mailing list or the BBS. This question will be received by all participating students as well as the instructor and the TA. Often the question is answered by a fellow student, and the instructor and TA provide corrections and guidance as the discussion develops. It should be emphasized that all these interactive resources can be accessed by the student using a simple web browser starting from the course home page. Once the students overcome their initial inhibitions toward active and collaborative learning, the online interactions become a key part of the learning experience.

Architecture Overview

A client/server model is used to deliver streaming content; in this case, the client is the user's installed RealPlayer application, and the server is the RealServer G2 software. The browser merely works to establish communication between the two in a manner described in Figure 8.3.

When a user clicks a URL link to Real Content within his browser, the browser sends an HTTP request to the web server, which then responds by sending appropriate metafiles to the browser. The metafile contents are interpreted by the browser so that the RealPlayer application is started as a helper application. RealPlayer now reads the URL from the metafile and subsequently interacts with the RealServer using RTSP (Real Time Streaming Protocol) to request the specified content. After a short period of buffering, the RealServer then streams the specified clip directly to the RealPlayer in real time without any further interaction with the user's browser.

Web-Based Utility: WebCT

The development of a sophisticated web-based educational environment is facilitated by a powerful tool called WebCT. WebCT is so flexible that it can be used to facilitate the delivery of entire online courses or simply to publish supplementary course material.

FIGURE 8.2

AUDIO AND VIDEO DELIVERY

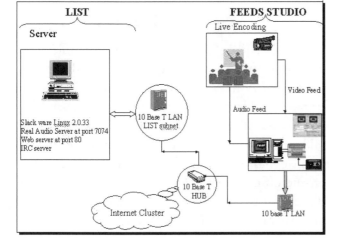

FIGURE 8.3

ARCHITECTURE FOR REAL STREAMING SYSTEM

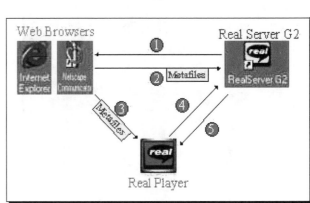

A significant advantage in using WebCT for online course development and presentation lies in its effective use of the browser. Not only does WebCT present online course material for browsers, but it also uses the web browser as the interface for its course building environment. Thus, even nontechnical users can quickly develop and administer high-quality online courses that might otherwise have required the services of web programmers.

An example of how these tools can be implemented into online course material is shown in Figure 8.4. This is the main student interface to the EEL 5718 Computer Communications course. In this example, relevant WebCT features have been sorted into five major links: The Lounge, Course Content, Lectures, Useful Utilities, and FAQs.

- Selecting The Lounge, students accesses three main facilities for interaction with others involved with the course. They can:

  1) Read a general overview of the course.

  2) Use Hypermail to view and to respond to various email sources—classmates, teaching assistants, or the instructor.

  3) Chat with fellow students, TAs, or the instructor, if they are currently online. Students can even make their own chat rooms using built-in WebCT features to facilitate class discussions.

FIGURE 8.4

WebCT TEMPLATE FOR COMPUTER
COMMUNICATION COURSE

- The Course Content link covers more detailed course information. Students can view a syllabus or a course outline.

- The Lectures, found in the classroom using the chalkboard metaphor, is where the streaming content is delivered. Students can watch the digitized video and audio of any lecture, chosen either by date or lecture number. The AV presentation can be reviewed at the student's own pace. Alongside the lectures, optionally in the same browser window, are presented Microsoft PowerPoint slides of main points from the selected lecture. The PowerPoint slides are synchronized with the video and displayed at appropriate junctures in each lecture. The PowerPoint slide appears in the browser in a separate frame or a separate window, the content of which changes as the lecture progresses. Each lecture is also subdivided into modular unites and can be nonlinearly navigated using a menu of topics.

- With the Useful Utilities, students can create their own web pages, use a personal and a class calendar, and download free software, such as RealPlayer G2 or ShockWave by Macromedia.

- Finally, Frequently Asked Questions (FAQs) offer students direction on how to best utilize the features of WebCT and the course.

WebCT provides an interface allowing the design and presentation of online course material for students, while offering a rich set of tools facilitating learning, communication, and collaboration. Further, WebCT provides browser-based administration and design of online course presentations, allowing the instructor full management of the entire course.

MEASURED RESULTS

The course, EEL 5718 Computer Communication, has been offered for several semesters using the *lectures on demand in ALN* method. This course is taken by first-year graduates and graduating seniors, and involves some 40 lectures, six homework assignments, a mid-term test, a comprehensive final examination, and a collaborative project. Over several semesters, both on-and off-campus students have taken parts or all of this course asynchronously in conjunction with a traditional on-campus class. Some students were actually able to join the class via live Internet broadcasts. The results of the learning experience were satisfactory and encouraging both from the student perspective as well as from a comparison of the performance of on-campus and off-campus students. The on-campus students who watched the lectures in real time or asynchronously over the campus network had much better video quality due to large available bandwidth, while the off-campus students who followed the course over 28.8 kbps modems had a less perfect video quality, but the audio stream was estimated by the users to be better than telephone quality and quite acceptable. The learning process through the synchronized multimedia format was evaluated by all participants to be better than videotapes, since notes and other auxiliary materials were displayed on the screen, so more attention was paid to the lecturer.

While the emphasis has been on the client/server streaming technologies, it was found that streaming audio/video material of each course occupies only about 400 Mb of storage so that the complete set of course materials, including lecture notes, slides, and assignments, can be stored on a standard 600 Mb CD. Thus, a CD with the multimedia content could be distributed to students taking the course, and they would have direct access to the streaming audio/video from the CD, while using the Internet for accessing interactive facilities such as online chat, mailing lists, and other frequently updated class materials. This alternative is especially desirable for those students who have very slow or highly congested connections to the Internet, as is, for example, the case with students in some international locations.

LESSONS LEARNED

The *lectures on demand in ALN* system we have described in this paper for delivering the computer communications course is still in the process of development and refinement as we gain more experience and assess our preliminary effort in terms of teaching and learning effectiveness. This methodology is now being used to offer an online MS degree in electrical engineering as well as courses toward a BS degree in electrical engineering

The use of asynchronous learning networks has become quite well-established in recent years as a mechanism for a networked community of learners to interact using Internet-mediated communication. The lectures-on-demand method provides a direct and cost-effective mechanism for content development using the time-tested metaphor of the traditional lecture. Active and collaborative learning models are encouraged by the effective use of mailing lists, bulletin boards, and chat sessions. Initial assessment confirms that this integrated approach has much cognitive value and facilitates learning (Gillet et al., 1994).

It is not difficult to imagine how traditional models of education might be threatened by the use of asynchronous delivery methods. Indeed, one can envision organizations, such as software firms that are not conventional providers of educational content, getting into this new business, as educational delivery becomes an attractive and lucrative proposition. The issue of choosing an educational provider would then become similar to choosing a provider for other online services. Clearly, the quality of the program must be measured by some recognized standard of accreditation; the reputation of the institution as well as overall costs will be important considerations. Only time will tell how these developments will fare when compared with more traditional forms of education. It is our view that the two modes of educational delivery will serve complementary purposes, with the traditional student/instructor model being preferred if at all possible, while the asynchronous mode will provide access to students whose circumstances would rule out the preferred mode of learning. Of course, the use of asynchronous online tools, such as electronic conferencing for mailing lists, will continue to grow as a complement to the traditional modes of learning.

ACKNOWLEDGEMENT

The work described in this paper was supported by a grant from the Alfred Sloan Foundation and the Southeastern University and College Coalition for Engineering Education (SUCCEED), funded by the National Science Foundation.

REFERENCE

Gillet, D., Franklin, G. F., Longchamp, R., & Bonvin, D. (1994, August). *Introduction to automatic control via an integrated instruction approach.* The 3rd IFAC Symposium on Advances in Control Education, Tokyo, Japan.

CONTACT INFORMATION

Haniph A. Latchman, Associate Professor
Electrical and Computer Engineering Department
University of Florida
Gainesville, FL 32611-6130
Email: latchman@list.ufl.edu
Phone: (352) 392-4950
Fax: (352) 392-0044

Using the World Wide Web to Teach Process Control in Engineering

Francis J. Doyle III, University of Delaware

Use of the World Wide Web (WWW) in several of my process control courses was aimed at generating a richer, more interactive learning environment for engineering students, who were already quite comfortable on the Internet. The web fostered an atmosphere of community, particularly effective for a course that had distance students distributed throughout the country.

This narrative describes the collective experiences of several engineering classes: 1) a required, senior-level, chemical engineering undergraduate course (CHEG 401); (2) an elective, senior-level, interdisciplinary course (CHEG 467); and 3) an upper-level graduate elective course (CHEG 801). The unique attributes of web-based education that will be stressed are the use of a web-based relational database in all courses, and the use of live video streaming in CHEG 801. The organizing framework for all three courses is an online course management software package developed at the University of Delaware.

COURSE ACTIVITIES

With the exception of CHEG 467, I had taught these classes in previous years without the use of any significant web-based component. Armed with online course management software and an extremely supportive staff, I embarked on the following innovations in these traditional courses.

Muddiest Point Forum

Borrowing from the classic one-minute quiz, we set up a discussion forum on the class web-page for the so-called "muddiest point" of each week. The students posted on the web the least clear concept from the two lectures in a given week so that all could see it and the identity of the posting party. Not only did this technique engage the students in dialog among themselves ("following up on the previous question, I would like to know..."), it also provided clear, timely feedback to the instructor on the pace of the class which enriched the contact between students and faculty. The students were rewarded by having the least clear concepts clarified at the beginning of the next lecture and their lowest quiz grade dropped, a not-so-subtle bribe. Participation ranged from a high of about 60% to a low of 25% of the class in a given week.

Electronic Syllabus

All three of the class web pages included an electronic syllabus with assignments and weights detailed to pro-mote time on task. Course objectives and detailed assignment listings also communicated the instructor's high expectations. A sample syllabus entry that illustrates these features is depicted in Figure 9.1.

Discussion Forum for Laboratory

The lab class (467) was populated by seniors from three majors (chemical/electrical/mechanical engineering). Teams were organized containing one student from each discipline. In a further effort to develop reciprocity and cooperation among students, a discussion forum was set up to enable a group that finished an experiment to post hints, suggestions, and valuable data to the next group that inherited the experimental station.

FIGURE 9.1

TYPICAL SYLLABUS ENTRY IN THE ONLINE COURSE MANAGEMENT PACKAGE
FOR MY UNDERGRADUATE PROCESS CONTROL COURSE
(CHEG 401). The icons on the top menu bar provide links to supplemental material (e.g., MATLAB resources)

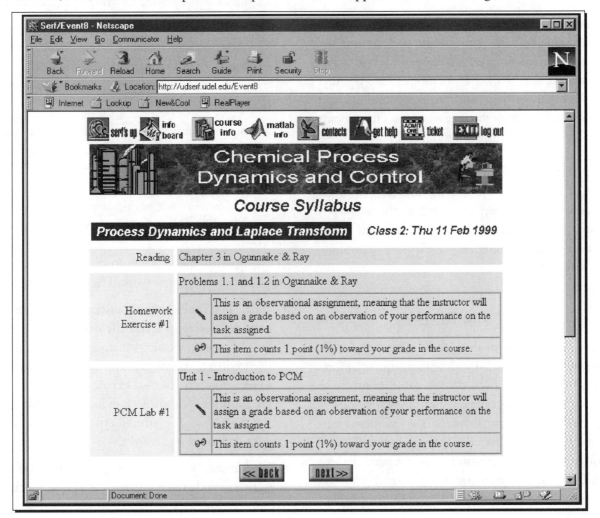

Internet Resources

All three courses relied heavily on an engineering software package, MATLAB, for homework and course projects. Links to various web resources, including MATLAB tutorials and help pages, were available from the main syllabus.

Live and Archived Video

The graduate course (801) had a population consisting of local graduate students, distance graduate students (on internship in industry), local continuing education professionals, and distance continuing education professionals. Distant locations included Indianapolis and Seattle, so time changes were a consideration as well. Using RealPlayer formatted video, we streamed the lectures live over the WWW during normal class time and simultaneously archived an electronic version that was accessible from the syllabus page. We wanted to offer a variety of media for access, especially for local students, in order to respect diverse talents and ways of learning.

Electronic Gradebook

Another valuable part of the online package was the electronic gradebook. It solved many of the traditional problems associated with anonymous grade posting, since the login was password protected, and enabled easy access to grades for distance students. The students uniformly appreciated the prompt feedback.

Computer-Based Simulation Modules

In one of the courses (401), a detailed set of process simulation modules was employed as the basis of a computational laboratory. The primary intent of the hands-on controller design experience was to promote active learning.

MEASURED RESULTS

As noted earlier, two of these three courses had been taught previously (1992-1996) without the use of extensive WWW tools. I was then an assistant professor and at a different institution, Purdue. These differences notwithstanding, I observed a significant and positive change in classroom interactions and, more importantly, student performance. Measurable changes included more focused questions, owing to the archived video and/or the muddiest point forum; live-

lier class discussion; and a drop in office hour attendance, with a simultaneous increase in email questions. The only direct quantitative measure other than the subjective GPA was the previously noted participation rate, approximately 40%, on posting to the muddiest forum on a weekly basis. In earlier course offerings, a primitive bulletin board-type discussion forum elicited only sporadic postings over the course of the semester.

LESSONS LEARNED

I have enumerated a few key insights that have been gained as a result of these teaching experiences.

- The muddiest-point forum proved to be a rather valuable tool to promote discussion in a class (401) that is generally considered cut-and-dried. The WWW forum was conveniently accessed immediately after lecture when questions were fresh in the students' minds. It was tremendously valuable to get quick student feedback on specific lecture topics and to identify students who might require extra attention.

- The full electronic syllabus listing encouraged the students to work ahead on readings and assignments, with expectations and priorities clearly articulated.

My biggest fear was that the archived video would promote absenteeism, but attendance was nearly perfect, and WWW access statistics revealed that the local students were using the archived video as a review tool. I discovered some restrictive local campus policies with respect to WWW access statistics, which are a factor to consider.

Along with the positive, come the not-so-good things that did not quite work. They included:

- Email live feedback: The distance education students were able to access the course lecture video live, but we only offered them an email option for live feedback. As one student explained, this is akin to requiring a traditional lecture class to write out a question for the instructor in longhand. It just will not work. Future course offerings will experiment with dedicated audio links.

- Modem rate video streaming. Our original intent was to provide the live video at a rate conducive to home access. This rate was acceptable for the audio portion, but the video was very broken up, and the instructor's slightest movement looked like an instantaneous jump. One distance student remarked that a whole semester of this would make him seasick. We learned quickly, and dialed up the streaming rate to ISDN.

SUMMARY

This new teaching experience, like most, has been a learning exercise for both the students and the instructor. I have a new appreciation for the power of web-based educational technology in both local and distance education. There is no question that the web-enhanced learning environment has promoted a sense of community with the students and the instructor.

CONTACT INFORMATION

Francis J. Doyle III, Associate Professor
Department of Chemical Engineering
University of Delaware
Newark, DE 19716
Email: fdoyle@udel.edu
WWW: http://www.udel.edu/present/best_practices/
Group: http://fourier.che.udel.edu
Phone: (302) 831-0760
Fax: (302) 831-0457

Vignette 10 A Multimedia Learning Environment in Statics

Siegfried M. Holzer and Raul H. Andruet, Virginia Polytechnic Institute and State University

INTRODUCTION

...for the computer to bring about a revolution in higher education, its introduction must be accompanied by improvements in our understanding of learning and teaching.

Nobel Laureate Herbert Simon
(Kozma & Johnston, 1991)

Simon's statement has been our guiding theme in the development of a multimedia learning environment in the subject area of statics. It was reinforced by Ehrmann's (1995) suggestion to select first the best methods for teaching and learning and then the technologies that support those methods.

Statics is a branch of mechanics that is concerned with the computation of forces acting on bodies (solids or fluids) in equilibrium. Drawing on the rich literature on learning and teaching, we developed a workshop learning environment (Laws, 1991) that includes physical models, interactive multimedia, traditional pencil-and-paper activities, and cooperative learning in the framework of experiential learning (Kolb, 1984). The course is designed to promote students' active engagement in learning. Our laboratory for evaluating and improving this learning environment is a junior-level course taught in architecture.

In this paper we provide a background for experiential and cooperative learning, describe a typical session, share lessons learned, and present some student evaluations.

EXPERIENTIAL LEARNING

Learning is the process whereby knowledge is created through the transformation of experience.

David Kolb (1984)

Experiential learning, modeled after the scientific method, has its roots in the works of Dewey, Lewin, and Piaget (Kolb, 1984). It focuses on the central role that experience plays in the learning process. Moreover, "learning from experience is the process whereby human development occurs" (Vygotsky in Kolb, 1984). Although experience is essential to learning, it is not enough; one has to transform it to construct knowledge (Piaget, 1954; Bringuier, 1980; Holzer, 1994). Kolb's experiential learning model (Figure 10.1) displays two fundamental activities of learning: grasping and transforming experience.

Each activity involves two opposite but complementary modes of learning. One can grasp an experience directly through the senses (sensory, inductive mode) or indirectly in symbolic form (conceptual, deductive mode). Similarly, one can transform experience in two distinct ways, by reflection or action. At any moment in the learning process, one or a combination of the four fundamental learning modes may be involved. Their synthesis leads to higher levels of learning (Kolb, 1984). For example, a student's retention of knowledge increases from 20% when only abstract

conceptualization is involved, to 90% when students are engaged in all four stages of learning (Stice, 1987). We found it helpful to view the four-stage learning cycle as a spiral in time that extends beyond a session. For example, a concept or principle may be developed or applied in different contexts at different times and through different learning modes.

Cooperative Learning

. . . early evidence suggests that students who work in small groups, even when interacting with high-tech equipment, learn significantly more than students who work primarily alone.

Light (1990)

Cooperative learning is not a new concept (Ercolano, 1994). Extensive research initiated in the late 1800s has demonstrated significant advantages of cooperative learning over competitive and individualistic learning in various learning characteristics; these include high-level reasoning, generation of new ideas and solutions, motivation for learning, personal responsibility, and student retention (Johnson et al., 1991).

Cooperative learning provides structures (Kagan, 1990) to engage students in meaningful activities that can be shared with others (Papert & Harel, 1991). Meaningful activities include authentic activities that represent future tasks and problems and are rich in learning resources (Beichner, 1993).

We have been experimenting with various group sizes and cooperative learning structures and found that pair activities work well in class. In groups of three, for example, one student is easily left out. We also tried different cooperative structures and arrived, with the help of student feedback, at a combination of think-pair-share (Lyman, 1987) and think-aloud-pair-problem-solving (Lochhead, 1987). For simplicity, we call the structure think-pair-share (TPS).

Think: Think about the solution of the problem individually to organize your thoughts.

Pair: Form pairs, a think-aloud problem solver and a listener, to solve the problem; reverse roles after every problem.

Share: Share your findings with another pair or a larger group.

FIGURE 10.1
EXPERIENTIAL LEARNING MODEL

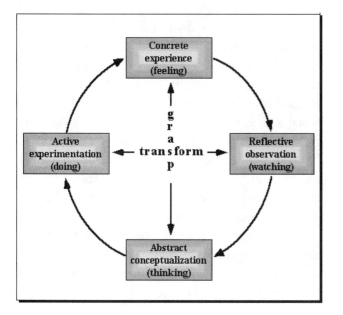

A Session

I realized how much more I learn when I help people.
(A student)

We meet in a computer lab where two students share one computer. Sessions generally consist of three parts: 1) a warm-up problem or a puzzler to engage the students; 2) ten- to 15-minute lectures interspersed with cooperative activities; 3) a minute paper (Cross, 1991), where students are asked to reflect and answer questions about the day's lesson and activities. Anonymous minute papers provide valuable insight into students' conceptions, achievements, and difficulties. This information allows us to evaluate and to improve the learning environment in a continuous fashion.

The multimedia program, constructed with Authorware 5 Attain (1999), is used in various ways: 1) to present minilectures; 2) to guide student teams in developing concepts, solving problems, and discussions; 3) to provide connections to the students' background and engineering structures; 4) to integrate traditional pencil-and-paper activities; and 5) to preview and review lessons.

Multimedia learning activities, for example, a discussion of characteristics of truss structures based on Figure 10.2, are illustrated in the paper by Holzer and Andruet (2000). The program is available on request (holzer@vt.edu).

Learning Outcomes

... research shows that when the conditions [for learning] improve ... through implementation of one or more of the Seven Principles of Good Practice ... learning usually improves.
Ehrmann & Zuniga (1997)

Although occasionally a student doesn't like the computer as a learning tool, on the whole the students are actively engaged in learning, and teaching is rewarding. The following excerpts from student evaluations provide some insight into their learning experiences:

FIGURE 10.2
CHARACTERISTICS OF TRUSSES

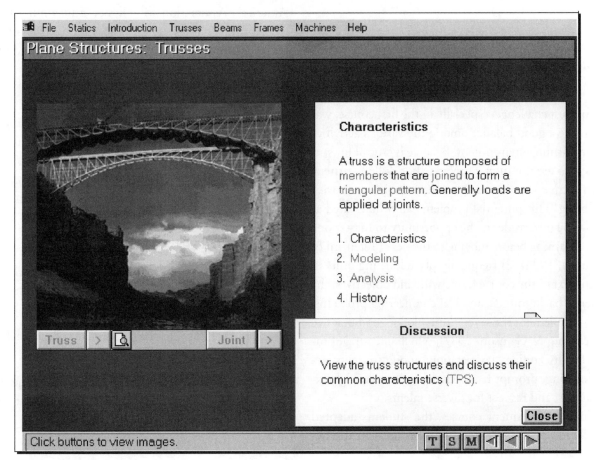

- *Yes, the* [multimedia program] *did facilitate learning by providing an interactive learning procedure where principles were developed and expanded upon active involvement with concrete and abstract example problems.*

- *Yes* [the multimedia program] *helped me a lot. It was really good to see examples and how they worked.*

- *I used it* [the multimedia program] *a lot out of class and found it very helpful.*

- *Yes* [the multimedia program facilitated learning]. *It worked very well in class time and with a partner.*

- *He created a strong learning environment, and his method was exceptionally strong for learning; I feel I took a lot from this course and professor.*

- [He] *taught us to think intelligently and learn.*

- *His system with the computer, "think-pair-share" learning teams, and in-class problem solving is the most effective way to learn such subject matter that I have encountered in 16 years of schooling.*

LESSONS LEARNED

Learning happens especially felicitously when the learner is consciously engaged in meaningful activities that can be shared with others.

(Papert & Harel,1991)

The biggest challenge, especially in the first course, was to achieve a good balance among the various activities in our learning environment. Balance is crucial for students who are not highly motivated or skilled learners; a rich, active learning environment can become overwhelming. This potential problem can be alleviated as follows: 1) give students the opportunity to master one unit of learning before moving to the next (Terenzini & Pascarella, 1994); 2) frequently place learning units in the context of the course framework and objectives, the students' backgrounds, and real engineering problems; and 3) implement the seven principles of good practice (Chickering & Gamson, 1987), which encourage student/faculty contact, cooperation among students, active learning, prompt feedback, time on task, high expectations, and respect for diverse talents.

In the subsequent courses, the students adapted quickly to the new learning environment. The follow-

ing comments selected from one-minute papers reflect their attitudes:

"Groups/pairs are great to work in."

"Good to have a few minutes to think/reflect before conversing with partner."

"Interesting learning concept; good to be part of this. Computer and partner interaction makes class seem easier. More ideas are aired with this environment."

"The group activities allow for personal interaction and verbal comparison. Then reverting to the computer to see the answer and diagram really helps."

"Computer is very user-friendly and set up well for learning."

"The computer diagrams really helped me to understand the concept of components."

"The program that we are using is so easy to operate and understand. Technology, isn't it wonderful?"

"I feel like I am getting a good grasp on the material. Seeing it on the computer helps so much."

"I enjoyed answering the questions of my partner."

"I am actually enjoying this class."

REFERENCES

American Association for Higher Education. (1996, April). What research says about improving undergraduate education: Twelve attributes of good practice. *AAHE Bulletin.*

Authorware 5 Attain. (1999). Macromedia, Inc.

Beichner, R. J. (1993, June). A multimedia editing environment promoting science learning in a unique setting—A case study. *Proceedings of the Educational-Media 93, World Conference on Educational Multimedia and Hypermedia*, Orlando, Florida.

Bringuier, J. C. (1980). *Conversations with Jean Piaget.* Chicago, IL: University of Chicago Press.

Chickering, A. W., & Gamson, Z. F. (1987, March). Seven principles for good practice in undergraduate education. *AAHE Bulletin, 39* (7), 3-7.

Cross, K. P. (1991, October). Effective college teaching. *Prism.* ASEE.

Ehrmann, S. C. (1995, March/April). Asking the right questions: What does research tell us about technology and higher education? *Change.*

Ehrmann, S. C., & Zuniga, R. E. (1997). *The Flashlight^{TM} evaluation handbook*. Washington, DC: AAHE.

Ercolano, V. (1994, November). Learning through cooperation. *Prism*. ASEE.

Holzer, S. M. (1994, Spring). From constructivism to active learning. *The Innovator, 2*.

Holzer, S. M., & Andruet, R. H. (2000). Experiential learning in mechanics with multimedia. *International Journal of Engineering Education*.

Johnson, D. W., Johnson, R. T., & Smith, K. A. (1991). *Active learning: Cooperation in the classroom*. Edina, MN: Interaction Book.

Kagan, S. (1990, January). The structural approach to cooperative learning. *Educational Leadership*.

Kolb, D. (1984). *Experiential learning*. Englewood Cliffs, NJ: Prentice Hall.

Kozma, R. B., & Johnston, J. (1991, January/February). The technological revolution comes to the classroom. *Change, 23* (1).

Laws, P. (1991, July/August). Workshop physics: Learning introductory physics by doing it. *Change, 23* (4).

Light, R. J. (1990). *The Harvard assessment seminars, 1st Report*. Cambridge, MA: Harvard University.

Lochhead, J. (1987). Teaching analytical reasoning through thinking aloud pair problem solving. In J. E. Stice (Ed.), *Teaching thinking through problem solving*. New Directions for Teaching and Learning, No. 30. San Francisco, CA: Jossey-Bass.

Lyman, F. (1987). Think-pair-share: An expanding teaching technique. MAACIE, *Cooperative News, 1* (1).

Papert, S. A., & Harel, I. (Eds.). (1991). *Constructionism*. Norwood, NJ: Ablex.

Piaget, J. (1954). *The construction of reality in the child*. New York, NY: Basic Books.

Stice, J. E. (1987, February). Using Kolb's learning cycle to improve student learning. *Engineering Education, 77* (5).

Terenzini, P. T., & Pascarella, E. T. (1994, January/February). Living with myths: Undergraduate education in America. *Change*.

ACKNOWLEDGMENT

Funding for this work was provided in part by the NSF to SUCCEED (Cooperative Agreement No. EID-9109053). SUCCEED is a coalition of eight universities working to enhance undergraduate engineering education.

CONTACT INFORMATION

Siegfried M. Holzer, Alumni Distinguished Professor
Virginia Polytechnic Institute and State University
Civil Engineering
Blacksburg, VA 24061
Email: Holzer@vt.edu
Phone: (540) 231-6073
Fax: (540) 231-7532

Vignette 11 The Use of Preclass Quizzes in Chemistry Classes

Angela G. King and Yue-Ling Wong, Wake Forest University

Regardless of the discipline in which they teach, many faculty members have similar concerns regarding both students' preparation for class and the quality of their interaction with students during class. Without the proper preparation, students often do not grasp the basic tenets of course content during the time it is being presented and discussed in class well enough to recognize their own questions and to seek guidance from their instructor. These problems are amplified when the lack of preparation is for a laboratory course, where uninformed students pose a safety threat to themselves and others and experience problems in completing the laboratory experiments within the allotted time.

Our goal was to improve student preparation for both chemistry lecture and laboratory classes in order to allow, respectively, the greatest in-class interaction on challenging topics and more efficient and accurate results in the chemistry teaching laboratory. Once our pedagogical approach was planned, we discovered that we could apply the technology resources available at our university to implement it with relative ease. The technology allowed us to rapidly gauge each student's mastery of assigned preclass material before class, and we could apply the same technology to lecture and lab classes, including chemistry courses for both science and nonscience majors.

EDUCATIONAL THEORIES

Success in chemistry is directly proportional to students' thorough understanding of chemical concepts and their ability to apply those concepts in solving mathematical problems. On their own, many students have difficulties in both grasping fundamental concepts and completing mathematical manipulations to solve problems involving these concepts. If students arrive at class having prepared and learned basics, such as the vocabulary referenced in the day's lesson, the instructor may use the remainder of class to both cover more complex topics and allow the students to work interactively in small groups on problem sets, ConcepTests, writing assignments or discussions. In lab sections, using the same approach allows the instructor to forego the elementary material in prelab lecture, which gives the students more time to complete experiments. Our approach to achieving the ideal scenario is based on a strategy developed to increase preclass preparation for physics classes at the US Air Force Academy and popularized in *Just-in-Time Teaching* (Novak et al, 1999). We now require preclass quizzes for each new topic in the general chemistry lecture and before every lab experiment in a nonscience-majors chemistry course.

COMPUTER-ENHANCED TECHNIQUES

Development of the preclass materials involves collaboration between the instructor, Angela G. King, and the chemistry department's Academic Computing Specialist, Yue-Ling Wong (Wong & King, 1999). These materials are presented in a web-based format and may include background material, animations or images if needed for visualization, online tutorials, practice quizzes for the students to monitor their own learning, and assigned readings from the textbook. Each set of preclass materials concludes with a computer-graded quiz that students complete before class.

Although the online quiz template described in this paper is an in-house project, factors considered in the development process can be applicable to any other campus environment, whether you are starting an in-house project or looking for a commercially available product.

While many faculty are already very familiar with creating course web pages on their own, creating an online quiz involves constructing online forms and mastery of cgi scripting, which are unfamiliar fields for most faculty. There is also a wide variety of quiz formats and styles. Our online quiz template was developed to make use of frames to separate the questions from the answer sheet form (Figure 11.1), a very different approach from many other online quizzes, which intermix form objects and the questions on the same page. Our approach was inspired by the opscan widely used for paper quizzes in that one generic copy of opscan is applicable for many different sets of quizzes. In our template design, the question page is a regular web page that faculty are free to create in any format, incorporating any multimedia elements they need as long as the web supports them. The question page does not even have to be a web page; it can be, for instance, a Microsoft Word document, an Adobe Acrobat file, or a paper copy of questions, using the online form to collect students' answers. The answer sheet (online form) is generated automatically with the cgi script. Therefore, the only page the instructor has to create for the quiz is the question page. Those who choose to have the questions and the form objects merged on the same page can type the questions directly on the generated form and do not have to use a frame setting.

When students submit their answers, the responses are electronically compiled into an Excel file (spreadsheet) for easy review by the instructor, and an email copy is sent to the students for their records. The tem-plate also provides several grading options for the specific purpose of preclass assignments. For example, since the students are completing the preclass exercises at different times, the instructor may or may not want to let them know the correct answers. If the completion of the exercise, not the score, matters, letting students immediately know the correct answers provides feedback.

For laboratory sections, student procedures are found on the class web page. Students must read the procedure and when they consider themselves adequately prepared for lab, complete an online graded quiz covering the experiment. These quizzes have replaced the prelab questions used in previous labs, which were collected and graded by teaching assistants. The advantage to using the online quizzes is that students must complete the quizzes before coming to the prelab lecture. This ensures that they are not writing out their answers instead of listening to tips and safety comments given by the instructor during this period. In both lecture and lab sections students are awarded points for correctly answering quiz questions (4.8% of

FIGURE 11.1

A SCREENSHOT OF AN ONLINE QUIZ

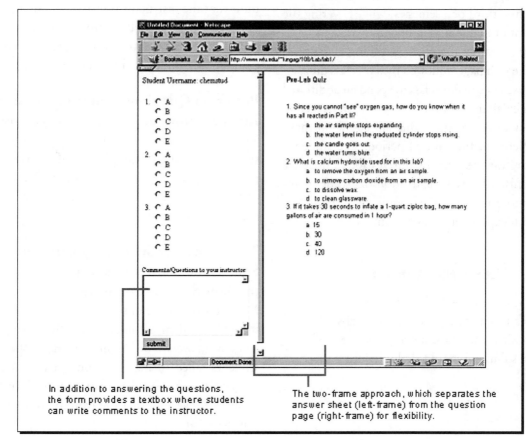

In addition to answering the questions, the form provides a textbox where students can write comments to the instructor.

The two-frame approach, which separates the answer sheet (left-frame) from the question page (right-frame) for flexibility.

the final grade and 2.8% of the final grade, respectively).

For both lecture and lab, the quizzes are generated from the same template. The template allows the instructor to choose the number of questions as well as the type (multiple choice, radio button, and short answer) and then generates an answer sheet. The instructor prepares the questions in html format, and students access the quizzes from the web. The quiz results are electronically compiled into an Excel file (spreadsheet) for easy review by the instructor, and a copy of each student's answers is emailed to students for their records. In addition to answering the questions, students have the option of writing comments to the instructor.

MEASURED RESULTS

Despite the small impact completing online preclass quizzes has on a student's final grade, the completion rate is very high (>96%). The students' average score on the preclass quizzes for general chemistry lecture is 75%. Use of the preclass quizzes and the resulting increase in student preparation have allowed four extra group work sessions (approximately 20 minutes each) during the first third of a semester, while covering the same amount of material as in previous years.

Putting all safety material, including a digitized video, on the web page, followed by a preclass quiz, allowed a nonscience majors class to spend an additional 40 minutes in lab determining the percent of oxygen in air. Without the extra time, this lab could not have been completed in the allotted period. The students' average score on the preclass quizzes for nonscience majors chemistry lab is 87%. In addition, students appear to be more at ease in the laboratory, and our success rate with experiments has grown.

LESSONS LEARNED

While our experience with incorporating graded preclass quizzes in chemistry lectures and labs has been generally positive, we have noted some areas of difficulty where solutions should facilitate future success.

Demonstrate the Quizzes Once in Class

Students who experience technological difficulties may quickly become frustrated by a poor performance, despite having prepared for class, reducing their motivation to prepare for future classes. In addition, demonstrating how to find and complete quizzes will save the instructor from replying to individual students just prior to the deadline for the first quiz. If possible, have an ungraded practice quiz that employs the same technology; students are reassured knowing the program works before it can affect their grade.

Develop Materials/Strategies Based on Your Priorities as an Instructor

Students are easily frustrated when they spend a lot of time mastering a technological application that does not emphasize important material and will not have an impact on their learning.

The Instructor Should Provide the Content for Preclass Quizzes

While writing the quizzes takes time, custom questions can give insight into what material students mastered and which concepts are presenting difficulties. Students are more motivated to work through questions that the instructor prepares, feeling that they reflect priorities that will resurface on exams. Quizzes should be at a level that forces preparation without being so difficult as to discourage students.

Proofread Questions, Watching for Alternative Interpretations of Multiple-Choice Answers

The ease of computer grading and spreadsheets of answers is lost when multiple sets of answers could be correct, depending on interpretation. This is often the case when "none of the above" and "all of the above" are possible answers.

The Format for Submitting Quiz Answers Should Include a Mechanism to Allow Student Comments

More information can sometimes be gleaned by reading a few student comments than by looking at a 100 student answers. For instance, it may appear that all students failed to master a concept presented in the preclass material, until an instructor reads one student comment revealing that the wording of that question was not clear.

If Possible, Provide Students with Instantaneous Feedback to Allow Them to Monitor Their Own Mastery of Material

Since all students in these classes take the same quizzes at any time before the deadline, correct answers and their scores are not supplied when they submit their quizzes to ensure that they are not tempted to circulate a set of correct answers. This caution makes it difficult to allow students to gauge their preparation for class and keep track of their accumulated points. It may be more efficient in the future to have a pool of questions from which a preset number are randomly picked for each student's quiz. Since each student would be taking a different quiz, scores could be instantaneously given on submissions without fear of promoting honor-code violations.

CONCLUSION

Our experiences using preclass electronic quizzes in chemistry labs and lectures demonstrate that these are useful tools for increasing student preparation for class if thought and effort are put into writing the quizzes and programming the grading mechanism. It is then the instructor's responsibility to make the most of a class population more ready to engage in discussion or learn advanced concepts.

REFERENCES

Landis, C. R. et al. (1998). The new traditions consortium: Shifting from a faculty-centered paradigm to a student-centered paradigm. *Journal of Chemical Education, 75.*

Lemke, J. L. (1990). *Talking science: Language, learning, and values.* Norwood, NJ: Ablex.

Novak, G. M., Patterson, E. T., Garvin, A. D., & Christian, W. (1999). *Just-in-time teaching: Blending active learning with web technology.* Upper Saddle River, NJ: Prentice Hall.

Tobias, S. (1992). *Revitalizing undergraduate science: Why some things work and most don't.* Tucson, AZ: Research Corporation.

Wong, Y. L., & King, A. G. (1999). Application of interactive web tools in teaching redox Chemistry. *Interactive Multimedia Electronic Journal, 1* (1). (http://www.wfu.edu/IMEJ)

CONTACT INFORMATION

Angela G. King, Senior Lecturer
Department of Chemistry
Wake Forest University
Email: kingag@wfu.edu

Yue-Ling Wong, Academic Computing Specialist
Department of Chemistry
Wake Forest University
Email: ylwong@wfu.edu

WWW: http://www.wfu.edu/~kingag/111/,
http://www.wfu.edu/~kingag/116/,
http://www.wfu.edu/~kingag/108/ and
http://www.wfu.edu/~ylwong/

Vignette 12 | Online Quizzes Facilitate Preparedness for the General Chemistry Laboratory

Christa L. Colyer, Wake Forest University

INTRODUCTION AND EDUCATIONAL THEORY

General chemistry instructors are often faced with the difficult task of maintaining a balance between coverage and conceptual understanding. The need for coverage is driven in no small part by an array of demands from various sources, such as requirements for medical school entrance, American Chemical Society accreditation, university divisionals, and so on. However, simply relating a multitude of seemingly disconnected facts to introductory chemistry students will do little to enhance either their real understanding of chemistry and chemical processes or their interest in the field. The incorporation of a laboratory component into the course is an obvious solution to some of these problems and one used by most universities. In a hands-on and highly student-centered way, the general chemistry laboratory illustrates the materials from lecture classes, thereby providing the opportunity for students to develop a much deeper conceptual understanding of the topics. The sense of discovery generated by carefully crafted laboratory experiments can motivate disinterested or disengaged students.

Effectively running a laboratory requires that everyone involved—instructors and students—be prepared in advance. Alas, students often fail to see the importance of preparation. Their reticence to prepare may be due, in part, to the little credit typically assigned to the laboratory portion of the class or to their unfamiliarity with laboratory tools and methods. However, being prepared frees students to experience and to observe all aspects of the lab with greater open-mindedness and curiosity. It also alerts them to possible laboratory hazards and ensures that labs that are more challenging can be tackled in the allotted time. General chemistry laboratory instructors must devise means to ensure student preparedness for each laboratory session.

COMPUTER-ENHANCED TECHNIQUES EMPLOYED

To facilitate student preparation, a web page was created for the general chemistry laboratory course. A single, common web page was shared by four sections, each section containing somewhere between 40 and 60 students. The web page contained links to the course syllabus, to various web resources, and to individual pages created for each laboratory experiment. On these pages, the objectives of the experiment were clearly stated, and lists of new equipment and skills to be used and acquired were also provided. Helpful hints, including last minute changes to procedure, sample calculations, and shared data, were included. Trivia and fun facts relating to the experiment were included to generate greater interest in the experiment. Most importantly, each experiment's web page contained a link to an online, prelab quiz. The quizzes were designed with several goals in mind:

- To emphasize salient theoretical and practical aspects of the upcoming lab

- To encourage students to prepare for the lab

- To help students assess their own weaknesses before coming to the lab

- To help the instructor assess common areas of misunderstanding within the student body

The online quizzes typically consisted of five to seven multiple-choice questions based on materials presented in the laboratory manual, lecture, textbook, and/or on the course web page. Some questions were specifically geared toward the methods that would be used, and others were geared toward data analysis and interpretation and the relationship between the data and concepts learned in lecture. The students were permitted to access and read the quiz questions as many times as they chose during the week leading up to the laboratory. This free access was intended to provide students with the opportunity to find all of the necessary information prior to beginning the laboratory, thus maximizing their preparation. Although students were encouraged to use as many resources as possible when preparing for the quizzes, they were instructed not to work with any other students when submitting their final answers. Answers were submitted online. The quiz forms included a text box in which students could enter any questions or comments to their instructor. After submission, students received an email message confirming the receipt of their answers by the instructor. This email message also indicated the student's total score and which, if any, questions s/he answered incorrectly. The correct answers, however, were not supplied in the email to encourage students to seek these corrections on their own. All student answers were compiled automatically in an Excel spreadsheet accessible only to the instructor. Along with total scores, the instructor's spreadsheet contained responses by each student to each question, so that trends or patterns in errors could be detected. Student comments from the quiz text boxes were also compiled in the spreadsheet, so that the instructor could assess any individual or common concerns.

MEASURED OUTCOMES

The outcomes of online quiz usage in the general chemistry laboratory were assessed for one section of the spring 1999 course (56 students). Although other sections made use of the laboratory web pages, they did not implement any regular plan of online quiz usage. Even in the one section being considered, online quizzes were supplemented with in-class quizzes. During the semester, eight online quizzes were given. Two of them were mandatory; four were optional, with a bonus mark added to the student's lab report for online quiz completion; and two were optional, with no bonus incentive.

To measure the outcomes of this venture, we must consider how well the online quizzes managed to achieve their stated goals.

Did the Quizzes Emphasize Salient Aspects of the Upcoming Lab?

Quizzes were made sufficiently challenging so that their completion required students to read the rele-

vant sections in the laboratory manual and to consult their lecture notes, textbook, and web page. The content of the quiz questions was selected so that it would guide students in their readings and preparations, thereby ensuring that all salient points were studied. The quizzes filtered the vast quantities of information available to the laboratory student.

Did the Quizzes Encourage Students to Prepare for the Lab?

First, let us consider whether or not the online quizzes encouraged preparation. The timeliness of this preparation will be considered separately. If submission of answers to the quiz is considered sufficient to indicate student preparation, then the response rates in Table 12.1 show that preparation is greatest when the quiz is made mandatory (94.5% completion rate). The incentive of being prepared for the lab, in and of itself, appears insufficient to motivate students to complete the quizzes, as completion rates dropped to as low as 38% on optional quizzes. However, even a token, such as a single bonus point toward students' prelab written assignments, which form part of their laboratory report, is sufficient to motivate more than two-thirds of the class (68.1%) to complete the quizzes in preparation for lab. This assessment of completion rates is predicated on the fact that students have full and easy access to computers and the Internet. In the laboratory class section considered here, only one student did not have a laptop computer. However, the chemistry department maintains a computer lab in the same building as the undergraduate labs, thus providing full and easy access to necessary computing facilities for students who would not otherwise possess such access.

The timeliness of student preparation facilitated by online laboratory quizzes is also presented in Table 12.1, where three categories of respondents are considered: last-minute respondents (those who submitted their answers less than 30 minutes prior to the laboratory), same day respondents (those who submitted their answers after 8 a.m. on the day of the laboratory, including last-minute respondents), and advance respondents (those who submitted their answers prior to 8 a.m. on the day of the laboratory). The occurrence of last-minute submissions increased as the perceived value of the quiz decreased. That is, only 10% of respondents waited until the last minute to submit their answers when the quizzes were mandatory. This number increased to almost 19%

when the quiz afforded the students just one bonus mark on their laboratory report, and to 33.5% when the quiz was optional with no bonus. Since one of the stated goals of these online quizzes was to ensure advance preparation on the part of the student, we should consider the number of students completing the quizzes prior to 8 a.m. of the day of the lab. Students completing their quizzes before this time are deemed to have had sufficient time to contact their instructor, teaching assistant, and/or classmate(s) to clarify points of question prior the lab. As the value of the quiz was perceived to decrease (from mandatory, through optional with bonus, to optional with no bonus), the number of advance respondents decreased. Mandatory quizzes saw almost 62% advance response, while optional with bonus quizzes saw just over 54% advance response, and optional with no bonus quizzes saw only 35% advance response.

These results can be compared to those of Tissue et al. (1996), who studied the use of web-based prelab exercises in chemistry. Tissue's studies, however, involved a senior-level instrumental analysis class, populated by 21 chemistry majors who were presumably already quite motivated and quite skilled in fundamental lab procedures. Their prelab exercises included a short online quiz in addition to other hypermedia text and ac-

tivities. Tissue found a 92.5% completion rate overall for the required prelab exercises, including the quizzes. Of these, 37% were completed in advance, 44% were completed the day of the lab, and 19% were completed after the lab class. Late completion necessarily defeats the purpose of using online quizzes for preparation.

Did the Quizzes Help Students Assess Their Own Weaknesses before Coming to the Lab?

Various observations would indicate that this goal was met. For example, recall that the students automatically received an email message confirming their quiz submission and indicating which of their answers were incorrect. On average, three students of 56 would resubmit the quiz immediately after their initial recorded submission, presumably with the intention of improving their level of understanding, even though no additional credit was awarded for such action. Sometimes students would resubmit as many as four times, until they finally selected the correct answers to all problems. Furthermore, an average of four students repeated each quiz at the end of the semester, presumably in preparation for the final laboratory examination. Thus, the quizzes were seen by the students as valuable study aids. The student comments that were submitted with the quizzes generally appealed for help with one or more

TABLE 12.1

RESPONSE RATES FOR GENERAL CHEMISTRY ONLINE QUIZZES
(corresponding to one laboratory section of 56 students in spring 1999)

Online Quiz	Completion Rate	Last-Minute Respondents[a]	Same Day Respondents[b]	Advance Respondents[c]	Respondents with Comments
Mandatory[1]	94.5%	10.0%	38.4%	61.6%	11%
Optional, with bonus[2]	68.1%	18.9%	45.5%	54.6%	8%
Optional, no bonus[3]	38.0%	33.5%	65.0%	35.0%	5%

[a] "Last minute" refers to the percentage of respondents who submitted their answers with less than 30 minutes remaining until the laboratory class.

[b] "Same day" refers to the percentage of respondents who submitted their answers on the day of the laboratory class, between 8 a.m. and 2 p.m. This percentage is inclusive of the last-minute respondents.

[c] "Advance" refers to the percentage of respondents who submitted their answers prior to 8 a.m. of the day of the laboratory class.

[1] These entries represent the average of two mandatory online quizzes.

[2] These entries represent the average of four optional quizzes with bonuses.

[3] These entries represent the average of two optional quizzes with no bonuses.

concepts that seemed to be eluding their understanding. Furthermore, the quizzes often prompted telephone calls or emails from the student to the instructor prior to the lab to clarify some aspect of the lab.

Did the Quizzes Help the Instructor Assess Common Areas of Misunderstanding within the Class?

The Excel spreadsheet compiled for each online quiz provided a clear indicator of student performance. Prior to the lab, instructors could check this file to determine which, if any, questions caused difficulties for a large number of students. Instructors were then quick to modify their laboratory lecture topics to provide the necessary explanations to resolve trouble spots. This approach represents a greatly simplified version of *Just-in-Time Teaching*, popularized by Novak et al. (1999). The instructor was often alerted to troublespots by way of the comments that students included with their quiz submissions. The inclusion of comments with quizzes was uniformly low but increased as the perceived value of the quiz increased. Eleven percent of re-

spondents to mandatory quizzes included comments, while only 5% of respondents to optional quizzes with no bonus did so (see Table 12.1).

For the online quizzes to truly serve their purpose, they must be perceived as worthwhile by the students themselves. Since the quizzes represented additional work, above and beyond the usual in-class quizzes and prelab and postlab written reports, it was expected that students might look upon them as inconveniences or additional burdens. However, students responded favorably (see Figure 12.1). Of 50 completed end-of-semester course evaluations, 15 students (or 30% of the class) strongly agreed that "the quizzes were helpful for learning course materials." An additional 64% indicated that they agreed with or were neutral toward the statement. Only 6% of respondents disagreed or strongly disagreed with the statement. In a more general sense, there was almost unanimous support for the web page itself. Everyone except one student strongly agreed or agreed that "the class web page was helpful." No students disagreed with this statement, and only one was neutral.

FIGURE 12.1

RESPONSES PROVIDED ON THE END-OF-SEMESTER (ANONYMOUS) COURSE EVALUATION BY 50 STUDENTS TO THE STATEMENTS: "THE QUIZZES WERE HELPFUL FOR LEARNING COURSE MATERIALS," AND "THE CLASS WEB PAGE WAS HELPFUL."

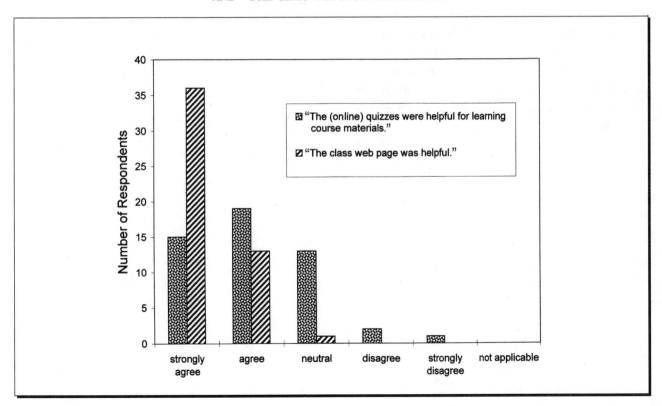

These student responses to the use of online quizzes for laboratories are not unlike those found by Tissue et al. In their work, 33.3% of students agreed or strongly agreed with the statement that "Doing the prelab exercises helped prepare me for the upcoming laboratory work," while almost 71% of students agreed or strongly agreed with the statement, "Doing the prelab exercises helped me to understand the underlying concepts." Tissue's senior chemistry students saw the exercises as most helpful for understanding concepts as opposed to teaching them laboratory skills. This distinction between concepts and skills was not made in the course evaluation given in our own general chemistry laboratory class.

LESSONS LEARNED

Online quizzes can serve as helpful tools to encourage students to prepare for general chemistry laboratories. Presumably, preparation will help students to function more effectively and quickly in the lab to understand the greater significance of their results, rather than simply going through the motions of the laboratory procedure. However, for online quizzes to be effective, the student must perceive their value. This can be achieved by simply including a bonus point for their completion or by making them mandatory. Mandatory online quizzes were, in fact, the most effective tools for ensuring student preparation. Although there has been no attempt to correlate quiz scores to laboratory performance, it seems safe to assume that students who are prepared by taking these quizzes will necessarily obtain a more fulfilling and meaningful laboratory experience.

ACKNOWLEDGMENTS

The author would like to thank Dr. Yue-Ling Wong, who is responsible for writing the script for the online quizzes employed in this general chemistry laboratory class, and for the cooperation of Drs. Swofford, Welker, Noftle, and Welder, whose laboratory sections shared the use of the general chemistry web page, even though the statistics regarding their usage are not documented here.

REFERENCES

Novak, G. M., Patterson, E. T., Garvin, A. D., & Christian, W. (1999). *Just-in-time-teaching: Blending active learning with web technology.* Upper Saddle River, NJ: Prentice Hall.

Tissue, B. M., Earp, R. L., & Yip, C. W. (1996). Design and student use of World Wide Web-based prelab exercises. *Chemical Educator, S1430-4171* (96), 01010-2.

CONTACT INFORMATION

Christa L. Colyer
Department of Chemistry
Wake Forest University
Winston-Salem, NC 27109
Email: colyerc@wfu.edu

Vignette 13 Instructional Technology for Assessment

Charles H. Atwood, Joel A. Caughran, and Jacob G. Martin,
University of Georgia

INTRODUCTION

In the late 1990s, the University of Georgia's freshman chemistry program increasingly incorporated instructional technology. There has been an increased emphasis on assessment of learning using two different forms of instructional technology. We presently use WebCT to give prelab quizzes to 1,700 students. We have also developed a computerized testing program to replace the multiple-choice paper test formerly given to 1,350 freshman chemistry students. Both testing methods have evolved into reliable and innovative platforms for testing large classes.

EDUCATIONAL THEORIES

Prelab quizzes have been given in the freshman chemistry program at the University of Georgia for over 30 years. Primarily, they were an attempt to motivate students to come to lab prepared for the day's experiment. The old written format abjectly failed to persuade students to study before lab. The average on these exams was typically 35% to 45%, proof that the students were ill-prepared. With quizzes now managed by WebCT, students have a week to take them and may use their lab manuals. While we have had to adapt WebCT to make the system easy for students to use, we are very pleased with how it encourages the students to study the lab material before coming to lab.

The computerized testing program grew out of several seemingly disparate initiatives. First, the University of Georgia switched from the quarter system to the semester system in the 1998-1999 academic year. The switch provided an impetus and a time frame for us to change. Second, the dean of the College of Arts and Sciences decided that mass night exams were interfering with the university's night school program and eliminated our old method of administering exams. Finally, the chemistry department has an excellent reputation in the field of computational chemistry and molecular modeling. However, little, if any, of

that information was trickling into the undergraduate classrooms. It was obvious that some impetus was necessary to bring molecular modeling to the undergraduates. An interactive, multimedia, testing program that included molecular models provided that impetus.

While our motivations do not cite Piaget or other learning theorists, they were sufficient to bring the project to fruition. The first two initiatives—semester conversion and no mass night exams—provided the financial resources to build a testing center and to develop the program. Inclusion of interactive molecular models in the quizzes provided the signpost to monitor our progress. In designing a testing system enhanced with molecular models, we also developed a testing system that has numerous pedagogical and administrative advantages over traditional multiple-choice exams.

COMPUTER-ENHANCED TECHNIQUES

WebCT Prelab Quizzes

A brief description of our presently operational prelab quiz system will shed light on the techniques we developed for administering these quizzes. At the start of the semester, the WebCT server is loaded with the class rolls, which include the students' names and the day that they attend lab. Students are assigned user IDs based on their names and initial passwords based on their university ID numbers. When students log into their WebCT sites, WebCT determines what day they attend lab. From that point forward, all information is released to the students based on their lab day. All the prelab quizzes for one semester, including dates and times to release the quizzes, are installed in WebCT at the beginning of the semester, and the server administers the exams.

Presently, prelab quizzes are released one week before the lab day and turned off at 3 p.m. the day before lab. For example, a student with a Wednesday lab has access to the prelab quiz for the following week beginning on Wednesday at 5 p.m., and must have completed that quiz by 3 p.m. on Tuesday, the day before the lab. Students can take the prelab quizzes up to three different times during the week. If students do poorly on their first attempts, they can take the quiz up to twice more to improve their score. The three scores are averaged for the final grade. No efforts are made to prevent students from using their lab manuals or discussing the quizzes with each other. This encourages group learning and students mentoring other students. However, each student has essentially a unique quiz.

When the prelab quizzes are built, WebCT is instructed to choose from a bank of questions on lab procedures, safety topics, or calculations required by that experiment. Student A might logon to the system and receive the first question on safety, the third question on lab procedure, and the sixth calculation question. Student B, after login, would receive a similar prelab quiz but with different questions. If students make a second or third attempt, the computer generates a new quiz for them. Thus, they cannot rely on getting the same questions but must grapple with the material, trying to understand the different questions. At present, our questions are not as interactive or multimedia as we wish but are improving.

COMPUTERIZED TESTING SYSTEM

Jacob Martin, an undergraduate computer science major, programmed our one-hour exam testing system, which incorporates a question and exam creator, posttest viewer, test regrader, and testing function. It is a completely separate system from WebCT. The program is written in Visual Basic, uses Microsoft Access for the database, and is designed to run on our local area network. The network limits access to the four or five people teaching freshman chemistry classes in any given semester, the three authors of this paper, and the 40 computers used to administer the exams. This arrangement provides excellent test security and severely limits access to the question database.

To test 1,350 students in groups of 40 at a time, we developed a registration system, using cold fusion, that allows students to choose a day and time to take their test. One week before the first exam session, a test registration icon appears on the students' WebCT site. Students open this icon, revealing the list of 35

sessions spaced over the five days available for the test. They can then choose a session and submit their choice. The program replies with a random code that they are instructed to write down. The code allows students who realize they have a conflict with their initial test session to reenter the program, submit the code, and choose a different test session. As the sessions fill, they are removed from the students' view, leaving only unfilled sessions. After registration is completed, our server knows when students are expected to take their exams. Students must attend their chosen session; otherwise, the system will not allow them to begin. Presently, we give 80-minute exams, with ten minutes in between sessions to reset the computers and to let the new students enter the testing room and begin the exam. The system has the flexibility to give exams of any length greater than one minute.

Students arrive at our Chemistry Learning Center usually ten to 20 minutes before their appointed testing session. After a session finishes, the teaching assistants (TAs) replenish the scratch paper, reset the computers, and call the next group of students into the Testing Center. Books, bags, and hats are dropped along a wall before the students sit at a computer. After the students logon to the system, the TAs check their IDs. The server is instructed to begin the exam, and timing for the test begins. At the end of the test session, the computer removes the test from the students and reports their score. Appropriate time provisions can be made for learning disabled students.

On a paper exam, students can work on the questions in any order. They can also mark a question as being difficult and come back to it. We wanted these paper exam advantages included in our system. We incorporated both features into the program using a series of numbered boxes that correspond to the test questions. By clicking on box three, question three will appear on the screen. As the questions are answered, the boxes turn from gray to blue. If question six is difficult, right clicking on box six will turn it red, providing a reminder to return to this problem.

Generating simple multiple-choice exams would have been easy but would grossly underutilize the computers and prevent significant change to our assessment procedures. Consequently, we built seven different types of test questions in the program: multiple choice, multiple answer, text entry, number entry, computational, clickable molecular models, and stoppable movie questions. Brief descriptions of each follow in order.

Multiple-Choice Questions

Multiple-choice questions are presented just as in a paper exam, except students click on their choice. The system can accommodate from two to five possible choices. Furthermore, either the question or the answers can contain images with sixteen million color graphic capability.

Multiple-Answer Questions

In multiple-answer questions, students must click on one, two, three, or more of the possible choices. An example of a multiple-answer question is:

Question: Choose the responses that describe physical, not chemical, properties.

A. Baking powder gives off bubbles of carbon dioxide when added to water.

B. A particular type of steel consists of 95% iron, 4% carbon, and 1% miscellaneous other elements.

C. The density of gold is 19.3 g/mL.

D. Iron dissolves in hydrochloric acid with an evolution of hydrogen gas.

E. Fine steel wool burns in air.

Both B and C are correct responses to this question.

Text-Entry Questions

Text-entry questions require students to type text responses. These are effective definition, fill-in-the-blank, or chemical nomenclature questions.

Number-Entry Questions

Number-entry questions, designed for calculational problems, require students to enter a number that is accurate within a range set by the exam writer. Students are also required to enter units (for example, meters, centimeters, feet) in their responses.

Computational Questions

In computational questions, every student can have the same entry question but with different computer-generated numbers. Computational questions provide instructor input to determine the range and number of significant figures for each question. Graphics capability is possible in any of the above questions.

Molecular-Modeling Questions

There are two kinds of molecular-modeling questions. Any of the four question types described above can include a molecular model. The second molecular modeling question involves clickable atoms. Molecular models can be displayed with the instructions to click on atoms containing particular characteristics, such as most acidic or sp^2 hybridized. As students click on the atoms, small, colored balls appear around the chosen atom or atoms.

Movies or Animations

Movies or animations can also be included. Any of the question types described above can include a movie, except the clickable molecular model question. Students can be shown a movie and asked to stop it at an appropriate point. For example, a titration movie could be displayed, and the students asked to stop it at the end point of the titration. For their response, students slide the movie bar to the appropriate point and leave it there. An error bar of several frames can also be included in these questions.

As students finish their tests and submit them, they are given the opportunity to retry missed questions, if the test writer so chooses. The program removes the buttons of correctly answered questions and returns the incorrect ones. Students can see their initial responses and change them for half credit. In multiple-answer questions, if correct answers have been chosen, they are grayed out, preventing students from changing them. Students receive partial credit for that answer and can receive additional credit on their second try. For number-entry questions that involve units, if the student correctly answers the units but misses the numeric answer, the units section is grayed out and appropriate partial credit applied. The converse is true if they have the correct number but the wrong units. A third retry of missed questions for one-fourth credit is also available.

The students' responses are stored in an Access database. By using appropriate Standard Query Language (SQL) queries, the database can provide detailed information on the students' performance on tests, particular questions, or any set of parameters. A statistical analysis package is also available. Access makes correcting a mistake in a problem relatively easy. After the students have finished the exam, the correction is made, and the test regraded, giving the students with the mistaken question appropriate credit—an obviously better solution than giving blanket credit as may be done on paper multiple-choice exams.

Because the exam is given over several days, using the same questions every day would favor the students who register for the late sessions. The exam-creating function permits choosing questions of similar difficulty for each exam session. For instance, if we wished to examine the students on density, we can create numerous questions in which the density of the material is changed, and the students are asked to provide either the mass or volume of the material. Thus, every exam session will receive a question about density, but they will differ. Furthermore, in a given exam session, every student has the same set of questions, but they are presented in random order. So Student A's question on density might be the sixth but the ninth question for Student B. In this fashion, we have created a unique, albeit highly similar, exam for each session. Furthermore, a sample exam which covers the material for the test, is generated about one week before the first test session. Thus, every student should be cognizant that they need to know about density before the exam is given.

The testing system is a shell that can be used equally well for any subject. Only a question database is required. It is possible to give an exam in drama containing scenes from a Shakespearean play. Images of Van Gogh's paintings can be embedded in art history exams. Biology exams that look at various parts of cells or anatomical structures of animals are possible. In effect, testing has taken on a new dimension with the inclusion of instructional technology.

MEASURED RESULTS

WebCT Prelab Quizzes

For the first two prelab quizzes of fall semester 1999, the average scores were 88.7% and 89.2%. A comparison to the paper test average of 35% to 45% on similar quizzes shows that the students are at least getting more involved with the material prior to lab. In that respect, some progress is being made. As we integrate more multimedia, such as lab techniques, into the system, students should become more efficient and safer in labs.

Computerized Testing System

With the ability to retry questions, students can learn and correct mistakes during an exam. This learning is reflected in how the average scores change after the first, second, and third tries. For the first exam in the fall 1999 semester of freshman chemistry, those averages are 67.6%, 70.6%, 71.0%, respectively. The average number of questions that the students correctly answered on the three retries are 16.9%, 18.4%, and 18.8%. The averages do not change greatly, but it is important to remember that the number of points earned for a correct answer is decreasing by half from try to try. The 3.4% difference in averages would be 13.6% if the values were not decreasing. It is true that some of the increase is from guessing correctly on multiple-choice or multiple-answer questions, but that argument cannot be made for text- entry or number-entry questions.

LESSONS LEARNED

WebCT Prelab Quizzes

The initial trial of WebCT prelab quizzes was a painful experience. The single biggest problem was that the university's server was inadequate to handle the large number of students who needed access. This problem was exacerbated by setting a Sunday midnight deadline for completion of the prelab quizzes. Essentially all students would wait until Sunday night between 10 p.m. and midnight to work on their quizzes, and the server crashed with amazing regularity. A larger, parallel quad processor server was installed in the spring semester. This alleviated some of the problems, but, in conjunction with a feature in WebCT—its ability to release material selectively—computer crashes have disappeared. We chose to release all material based on a day that lab meets. Students who meet on Thursday can only see quizzes and other information that are related to Thursday's lab. The instructor pays a price for this feature. The quizzes must be set up in several parallel sessions that are released on a given day. Most of this work can be done before the semester begins. The effort is worthwhile because it groups the students and simplifies the information they are presented.

Second, our students are computer illiterate enough that they have a difficult time responding appropriately to the prelab quiz questions. Some common inappropriate responses were not entering words properly, not knowing how to enter numbers in exponential notation, and not clicking in the correct fields. We instituted a sample quiz that the students must complete and make 80% or higher on before their prelab quizzes are released. The quiz asks such questions as, "What is Fred Flintsone's wife's name?" as it instructs the students in the vagaries of WebCT quizzes. Many of the problems encountered on the first use of WebCT were eliminated through this quiz.

Initially, students could take the prelab quizzes up to five times, and only their highest grade was averaged. However, students wasted their first two or three attempts, hoping to guess and get the correct answer. Reducing the attempts to three and averaging has quickly focused the students' attention on studying the lab material before they sit down at a computer.

Computerized Testing System

As with the WebCT system, we have initiated an exam to orient the students to our program. It serves as both a diagnosis of the students' skills and an orientation to the program's capabilities. This has effectively removed many of the students' complaints of "I did not know how to ____."

We supply the 40 students with TI30Xa calculators and scratch paper. We could have used the Windows calculator in our program, but students want a calculator in their hands. Issuing a calculator also eliminates the possibility of students bringing to the tests programmable calculators that are loaded with information for the test.

The Chemistry Testing Center contains 40 computers, but we do not release all 40 spaces for any session. Spaces are intentionally left open so that students who failed to register, forgot to take their exam, slept through their exam, got sick, or had family problems earlier in the week can be accommodated.

CONCLUSION

Freshman chemistry at the University of Georgia has instituted instructional technology in its teaching and testing. The prelab quizzes and hour exams are now computerized and interactive. Improvements are being made in how tests are administered in both systems. However, it is accurate to say that testing in these classes is now radically different from the old paper multiple-choice exams. Inclusion of molecular modeling, video clips, animations, and graphics herald a new era in testing for large university classrooms.

CONTACT INFORMATION

Charles H. Atwood
Chemistry Department
University of Georgia
Athens, GA 30602
Email: batwood@chem.uga.edu
WWW: http://www.chem.uga.edu/DoC/
ResFacCHA.html
Phone: (706) 542-1917
Fax: (706) 542-9454

BIOLOGICAL AND HEALTH SCIENCES

 **Using Computer Technology to Supplement a Traditional College Agriculture Class**

James R. McKenna, Virginia Polytechnic Institute and State University

INTRODUCTION

For almost a decade, the computer has assumed a significant role in enhancing my undergraduate crop production classes. Initially, I used the computer to provide interactive, multimedia, self-paced programs to teach basic course information. We renovated a classroom to create the Supplemental Learning Center, a workstation for hands-on learning to complement the visual presentation in the multimedia programs.

The addition of web-based notes presented the primary class information and detail not provided in the interactive, multimedia programs. These notes contained links to the library, reading lists, and electronic journal search sites for enrichment and term paper preparation.

The next generation of electronic pedagogy improved student-to-student and student-to-faculty interactivity. I added a bulletin board, chat line, and electronic office visit features to each of the Internet class pages. This allowed nearly seamless communication of course information, online reviews, and discussions, which enhanced faculty availability for student advising and counseling.

I also added a short video to the beginning of each web lecture, which provides an overview of the notes and attempts to emphasizes the most important concepts. With the completion of this phase, all four of my classes have the framework to be offered online, as well as on-campus.

EDUCATIONAL THEORIES

As on most campuses, the classrooms that I've taught in are not equally equipped for audiovisual presenta-tions. Often shades were broken, bulbs blown, equipment missing, not to mention the fact that you had to set up and tear down as students entered and left the room. Bringing in live plants, seeds, or soil profiles to classrooms in other buildings and across campus was difficult at best and usually abandoned after a period of resolve.

To address this issue, we developed the Supplemental Learning Center, a lab that connects to my office. Ten computer workstations were set up with accompanying bench space for microscopes, soil samples, seeds, and plants to complement the electronic presentation. Over two years, twenty-four 45-minute interactive multimedia programs were created for CSES 2444 (Agronomic Crops) and CSES 3444 (World Crops and Systems). The 2444 programs taught agricultural literacy, often to urban students; that is, the difference between wheat and barley or a combine and haybine. The programs allowed a self-paced presentation with interactive questions and a 20-question, multiple-choice quiz at the end of each program. I could concentrate more on higher order instruction in the classroom and leave the terminology and identification to self-study. In 3444, each of the 12 multimedia units took students electronically to a different world agroecosystem based on temperature and rainfall. Each had the same interactive questions and quizzes.

The unexpected benefit was that the multimedia took the place of a class period in a M-W-F class. Both CSES 2444 and CSES 3444 normally have between 90 and 110 students. The class is awkward to teach because it is too large for small rooms and too small for large, usually well-equipped, lecture halls. I was able to split the classes into two sections, teach them back-to-back on Monday and Wednesday, and use Friday's time for lab visits throughout the week. (Lab is open 8:00 a.m. to 5:00 p.m., Monday through Friday.) With only one additional lecture, I was able to have smaller, more interactive classes.

Another problem was the availability of a single text that covered these classes' wide range of subject matter. The answer was to put the class notes up on the web and no longer require a text. To make the notes more interactive, I added good URL addresses to supplement the notes. I filtered the locations so that I was comfortable with the site quality and sent students up-to-date information. Throughout the notes, I was able to highlight important concepts with blinking red text. I structured the lectures to include learning objectives, overview, notes, summary, and self-evaluation questions.

For each class, I provided links to the library, electronic journals, old exams, and reading lists. These resources made obtaining information for term papers easier, and I believe the overall quality of the students' work on these papers improved, although I cannot document this. In addition, each class page contained the class organizational information and the syllabus.

As more and more pressure is placed on us to make our classes web-ready, the missing components were those electronic tools that allowed for communication. To address the needs of an at-a-distance class, I added a chat room to facilitate both student-faculty and student-student discussion. The line is available all the time for student-student dialogue, and at a set time, the instructor is online in the chat room to interact in real time. The instructor can also read over the dialog and comment when relevant. There still also was a need for a private office visit. A student can use email to set up an appointment, and a private chat room allows for a real time faculty-student conference.

The final addition to these classes was an online test component. Online testing allowed both multiple-choice and essay-type exams. We are also adding a five-minute video to begin each lecture. These videos will add a human touch to the notes and attempt to highlight the most important concepts to draw from the web lecture notes.

COMPUTER-ENHANCED TECHNIQUES USED

- Interactive multimedia with quizzes
- Email
- Web-based class notes with major concepts highlighted
- Filtered URLs to supplement web notes
- Links to resources/old exams/syllabus/reading lists
- Class bulletin board
- Online multiple-choice and essay quizzes and exams
- Chat rooms
- Private chat room with instructor
- Video clips to highlight concepts

MEASURED RESULTS

Each class evaluates the instructor and the technology each time the class is taught. The average evaluation of these computer-aided classes over the past five years has been consistently 3.8 on a 4.0 system. Early in the development of the interactive multimedia programs, supplementary evaluations were added to the standard university evaluation. The results of two years provided a positive response, with the programs receiving a 4.3 on a 5-point scale for student satisfaction. Comments continue on how the multimedia enhances the lectures.

Evaluation of the web-based tools has not been as systematic, as these are more recent additions. However, the number of hits on the pages indicates significant student use. The email traffic has increased ten times in the last couple of years. More students are taking advantage of the chat room, and access to the instructor has been greatly improved. More and more web-based information is being used in term papers, and the quality of references on term papers has definitely improved.

Overall, students seem to enjoy the technology. A significant number of students still come to us without a lot of computer experience. Just using the computer tools in these classes forces them to learn and to become comfortable with the computer.

Lessons Learned

The computer is a supplemental tool. Personally, I do not feel it will completely replace the teacher in the classroom with the student; however, the computer can greatly enhance the quality of the time spent in the classroom. I can address a wide variety of learning styles using multimedia, notes, interactive questions, and chat rooms, although chat rooms are more effective when the instructor is online to interact. The computer aids in leveling the playing field by bringing my students to a similar knowledge level when they come to class. I find I can spend more time with higher-order learning in the traditional class. We do not need to identify barley. We can talk about why you would grow barley when wheat is a more valuable commodity. The computer has allowed me to meet with smaller, more interactive classes and to provide students with a wide range of supplemental material that has greatly expanded the parameters of my classes.

In the spring 2000, I took a student group to South Africa on a semester-long exchange and am offering CSES 3444, World Crops and Systems, online from Bloemfontein, South Africa. We will see how the at-a-distance toys function. Please visit my home page and links to my classes. I have four classes, all constantly under construction. The two other classes are CSES 4444, Sustainable Ag Systems, and HIST 3124, History of American Agriculture. You are more than welcome to visit, make comments, and/or suggestions.

Contact Information

James R. McKenna, Professor of Agronomy
     and Coordinating Academic Advisor
Virginia Polytechnic Institute and State University
235 Smyth Hall
Blacksburg, VA 24060
Email: jamckenn@vt.edu
WWW: http://teach1.cses.vt.edu/jrm/jim.html
Phone: (540) 231-9786
Fax: (540) 231-3431

Vignette 15 | Computer-Enhanced Learning in Introductory Biology Classes

Robert C. Hodson, University of Delaware

INTRODUCTION

I have been dismayed by the general passivity of students listening to lectures and conducting cookbook laboratory exercises, and I have begun trying student-centered learning techniques. To support collaborative activities, I wanted to incorporate technology. I felt that I could make the most impact in the discipline of biology teaching through communication, visualization, and laboratory experimentation. I have had the pleasure of teaching each year one, sometimes two, sections of honors introductory biology, a two-semester, first-year course with a maximum of 20 students per section. Some successes have migrated into nonhonors sections. Over the last several years, this course has provided opportunities to try various classroom teaching methods and, in particular, investigation-rich laboratories with classes averaging eighty students per section.

Honors introductory biology, offering four credits each semester, is for biology majors, but there are always students from other majors, such as animal science and biochemistry. The lecture meets the usual three times a week for 50 minutes each, and the laboratory is three-and-a-half hours (three hours is standard). In the fall, a required one-credit freshman seminar that meets once a week for 50 minutes and is graded pass/fail is tied in with the laboratory and provides the opportunity to learn various skills, such as Internet information and evaluation, and to discuss the results of laboratory investigations.

The following is a summary of those aspects of the courses that are computer assisted.

EDUCATIONAL THEORIES

Biology is intrinsically a hierarchical subject, usually taught in a sequence of topics from molecules to ecosystems. I wanted to retain an order that seems embedded in my discipline yet allow students working in collaborative groups to "uncover rather than cover" (Bass, 1999) biological facts and concepts, to have more real-world scientific experiences in the lab, and to use technology to increase active learning. In addition, by providing easy-to-use communication mechanisms, I hoped to increase my interaction with the students, especially in developing and analyzing their written and experimental work.

The result is a course built around groups of three to four students with an emphasis on collaborative learning. The lecture has a focused-discussion format. Students are challenged with questions that are delivered online in advance of class meetings. Some questions require only careful reading of the textbook and no group interaction. Other questions require supplemental sources from the library or Internet and group interaction.

The same groups carry over into the laboratory. Each week, on a rotating basis, one group member attends a half-hour training session and then leads the group during the remaining three hours of laboratory. Training is provided in the use of equipment, the materials and their locations, and aspects of leadership, such as how to distribute work loads and decision-making strategies. The laboratory engages students in all aspects of the scientific process. They must propose a testable hypothesis, design an experiment, collect, analyze, and interpret data, and communicate their findings. The use of electronic probes provides data with less experimental error fast enough that follow up experiments can be performed in the same laboratory period. Two communications are required each semester. One is a written report modeled after a primary journal article, with tables and figures (graphs) prepared in a worksheet and submitted as a text or html document on disk. The second report is either a group poster or a group oral report using presentation software.

COMPUTER-ENHANCED TECHNIQUES

The primary technology used to guide and to support students in my course is a web site (http://www.udel.

edu/hodson/hodson.html) that includes all of the following components:

- Course guide (syllabus) with email links to faculty and staff

- Lecture and laboratory schedules (updated regularly)

- Study questions

- Old interactive tests

- Anonymous suggestion box

- Chat room

- Class list with photos, names, and email addresses

- Archive of links to online resources referred to in class discussions by students or myself

- Forms: interactive Java applets written with Jamba (e.g., technology survey, course evaluation)

- Online version of the laboratory manual, enhanced with interactive Java applets such as those that show how to carry out dilutions

CLASSROOM ACTIVITIES

- A structured discussion format, with questions delivered online in advance

- Computer-delivered images provided on CD-ROM by the textbook's publisher and personal digital camera

- Display of Internet resources

Seminar Activities

- Finding and evaluating online information

- Using spreadsheets for constructing tables and graphs taught by a self-paced tutorial enhanced with screen capture images

- Virtual Flylab: presents online *Drosophila* genetics problems

Laboratory Activities

The typical technology-rich laboratory session has teams of three to four students, each with a laptop computer connected to an electronic probe through an analog-to-digital interface. The extremely stable and sensitive probe sends output to the computer, so students quickly get data they can save and later transfer electronically to a spreadsheet, avoiding tedious note-taking. Since they save time in the initial, structured investigation, students can then form their own, new hypotheses about what would happen if they changed conditions and proceed to test them. At the end of the laboratory period, data are collected from all teams and converted to html so that they can be shared. This method breaks a complex investigation with multiple variables into several different experiments that can be recombined, giving a richer dataset. Students are engaged in the actual practice of science and scientific inquiry. (Our laboratories have been technologically enhanced with a generous grant from the Howard Hughes Medical Institute.)

A specific example of how this laboratory protocol works is a photosynthesis experiment. An infrared gas analyzer probe detects the amount of carbon dioxide leaf tissue removes in a flowing stream of air. Each measurement takes as little as 15 minutes, leaving ample time for multiple experiments in which light intensity or some other parameter is varied. Some teams study different variables, and they compare their data in a report. We also make use of a digital camera to capture the experimental set-up and to record qualitative observations that can later be incorporated into a report and laboratory manual instructions.

Finally, students report laboratory results using three different formats: 1) word-processed documents containing spreadsheet tables and graphs, 2) web pages, and 3) oral reports using presentation software. Students learn the technology to communicate results. I find it easier and quicker to make comments electronically than on paper. This nearly instantaneous feedback is an important part of mentoring that technology helps to facilitate.

MEASURED RESULTS

We have begun to assess attitudinal data, and preliminary results indicate that students appreciate working with sophisticated equipment like electronic probes, although some procedures must be refined. Students noted that the digital camera has enhanced their reports and posters significantly. Students, even those who profess little computer knowledge or computer phobia, appreciate the technological skill instruction. We have some anecdotal data indicating that the technology is effective in increasing communication. Here is an excerpt from one student's email that substantiates this inference:

At any rate, the extent to which technology has taken a role in your class is absolutely wonderful in my opinion. . . . Having such a well designed and informative web page up and running for a class makes it a million times easier for me to keep up on what we're supposed to be discussing in class, as well as where we are in the lab, due dates, etc. I don't have to run around calling people or trying to find you if I have a question about what I should do or have done before I go to class. I just plop down at my computer, bring up the page, a couple clicks and I know what's going on. I must especially give you kudos for updating the web page regularly.

Student laboratory reports are more sophisticated and biologically relevant. High-quality data moves students away from explaining negative or artificial results to interpreting meaningful data.

One can roughly gauge how a course is going from the ratio and content of anonymous email. No anonymous email messages have been received criticizing the course in the first third of the fall 1999 semester.

LESSONS LEARNED

The first attempt at the discussion format in spring 1999 was less than successful. Questions required only regurgitation of facts and concepts and no group interaction. Although students found this boring, they still scored better on short essay exams than previous students, so they were learning from reading, which was a significant achievement. The second attempt, in fall 1999, encouraged more group interaction and posed questions that built on textbook material but combined ideas to reach new insights. Students seem to appreciate opportunities to test their comprehension of the material, and we have had some great discussions.

The old question, "What are you going to test, the book or your lectures?" disappears when students have access to study questions and discussion ques-

tions at all times. These questions also help students choose and emphasize reading material.

Computer-assisted instruction provides ways of delivering course material better and providing new course material, such as images and information gleaned from the Internet, but it is definitely not an end in itself. If it does not improve instruction in some tangible way and/or increase the instructor's enthusiasm for teaching and students' enthusiasm for learning, why use it? In biology, its ability to make topics less abstract is very powerful, and its ability to increase opportunities for communication between students and with the instructor increases learning opportunities.

Seeing photographs not only helps those who learn visually; all learners are helped by actually seeing what we have been describing.

The laboratory group leaders free the teaching assistants, who are advanced undergraduate students, and the instructor from repetitious instruction, and the students are able to get more done in less time with fewer mistakes. This innovation has been adopted by all sections of Introductory Biology, honors and nonhonors alike.

The research-grade electronic probes (Qubit Systems, Inc., Kingston, Ontario) interfaced with laptop computers were no more difficult for students and teaching assistants to learn than older procedures with less technology, and the results were much more satisfying. Students applied most of their thinking to understanding the biology of the system rather than explaining artifacts. The ability to collect high-quality data quickly provided more opportunities for critical thinking.

Although the learning curve for technology may be steep, in the long run, it can save time. For instructors, it can release time for more scholarship in research and/or teaching.

CONCLUSION

My experiences encourage me to make more use of technology. Combined with appropriate teaching strategies and firmly set pedagogical goals, it seems to increase learning or at least the opportunities for learning. I have more communication with my students than ever before. They obtain more results more quickly in the laboratory. We can spend more time in the laboratory performing "what if" analyses rather than just following sets of instructions. I feel that these tools create more opportunities to engage in collaborative work and critical thinking. Students will be able to use these skills no matter what career paths they choose after leaving the university.

REFERENCE

Bass, R. (1999, October). *Exemplary models for web-based learning.* PBS live satellite downlink.

CONTACT INFORMATION

Robert C. Hodson, Associate Professor
Biological Sciences and University Honors Program
University of Delaware
225 McKinly Laboratory
Newark, DE 19716
Email: hodson@udel.edu
WWW: www.udel.edu/present/best_practices/
Course Page: www.udel.edu/hodson/hodson.html
Personal Page: www.udel.edu/hodson/myprofile.html
Department Home Page: www.udel.edu/bio/
Phone: (302) 831-8440
Fax: (302) 831-2281

Vignette 16 Multimedia Animation and the Insects

Donald W. Hall, University of Florida

My course, The Insects, is a lower divisional course for nonscience majors, with an enrollment of 320 students (mostly freshmen and sophomores). On the first day of class, I ask the students how many of them dislike science and science courses. Typically, about 90% raise their hands. My goal, in addition to teaching the students about science, is to change their attitudes toward science. For this to happen, I believe it is imperative that I present the material in the most exciting and organized way to make it easy for the students to learn.

COGNITIVE BASIS

Learning is believed to take place in two memory compartments—working memory and long-term memory. For learning to occur, new information must be taken into working memory, integrated with previously learned information retrieved from long-term memory, and then itself be encoded into long-term memory—

a process known as cognitive transformation (Farquhar & Surrey, 1995). Information entering working memory must be reinforced continuously or encoded into long-term memory, or it is rapidly lost. Working memory has a very limited and short-term capacity and is readily overloaded. There is evidence from a variety of fields that information is organized into chunks for long-term storage. Therefore, a knowledge of chunking theory (Simon, 1974) should be helpful in avoiding overload of working memory. Simon presented evidence that the chunk capacity of working memory is in the range of five to seven (probably closer to five) chunks. He gave the following working definition of a chunk: "a chunk of any kind of stimulus material is the quantity that short-term memory will hold five of." In lecture situations, it is imperative to organize material into a manageable number of chunks to avoid overloading students' working memories.

Working memory is believed to be composed of three compartments: the central executive and two slave systems—the phonological loop and the visuo-spatial sketch pad (Baddeley, 1992) (see Figure 16.1). The central executive is an attention controller and task manager. The phonological loop is responsible for holding speech-based material, while the visuo-spatial sketch pad forms and manipulates images.

Because working memory has a very limited capacity, each additional cognitive process performed places additional demands on the system. The total load on working memory, including learning and non-learning events, is known as cognitive load. Farquhar and Surry (1995) have divided cognitive load into three categories: learning events, message comprehension events, and nonlearning events. Learning events are the mental manipulations and reinforcement that assist in transferring information from working memory to long-term memory. Message comprehension events are the load on working memory to understand the material. Complexity of information, unfamiliar terms, and the number of competing sensory stimuli are factors that contribute to message comprehension. Nonlearning events include anything that distracts from the learning process (e.g., daydreaming, personal problems, and banging doors). When message comprehension events and nonlearning events place significant load on working memory, low cognitive engagement occurs, and little learning takes place. Also, when excessive demands are placed on working memory, students become frustrated and tune out.

FIGURE 16.1

THREE COMPONENTS OF WORKING MEMORY

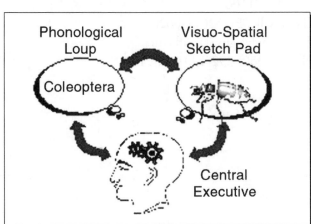

COMPUTER-ENHANCED TECHNIQUES USED

I have attempted to address the cognitive issues of chunking, cognitive load, and the three compartments of working memory by the use of a wide range of computer-based multimedia, including colorful text, graphics, digitized photographic images and sound, CD audio, computer-controlled video laser disc clips, and computer-based animations (Hall, 1996b). Because it is a visually rich subject, entomology is ideally suited for multimedia. Of course, multimedia is not limited to the computer. Therefore, whenever possible, I bring live insects to class for demonstrations under the document camera. Also, I still occasionally use slides, and due to copyright restrictions I still use some VHS videotapes. When possible, I prefer computer media, because they allow seamless presentations. Significant pauses in a presentation invite loss of attention by the students.

Multimedia has forced me to think more carefully about how I should organize the subject material to most effectively achieve my learning objectives for the students. Chunking theory suggests no more than five related points per computer slide. To enforce that limit on myself and to make text easily readable in the rear of the room, I use a font large enough to discourage myself from putting too much on a slide. Also, to help maintain student focus, I dim points after they have been covered. I rarely animate text, because I believe flying text has only a very transient effect in maintaining attention. After that, I believe it is distracting.

Digitized slides and video can provide rich visual images for the visuo-spatial sketch pad of working memory, while the computer text and accompanying verbal commentary provide the speech-based material for the phonological loop. Theoretically, this should assist the student with working memory tasks.

Motion is known to be a powerful force in maintaining attention, especially when used in a relevant context. I make use of extensive video- and computer-based animations in my course in an attempt to hold the students' attention. When possible, I prefer to use video laser discs. Laser discs, unlike videotapes, allow nearly instantaneous, random access to sequences of frames. With multimedia authoring software, it is possible to control the video laser disc player directly from the computer. However, this method results in longer pauses before the video is played. I prefer to create computer-generated barcodes for the video clips and then to control the laser disc player with a barcode reader. This approach avoids undesirable pauses that may result in students becoming distracted.

Computer-based animations can also provide visual images and maintain student attention. I have created a series of animations for my course that illustrate a variety of insect behaviors (Hall, 1996a). Some of the animations were created with multimedia authoring software that has a scripting language. With this type of software program, computer graphics may be manipulated and moved on the screen very precisely. For example, graphics of multiple sets of wings or legs in different positions may be grouped onto a single insect body and then repetitively shown and hidden as the whole group is moved across the computer screen to make the insects fly or crawl.

Simpler animations may now be created with newer versions of standard presentation software (e.g., PowerPoint) by using the software's custom animation feature. To demonstrate the phenomenon of butterflies' response to post-pollination color changes in the common ornamental plant *Lantana camara*, I insert a full-screen photograph (jpg format) of a flower cluster onto a PowerPoint screen. Then I use the custom animation feature to cause butterflies (as Windows™ metafiles) to fly to the flowers and begin to feed. Animations can be powerful learning tools to illustrate difficult concepts as well as to maintain student attention.

MEASURED RESULTS

At the end of the semester in which I first used multimedia, students were asked to evaluate the effectiveness of the multimedia on a Likert-type scale (Hall, 1996b). Ninety-five percent of the students responded that the multimedia stimulated and enhanced their interest in the course. There is also anecdotal evidence for the effectiveness of the multimedia. Many students have commented to me in person and via email that the multimedia has been helpful to them. For example, one student came up after class and commented, "I'll never forget aphid alarm pheromone after that animation!"

LESSONS LEARNED

I have had to develop a presentation style that is natural and not tied down to the computer area. Initially, I think my lectures might have been a little mechanical, because I was concentrating so much on the technology. Also, early LCD projectors and three gun projectors were not very bright and required dimming the lights—an invitation to tired students to go to sleep. Newer projectors are sufficiently bright that this is not a problem. Overall, I believe that the use of multimedia technology has greatly enhanced student learning in my course.

REFERENCES

Baddeley, A. (1992). Working memory. *Science, 255,* 559.

Farquhar, J. D., & Surrey, D. W. (1995). Reducing impositions on working memory through instructional strategies. *Performance and Instruction, 34* (8), 4-7.

Hall, D. W. (1996a). Creating computer-based instructional animations. *NACTA Journal, 40,* 8-11.

Hall, D. W. (1996b). Multimedia in the entomology classroom. *American Entomologist, 42,* 92-98.

Simon, H. A. (1974). How big is a chunk? *Science, 183,* 482-488.

CONTACT INFORMATION

Donald W. Hall, Professor
Department of Entomology & Nematology
University of Florida
P. O. Box 110620
Gainesville, FL 32611-0620
Email: dwh@gnv.ifas.ufl.edu
Phone: (352) 392-1901, ext. 113

Pascal de Caprariis, Indiana University-Purdue University Indianapolis

Environmental Problems was developed as an online course for two reasons. First, I felt that students should spend a substantial amount of time contemplating how to learn about a subject rather than concentrating entirely on content. The asynchronous format of an online course seemed suitable, because it requires the instructor to develop active learning exercises, which tend to be introspective. Second, I wanted a course in which students could interact with each other on an equal footing. I felt that email communications would be less intimidating to those students who are reluctant to express opinions in a classroom, so collaborative learning would be more likely to succeed in an online course.

Administrative information is provided on a web site, and all communication is by email. Students communicate with each other on a listserv; they post their assignments on the discussion forum component of Microsoft Frontpage™, and papers written on the topics covered are submitted to me as email attachments. Enrollments were 25 and 46 students, respectively, the first two times the course was offered. To reduce confusion, the larger group was broken up into two groups of 23 students, using two listservs and two separate sections on the discussion forum.

COURSE DESIGN

Course design was based on standard instructional design principles. The pedagogical component was achieved by constructing tables with three columns, consisting of things I want students to be able to do at the end of the course, skills students needed to achieve the goals, and things I must do to ensure students had those skills. So my design algorithm consisted of goals, skills, and teaching strategies. Table 17.1 addresses cognitive goals, including making decisions about what aspects of the subject are important, prioritizing them, searching for articles on each one, and, finally, synthesizing the material found by writing a short paper on the subject.

In Table 17.2, I considered the affective component of knowledge, involving metacognitive activities, which also consisted of goals, skills, and teaching strategies. Ideally, in achieving affective goals, students will learn to determine the relevance of what they read to their cognitive goals; they will become aware of how their response to material is affected by their prior knowledge, especially if that knowledge is biased; and they will recognize when what they learn conflicts with their beliefs and decide how to respond to that realization.

To achieve the cognitive and affective goals in an online course, I used the following principles:

Collaborative learning. This approach is desirable because peers are more closely attuned to other students' zones of proximal development (Vygotsky, 1962), so interactions between students are more likely to be effective than the passive reception of information from an instructor.

Rapid feedback. The use of conferencing software allows an instructor to monitor individual and group progress and to interject comments and suggestions at appropriate times.

Active learning. An online course is ideally suited to active learning exercises because the format precludes the traditional, passively received lecture presentation.

COURSE ACTIVITIES

The activities discussed here do not require elaborate equipment or esoteric knowledge on the part of the instructor. Everything is accomplished using a web site for administrative information, a listserv for communications, and a discussion forum as a place where students can post their work. I begin each semester by giving the students practice in each skill before moving on to graded projects. To save space, the practice exercises are not discussed here.

The cognitive goals of the course are first addressed by providing students with some background material on the subject to be studied. For example, I wrote some text on how nutrients are recycled in a rain forest and posted the material on the course's web site. Students were then asked to create an outline for a study of rain forests. They were asked to decide what aspects of the subject should be included and how each aspect is related to the others. They posted their outlines on the discussion forum and were expected to critique each other's submissions. Most of the outlines were similar. Eventually, someone took the best parts from each and constructed a composite outline. Sometimes, there were two or three competing composite outlines. Then I asked the students to vote on which one they wanted to use for their study. I posted the one that got the most votes on a new page in the discussion forum, and it became the one they used for the remainder of the project.

After the composite outline is posted, students search the Internet for articles on the different aspects of the topic. Most of them find articles on several of the aspects. Students post their summaries of the articles and their URLs in the appropriate places in the discussion forum. Each summary is expected to be sufficiently characteristic of the article that another student could use it as a source, while writing the paper on the subject. This component of the project requires students to recognize that articles on the Internet are not peer-reviewed, so they must evaluate the credibility of the articles.

When enough summaries have been posted, everyone uses a selection of them as source materials for their papers. Because different students choose different summaries, the papers are not identical, but because they all follow the same outline, the similarities are sufficient that the papers are easy to grade.

The affective goals are addressed through the interactions between the students. Creating the composite outline requires each student, or most of them, to

TABLE 17.1

EDUCATIONAL STRATEGIES FOR COGNITIVE GOALS

Cognitive Goals	Skills Needed	Teaching Strategies
Know basic facts about the subject.	Find information about environmental topics.	Provide some relevant information on the course's web site to get students started.
Recognize relationships between systems and parts of systems.	Be able to organize information in different ways	Show students how to construct hierarchically structured outlines.
Synthesize information	Develop a coherent explanation for a phenomenon.	Give practice in writing short papers that follow the outlines.

TABLE 17.2

EDUCATIONAL STRATEGIES FOR AFFECTIVE GOALS

Affective Goals	Skills Needed	Teaching Strategies
Monitor one's learning.	Recognize the relevance of information to one's cognitive goals.	Introduce the subject of schemata as a way to develop metacognitive activities.
Evaluate motives as well as information.	Recognize the goals of the authors of the source materials.	Give instruction and practice on reading articles critically.
Recognize the components of one's value system.	Recognize any conflicts between what one learns and what one believes.	Discuss the relationship between the outline developed and how one thinks about the subject.

Teaching with Technology

work with everyone else in the group. They have to submit their ideas to evaluation and evaluate the ideas other students have submitted. It is not easy to have one's ideas ignored or criticized, and some students are reluctant to criticize the work of others, but this approach to collaborative work forces students to deal with these problems as they work on the cognitive goals.

GRADING THE PROJECTS

A common complaint of students involved in collaborative learning exercises is that although some students do most of the work, everyone gets the same grade for the project. I do not give group grades in this course. Grades are assigned to individual students, based on their outlines, summaries, papers, and interactions with other students. The outlines are graded on the basis of their quality and the quality of the comments made about other students' outlines. It is not enough to say, "That is a great outline." I am looking for comments that show how to improve it or suggest how to meld it with someone else's outline. By the time the composite outlines have been constructed, a good deal of group work has occurred, but each student receives a personal grade based on his/her contributions to the group effort. With regard to the summaries, students are graded on the number and quality of the ones they submit. Someone who just copies an article and posts it gets nothing for the effort, and someone who posts a sentence or two gets very few points. I am looking for thought, not volume or cryptic comments. Of course, each student gets an individual grade for each paper, based on how well it is written (grammar and adherence to the outline) and its accuracy.

MEASURED RESULTS

By the time students finish the course, they learn a good deal about topics, such as rain forests or global warming, but they learn more than content, because they have had to do all of the work themselves, albeit under a certain amount of supervision. For example, because I insist that they construct an outline on each subject before they begin searching for source materials, they eventually realize the importance of focusing their work by thinking about the structure of a topic

before beginning to study it in detail. Other valuable skills students develop are the ability to read articles critically, evaluate their credibility, and summarize them succinctly. These skills are valuable because they are transferable to other courses and other disciplines. Achievement of the affective goals is more difficult to assess; changes in intrapersonal skills are subtle and probably will not be significant in just one semester, but over the course of a semester, the number of students who participate in the discussions increases, suggesting that interpersonal skills are developing.

How is achievement of the goals enhanced in an online course? The influence of the asynchronous format is indicated in a number of ways. First, the pace of the course is necessarily slower than that of a traditional course, so the lag between sending a message and receiving a reply gives students time to think about what they are doing. I find that the work turned in is usually superior to the papers submitted by students in my traditionally taught lecture courses. The lag also gives students time to cool off if they are offended by another student's response to their work, so the format facilitates learning to accept criticism. Another advantage involves reticent students. Many students find it difficult to believe that their ideas are as worthwhile as those of the extroverted students, so they rarely participate in discussions. In an online course, these students can submit ideas nearly anonymously, so some of them (not all, of course) will participate more freely in this format.

LESSONS LEARNED

1) The slow pace of an online course prevents covering the same amount of material as in a course that uses the lecture format. If it is important to cover a specific amount of material in a specific manner, the online format is probably not a good choice.

2) If an active-learning, collaborative environment is desired, the online format should be considered; it can provide a valuable experience to both students and instructors.

3) The amount of email traffic involved in an online course can be formidable, so some instructors respond to messages only on specific days. On the other hand, I have found that students really appreciate rapid responses to their questions, so each

instructor must decide how to manage the time involved.

4) Giving individual grades for collaborative activities is difficult to do fairly in most courses, because we never really know who has done the bulk of the work. In an online course, every message to the listserv or discussion forum comes with the sender's name on it, so I know who is doing the work and who is not. After each paper is turned in and graded, I can provide each student with a detailed explanation of how many points he/she received for each component of the project, and I can easily justify each decision.

5) Writing the background material for each subject myself avoided the copyright infringement problems associated with using material already posted on the web.

CONCLUSIONS

The learning that occurs in my online course cannot be compared with that in a traditional lecture course, because the activities differ markedly. In a lecture course, I present content arranged in a logical manner; students take notes and then are tested, largely on recall, at a later time. The emphasis is on the teaching, because we assume that learning will occur if the material is presented adequately. The attrition in large enrollment service courses is sufficiently large that this assumption is clearly flawed. In an online course, the emphasis must be on the learning, because the traditional model of teaching is not relevant. An observer in a traditional course would pay attention to the rhetorical skills of the instructor, whereas in an online course, the activities of the students would be of interest.

REFERENCE

Vygotsky, L. S. (1962). *Thought and language.* Cambridge, MA: MIT Press.

CONTACT INFORMATION

Pascal de Caprariis, Associate Professor
Department of Geology
Indiana University-Purdue University Indianapolis
723 W. Michigan Street
Indianapolis, IN 46202
Email: Pdecaprr@iupui.edu
WWW: http://www.geology.iupui.edu/labs/teachinglab
Phone: (317) 274-7484
Fax: (317) 274-7966

Vignette 18 — Digital Digging: A Problem-Based Approach to Undergraduate Education in Archaeology

Jeanne Sept, Indiana University, Bloomington

INTRODUCTION

You would think that it would be easy to teach archaeology classes in Indiana. After all, our students are often motivated by the exploits of Indiana Jones, a famous fictional archaeologist portrayed in several films. But Hollywood has done us no favors. Students come into my classes assuming that the goal of archaeologists is to discover ancient treasures and whisk them off to museums or private collections to save them from uncertain fates. In fact, archaeology is less an adventure of discovery than a science of interpretation. My challenge is to help students learn to think like archaeologists, to engage them in the process of critical inquiry we call science. I have found that the tools of our Information Age can really help my students investigate the Stone Age.

INSTRUCTIONAL GOALS

In the average archaeology classroom, university students play a passive role; they are told a story of the human past that weaves the names and dates of different sites and prehistoric cultures, illustrated with slides, videos, museum exhibits, or artifact replicas. I think this traditional approach is flawed, because students leave such courses with heads full of memorized facts and principles, sometimes without understanding the relevance of this knowledge to their own lives and having learned very few skills that they can transfer to other learning contexts. It is rare for undergraduates to get any experience in the collaborative teamwork and interpretive debate that are so central to archaeological inquiry until they take advanced seminars or lab classes.

To counteract this, I think it is vital to challenge our students to work through real prehistoric problems and to learn to analyze and to interpret archaeological data for themselves. Therefore, I have focused on developing instructional strategies in my classes that allow me to spend less time lecturing about basic information and more time modeling and discussing the logic of interpretation. I try to coax students to spend less time just listening and more time deciding how to evaluate complex issues, to spend less time just memorizing and more time using information to solve actual problems.

One way to engage archaeology students in data analysis is to give them problem sets asking them to interpret site data. Because real archaeological data is voluminous and complex, such class exercises are often based on small, simplified datasets. Unfortunately, this simplification can reinforce a student's notion that there are right answers to dig for, rather than tantalizing problems that are difficult to solve with ambiguous, long-buried clues. Could there be an alternative way to give students access to the rich reality of archaeological data without overwhelming them with complex detail? I became convinced that computers could help.

TEACHING WITH TECHNOLOGY

In general, I emphasize written work and problem-based learning focused on case studies. In this context, computers can be effective teaching/learning tools that can both support and challenge students intellectually. I have used a range of standard software packages and also developed two new computer applications designed specifically for archaeology courses: a case-study exercise that runs off a CD-ROM and a data visualization tool that runs over the Internet.

PRESENTATION AND DISCUSSION TOOLS

I use a standard set of computer applications in two ways to help students explore the content of my courses. First, I maintain extensive course web pages with basic lecture notes and embedded hypertext links. Students also take self-paced, weekly electronic quizzes available from the web page. Colleagues often wonder why my students continue to attend classes when I provide such web materials for them. I have always had good class attendance, and I suspect that this is because I try to use class time to do more than merely present information, which would be duplicated in my virtual lecture notes. Face-to-face with students in class, I discuss the challenges of archaeological interpretation by working through examples. These discussions continue outside of class through email.

During the last three years, I have increasingly used multimedia presentations to complement my lectures and stimulate discussion or activities in classes. My presentations rely heavily on visual materials, and the computer slides allow me to easily write on or highlight the images during the lecture, often directly in response to student comments. In particular, computer slides allow me to easily integrate vocabulary and concepts with the visual images and also to insert information generated by the class into the presentation I have prepared. For example, in my junior-level class on prehistoric diet, the students read an article about how taste sensitivity varies. During class, the students taste different strengths of sugar and salt solutions, and we use the computer to generate descriptive statistics of their lab results and plot them on a graph of data from the article. This facilitates class discussion of the article and related concepts.

Analytical Tools

I wanted to give students a real dataset from a famous archaeological site, important to my own research in Africa, and ask them to analyze different aspects and develop interpretations, building from short answers into essays. Working with staff in our campus Teaching and Learning Technology Lab, I designed a multimedia CD-ROM called *Investigating Olduvai. Archaeology of Human Origins*, published in 1997. It is organized into three parts: 1) a set of research questions and problems that archaeologists have posed about the site, 2) a complete set of data from the site and additional background information, 3) a set of methodologies and analytical tools. The CD-ROM contains a complete set of actual data from the site and a suite of research questions with different levels of difficulty. I can use it in all the archaeology classes I teach because it is accessible to students with different backgrounds and levels of expertise.

My students work with *Investigating Olduvai* for a series of case study exercises. For example, in my fresh-

man-level introduction to archaeology class, students use the CD-ROM for one assignment in class and one out of class. In class (in a computer cluster), they first work collaboratively to integrate multidisciplinary data and interpret the age of the site, and then each team interprets evidence for the site's ancient environment. Out of class, they analyze information on artifacts and fossils from the site. My prehistoric diet class uses the CD-ROM to work on a more complex exercise; they analyze detailed data on fossil bones from the site to reconstruct the diet of early toolmakers.

As I was revising my CD-ROM for publication, web browsers were just beginning to emerge as a powerful, new Internet technology for teaching and learning. On the one hand, the web seemed limitless and flexible, compared to the fixed format of a CD-ROM. And yet, most of the web materials at the time were no better than static textbooks; they encouraged students to passively browse for information, rather than engaging them in any active way. Frustrated, I decided to collaborate with Martin Siegel, the research director for IU's Center for Excellence in Education, to develop a rich, interactive digital learning environment for the web, in which archaeology students could explore and learn to interpret authentic data from a wide range of archaeological sites in Africa. The goal of our project, titled Prehistoric Puzzles, is to develop web learning tools in the Java programming language that will lead students away from their current, passive experiences of surfing through web information into powerful instructional interactions that will help them develop collaborative problem-solving and research skills. Just as my CD-ROM was built on the three pillars of problems, data, and analytical tools, so Prehistoric Puzzles has three structural elements:

1) Instructional modules and web-based activities designed to pose research problems and help students to apply analytical methods and principles

2) An African archaeology database that contains complex multimedia data on sites from all regions and prehistoric time periods in Africa. This relational database can be viewed as a series of web pages or explored with our visualization tool TimeWeb

3) A web-based tool called TimeWeb, written in the Java programming language, that helps students to

visualize and to explore the space/time dimensions of archaeological data

TimeWeb allows users to query our archaeology database. Students choose selection criteria for each query from a menu of variables and different classification systems.

MEASURED RESULTS

When surveyed, students in all my classes have unanimously approved the use of computers to present class materials, whether on my web pages or in class presentations. It is time-consuming to create these materials, but I believe they provide good scaffolding for student learning.

Has my CD-ROM been an effective teaching/learning tool? Yes. During seven years of use, in four different archaeology courses, most students have found the CD-ROM challenging and interesting and frequently comment that they have learned a lot more working on exercises with the Olduvai data than they have in other archaeology classes. For example, 96% of the students agreed with the statement, "The Olduvai program allowed me to apply the concepts I've learned in this class"; 93% agreed with the statement, "The Olduvai program made anthropology concepts more relevant for me"; and 90% thought that the CD-ROM required them to use higher-level thinking skills than other assignments. Meanwhile, Prehistoric Puzzles is still in its formative evaluation phase, but it promises to provide an even more challenging learning environment than the CD-ROM.

LESSONS LEARNED

Overall, my goal is to create an active, collaborative classroom where the traditional survey course is replaced by a creative, problem-centered environment. My use of presentation technology and my CD-ROM have helped me to do this, and I expect that Prehistoric Puzzles will also enhance the opportunities for me to help students piece together the puzzles of the past for themselves. The key ingredient to the use of any of these technologies in the teaching/learning process is the investment of time. It takes considerable time to think through and to develop challenging, authentic materials to enhance instructional interaction, essential time to communicate with students in class and over email, and, most importantly, critical time to allow students to engage in these activities in class. This results in the classic trade-off of any problem-based learning environment, where depth of engagement can only be achieved by sacrificing topical coverage. My experiences have convinced me that teaching with technology can help make problem-based activities authentic, valuable learning experiences for both students and instructors.

REFERENCE

Sept, J. (1997). *Investigating Olduvai. Archaeology of human origins CD-ROM*. Bloomington, IN: Indiana University Press.

CONTACT INFORMATION

Jeanne Sept, Professor
Anthropology Department
Student Building 130
701 East Kirkwood Ave
Indiana University
Bloomington, IN 47405-7100
Email: sept@indiana.edu
Course Web Page: http://www.indiana.edu/~origins
Prehistoric Puzzles Web Page: http://www.indiana.edu/~puzzles
Information about author's CD-ROM: http://www.indiana.edu/~origins/teach/Olduvai.html

 **Prescription for Excellence: A New Computer-Based Medical Curriculum for Wake Forest University**

J. Charles Eldridge, Wake Forest University

To celebrate the centennial of the founding of the Wake Forest University School of Medicine in 1902, the medical student curriculum has been professionally and technically renovated. Beginning with the class of 2002 (entering in the fall of 1998), each of the 108 incoming students has been issued an IBM ThinkPad computer to be used in conjunction with a dedicated server network. In addition to raising tuition, the school has underwritten a multimillion-dollar infrastructure from multimedia display systems to a fiberoptic cable and router network to a specialized support staff. This chapter summarizes the background, expectations, achievements, and remaining challenges after one-and-a-half years of operation.

MEDICAL EDUCATION FOR THE 21ST CENTURY

Medical school faculty have increasingly recognized that the changing health care environment mandates a new educational philosophy. For example, the modern MD degree represents only the midpoint of a physician's training and education. Several more years of specialized training remain, and most of a physician's expert knowledge and skill are acquired during the residency years. Because a medical school presents a single curriculum to all students, our charge has become the instruction of fundamental material essential to future obstetricians, radiologists, psychiatrists, or hand surgeons.

SKILLS ARE AS IMPORTANT AS KNOWLEDGE

The quantity of important biomedical knowledge seems to expand explosively, yet the MD program remains four years long. We concluded that we must impart essential basic concepts and teach students how to fill in the details for themselves. Computerization brings a resource development strategy that experienced professionals use to find essential facts. Indeed, as health care becomes increasingly resource-driven, management of the growing mountains of patient records and test results, new diagnostic and treatment information, and lists of rules and policies would be unbearably complex without electronic storage and retrieval. Our students must practice management of electronic material early and often.

THE COMPUTER'S CENTRAL ROLE

The 1999 student version of the ThinkPad laptop computer has a modem connector, an Etherlink network card, a 6.4 GB hard drive, a CD-ROM drive, active matrix display, and operates with Windows 98. Some 1,000 DHCP 100 Mbit data ports, accompanied by electrical power outlets, have been installed by each seat in lecture halls, and in conference rooms, teaching labs, and the library. The ports are linked by fiberoptic cable to a separate, dedicated curriculum server. Everything the students will study or use is posted on the server and can be downloaded to the laptops for offline work.

The system is accessed by opening an intranet home page that moves to a set of calendar pages. Student activities are generally blocked in a series of lectures, labs, and conferences attended by all, and each scheduled event contains at least one hyperlink to a file of reading material or an image set. In addition to Microsoft Office Pro 97, each laptop computer has a medical dictionary, online testing software, Reference Manager, the Web Snake Offline Browser, and a CD library of anatomic and radiologic images.

Figure 19.1 illustrates a typical weekly calendar during the first year. Underlined lecture titles are hyperlinks to faculty-prepared notes on html-formatted pages. The designation "slide" is a link to a PowerPoint image set, prepared and shown by the instructor during the class session. On Monday and Friday afternoons, groups of six students engage in a clinical case session with two faculty facilitators ("Small Groups"). Case pages are stored on the server in html format with appropriate exhibits attached and examined using an overhead monitor in each conference room. Student laptops can access the case after the session is finished, as a hyperlink from the patient name ("Zebulon Kincaid").

COMPUTERIZATION SERVES THE FACULTY

An MD curriculum is a standardized program of clearly established learning objectives, so the computer's principal advantage is in centrally locating all instructional materials. Curricular planners and staff can easily cross-reference, identify, and quantify any item. Demographic questions are easily answered, and various teaching modalities or topics are quickly and accurately analyzed.

Faculty teaching styles have been greatly improved by the addition of digital multimedia projection, electronically prepared class notes, and web and CD-based resources. Quizzes can be administered through student computers on weekends or evenings without using class time. Faculty/student email communication resolves many issues without appointments and meetings. A web-based online grading system assesses individual activity in small groups. Every week, faculty

pull up their group page which includes student photos, and check off scoring levels for each of several assessed characteristics. Scores are saved in background for computation of overall grades.

COMPUTERIZATION SERVES THE STUDENTS

Laptops have reduced the burden of textbooks and paper note pages; the entire curriculum is gradually downloaded onto the laptop hard drive. Indeed, the instant resource base now includes the entire World Wide Web. Faculty-provided materials are more graphic and identically formatted. The detailed calendar is easily accessed and can be changed quickly for all to see.

Case sessions, which include a patient scenario and task questions for study, are held twice weekly. Case pages are available for student downloading after the session ends. Email facilitates communication among students, particularly groups of students. Finally, students become adept at computer use at a time when these skills are becoming central to health care. It is always interesting to hear students describe the reactions of their private practice preceptors, who see them fishing information from a computer logged on to the distant medical center.

FIGURE 19.1

CALENDAR OF WEEK

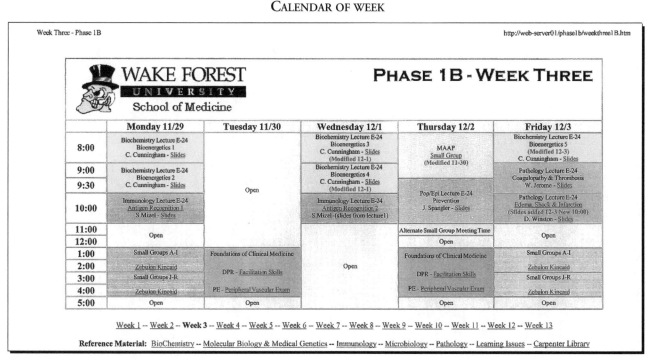

Upon survey, nearly every student reports using the computers to search the Internet and to access lecture and lab materials. About one-third key in notes during lecture. Complaints focus primarily on the laptops being too bulky to carry everywhere or too slow to permit effective use of the web over modem. Hardware breakdown has been rare. Overall satisfaction is 100%.

DRAWBACKS AND CHALLENGES

A significant drawback for those contemplating the computerized curricular approach is the price tag. The medical school underwrote $300,000 of one-time installation cost and incurs an annual operating budget of nearly $1 million for academic computing. A full-time staff of three technicians is continually busy uploading and editing instructional materials, training students and faculty, and responding to equipment problems. In addition, each student is charged a $1,500 tuition supplement for each of the first two years to fund the direct cost of a laptop computer and core software.

Although new technology has improved classroom presentations, the images are much harder to create initially and often require faculty training combined with staff assistance. Creating and posting material for the initial rollout often produced moments of stressful crisis. In addition, electronic testing formats are not yet ideal, principally due to concerns about security and hardware reliability. Large and important exams continue to be administered on paper.

SUMMARY

Wake Forest School of Medicine has introduced a bold, new MD curriculum that is more profession-based, interdisciplinary, and student-centered. The addition of computerized technology, from powerful laptops for each student to a fiberoptic server network to digital multimedia instructional equipment to World Wide Web access, has facilitated this renovation process at every step. Despite the costs, occasional setbacks, and continuing challenges, the WFU experience has produced a more energized teaching faculty, a better organized curriculum, and a significant addition to our student recruiting strategy. We firmly believe that professional programs of all types will be moving toward the design that Wake Forest is operating now.

CONTACT INFORMATION

J. Charles Eldridge
Department of Physiology and Pharmacology
Wake Forest University School of Medicine
Winston-Salem, NC 27157-1083
Email: eldridge@wfubmc.edu
Phone: (336) 716-8570

Vignette 20 Web-Enhanced Learning for Public Health Graduate Education

Christine L. Pistella, University of Pittsburgh

INTRODUCTION

The purpose of this chapter is to describe the use of web-based instructional materials for a graduate course addressing the social and behavioral aspects of public health practice. During 1999, the instructor used web-enhanced instruction to promote an adult learning environment that facilitated active learning and the use of current Internet resources and promoted student and instructor communication. Like many core courses, this one faced several barriers to effective learning: a large student group, diverse levels of familiarity with the topic, a high proportion of adult learners with ongoing professional commitments, its required status, and time limitations for course content (1.5 credits for a seven-week session). Students in the course were drawn from departments studying infectious diseases and microbiology, epidemiology, biostatistics, environmental health, occupational health, genetics, and health services administration. Students' professional backgrounds were diverse: medicine, nursing, social work, pharmacy, engineering, and administration, among others. Many students also had extensive scientific backgrounds in such fields as chemistry and biology. The majority of the students also had clinical and professional experience. Approximately 20% of the course participants were international students, representing nations in Africa, Asia, South America, and Europe.

The 1999 class consisted of 80 students. Class meetings were held in a large, media-enhanced auditorium with Internet access. CourseInfo (course management software) was used to develop the web-based instruction. The University of Pittsburgh Center for Instructional Development and Distance Education (CIDDE) provided instructor orientation to the classroom technological capabilities as well as student orientation to CourseInfo during the first class meeting. CIDDE also provided in-class technical support as needed for individual class sessions and online technical support for student and instructor questions throughout the course.

PEDAGOGICAL APPROACHES

CourseInfo offered many planning and communication features that enhanced implementation of the course. Several factors influenced the choice of pedagogical approaches. First, promotion of active learning of social and behavioral content in a large lecture hall seemed more likely with the use of CourseInfo features. Second, many social and behavioral theories and concepts are relatively complex. Student familiarity with these concepts varied, as some had considerable professional experience with public health practice, while others reported no professional experience. Therefore, the use of the courseware permitted more individualized learning and pacing as well as promotion of lifelong learning, with recommended readings and web sites for advanced learners. Third, the web-enhanced package offered features that promoted integration of learning strategies. Students used multiple tools, including readings, web site links as resources, lecture materials, and case examples within web sites. Therefore, complex materials from a variety of sources fostered an active learning experience.

COURSE ACTIVITIES

The course activities involved the traditional face-to-face format, including lecture, discussion, and student presentations. The CourseInfo features used for course activities included the following.

Precourse communication with students. This included a student questionnaire, email communication related to the use of CourseInfo, access to the entire syllabus, and email access to the instructor and students enrolled in the course.

Student questionnaire. Students completed an online questionnaire that elicited self-reported knowledge and experience with the primary course topics as well as expectations for the course and interest in the course content. The results were shared online with the students and used to adapt individual content modules to meet class needs. For example, the student questionnaire indicated that 90% of the students considered themselves inexperienced in one topic, so the lecture and class activities reflected a beginner level for this material.

Course documents. All course documents, such as syllabus and assignments, were accessible via CourseInfo.

Web site hyperlinks. Hyperlinks to multiple sites were added for each class module, so students could integrate web resources with lecture, discussion, and journal readings.

Gradebook. Students could view quiz and exam grades using the courseware.

Web site critiques. Students selected a relevant web site and provided a critique of its usefulness, accuracy, and value for public health professionals or consumers.

Online submission of student reports. Students submitted papers using a courseware drop-box feature.

Announcements. Instructor communication increased with use of the announcement feature that alerted students of the posting of new resource materials, grades, or a current event related to the course content.

MEASURED RESULTS

The course evaluation indicated that several highly rated components of the course might be attributed to the use of web-enhanced courseware. These included instructor/student communication, organization of the course, and timeliness of the course content. The course also was highly rated as encouraging students to learn more about the course content. These findings showed that the instructor's course goals to foster adult learning, to create a collaborative learning model, and to promote motivation for lifelong learning about the content were met.

LESSONS LEARNED

1) Effective use of web-enhanced teaching methods requires significant time and commitment to instructor training. For example, as preparation for this course, the instructor participated in workshops related to course design, distance learning techniques, instructional design, and adult learning. The instructor commitment to continued training in instructional strategies for distance learning as well as technical training is critical to the implementation of web-enhanced courses.

2) Preparation and implementation of a web-enhanced course requires additional staff and teaching assistant training as well as time commitment. Student expectations for access to the instructor and support staff as well as for quantity and quality of educational materials increase with the use of web-enhanced courseware. Likewise, staff and teaching assistants must receive ongoing training related to courseware and other technical support functions so that they may assist the instructor with implementation of the course.

3) University-based support for faculty, staff, and students is essential for successful distance and distributed learning. The centralized support system available through the University of Pittsburgh offered multiple workshops for faculty and staff training as well as technical support. Technical support must be integrated with the necessary changes in instructional methods, course design, and student evaluations.

4) The use of the integrated learning model offered multiple strategies for students to understand these concepts and to view web sites relevant to public health practice and research. This feature was helpful with a large enrollment with diverse professional and cultural backgrounds.

5) Timeliness of content could be immediate, since access to the Internet facilitated use of multiple web sites describing current events related to social and behavioral aspects of public health for class projects. Real-time examples could be used for group projects, exams, and class discussion, thereby fostering students' understanding of the applicability of the

course content to their own professional and personal experiences.

6) Web-enhanced instruction facilitated communication among students as well as with the instructor. This was helpful, as many students did not know each other because of the multiple departments and schools represented in core courses. Student lists of email addresses increased their communication with each other and helped to reduce the social and educational isolation often experienced in large enrollment courses.

7) The use of web materials, such as hyperlinks to multiple public health sites, in course readings and assignments promoted application of Internet resources and increased Internet critique skills for professional development.

8) Web-enhanced learning increased and improved access to course materials and email communication between the instructor and classmates by removing logistical barriers often experienced by adult learners with professional and family responsibilities.

Conclusions and Recommendations

Web-enhanced instruction has the potential to improve the quality of the educational experience for most students. Electronic courseware meets many of the needs of the adult learner, such as greater communication access to the instructor and fellow students and immediate access to current events and health research of relevance to course content. However, faculty considering web-enhanced courseware and other distance learning techniques should be aware of both the planning and training commitment. Faculty also should recognize that the use of web-enhanced courseware, especially many communication features, involves a collaborative learning model in which student expectations for instructor accessibility and performance are raised. Student communication with the instructor markedly increases an expectation for email feedback.

The positive aspects of web-enhanced education are particularly beneficial for interdisciplinary courses, such as public health education. The capacity to introduce individualized and self-paced learning modules and to involve web-based educational materials representing diverse professions, disciplines, and cultures adds value to the educational experience for the adult learner. Likewise, the availability of Internet hyperlink resources, such as newspapers, journals, and government hearings, offers the immediacy required for the health professional student who must be able to apply academic courses to public health practice. In summary, courseware management packages introduce communication and resource features that have the potential to increase the quality of the educational experience for the health professional student, particularly the adult learner seeking a collaborative learning experience.

References

Carbone, E. (1998). *Teaching large classes: Tools and strategies.* Thousand Oaks, CA: Sage.

Cyrs, T. E. (1997). *Teaching at a distance with the merging technologies.* Las Cruces, NM: Center for Educational Development, New Mexico State University.

Draves, W. A. (1997). *How to teach adults* (2nd ed.). Manhattan, KS: The Learning Resources Network (LERN).

Contact Information

Christine L. Pistella
University of Pittsburgh
216 Graduate School of Public Health
Pittsburgh, PA 15261
Email: chrisp+@pitt.edu
Phone: (412) 624-3162

Introduction of Computing Competencies for Future Healthcare Professionals

Ellen R. Cohn, University of Pittsburgh

PEDAGOGICAL APPROACHES TO CLINICAL COMPUTER COMPETENCY ACQUISITION

Common pedagogical approaches for clinicians have been to teach computer competencies in contexts devoid of clinical content. Various schemas for such instruction have included:

Instructional modules and support. Students can take university-supported, noncredit workshops and access support personnel in computer labs and telephone/email-based help desks.

Preprofessional computer course. Students are required to take one or more computer courses, typically offered by the computer science department.

Computer-assisted learning. The instructor adopts one approach, such as computer-assisted instruction in pharmacy calculations, and uses it to teach a body of knowledge.

Computer-based assignment. The instructor constructs one or more computer-based assignments, such as construction of a web site, or an Internet-based assignment.

Clinical practicum. The student is immersed in the clinical site and expected to acquire functional computer skills.

When a student has not yet acquired a repertoire of either clinical or computer competencies, the latter approach can be overwhelming to both the student and the clinical instructor. In addition to acquiring the computer competency to function in the clinical site, students must develop professional poise, become acclimated to the clinical site, acquire the interactional skills to relate to a new patient population, and expand their body of knowledge of the disorder and the therapy.

Even more important than their computer skills per se, students must approach the clinical setting ready to learn new technological competencies. Schumacher et al. (1997) reported that, in therapists, the greater the computer experience, the lower their computer anxiety.

COURSE EXPERIENCE

Class Characteristics

The basis of this vignette is a three-credit undergraduate class taught for the first time by the instructor in spring 1999. The class consisted of 52 undergraduate students in communication science and disorders and met for three hours each week in a classroom with Internet access. A doctoral-level teaching assistant was assigned to the course. A digital projector was routinely used to project PowerPoint lectures. The CourseInfo software program was supported by the University of Pittsburgh's Center for Instructional Development and Distance Education. The instructor had received prior training in CourseInfo, and both students and the instructor had access to 24-hour, seven-day-a-week technical assistance. Students were initially introduced to the CourseInfo program by the instructor in the school's computer laboratory.

Each class incorporated instructor lectures and active learning in pairs and groups. Course products included completion of a precourse survey, a student home page, multiple writing assignments, literature searches, and two group-generated, poster-session assignments.

INTEGRATION OF TECHNOLOGY COMPETENCIES

Healthcare professionals are increasingly called upon to use computer-based technologies in all aspects of their clinical practice (Anderson-Harper et al., 1998; Carlucci, 1999; Chandra & Holt, 1996; Cochran et al., 1993; Iskowitz, 1999; Masterson et al., 1999; Mormer & Palmer, 1998; Sylvester, 1997; and Wynne, 1993). Computer usage by healthcare professionals can be organized into the five overlapping functional categories which are presented below and are based, in part, on the work of Cochran et al. (1993).

The following list details the technology competency categories and activities designed to introduce these competencies.

1) Acquisition of Current Knowledge

Competencies

- Pre- or post-professional use of computer-assisted instruction

- Use of Internet knowledge sources

- Electronic access to colleagues or external experts via email and listservs

- Online conference attendance

Activities

- The CourseInfo course document section contained a syllabus with hyperlinks to electronic readings, including an online statistics textbook.

- The CourseInfo external links section provided hyperlinks to web sites, search engines, and sources of technical assistance.

- Students used the CourseInfo communication section to email the instructor and other students, conduct group work, participate in a virtual discussion, and contribute to a threaded discussion.

- Class assignments were posted in the CourseInfo assignments section. The instructor's "whole class feedback" on assignments and examples of outstanding papers were also posted.

- Students took practice quizzes in the CourseInfo assessment section and completed a computer-based precourse survey.

- Three lectures were delivered from the Supercourse in Epidemiology, the Internet and Global Health, http://www.pitt.edu/~super1/. This site was also hyperlinked in the CourseInfo course documents section.

- Instructor-generated PowerPoint lectures were posted for students to download.

2) Clinical Research

Competencies

- Use of Internet knowledge sources

- Use of software and internet for data acquisition

- Use of software for data analysis

- Dissemination

Activities

- Use of Internet sources was required to complete the group-generated poster sessions and a research paper.

- Students became facile with email and word processing, two dissemination tools.

- Students became acquainted with use of an online survey tool in the CourseInfo assessment section.

- Students tracked their performance using the CourseInfo gradebook.

3) Program Administration

Competencies

- Use of word processing and graphics software to develop reports, treatment plans, and correspondence

- Use of spreadsheet software to track billable hours, construct and track budgets, accounts receivable, and business expenses

- Use of calendar tools to schedule patients, meetings, and staff time and to track productivity

- Use of web site to represent and promote program

- Use of computer-linked telecommunication to send and to receive documents and to conduct videoconferences and teleconferences

Activities

- Students used word processing software to develop reports, treatment plans, and correspondence. Some used PowerPoint software to develop presentations.

- Students had access to the CourseInfo calendar tool.

4) Service Delivery

Competencies

- Use of computer as a diagnostic tool

- Use of computer to score and to analyze diagnostic tests

- Use of computer-based materials as a context for instruction

- Use of computer as an instructor

- Use of computer to support decision-making

- Use of computer as a clinical data recorder/analyzer

- Use of computer as a clinical materials generator

- Use of computer to generate biofeedback

Activities

- Students used word processing to generate a therapy plan and behavioral objectives.

5) Career Development

Competencies

- Use of email and Internet to investigate career opportunities

- Use of software, email, and Internet to develop and disseminate résumé

- Use of Internet to display personal web site

- Use of email and Internet to network and to interact with professional organizations

- Use of computer-mediated communication to engage in intrapersonal, interpersonal, and small group communication

Activities

- Students used the CourseInfo student page to develop personal home pages.

- Hyperlinks to professional organizations were included in both the CourseInfo course documents section and the CourseInfo external links section.

- Students became accustomed to using email in the CourseInfo communication section. Many participated in an online virtual chat when a winter storm prevented class attendance.

RESULTS

1) Students successfully achieved the targeted computer based competencies.

2) Students made frequent use of the CourseInfo course site:

- Total course hits: 18,932

- Content hits (i.e., main page, course information, staff information, course documents, assignments, and external links): 15,576

- Communication hits (i.e., email, student homepages, group homepages, discussion board, virtual chat, and student roster): 960

- Group hits (i.e., group area, group email, send file to group, and group virtual chat): 53

LESSONS LEARNED

1) Introducing selected computer competencies in incremental steps and recognizing that not all competencies would be introduced in one course was useful.

2) CourseInfo use raised students' expectations of instructor preparedness (Mormer, 1999). Students wished to download PowerPoint outlines the day before they were to be used in class, and preexamination quizzes were requested. The quantity of student emails to the instructor increased dramatically as compared to prior courses; many contained statements of appreciation for the CourseInfo use.

3) Students reported acquiring computer skills when required to research and to complete assignments.

4) Both students and the instructor were motivated by building a social component into the use of CourseInfo. Students enjoyed receiving a welcoming email with the course site address before the first class meeting. Many took this opportunity to read about the instructor and class requirements. Student pages were read by most students and seemed

to create greater class cohesiveness. These, along with the precourse survey, enhanced the instructor's knowledge of individual students.

5) A precourse survey provided the instructor with valuable information about students' expectations, learning styles, attitudes toward computer use, and professional goals.

6) The posting of PowerPoint lectures for students to download prior to class enabled the instructor to progress more rapidly through the material. Since students were not as burdened with "stenographer" duties, more time was available for active learning activities designed to promote higher-order reasoning, integration, and generalization.

7) Student learning styles varied for CourseInfo acquisition. Some requested structured didactic instruction, while others made use of intuitive learning strategies (Mormer, 1999).

8) Technology-savvy students were effective informal peer mentors.

9) Student and instructor reactions to CourseInfo were overwhelmingly positive. Minor difficulties related to log-in problems and, initially, to printing PowerPoint presentations.

Conclusions and Recommendations

1) Future healthcare professionals must acquire technology competencies. This process should be initiated prior to immersion in clinical training and be systematically introduced and tracked. The ultimate goal is for the healthcare professional to assume a life-long sense of responsibility for competency acquisition.

2) Course-management software facilitates the acquisition of these skills.

3) Courses that incorporate an intensive introduction to computing competencies, "technology-intensive courses" (TICs), might be required in the same way that many universities mandate "writing-intensive courses." The University of Hawaii's four-year experience with TICs provides a model (Nagata, 1999). Based upon our experience, TICs would best be taught by instructors with computer com-

petence, access to computer labs, technical support, instructional-design support, and adjusted class size or teaching assistant support.

References

Anderson-Harper, H., Kavookjia, J., & Munden, C. D. (1998, Fall). Teaching students to develop a web site as a tool for marketing pharmaceutical care services. *American Journal of Pharmaceutical Education, 62* (3), 284-289.

Carlucci, D. (1999, March 8). Building clinical computer competency. *ADVANCE for Speech-Language Pathologists,* 7-9.

Chandra, A., & Holt, G. (Fall, 1996). Need to enhance computer skills of pharmacy students. *American Journal of Pharmaceutical Education, 60,* 297-303.

Cochran, P. S., Masterson, J. J., Long, S., Katz, R., Seaton, W. H., Wynne, M., Lieberth, A., & Martin, D. (1993, September). Computing competencies for clinicians. *ASHA,* 48-49.

Iskowitz, M. (1999, March 8). What can technology do to improve your practice? *ADVANCE for Speech-Language Pathologists,* 10-11.

Masterson, J. J., Wynne, M. K., Kuster, J., & Stierwalt, J. A. G. (1999, May/June). New and emerging technologies: Going where we've never gone before. *ASHA, 41,* 16-20.

Mormer, E. (1999). Personal communication.

Mormer, E., & Palmer, C. (1998, June). A guide to using the Internet: It could change the way you work. *The Hearing Journal, 51* (6), 29-30.

Nagata, C. (1999, September 29). University of Hawaii at Manoa, Educational Technology Department [personal email].

Schumacher, K., Brodnik, M., Sachs, L., & Schiller, M. R. (1997, Fall). Therapists' anxiety and attitudes toward computerized documentation in the clinical setting. *Journal of Allied Health,* 151-158.

Sylvester, R. R. (1997, Spring). Incorporation of Internet databases into pharmacotherapy coursework. *American Journal of Pharmaceutical Education, 61,* 50-55.

University of Hawaii Technology Intensive Standards. (1997, July 1; last modified 2/22/99). What should our graduates know? <http:www.Hawaii.edu/ti/TIC/te_in st.tm> (9/29/99).

Wynne, M. K., Seaton, W. H., & Allen, R. (1993, September). Integration into office management. *ASHA*, 50-51.

CONTACT INFORMATION

Ellen R. Cohn, Director of Instructional Development
School of Health and Rehabilitation Sciences
University of Pittsburgh
5026 Forbes Tower
Pittsburgh, PA 15260
Email: ecohn@pitt.edu
Phone: (412) 647-1357

 **Using Internet Technology to Enhance Learning in Large Lecture Classes**

Charlene Hamilton, Donnarae Paulhamus, and Mary Beth Cochran, University of Delaware

A trend in higher education is to involve students to a greater degree in their own learning. Increasing the use of technology can accomplish this involvement even in large lecture classes. Internet newsgroups are an ideal way to increase student interactions and to give them a forum for addressing their nutrition-related questions and concerns. However, designing a large lecture class (250 students) to include Internet newsgroups poses a logistical problem related to how an instructor can reasonably manage the volume of electronic postings. In this case, the use of senior undergraduate nutrition students as peer mentors proved an ideal solution. Mentoring undergraduate students in a newsgroup ideally allows the seniors to begin applying principles learned in the classroom to a real-life situation.

IDEAS BEHIND COURSE DESIGN

I regularly teach an introductory nutrition course to large groups of students in a traditional lecture-style auditorium. I routinely teach two sections of the course each semester, with about 225–250 students in each section. The course fulfills a general education science requirement for students enrolled in the College of Arts and Sciences. As a result, the majority are taking it as a general education requirement, not as a requirement for their major. Most are either freshmen or sophomores. Course evaluations from previous semesters revealed that students frequently wished for more class discussion, more involvement with each other, and more contact with the instructor. These student comments, along with a growing frustration with the problems of teaching large lecture classes—low attendance, inattentiveness in class—led me to consider other teaching methods.

At the same time, the rapidly growing development of the Internet, with all of its potential for exploratory inquiry, presented an opportunity to modify the way I had been teaching this course. Could the Internet be incorporated into my course? Could I show students how to find useful information related to health and nutrition through web searches? Would I be able to help them be critical in their evaluation of the information they located on the Internet and to sort out what was scientifically valid from what was not? The most important consideration from a teacher's perspective was related to the volume of electronic comments that a revision of the course design to include Internet inquiry would generate. How could I reasonably manage a course involving the use of the Internet, with only one graduate teaching assistant and 450 students?

The educational principles that emerged from the redesigning of my introductory nutrition course included the following:

1) Includes personal interaction with teachers

2) Gives them an opportunity to ask questions, both of each other and the teacher

3) Offers support and encouragement in a safe environment

4) Lets them do independent work on topics of interest that relate to real issues in their personal environment

COMPUTER-ENHANCED TECHNIQUES USED

In redesigning this course, the first step was to decide what type of computer technology would best fit with these educational principles. Some form of interactive technology was required. For example, the use of email or listservs allows students to interact with the teacher and classmates. However, because of the large number of students involved, the volume of email generated from class interactions would be so large that it could overwhelm the university network. I also decided against using listservs because of the volume of messages. The technology that I chose for my course revision included Netscape Newsgroups as a required component. Newsgroups function as electronic bulletin boards, with a message from a student posted in a central site that can be read by anyone who signs into that newsgroup. Students can read each other's messages and respond to them at any time. The instructor can read all messages and make comments and post course announcements. No messages are duplicated as they would be if they were delivered by email or listservs. The introduction of newsgroups into my nutrition course has fulfilled all of the educational principles.

To accomplish the planned course objectives with Netscape Newsgroups, I recruited ten senior nutrition majors who would act as peer mentors. With the help of a consultant from the university Information Technology User Services office, the mentors were introduced to the use of newsgroups through two training sessions held in a computer lab. The mentors learned how to navigate through newsgroups and how best to respond to students' questions. Discussions were held on issues of confidentiality, since there could be questions of a personal nature. Mentors were provided with a list of referral sites (e.g., health services or counseling center) in case a student requested such information.

The two large classes were divided into smaller groups of approximately 40-45 students. Each mentor was assigned to one group. In each large lecture class, I demonstrated how to use Netscape Newsgroups and provided students with a handout of instructions provided by the user services consultant. Students were advised to which newsgroup they belonged and would be given credit only for questions and assignments that they submitted to the correct newsgroup.

During the first part of the semester, students were required to sign into their newsgroups and either to ask a question related to some aspect of nutrition in which they were interested or to respond to the questions or comments from other students. The questions or comments could be on any topic related to nutrition and health. Each mentor was responsible for answering newsgroup questions and providing resource information when requested. During the remainder of the semester, students in the course were required to complete a series of assignments using the Internet as a source of information. They were given specific directions on how to evaluate an informational web page and requested to use this evaluation technique when they found specific information on the Internet. The mentors read all of these assignments and gave the students specific feedback. Mentors were responsible for all of the record keeping in their respective newsgroups. During the first semester of this project, students and mentors posted more than 6,000 messages to the newsgroups.

For the fall 1999 semester, the course was revised to include videostreamed lectures. We used course management software developed at the University of Delaware that allows us to manage all aspects of the course online and includes posting lectures in digital format to the online syllabus where students may access them the next day. These videostreamed lectures include a full set of PowerPoint slides, which may be viewed independently from the lecture or printed and used as lecture notes. A graduate student in the department of nutrition and dietetics is evaluating the web-supported class along with a course taught by traditional methods and is comparing the attitudes, educational outcomes, and interest in technology of the two groups.

My role in this system included the following:

1) Taught the undergraduates how to use newsgroups

2) Supervised the mentors in their work with students in their assigned newsgroups

3) Read all of the postings from students and responses from the mentors

4) Served as a nutrition resource for the mentors, to assist them in answering difficult questions or providing additional resources

MEASURED RESULTS

Two nutrition graduate students evaluated this project as a master's thesis and an independent research project. The master's thesis focused on the specific content of the students' questions and the students' ability to evaluate informational web pages according to evaluative criteria. Men and women asked different questions. Men were more likely to be interested in topics related to sports nutrition, while women were more likely to ask questions related to weight and dieting. The topic of most interest to the group as a whole was related to diet and disease, with diabetes being the most commonly mentioned disease.

Another graduate did an independent research project assessing students' attitudes toward the use of newsgroups in an introductory nutrition course. Analyses of student evaluations showed a significant relationship between the frequency of participation and attitudes toward the newsgroups. Students who participated on a weekly basis indicated that, as a result of the newsgroup, they felt more involved in the class, would change a behavior based on information gained from the group, and/or would recommend this format to other large classes.

LESSONS LEARNED

I felt that the course objectives were enhanced by, and students who participated said that they enjoyed, the use of technology. However, there were drawbacks as well as successes. The successful introduction of technology into large classes depends on a dependable support network. Without a support system, the system could easily degenerate into chaos.

One factor that I did not anticipate was the students' varied familiarity with technology. Sophisticated computer users had no difficulty whatsoever, while the novices had difficulties that were extremely frustrating both to them and to the instructor and mentors who tried to offer advice. Even in this day of wide-scale computer usage, it is unwise to assume that all students will have a similar degree of familiarity with technology. Time must be allotted for repeated demonstrations and reminders about how the system works to ensure that all students become successful users.

One very successful outcome of this project was the mentors' unanimous approval. It was so successful that the format of the mentor experience was changed from a two-credit independent study to a three-hour course, titled Peer Nutrition Mentoring. The new course is being offered this semester as an experiment through the honors program and taught by a master's level nutrition graduate student under the supervision of the professor. The purpose of the course is to offer a preprofessional practice experience to aid seniors in offering education to undergraduates and expanding their knowledge of consumer issues in nutrition. Internet discussion fora will be used to increase the interaction of students in the large classes, supervised by the senior students in the Peer Nutrition Mentoring course.

CONTACT INFORMATION

Charlene Hamilton, Associate Professor
Department of Nutrition & Dietetics
University of Delaware
315 Alison Hall
Newark, DE 19716
Email: Hamilton@udel.edu
WWW: http://www.udel.edu/present/best_practices/
Phone: (302) 831-1677
Fax: (302) 831-4186

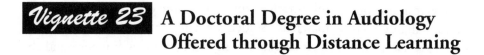 **A Doctoral Degree in Audiology Offered through Distance Learning**

Kenneth J. Gerhardt, University of Florida

The discipline of audiology is a relatively young profession, with roots emerging from the need to help World War II veterans cope with noise-induced hearing loss. A half-century later, the entry-level requirements are changing from a master's degree to a doctoral degree. Overwhelming demands by practitioners, employers, and national professional organizations have compelled some universities to seek new degrees, to restructure curricula for full-time, on-campus students, and to develop ways to accommodate thousands of working professionals who cannot leave their jobs nor close their businesses to relocate to campuses offering advanced degrees. The profession has embraced the doctor of audiology (AuD) as a professional degree for practitioners rather than the doctor of philosophy, which is a degree intended for individuals interested in teaching and research.

The audiology faculty at the University of Florida adopted distance learning as an educational opportunity that does not require a physical presence on campus. However, we felt that it was important for students to have face-to-face interactions with instructors as well as with fellow students. The model we developed requires students to meet in small groups at regional sites for a day at the beginning of the course and again at the end of the course. The majority of the learning experiences occur through videotapes, readings, and web-based instruction. A discussion of the specific components of our delivery model follows.

COURSE DESIGN

Individuals with a master's degree in audiology and at least one year of full-time employment are eligible for enrollment in the AuD Distance Learning Program.

Degree requirements include successful completion of nine eight-week courses, offered sequentially, as well as a written comprehensive examination. Students can complete the degree in a minimum of 18 months.

Regional facilitators, employed by the university, meet with small groups of students for a day at the beginning and again at the end of each course. Because the discipline has a strong clinical component, the first meeting is used to assess specific skills and to develop strategies for overcoming deficiencies in particular clinical areas. After the initial class, the students return home to review videotapes prepared for each class, complete assignments, take web-based quizzes, participate in weekly real-time conversations in regional and national discussion groups, post messages and ask questions in an asynchronous manner on a web board, and use email to communicate with their facilitators and the course instructor. During the final day of the class, the facilitators evaluate all assignments, assess the new clinical skills acquired by the students, and administer the final examination.

Instruction

University of Florida faculty members serve as instructors for the courses. Regional facilitators, all of whom hold doctoral degrees, are employed to assist with instruction. As new students enroll in the program, additional facilitators are added to maintain an approximate ratio of one to 15. The current enrollment approaches 350. Regional sites are selected in cities convenient to most students, and facilitators are located within that region. Facilitators are selected, in part, on their expertise in the course content.

The instructional model is based on positive and direct interactions among the students and with their facilitator. Students become acquainted during the first day of class and collaborate on joint assignments from their homes. Creating an interactive environment during the first day fosters a cohesive group that encourages and stimulates learning and professional networking.

Videotapes

The course instructor invites nationally recognized experts to lecture in specific content areas. These lectures are videotaped in a recording studio, edited by professionals, duplicated, and distributed to each student. On average, ten hours of lectures from three to five ex-

perts are prepared for each course. Visual aids in PowerPoint are digitized directly from a computer and edited into the final videotape. Transcripts of the videotapes are made available to hearing-impaired students enrolled in the program.

Readings and Assignments

A packet of materials is sent to each student before the beginning of the course. It is prepared by the instructor and includes a detailed syllabus, listing of required textbooks, copies of the PowerPoint slides used in the videotapes, listings of web sites, supplemental readings, descriptions of all assignments, grading scale, and so on. Printed materials are also available on individual faculty member's web sites.

Web-Based Activities

Web-based activities play a central role in the delivery model. Email offers a fast and convenient mode of communication that provides opportunities for personal contact with facilitators and the instructor. Regularly scheduled communications among students and facilitators cover a range of subjects from purely administrative topics to specific questions about course materials. Students email completed assignments to their facilitators and send examples of reports and abstracts to fellow classmates for inclusion in required notebooks.

Our program maintains a web board or message board for threaded discussions that is accessible with passwords provided to registered students. A web board is like a bulletin board divided into sections. It allows students to post and to read messages at any time. Most of the headings of the web board are identified by the city where students meet. Other headings include "Important Messages from UF," "Ask the Instructor," and "National Sounding Board." The latter web board is dynamic and unstructured. Students can engage in unlimited conversations, organize study sessions, recruit employees, advertise, etc. Students use the web board for many purposes, including posting drafts of projects for critique and disseminating abstracts and reports. Postings remain for two weeks before removal.

The program supports numerous chat rooms that serve as virtual living rooms where students can congregate and have real-time conversations with each other and their facilitators. Because students get to know each other during the weekend meetings, the chat rooms have an atmosphere of intimacy that promotes good learning. A sense of camaraderie and common purpose is very apparent during these discussions. Each week at predetermined times, usually in the evening, students enter the chat room and join into discussions related to the assignments for that week. Generally, facilitators assign two students per week to assist with the flow of the conversations. This technique has been very useful in maximizing the time spent in the chat rooms by focusing the topics under discussion.

Each week, again at predetermined times, the instructor is available in a national chat room for students to pose questions and to hear directly from the instructor. It is not surprising that the discussions often revolve around the upcoming examinations and assignments. The text of the national chat room is posted the following day for review by students unable to attend the discussion.

Clinical Experiences

Applied clinical or related experiences are components of every course. For example, I teach a class titled Occupational and Environmental Hearing Conservation. This course addresses the serious problem of noise-induced hearing loss from theoretical, basic science, and applied perspectives. Students study the federal regulations governing Occupational Noise Exposure and learn how to apply the law to environments in which individuals are exposed to noise. Measuring the noise levels in the worker's environment is a critical component of a hearing conservation program. Ideally, students would have opportunities to go into factories, interview workers and supervisors, conduct noise surveys in the plant, analyze the data, and apply the appropriate federal regulations. Organizing this type of experience for distance learning students was not feasible, so a computer-based experience, the Virtual Factory, was developed to simulate an industrial setting. The original idea was to have the Virtual Factory available through the web, but CD-ROM proved to be faster from the student's perspective. Prior to completing the Virtual Factory exercise, students read assigned materials, review videotapes of lectures that discuss the federal regulations, and interact with fellow students and facilitators regarding the specific aspects of the assignment.

The Virtual Factory was designed like a computer game. Students enter the main office and question the manager about the operation of the plant. Then they move about in the two-dimensional factory and interact with avatars (simulated employees). Virtual sound-level meters and dosimeters used for assessing noise exposures are built into the experience. The machinery produces simulated noise, and the students use appropriate sampling strategies to calculate the levels. After completing the survey, students write a report and email it to the facilitators for evaluation.

A Virtual Clinic modeled after the Virtual Factory is under development. Students will be able to enter the clinic and gain experience interacting with simulated patients using a wide array of diagnostic strategies. These clinics will be made available via the web or on CD-ROM. The technologies have advanced to the point where entire Virtual Worlds can be created in three-dimensional space, with video simulation allowing for tremendous educational opportunities. Only our imaginations limit what can be achieved.

Infrastructure

To deliver the educational product to the distance-learning students, the university formed a public/private partnership with a professional management group. This group serves as the business interface with our faculty. They are the conduit for applications and most nonacademic contact with the students. Their responsibilities include recording and editing videotapes; mailing all materials; maintaining the computer servers, web boards, and chat rooms; providing computer instruction for new students; copying all printed materials, videotapes, and CD-ROMs; marketing analysis; and advertising. The faculty governs the academic enterprise under the leadership of a faculty member who serves as the director of the distance learning program.

COURSE ASSESSMENT

Course evaluations are a critical component of the program and are used to shape the instructor's skills, to make adjustments in the class's content, and to assess the effectiveness of the facilitators and expert presenters. Specifically, we use a student/teacher evaluation form that includes ratings on ten indices of instruction and has space for written comments about the teaching skills of the instructor and appropriateness of the course. In addition, a second evaluation form is completed that probes the effectiveness of the facilitators, adequacy of the printed materials, and quality of the videotape lectures.

Clinical skills are assessed using pre- and post-evaluation forms developed by the individual instructor. These are self-assessment tools from which the faculty determines if appropriate clinical activities were available to assure growth in areas of deficiency.

CONCLUSION

Distance learning represents a very powerful technology that can deliver a high volume of information in an efficient and effective manner to a wide audience. The learning experience is greatly enhanced by providing class meetings at regional sites so that students can become acquainted with each other. We have learned that this type of program works very well for the working professional. However, distance learning may not be appropriate in some disciplines or as a replacement for an on-campus experience, which is important for the intellectual and social development of younger students.

CONTACT INFORMATION

Kenneth J. Gerhardt, Professor of Audiology and
 Associate Dean of the Graduate School
University of Florida
338 Dauer Hall
Box 117420
Gainesville, FL 32611
Email: gerhardt@csd.ufl.edu
Phone: (352) 392-2113
Fax: (352) 846-0243

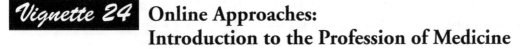

Vignette 24 Online Approaches:
Introduction to the Profession of Medicine

Samuel R. Browd, University of Florida

COURSE OBJECTIVES AND TEACHING PHILOSOPHY

It has been an unfortunate reality that many bright students who apply to medical school do so without any idea whatsoever of the history and culture that is the bedrock of the profession. Most premedical courses are highly complex and technical. During the first hour of the first day, formulas and equations are the matter of business. What is lost in the specifics of formulas and equations are the personalities, the creativity, and the underlying inquisitiveness that facilitated the great discoveries upon which most contemporary scientific teaching is based. Our course has sought to do two things. First, we want to provide what is often disregarded—an understanding of the history behind the basic and clinical sciences. How did the field of neuroscience come about? Who is the father of internal medicine? Why are medical residents called house officers? The second goal of the course is to promote individuality, creativity, and inquisitiveness. We designed our course to be interactive, thought-provoking, and fun. We strive to provide an antitraditional lecture every course period.

Antitraditional teaching has three basic premises: 1) make class fun—if the course is fun, students retain information better and become eager to participate and learn; 2) make class interesting—lectures should be graphically intensive, incorporating new technology, such as computer-based slide-making programs, video, and audio; a multimedia experience is far more interesting than monochrome text slides; 3) make class interactive—gone are the days when students solemnly took notes, never to interject their own ideas and feelings. Interaction is promoted in our model and highly valued both within the class and as a foundation for grading students.

TECHNOLOGY AND THE COURSE

The introduction to the profession of medicine course (IPM) targets two groups: those who are present in the lecture hall and those who virtually attend class from home or elsewhere. Each week, students are expected to attend class prepared for a group discussion. Weekly preparation entails viewing archived lectures and reading assignments on that week's topic. For example, during the cell biology block, students are required to view lectures archived to the course web page, typically three 50-minute lectures recorded during a prior semester, and to read related articles that may be downloaded in Adobe Acrobat from the course web page.

Class is a multimedia, interactive event designed to make the experience of the student who virtually attends the same as that of the student who is physically present. The classroom layout plays a large role in facilitating class discussion, and by extension, creates an on-camera experience that is aesthetically pleasing for the at-home student (see Figure 24.1). In the classroom, we employ two state-of-the art white boards for computer-generated display (slides, video, web pages, and chat browsers). One board projects the lecturers' slides or other multimedia displays, while the other displays questions submitted from at-home students using a web-based chat program. In turn, live video of the class lecturer, multimedia lecture displays, and general classroom discussion and questions are broadcast live over the Internet. A camera operator switches between broadcasting live video from the lecture hall camera to live video of the multimedia displays. This is done using video conferencing technology that takes S-video and converts it from an analog to a digital signal and encodes the digital signal on the course web server. This process introduces a 30-second delay, which must be kept in mind as the students at home submit questions. All live transmissions are archived for future reference, teaching, and review. In the event of a technical problem (e.g., a student loses an ISP connection) lectures can be reviewed at a later time. This also enables the course directors to update archived lectures, which promotes growth in the curriculum from year to year.

The experience for the virtual class participant works as follows. The at-home student logs onto the course web page and accesses the link for the live web broadcast. During the assigned class period, these students view the class lecture and discussion in real time. They also bring up a web-based chat program from a link on the course web page. At-home students are required to submit at least two questions per class. Our goal as instructors is to create a realistic in-class experience for the students who attend from home. This includes incorporating their questions and comments.

All aspects of the course are handled electronically. Students take two multiple-choice tests per semester over the Internet. In addition, a five-page term paper is submitted by email attachment. Course instructors and teaching assistants are reached by email, precluding the need for office hours. General course rules, regulations, class schedules, and information are obtained from the course web site. Students can submit specific questions to the instructors electronically through a questions-and-answers link on the web page. Every single aspect of the course is done electronically, using the latest web-based technology.

The IPM course takes students through an overview of the basic sciences that impact the current practice of medicine and the clinical disciplines that constitute the profession. Archived lectures recount the field's history, current status, and future directions/contributions as put forth by the distinguished lecturers. Students attend class once per week for two hours. Typically, the first hour is a new, live lecture that expands on the subject of the week. The format of the presentation varies each week and may include a faculty member giving a traditional didactic lecture but with an interactive twist, such as accepting questions as the lecture unfolds, a video related to the current topic, or even guest speakers, live patient examinations, or panel discussions. The second half of the class period is devoted to an interactive class discussion. Instructors walk the aisles starting conversation with broad-based questions often generated from current events. A strong focus is placed on intelligent conver-

FIGURE 24.1

CLASSROOM DESIGN

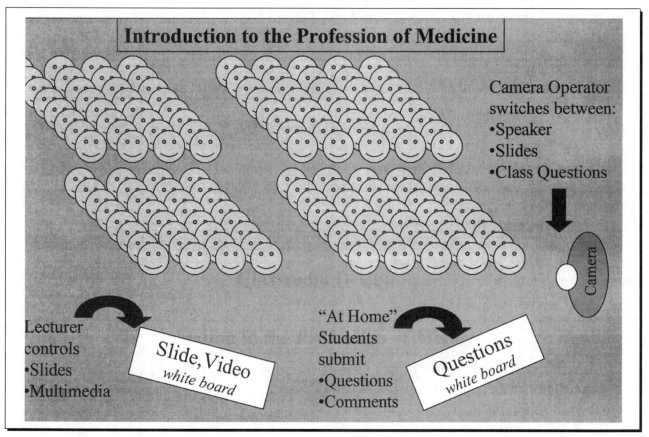

sation, as students are encouraged to interject their thoughts. We want students to come to class prepared to discuss the week's topic and to apply the principles and ideals about which they learned. Students at home are required to participate in the discussion by submitting questions using the web-based chat program. Submitted questions are displayed on the whiteboard for the entire class to see. Instructors proctor the electronic questions, fostering the feeling that virtual attendees have a stake in the discussion and can make meaningful contributions. Participation is a large portion of the course grade (40%) with required attendance and in-class or virtual participation a must for full credit.

Any course is only as good as the faculty who teach it; thus, we make every effort to recruit the most distinguished faculty from each discipline. We make a special effort to recruit professors with exceptional teaching skills as determined by prior student surveys. Once we have identified the best lecturer for each subject, the course director meets with that professor to discuss the course format and provide suggestions on how to design an interactive lecture. Great care is taken to explain the overall course goals and technical format so that continuity between lecturers is achieved. As with the students, we try to promote the individuality of each lecturer, accommodating his or her unique teaching style within the constraints of our course model.

RESULTS

Based on prior class surveys, we feel the course has made an impact on the students. When asked, "How would you rank the class overall?" 93% gave a rating of above average or excellent. "Would you recommend this class to a friend?" 94% said yes. "How do you rate this class compared to other undergraduate courses you have taken at the University of Florida?" 91% said among the best or "the best." Ninety-four percent used the web site to study or to review lectures; 93% rated the web site as excellent. Direct quotes include, "It was interesting and made me get up in the morning," "One of the best courses I have taken," and "Overall, the class was very interesting, informative, relaxed, and fun."

LESSONS LEARNED

Computer-based interactive teaching is not easy. Several hurdles make success a labor-intensive process.

1) The infrastructure to provide for live video and audio broadcasting over the Internet is expensive and requires expert support by systems administrators and other technologically savvy individuals.

2) A second problem is humanistic. People in general are comfortable in their old routines. Approaching tenured professors and asking them to make a multimedia lecture is often a harrowing experience for both course director and invited lecturer. It typically requires the invited speaker to learn a computer-based slide-making program and to redo slides that may have been used for 20 years. This is a very hard job indeed.

3) A third pitfall is faculty acceptance of interactive lectures. The traditional way of lecturing is stoic and stuffy: Interaction is bad and audience silence is good. Suggesting that faculty reevaluate their teaching methods is a difficult subject to broach. Importantly, if faculty are disturbed by interactive teaching, this will limit the effectiveness of the lectures and create the opposite of the desired effect. Lectures can become disorganized and difficult to follow, an issue that would significantly impact the students attending from home using a computer. Offering classes in a virtual medium will require a whole new way of lecturing that takes into account the pitfalls and technical requirements.

THE FUTURE

Multimedia web broadcasting is the future of higher education. Courses will be available to anyone, anywhere, with a desire to learn. We as educators cannot let this opportunity slip by; however, to make full use of the growing technology, we must be willing to change our concept of what makes a good lecture and, more importantly, what makes a good educational experience. Never before have so many tools been at our disposal. It is incumbent upon us to make lectures antitraditional. The introduction to the profession of medicine is a course for the 21st century and will serve as a model for future classes that aim to make learning interactive and fun.

CONTACT INFORMATION

Samuel R. Browd, MD/PhD Candidate
University of Florida Brain Institute
P. O. Box 100244
Gainesville, FL 32610-0244
Email: sbrowd@ufbi.ufl.edu
Home Page: http://www.ufbi.ufl.edu/~sbrowd
Course Home Page: http://www.medinfo.ufl.edu/other/profmed
Phone: (352) 219-7788
Fax: (419) 715-2843

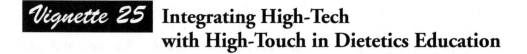

Vignette 25 Integrating High-Tech with High-Touch in Dietetics Education

Elizabeth M. Lieux, University of Delaware

INTRODUCTION

Since 1993, I have been using problem-based learning (PBL) as a teaching method for my class, Quantity Food Production and Service. I firmly believe it develops skills that facilitate lifelong learning. I developed a set of problems that students use to learn food safety and sanitation, menu planning, purchasing, production planning, service, and cost control. PBL allows for learning the course content in groups, developing greater facility in communication, working in teams, and research skills.

In the past I made many references available through the library, but students frequently did not use them. I shifted to using the web and online library resources to provide the rich context necessary for students to learn by solving the problems. PBL has certainly encouraged students to engage in self-directed learning and interests most more than listening to lectures three times a week. This method of learning appeals to both faculty and students who wish to create a shared learning environment, providing many opportunities to engage in conversation around the problems. My approach creates a high-touch and high-tech learning environment.

PBL is less efficient in some ways than the lecture method. It requires different assessment methods and a considerable amount of coaching and identification of appropriate resources. It occurred to me that I could use technology for coaching.

EDUCATIONAL THEORIES

I had several important expectations when incorporating more technology into a PBL course. I wanted to maintain the collaborative learning inherent in PBL and provide easier access to a rich variety of learning resources.

Active and Collaborative Learning

PBL inherently was active learning and collaboration. I hoped the use of email and newsgroups would increase the opportunities for students to collaborate outside of class among themselves and with me.

More Student Time on Task

At the completion of each problem, I provide a wrap-up to highlight the major concepts that should have been learned. In some classes, the students have paper copies of the slides that I plan to use. They annotate these during my short lectures and find notetaking much easier and quicker. I anticipated that the use of PowerPoint would allow more information to be presented more imaginatively.

Access to a Wide Variety of Resources

I hoped that by providing easy access to appropriate resources that the students would incorporate more references and, thereby, more depth into their problem solutions.

COMPUTER-ENHANCED TECHNIQUES USED

In 1997, I converted my syllabus and reserve readings to material that could be posted to the web. I revised the wrap-up presentations into PowerPoint presentations. The University of Delaware provided a high-level technology support and classrooms with powerful multimedia support (see web page http://copland.udel.edu/~lieux/ntdt321/syllabus321.html).

I created a web page that includes the electronic syllabus, grading information, a list of tentative topics, and photos of each of the student learning groups. All of the problems are found in a textbook, *Exploring Quantity Food Production and Service Through Problems* (Lieux & Luoto, 2000). An interesting enhancement is that each problem has its own section in the web page, which contains a brief explanation of what is expected, a collection of hyperlinks to sites where more information may be obtained, and a connection to the library, where articles may be retrieved from electronic reserve readings (http://copland.udel.edu/~lieux/companion/companion.htm).

One of the problems students explore is "David Bedford." It presents difficult concepts related to the delivery and service of food to patients. Frequently, students do not understand how a patient tray line functions. I developed a web page that helps students understand the variables associated with delivering patient food. This web page (http://copland.udel.edu/~lieux/patients/FoodtoPatients.html) includes text and pictures that take the students on a virtual field trip to a hospital food production area.

Electronic Library Reserves

For the problems normally used in a semester, a wide variety of resources were collected. The major references are textbooks, but all of the problems require a variety of other resources for complete understanding. I collected over 250 articles that were useful in understanding the various problems. These articles were scanned and placed in electronic library reserves. Students could click on library reserves for each problem and found from five to about 40 articles available. Using Adobe Acrobat, they could read the article and print it.

Email

We have used email for many years, and all students receive an account when they arrive at the university. They are accustomed to sending and receiving email and seem to prefer this method to telephone or face-to-face communications. Many course-related questions are quickly resolved through email or voicemail, and my office hours are reduced.

PowerPoint Presentations

I developed PowerPoint for wrap-ups and discovered how rich these presentations can be. What surprised me was that using multimedia presentations was faster than using overhead transparencies. In the past, I had spent time during the presentation writing on each transparency to enhance the presentation and to highlight the points I wished to make. My handwriting is not very legible, and the computer script is much clearer for students. Now these presentations take less class time and allow for the incorporation of graphics, images, and movement, which otherwise would have been impossible.

Asynchronous Discussion Groups

One of the greatest difficulties in organizing group work for college students is their inability to find times to meet outside of the classroom. In my PBL class, it is possible to avoid face-to-face meetings outside of scheduled class time. I expect students to develop the questions they plan to research, to prioritize these questions, share the questions with each other, and to discuss what they learn during class time. They are to independently research each question during their own time.

Some groups, however, have felt the need to meet outside of class because they did not believe the class time was sufficient. I thought that using newsgroups might be an effective way to allow this type of interaction without the necessity of a face-to-face meeting. I developed multiple newsgroups for the class, one for each learning group. They were trained on newsgroups using Netscape and required to submit two messages to their groups. Then they were encouraged to continue these conversations throughout the semester. I monitored each group and provided feedback on the conversations that developed. Unfortunately, very few conversations went beyond the required two submissions, and newsgroups were abandoned.

TABLE 25.1

PRE- AND POST-TERM EVALUATIONS OF STUDENTS ENROLLED
IN QUANTITY FOOD PRODUCTION AND SERVICE, FALL 1997

As a result of my experiences in this course:	Sept.*	Dec.*
1. I can work cooperatively as a member of a group or team.	1.72	1.59
2. I can learn effectively by working in a group.	2.33	1.76
3. I can contribute to a group discussion.	1.61	1.41
4. I have good oral communication skills.	2.33	2.00
5. I can express myself well in writing.	1.89	1.82
6. I can use a variety of resources to help me answer questions.	1.72	1.82
7. I can find appropriate resources in the library.	2.06	1.76
8. I can find appropriate resources on the Internet.	2.11	1.65
9. I can evaluate the accuracy of published materials.	2.56	2.12
10. I can learn course material without having a lecture on it.	2.35	2.06

1= strongly agree, 5= strongly disagree - * average

TABLE 25.2

COMPARISON OF QUANTITY FOOD PRODUCTION AND SERVICE
WITH OTHER COURSES EVALUATED, FALL 1997

As a result of this course:	Quantity Food *	All classes *
1. My ability to locate relevant information has improved.	1.71	2.18
2. My ability to critically evaluate the reliability and accuracy of published information has improved.	2.35	2.47
3. I have gained good experience in cooperative teamwork.	1.65	2.06
4. My oral skills have improved.	2.06	2.55
5. My written communication skills have improved.	2.06	2.49
6. I have become a more active participant in my learning.	1.71	2.28
7. I have learned how to solve real world problems.	1.94	2.34

1= strongly agree, 5= strongly disagree - * average

Measured Results

In the middle of each semester, I ask students to submit an evaluation about how the course is going and what they would like to see changed. They are uniformly positive about the materials available on the web page and the electronic reserves. They like the PowerPoint wrap-up presentations but want me to slow down, so that they can take more notes. They would also like to have the wrap-ups before the quizzes. This is not possible, because they would not view their own work as valuable, if I were to lecture on the topic and then give a quiz.

The first time this course was offered using computer enhancements and PBL together, the University of Delaware Institutional Research Office evaluated it as part of a National Science Foundation grant to transform undergraduate education. Using two evaluation instruments, the students reported their perceptions at the beginning and the end of the course on a variety of criteria, and then the students in my course were compared against many others. These surveys show that there was improvement in my course in all criteria but one from September to December (Table 25.1) and that my course was better in all criteria when compared with the other courses evaluated that fall (Table 25.2).

Lessons Learned

Asynchronous Discussion Groups

I assume that the failure of the newsgroups was because the students felt they had sufficient opportunity in class and through use of email and telephone for discussion. Some students indicated that living off-campus limited their opportunity to be connected by computer. For whatever reason, newsgroups were not successful in this class.

For my class, the combination of a high-tech approach using computer-enhanced techniques and a high-touch approach, problem-based learning, has led to a higher level of involvement and greater critical thinking ability among students. Many learning styles are accommodated. Students seem pleased with the mix of technology and active learning. Computer technology has enriched the PBL course and provided access to a large amount of information needed for student directed-learning.

Reference

Lieux, E. M., & Luoto, P. K. (2000). *Exploring quantity food production and service through problems.* Upper Saddle River, NJ: Prentice Hall.

Contact Information

Elizabeth M. Lieux, Associate Professor
Department of Nutrition and Dietetics
University of Delaware
Newark, DE 19716
Email: lieux@udel.edu
WWW: http://www.udel.edu/present/best_practices/
Course: http://copland.udel.edu/~lieux/
Phone: (302) 831-2732
Fax: (302) 831-4186

Joyce Perry, University of Delaware

INTRODUCTION

Wellness is a required course for health and exercise science majors at the University of Delaware, taken primarily as a freshman-level course. Having taught the course two years earlier in a primarily lecture format with some group work in class, I decided to improve pedagogy while incorporating technology. I used a password-protected course management system for the class to allow online discussion, an interactive syllabus, and an online view of grades. The online syllabus had links to assignments and references that were helpful for class topics. I also put most of the prepared lectures into PowerPoint, using many graphics and diagrams. I decided to develop some of my own wellness multimedia resources that would serve several functions. I planned to use them as a direct teaching resource, as a stand alone resource and review method for individual students, and as a place from which to hang other resources, including PowerPoint slides and web links. I also wanted to develop activity modules that would allow group collaboration with real-world scenarios in the wellness area. After having taken a course in interactive multimedia the previous year, I developed these teaching resources in Macromedia Director.

change their lifestyles, which is a major focus of this class. In developing my own teaching resources, I sought to emphasize lifestyle changes in such topics as coronary artery disease risk factors and the consequences of birth control decisions and sexually transmitted diseases. Not many real world scenarios and case studies were available to supplement the course. Although cases are widely available in the legal and medical fields, very few have been developed specifically in the health and wellness curriculum.

The area of coronary artery disease risk factors overlaps across many units in the course and was a natural place to use problem solving skills. I liked the idea of using cases to teach wellness, because they conceptually tie the disciplines together. Technology allows an instructor to make case-based experiential learning richer and more feasible. Similarly, the effect of risk factors on the whole person and on different interrelated concepts can be examined. I used my own Director movies to demonstrate the definition of wellness to begin the course and revisited this interactive multimedia program with a class discussion and group collaboration in coronary artery disease risk factors later in the semester (see Figure 26.1).

EDUCATIONAL THEORIES

I felt that this course could best be taught with short lectures and in-class and out-of-class activities with the students. I thought interactivity could be introduced in class and with asynchronous discussions online. In integrating technology, I wanted to address diverse learning styles by providing visual, experiential activities.

An important concept for the wellness course is not just mastery of the content but realization of consequences for lifestyle choices. I used a commercially produced CD-ROM (Alcohol 101) that emphasized decision-making in learning about the effects of alcohol. Traditional methods of transmitting knowledge fail to help students develop the experiential basis to

FIGURE 26.1

RISK FACTORS

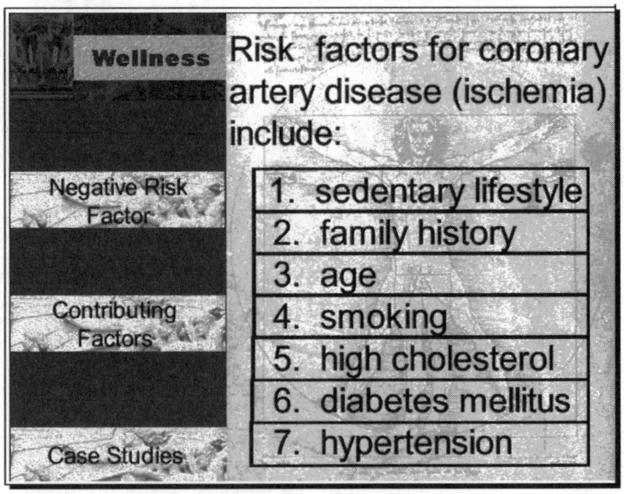

COMPUTER-ENHANCED TECHNIQUES

Multimedia. Multimedia was developed by faculty specifically for the course to enhance experiential learning and provide feedback on simple and more complex real-life scenarios.

Course management system. I managed the entire course with a course management system that is a web-based teaching and learning environment. The course was password protected to allow access only for the class and included an online discussion forum, email links to classmates and instructor, and hyperlinks to related materials and activities.

PowerPoint. I used PowerPoint to teach some lessons or as an introduction to a new unit.

Computer lab. I used the computer lab for some in-class activities—online sites and as an introduction to Alcohol 101, a multimedia program illustrating the consequences of negative and positive decision-making in teens and young adults.

MEASURED RESULTS

Feedback from evaluation forms indicated that students enjoyed the interactivity and were comfortable with the technology. Our class had access to a computing lab for class, and technology was available for presentations in the classroom.

Getting instant feedback from the instructor through the discussion forum in the course management system was a positive aspect of the course. Students commented or asked questions by topic. I was more active in the forum early in the semester. As other students responded to each other, I tried to lurk, unless I had to answer an administrative question. The discussion forum was also a place for feedback on class presentations by students.

Feedback from students regarding PowerPoint lectures was not always positive. The students enjoyed presenting in this manner, but the tendency to read the screen to the class thwarted the spontaneity of audience participation.

LESSONS LEARNED

Most students who take wellness are freshmen, so their exposure to a course management system is limited. Some students had taken a two-credit introduction to personal computers course, which gave them familiarity with Internet resources and the PC, but most had very little opportunity to apply it to other coursework. I found the course management system to be a tremendous help with organizing the course and my executive functioning. Grades and assignments were online in a syllabus that could be updated at any time.

I found PowerPoint to be most effective as an introduction to a new topic in class and helpful in presenting a broad overview of what we would be covering in greater depth later. If used too often, the darkened room seemed a deterrent to spontaneous discussion, and the students became a more passive audience. The posting of the PowerPoint outline to eliminate notetaking and gain greater attention was also helpful.

Introducing more interactivity, quizzes, and modules to the design can strengthen the multimedia program developed for the course. I have decided to use animations to improve the teaching and learning materials for the class. I have continued to develop the teaching resources with Authorware with help from a team of students, whose training in computer technology provides different skills, including graphics and programming. Developing a common user interface has proved helpful.

Time is the biggest obstacle. Online technical support with multimedia programming helps, as small problems with simple solutions can cause several weeks delay. Artistic assistance is beneficial. As a doctoral student in educational technology, I have had exposure to new media and some technologies that have increased my productivity that other faculty may not have had.

I feel the integration of technology has improved my teaching and productivity. By developing instructional materials, I have learned that you are never finished. The flexibility of being able to assess and update materials continually and easily and to stay current with the latest information is a tremendous asset for any faculty member.

REFERENCES

Alcohol 101, available from http://www.centurycouncil.org/

Hofstetter, F. (1998, October). *Three waves of the SERF web-based teaching and learning environment.* PBS Online. <http://www.udel.edu/fth/serf/serf1-3.html>

CONTACT INFORMATION

Joyce Perry, Assistant Professor
Health and Exercise Science
University of Delaware
15 Carpenter Sports Building
Newark, DE 19716
Email: jperry@udel.edu
WWW: http://www.udel.edu/present/best_practices/
Phone: (302) 831-4167

Vignette 27 Using Web-Based Materials to Enhance Future Veterinarians' Clinical Skills

S. Dru Forrester, Jeryl C. Jones, Beverly J. Purswell, Karen D. Inzana, and Michael S. Leib, Virginia Polytechnic Institute and State University

The goal of the four-year curriculum at the Virginia-Maryland Regional College of Veterinary Medicine is to provide students with the skills needed to be successful veterinarians. During years one through three, students spend their time in lectures or laboratories learning about anatomy, physiology, diseases of animal species, and other subjects. In year four of the curriculum, students work in a variety of clinical settings, including the Veterinary Teaching Hospital (VTH). In the VTH, they work under the supervision of clinical faculty and interns or residents to diagnose and to treat diseases in client-owned animals. The transition from third to fourth year is challenging for veterinary students, because they are expected to use the information they have learned to solve clinical problems in their own patients.

To make this transition smoother for students, we are increasingly using clinical case problem solving exercises in year three. These exercises include handouts describing patients with various problems, their background, and physical examination findings. Students are expected to evaluate the information and come to class prepared to discuss the cases. In class, the instructor projects photographs of patients and explains results of diagnostic tests, such as radiographs, blood analyses, and other visual tests. The instructor then facilitates case discussions to help guide students to a final diagnosis.

LEARNING IDEAS

For large classes, the Internet allows a more personalized approach to learning. We have recently begun using web-based case materials to apply the following educational principles.

Active learning. Students are able to access diagnostic test results, interpret their significance, and spend time reading reference materials before class discussions.

Collaborative learning. Students are encouraged to discuss the cases and results of all diagnostic tests with their classmates in small groups before class.

Application of knowledge. Web-based cases allow students to use their knowledge and hopefully retain information for which they can see a practical application.

Increased confidence. Increased practice using problem-solving skills on web-based cases allows students the opportunity to increase their confidence prior to seeing real cases in year four of the curriculum.

COMPUTER-ENHANCED TECHNIQUES

Since 1997, the authors have made web-based case materials available in three courses taught during year three at our college. These courses include Veterinary Urology, Respiratory System, and Small Animal Problem Solving. A web site was created for each of these courses by the primary author. From the home page for each course web site, students are able to access general information about the course, the syllabus, and schedules for lectures and laboratories. A description of additional features follows.

Electronic Mail Addresses of Course Instructors
Electronic mail (email) addresses of all course instructors are available on the web site for convenient student access. Students are encouraged to use email to contact instructors when they have questions. In addition, faculty use email to send announcements to all students and to disseminate clarifications prompted by individual student questions.

Grades for Assignments and Examinations
CheckGrades, a program available at Virginia Tech (www2.cyber.vt.edu/grades/), is used to provide students access to their grades. A single spreadsheet file containing all students' grades for assignments and their identification numbers can be exported to a comma-delimited file that is uploaded to the server containing the CheckGrades program. Students are able to access their grades by entering their social security number; individual students can view only their grades. Students who do not wish to have their social security numbers used can have them replaced with a nickname alias.

Lecture Handouts
Lecture notes are made available on the course web site as either hypertext markup files or portable document format files for access using Acrobat Reader. For Veterinary Urology, radiographic images were set up as links within the electronic versions of the student handouts. By choosing a link, students can view normal and abnormal radiographic examples that illustrate concepts described in that section of the handout.

Links to Other Web Sites
A list of links to other web sites with useful information is available in two courses. From this list, students can visit web sites for similar veterinary courses at other universities or view information about products available from pet food or pharmaceutical companies.

Study Guidelines
Online study guidelines are available for Veterinary Urology and Respiratory System courses. Students are provided with study questions about major topics covered in each lecture. On the web site, students can read each question, think about the most appropriate answer, and then click on a link to the correct answer.

Case-Based Laboratories
Instructors were asked to provide all materials they had been using to teach case-based laboratories, including word processing files, photographs of patients and endoscopic images, and color slides of biopsy specimens. Word processing files for laboratory cases were converted to hypertext markup files. All web images were created by scanning photographs, slides, radiographs, or computed tomographic scans. Sound files were obtained from several web sites that had examples for educational use. Files were transferred to the college's educational server for student access from home or computer laboratories on campus.

For each laboratory, students can view information about patients, including a photograph of the patient, close-up photographs of lesions, and a description of history and physical examination findings. For some cases, students can click on links that activate examples of sounds, such as abnormal breath sounds and cardiac murmurs. After initial patient information, students must answer a list of questions about the case. In order to answer some questions, they have to click on links to additional information; for example, images of radiographs, ultrasonograms, endoscopic photographs, and cytologic or histologic specimens. In addition to providing radiographs and ultrasonograms on the web, original patient radiographs are placed in the classroom for viewing by students. Students are encouraged to discuss cases with their classmates before class, although they are ultimately responsible for answers written on their handouts. In class, the instructor and students discuss cases, and assigned questions are answered. Students can ask questions about different ways to interpret diagnostic tests or any other items of interest.

OUTCOME ASSESSMENT

At the end of each course, students were asked to rate areas of the web site on a scale of 1 (not useful) to 6 (very useful) and to provide written comments about the course web sites. The highest rated feature of all three course web sites was the usefulness of having diagnostic test results available before class discussions of web-based cases. Overall, students felt that this access was critical, because it allowed them to interpret the results on their own or in small groups. This also gave them the chance to consult reference texts and class notes prior to making a final diagnosis. Although radiographic images were available on the web sites, many students commented that having the actual radiographs available for viewing was very important. Depending on what computer students used, they were not always able to clearly visualize radiographic images on their monitors and appreciate subtle lesions. Students uniformly commented that the online study guide was helpful when preparing for examinations. Many students commented about convenience of using email to contact faculty members with specific questions and stated they were much more likely to ask a question by this method than by speaking up in class or approaching an instructor in person. Although not all students accessed their grades using the web site, those who did commented that it was convenient, and they appreciated being able to see only their own grades.

LESSONS LEARNED

We feel that the use of web materials has enhanced the learning experience for our students. They seem to be more actively involved in evaluating the case materials than classes who previously were taught using cases described in handouts only. During class discussions, students seem to ask higher level questions, perhaps because they have spent more time evaluating the cases and reading and consulting reference materials. In addition, students like being able to see results of visual diagnostic tests prior to class discussions and seem to enjoy working through the web-based cases, because they are more similar to real-life cases.

Although our courses use computer-enhanced technology, we do not necessarily use computers in the classroom. Our students use the web-based course materials before class, and time spent in case-based laboratories is devoted to discussion between the instructors and students about the cases. We feel that the use of web-based technology provides students with a convenient method of accessing information about cases, so they are prepared to actively participate in laboratory discussions.

Based on our experience, we have identified some areas for future improvements. Until all students have equal access to appropriate computers, results of some diagnostic tests must be provided in standard ways (e.g., hard copies of some images in handouts or patient radiographs in addition to images of radiographs on the web site). In addition, the quality of web-projected images, especially radiographs, remains a limiting factor. Students have expressed concerns that image quality on their computer monitors is often insufficient for them to feel comfortable making a diagnosis.

As with any new method of teaching, some questions about web-based instructional materials remain to be answered. Does availability of web-based course materials increase student learning compared with more traditional instructional methods? Would using cases described only in handouts provide a similar learning experience compared with web-based cases? Improved learning may be difficult to evaluate objectively; however, if students feel they are learning more, and they enjoy using the web-based materials, perhaps their subjective impressions should be considered as much as objective measurements. Does use of web-based case materials require more time; for example, time needed for faculty members to prepare the materials and time required for students to use the materials? Time is of particular concern in professional schools, where students usually spend eight hours each day in class and often must balance their personal and professional lives with time devoted to studying. In addition, faculty members have increasing demands placed on their time, and devoting additional time to creating web-based materials may not be possible. Fortunately, web-based course materials can be created with the assistance of others; for example, work/study students or instructional technology staff. Lastly, is it necessary for all students to have their own personal computer, or can students adequately prepare for web-based courses using computers available in laboratories? Based on informal comments by students, they find it much more convenient to use web-based course materials when they have their own personal computer at home.

CONCLUSION

Based on our initial experiences in these three courses, we feel that web-based course materials provide stu-dents with additional learning opportunities. We plan to revise the current web sites each year and add new web materials to promote student learning. At some point, we plan to provide self-assessment questions on the web sites so that students can evaluate themselves prior to examinations.

CONTACT INFORMATION

S. Dru Forrester, Associate Professor
    and Director of Student Affairs
Department of Small Animal Clinical Sciences
Virginia-Maryland Regional College
    of Veterinary Medicine
Virginia Polytechnic Institute and State University
Blacksburg, VA 24060
Email: sdru@vt.edu
WWW: http://education.vetmed.vt.edu/curriculum
    /sdru/sdruhome.htm
Phone: (540) 231-4621
Fax: (540) 231-7367

 Development of an Internet Course
for Graduate Nursing Students

Janie Canty-Mitchell, Indiana University-Purdue University Indianapolis

Nurses make up the largest group of health care professionals. However, few nurses are knowledgeable or experienced in the political processes that influence health policy decisions at local, state, or national levels (Cohen, Mason, Kovner, Leavitt, Pulcinci, & Sochalski, 1998; Mason & Leavitt, 1998; Winter & Lockhart, 1997). The graduate health policy course at Indiana University School of Nursing provides a basis for understanding the political forces that shape nursing practice and health care delivery so that nursing students can influence the development of health policy through political involvement. Computer-mediated technology was used to enhance the course by 1) developing an asynchronous web-based learning format for graduate students across the state of Indiana; 2) increasing access to global information resources; and 3) improving interactivity and networking with the professor, other students, and political representatives.

COURSE DESIGN

In the 1997 spring semester, I incorporated local, state, and national Internet references into the health policy syllabus. Students were encouraged to use Internet references when completing policy papers and projects. Introducing students to Internet references produced mixed results. I assessed students' comfort with using computers and completing Internet assignments through the use of an in-class survey. In general, students became more comfortable using computers and the Internet during the class. However, some students who lived outside the Indianapolis area claimed they did not have access to computers and were limited in their participation. Others thought Internet assignments were time-consuming, while others claimed they did not know basic computer skills. The in-class survey helped me to reformulate the requirement that all students use the Internet to complete class assignments. Students were encouraged to use Internet references when completing policy papers and projects.

Internet Course Development

Based on my increasing level of interest in using the Internet to access health policy information and desire to enhance the course, I applied for and received a Network for Excellence in Teaching (NET) grant through the campus Office of Faculty Development.

Many individuals assisted in planning and implementing the web course. Since the course syllabus needed further development before placing it on the web, I consulted with graduate faculty who were experts in health policy. The School of Nursing faculty involved in web course development provided support during the planning and mapping of the web site. Weekly workshops required for NET grant recipients were helpful. They included hands-on training in the use of various computer programs and technology, problem-based instruction, classroom assessment techniques, computer technology evaluation, copyright laws, and teaching techniques. A multimedia and web design expert and Center for Teaching and Learning staff provided support and consultation. The initial web site included the syllabus; an interactive preassessment of students' knowledge, skills, and experience in policy and politics; a comprehensive bibliography; Internet linkages to state, national, international, and nursing resources; class notes; an interactive bulletin board; and private email for students to communicate with each other and the instructor

Pilot Testing/Evaluation

The initial web page for the policy course was simple in design. Graphics were intentionally kept to a minimum because students' computer capabilities were unknown. During the second 1997 summer session, 31 students (13 located at seven distant sites) enrolled in the policy class were using the pilot web site. I required them to complete the interactive student assessment over the Internet, and it was automatically forwarded to my university email address. During the first 48 hours, I received 13 responses. By the end of seven days, 27 students had responded. In previous classes, students at distant sites had to fax or mail their student assessment forms. The four students who did not respond could not access the site because the server was down. The bulletin board (online group discussions) and Internet linkages were used the same evening as the first class, as evidenced by student postings.

Further piloting of the web site occurred in the 1997 fall semester. Students received an orientation during the first night of class. They were given individual identification numbers and passwords to access the home page and allowed 30 minutes of class time to use computers in the nursing school's computer laboratory. After the first three weeks of the semester, they met in class for two hours every other week. During weeks that students were not in class, they were involved in online asynchronous discussions of assigned topics. Students liked meeting every other week and participated in discussions online. This format increased faculty workload, because weekly oral discussions in class were now replaced with online written discussions that needed written instructor feedback.

Pilot Evaluation

At the end of both the 1997 summer and fall semesters, students were asked to evaluate the use of the Internet and web for conducting research and communicating with other students and faculty. Many students noted that they did not have access to computers except those on campus. Computers in the nursing building were not accessible to students on the weekend. For one student, the server was down at times, which limited access. Others felt scared of technology and thought that too much time was needed on the computer. A few students were concerned that their families could not make or receive telephone calls while they used the Internet. Overall, students commented that practice using the World Wide Web was an asset in preparing class assignments.

IMPLEMENTATION

The web-based course was fully implemented in the 1998 spring semester. Instructional letters were sent to students one month prior to class informing them of the course format, required books, computer and software requirements, and computer/software classes available. In addition, two optional in-class sessions were scheduled. The first optional class oriented students to the Internet

course, library and Internet research resources, and unit assignments. Fifteen of the 25 registered students attended the first orientation session. Only five students attended the second. Only two students withdrew from the courses. Since the 1998 spring semester, the Internet course has been offered six times. Tables 28.1 and 28.2 list strengths and weaknesses of the Internet course from both student and faculty perspectives.

COMPUTER-ENHANCED TECHNIQUES USED

The course uses the WebCT program, which allows interactivity among the professor, students, and local, state, and federal agencies concerned with health policy and advanced practice nursing. Included on the health policy home page are the following:

1) A course calendar allows students to access monthly course information, deadlines for assignments, and upcoming events.

2) A course content section includes information about the instructor; the course syllabus; evaluation criteria for the course; a comprehensive bibliography; Internet linkages to local, state, national, and international policy resources; a list of community resources; and learning activities for the semester. Units of learning include a brief overview of the unit, objectives, reading assignments, learning activities, evaluation criteria, and estimated time frames for completing the unit. Unit assignments may include readings from textbooks, journal articles, newspapers, and Internet resources; online quizzes; online asynchronous discussions; evaluation of Internet policy resources; evaluation of health-related laws, regulations, and proposed bills obtained from online legislative sites; letters to influential policy representatives and written critiques of policy meetings attended or interviews with influential people involved in health policy decisions.

3) A bulletin board allows students and instructor to interact. Information posted is accessible to all students in an ideal forum for discussing issues, disseminating new information, and responding to guided case studies. It also allows students to interact to complete a final group project or paper.

4) Private mail allows students to send individual messages to each other and the instructor and allows the instructor to send messages to an individual or group of students.

5) Other tools include course exams, grades, an online chat room, and student home pages. The latter tool allows students to design personal home pages that are accessible to classmates and may also be used to post creative health policy projects. The course quizzes are completed online; grades are received immediately after students take the quiz.

MEASURED RESULTS

An interactive evaluation tool is used to assess students' use of electronic communication systems and Internet resources to conduct research. The items for the interactive evaluation tool come from the Flashlight Current Student Inventory, a tool for local evaluation of educational technology. This evaluation was piloted on students taking the course during the second 1997 summer semester and has been used for each of five semesters since that time. Table 28.1 outlines students' perspectives on the strengths and weaknesses of the course. Table 28.2 outlines the faculty members' personal evaluation of the web course.

Students' final projects and papers were used to evaluate student learning. They required students to synthesize knowledge learned from the preceding four units and to develop a creative strategy to influence health policy in the workplace, government, or professional and community organizations. Two students created a video to increase tuberculosis awareness and arranged screenings at adult day care centers. They invited a newspaper reporter to assist them in influencing

TABLE 28.1

REWARDS AND PITFALLS OF AN INTERNET COURSE: STUDENT PERSPECTIVES

Rewards or Strengths
1) "The course is easily accomplished over the web."
2) "I liked the flexibility of the course. [I can] work within the time frame of my own choosing."
3) "I liked the flexibility of students choosing different topics for completion of the course."
4) "The challenge of the assignments spurred learning and a movement toward advanced practice nursing."
5) "[The course was] enjoyable, challenging, spurred critical thinking."
6) "I gained a lot of Internet/computer skills from the course."
7) "The course allowed me to explore a new area of professional nursing."
8) "[The course] forced my attention to politics."

Pitfalls or Weaknesses
1) "[A] required orientation [is needed] at the beginning of the semester."
2) "The amount of material covered could be compared to a three hour class."
3) "Too many assignments. Have fewer projects and papers."
4) "Internet courses take twice as long for class discussions to occur."
5) "I miss the face to face interaction with peers."
6) "Good for core courses, but not for specialty courses required for nursing majors."
7) "Having questions answered is more difficult than an immediate response in a classroom."
8) "The course is more like an independent study than a regular course. I feel cheated by not having met the instructor."

policy on World Tuberculosis Day. Four students created a newsletter entitled, "Nurses Link in Ink," a resource for Indiana nurses on legislative issues affecting health. Newsletters were distributed to classmates and nurses in policy-making positions across the state. Two students created a brochure entitled, "How Safe are You?" which highlighted problems with Unlicensed Assistive Personnel. They addressed the public's need to encourage legislators to vote for the Patient Safety Act (HR 1165), a bill before the US Congress. Brochures were distributed to the public and nurses throughout Indiana. Four students conducted a telephone survey in four counties regarding the public's perceptions and satisfaction with managed care plans. They analyzed the results and distributed them along with policy recommendations to legislators and the *Indianapolis Star*. Three students created a PowerPoint presentation on stroke awareness programs to increase awareness among policymakers and influence funding for more stroke prevention programs.

Peer-review evaluation was conducted in summer 1999. Results were positive as they related to the organization of the course, required readings, and assignments. A weakness was the number of written assignments, which required the faculty member's time. The peer reviewer noted the need for further development of interactive elements that could enhance the course.

The following recommendations are based on three years of experience in the field.

1) Faculty should negotiate for a reduced workload when developing an Internet course and during the first semester of its implementation. The web-based

TABLE 28.2

REWARDS AND PITFALLS OF AN INTERNET COURSE: FACULTY PERSPECTIVES

Rewards or Strengths

1) Developed and implemented a new method of learning for students in a one-year time frame
2) Learned about computer technology, health policy/politics, and global Internet resources available for research and teaching
3) Presented course development activities at three national conferences
4) Students communicated with faculty more than in classroom sessions
5) Students were more creative in final health policy projects
6) Students used background research literature from diverse sources in papers and projects
7) Evaluation of classroom learning was ongoing throughout the semester

Pitfalls or Challenges

1) Time taken for the course was twice that of classroom teaching, related to:
   • Increased online discussions among students and students and faculty
   • numerous questions that needed written responses
   • written assignments to grade versus in-class oral discussions
   • more assignments given to measure learning
2) Limited face-to-face interactions with students
3) Insufficient secretarial support for web-based courses
4) Students' skills in computer technology varied widely
5) Increased workload
6) No reduction in teaching assignment when web course implemented

course required double the work of an in-class course.

2) Ensure that departmental secretaries and support staff are trained in web course development to ensure adequate support for faculty.

3) Ensure that students have training and education in the World Wide Web, Internet, computer software, and the particular online course. Students vary in their computer knowledge and skill levels.

4) Partner with another faculty member when developing and implementing an Internet course. Because Internet courses are demanding, alternate the teaching periodically. In my case, after teaching the Internet course to 135 students in five semesters (and 255 other students in the same time frame), I experienced burnout.

SUMMARY

The Internet policy course helped to create a new educational paradigm where the faculty is not the "sage on the stage" but the "guide by the side." Barr and Tagg (1995) describe this paradigm shift from teaching to learning. In the old teaching paradigm, the faculty delivers instruction. In the new learning paradigm, the instructor facilitates learning and elicits student discovery and construction of knowledge. In the teaching paradigm, the faculty lectures. In the learning paradigm, the instructor designs learning methods and environments. A faculty in the learning paradigm is evaluated on the effectiveness of student learning rather than faculty teaching. This new method of learning challenges both students and faculty who are accus-

tomed to the old paradigm. The challenges, however, are outweighed by the students' excitement over gaining new knowledge and requisite political experience in the health policy arena.

REFERENCES

Barr, R., & Tagg, J. (1995, November/December). From teaching to learning: A new paradigm for undergraduate education. *Change,* 13-25.

Cohen, S. S., Mason, D. J., Kovner, C., Leavitt, J. K., Pulcini, J., & Sochalski, J. (1996). Stages of nursing's political development: Where we've been and where we ought to go. *Nursing Outlook, 44,* 259-266.

Mason, D., & Leavitt, J. K. (Eds.). (1998). *Policy and politics in nursing and health care* (3rd ed.). Philadelphia, PA: WB Saunders.

Winter, M. K., & Lockhart, J. S. (1997, September/October). From motivation to action: Understanding nurses' political involvement. *Nursing and Health Care Perspectives, 18,* 244-250.

CONTACT INFORMATION

Janie Canty-Mitchell, Assistant Professor
Indiana University School of Nursing
1111 Middle Drive, NU 461
Indianapolis, IN 46202
Email: jcanty@iupui.edu
WWW: http://nursing.iupui.edu/online
Phone: (317) 278-1380
Fax: (317) 278-1378

LANGUAGES, LITERATURE, AND THE HUMANITIES

Vignette 29 — A Web-Based Reading Assistant for Intermediate Italian

Katrien N. Christie, University of Delaware

The idea behind this project is to help students become better and happier readers in Italian. The curriculum for the third semester of Italian at the University of Delaware includes the reading of five short stories. Typically, part of a story is first assigned as homework and then discussed in the next class. However, many students struggle with these readings at home and on their own. They lack good reading skills and become frustrated from looking up many words in a dictionary. Clearly, students would have a much better understanding of the story and, consequently, a much more pleasant reading experience if we could provide them with a personal tutor. I turned to the World Wide Web to design such an assistant, available when and wherever students would need one.

The web-based reading assistant divides each story up into passages of manageable length and guides students through each with a variety of comprehension aids, including images, paraphrases, translations, and cultural information on Italian web sites, and graded comprehension checks with feedback. By interacting with the reading assistant, students reach a basic understanding of the story independently and are better prepared to achieve a deeper understanding of the short stories in subsequent class discussions.

EDUCATIONAL THEORIES

The advent of the Internet is starting to have a major impact on foreign language teaching, in part, no doubt, thanks to the enormous potential for the authentic and up-to-date linguistic and cultural resources it offers. Collins (1991) identifies several shifts in teaching/learning in the classroom due to the impact of new technologies. The following four touch on issues that have been much talked about in the literature on innovative classroom approaches within the foreign language profession. They include:

1) A shift from lecture and recitation to coaching, where the teacher is a resource rather than the authoritative transmitter of knowledge. The web-based reading assistant is designed to be such a resource, promoting interactive and collaborative learning, providing, for instance, prompt feedback to comprehension-checking questions, and different levels of help (different strokes for different folks). Moreover, it facilitates the teacher taking on such a role in subsequent classes.

2) A shift from the primacy of verbal thinking to the integration of visual and verbal thinking. The reading assistant provides many glosses, both textual and visual, as well as links to relevant web pages, all of which help students to visualize concepts.

3) A shift to more motivated and engaged students, who see technology as encouraging and supporting their learning efforts and who will increase their time on task and their personal investment in their work. The reading assistant gives students the tools they need to become more proficient readers in Italian.

4) A shift from a competitive to a cooperative social structure. The reading assistant provides a discussion forum where students are encouraged to share their insights and problems. This enhances the students' sense of initiative and responsibility.

COMPUTER-ENHANCED TECHNIQUES AND TOOLS USED

The entire course is presented to students on the web via the University of Delaware's online course management software. This software is a password-protected system that only students who are registered for the course can access for the duration of one semester. This protection is important for this particular course, since we are working with copyrighted materials. I made use of the UD online course management software to generate the reading assistant, other class assignments, a daily syllabus, and a grade book. The entire course is electronically managed.

Reading Assistant

Each of the five stories is segmented into manageable reading passages. Each segment is first presented without glosses and followed by several comprehension-checking questions that allow students to ascertain whether they have understood the main gist. After students have answered these basic questions, which are usually multiple-choice or true/false questions and which also provide explanatory feedback, the same segment is presented a second time, now with many italicized words or phrases. The latter are glossed either as a picture or text in a designated box to the left of the reading. The glosses are activated by mouse-overs; that is, when students move the mouse over an italicized word or phrase, a picture or text appears in the gloss box. When students then click on the same italicized word(s), the box flips over and displays additional help, either an Italian synonym, paraphrase, or English translation if the first gloss was a picture, or an English translation if the first was a synonym or paraphrase. This system of glossing thus has two built-in levels of access: the first by mouse-over, the second by clicking. This provides different levels of help for students with different levels of ability and steers students away from reverting to their native language to achieve comprehension. They focus first on pictures and paraphrases in Italian, but those who need it still have access to translations. Some glosses also contain links to relevant Italian web pages that provide culture-specific background information. After the second presentation of the segment, students again test their comprehension through further questions that probe their understanding somewhat deeper. Again, feedback is given for each response. In addition to all the passages that make up each story and the accompanying comprehension checks, each story begins and ends with a reading activity. The former is designed to activate knowledge students already have about the main topic of the story, while the latter reinforces a global understanding of the whole story.

Assignments

In addition to the activities contained in the reading assistant, other assignments associated with the course are incorporated into our online course management software. These include compositions, presentations, and quiz content and preparation information. Here again, the software serves as an electronic assistant to the teacher, because students can readily access these materials and need not contact me to find out the details of an assignment or what will be on a test.

Syllabus

Every day the course management software serves up the class du jour on the web. Students instantly know what they are doing today, what they did yesterday, and what is expected for the next class. Each class is a self-contained unit, and students use back and next buttons to navigate through the syllabus. The course content itself is sometimes linked to web sites outside of the online software. For example, when the use of present perfect and imperfect tenses is compared, students can link to another web site that provides additional explanation and practice on that topic.

Grade Information

All comprehension-checking questions in the reading assistant are automatically graded and recorded in the students' grade books. The grade book records all other grades too, and students know which assignments they have completed. It displays a running average based on all assignments completed so far. Again, the software takes on the role of my electronic assistant, recording and averaging grades and making them readily accessible to students.

MEASURED RESULTS

The jury is still out on students' experiences in this course, since it is being implemented for the first time. Nonetheless, I used the online course management software in a similar but more limited fashion for a business Italian class. That class was also electronically managed, with the syllabus, grade book, and course materials available on the web, although the reading assistant was more limited. Pairs of students were observed in their interaction with the course material at several intervals during the semester. They were also given questionnaires to collect information on their experience with this web-based course.

Overall, students' reactions were almost unanimously positive. Their positive reaction is especially significant since a questionnaire given at the start of the semester revealed that the students were not frequent users of foreign language computer software or of the Internet and that they had a fairly negative view of the potential benefits of this type of technology in the foreign language classroom. Nevertheless, at the end of the course, students thought they had learned a lot in one semester, not only about business Italian, but also about the Internet and computers in general. In learning Italian, students were also learning valuable computer skills that may prove useful in their later academic or professional careers. One student commented: "It helped me understand how computers can be used in different ways."

Students also appreciated having the syllabus presented to them on a daily basis. They remarked that this helped them to organize and to keep up with the work. One student said: "It was day-by-day. If you missed a class, you could see the work you missed and know what to do for the next class." With regard to reading on the web, students thought that it was "nice to do homework on the computer," and one even commented that it "almost made homework fun!" Finally, students also mentioned that "being able to see your grade" was useful.

The few negative points mentioned had to do with problems of access, for example, no Internet connection at home, and technical difficulties, for example, the server down.

LESSONS LEARNED

The students' satisfaction may be related to an observation mentioned at the beginning of this paper: that technology can create more engaged students. Whether it is a novelty effect or not, I believe students did spend more time on task; that is, they spent more time cognitively engaged with the Italian language and culture, thanks to the web-based materials, to an extent that would otherwise not have taken place. For that reason alone, I would evaluate this technology as a beneficial tool. As a consequence, classroom time was more productive, more interesting, and more engaging. Because some of the mechanical work required to achieve basic comprehension is done outside of the classroom, class time can be devoted to more cognitively demanding and engaging tasks. This, in Collins's terms, illustrates the shift from lecture and recitation to coaching, which new technologies like the Internet make possible. Or as Lee and Van Patten (1995) put it, the teacher becomes more of a facilitator, an architect, and resource rather than an authoritative transmitter of knowledge.

My experience as a teacher was, therefore, equally positive. Although I invested a lot of time in designing pedagogically sound learning activities and learning how to implement them, it was worth it to see the students enthusiastic about what and how they were learning.

REFERENCES

Collins, A. (1991, September). The role of computer technology in restructuring schools. *Phi Delta Kappan*.

Lee, J. L., & Van Patten, B. (1995). *Making communicative language teaching happen*. New York, NY: McGraw-Hill.

CONTACT INFORMATION

Katrien N. Christie, Assistant Professor
    of Foreign Languages and Literatures
326 Smith Hall
University of Delaware
Newark, DE 19716
Email: katrien@udel.edu
WWW: http://www.udel.edu/katrien,
    http://www.udel.edu/present/best_practices/
Phone: (302) 831-2183
Fax: (302) 831-8000

Vignette 30 Computer Enhancement of Latin 211: Introduction to Latin Poetry

Mary Pendergraft, Wake Forest University

Wake Forest University has traditionally felt a strong commitment to a well-rounded liberal arts curriculum. As an example of that commitment, we require our students to study a second language through the fourth-semester level; that is, to complete successfully at least one course in which authentic texts in the target language are read. The most popular of the Latin courses that fulfill this requirement is Latin 211, Introduction to Latin Poetry. Fall semester of 1998 saw the first offering of Latin 211 in its current format, as an "anthology" that included representative texts from major Roman poets.

This course exposes students to a selection of important Latin poetry placed in the context of literary history and criticism. The skills that are essential to this enterprise are those also required to read Latin prose: a general competence in the Latin language, including a strong vocabulary and a solid understanding of morphology and syntax. Areas of knowledge that are particular to the study of poetry include Latin metrics and poetic devices.

In any semester, the students enrolled in this course represent a range of ages, from first-year students to seniors, and a variety of backgrounds; some have done all their Latin study at Wake Forest, whereas others come directly from high schools in all parts of the country. Their skill levels vary widely. It is difficult to predict what poems will already be familiar and which poets will particularly interest them.

When I had to choose a textbook for this class, I identified the characteristics I considered most important. The ideal choice would be inexpensive and include a range of poets, enough to allow us flexibility in choosing those whom we would read. It would also offer commentary at my students' level. No published anthology met all these criteria: Their selections were too few, or their commentary wasn't appropriate, or they were too expensive. However, Wake Forest is in the midst of a computer initiative that, as of fall 1999, put in the hands of every student an IBM ThinkPad and provided widespread access to Internet connec-

tions. Faculty have been encouraged to use our electronic capabilities creatively and constructively.

These considerations, taken together, encouraged me to develop an electronic anthology and to supplement it with other electronic documents.

EDUCATIONAL THEORIES

Electronic Course Materials

Primary resources. In fall 1998, the course shell available at Wake Forest was a web-based version of Lotus Notes. In the cabinet established for Latin 211, I first filed a selection of electronic texts, downloaded from the Latin Library at Ad Fontes Academy (http://patriot.net/~lillard/cp/latlib). William L. Carey's excellent collection of public-domain texts is extremely comprehensive and attractively formatted. Relying on out-of-print editions, its texts cannot represent the most current scholarly consensus about correct manuscript readings or spelling or appropriate punctuation. In the small number of situations where those considerations are important, however, it is not difficult to make changes for the sake of clarity. The greatest advantge in using electronic texts is the flexibility to choose poems in response to the class's interests without incurring additional expense of delay. When it became clear how much they enjoyed Ovid, I was able easily to increase the number of selections we read from that poet.

Note: Two additional archives for Latin texts in electronic form are the Bibliotheca Latina (http://ployglot.lss.wisc.edu/classics/biblio.htm) and the Bibliotheca Augustana (http://www.fh-augsburg.de/~harsch/a_summa.html#la).

Secondary resources. The Latin Library contains only texts without commentary or grammatical notes. Consequently, I developed notes and reading aids for each text, drawing on a number of print or electronic editions as well as my observations of my students' needs. I was able to refer to specific parallels in texts we had read together.

In addition, I alerted them to the excellent resources of the Perseus Project (www.perseus.tufts.edu), where the Latin texts have both a "look up" and a parsing function, which, respectively, reveal a dictionary entry and a morphological identification for a given word. Their texts are hyperlinked to English translations for the truly desperate, and recently, many have acquired links to standard commentaries. Although Perseus provides direct access to Lewis and Short's *Latin-English Dictionary* and to Allen and Greenough's *Latin Grammar,* I nonetheless ordered for my students a less expensive paperback dictionary and grammar as an optional purchase.

Finally, I made available an introduction to Latin poetic meter and created handouts on specific grammatical topics as the need arose.

Because the students expressed some skepticism about the value of making texts available electronically, I offered them the following list of suggestions for preparation strategies:

"How can you use your electronic texts to help you study?"

1. You can put the text and the notes in parallel columns:

Arma gravi numero violentaque bella parabam	gravi numero: here "in solemn meter"— this reference to dactylic hexameter as the proper form for epic is, through ring composition, taken up again in the poem's penultimate couplet.

2. You can cut vocabulary words from the text and paste them into a list. You can then use the sort function on table menu to alphabetize them before you look them up, either in your paper dictionary or electronically.

3. You can use the search function to locate other instances of a vocabulary item in passages we have read.

4. You can print out passages to practice scansion.

5. You can make multiple copies of the text; on one you may keep marginal notes on vocabulary or syntax, while you can still have a clean copy to study.

In the Classroom

My classroom has a widescreen television monitor to which I can attach my ThinkPad in order to display to the class what I see on my screen. Generally, I put the text we are reading before their eyes, to reduce the temptation to read, not Latin, but their notes. As we discuss a passage, I can highlight words, change the font color to associate nouns and adjectives, for instance, or open a new window to reveal paradigms, or review points of syntax.

The potential value of this use of technology had become clear earlier when I was searching for a way to respond to the needs of hard-of-hearing students in Greek and Latin classes over the years. For them, a visual supplement to oral discussion makes any class hour more valuable. Our experience bore out the frequently heard belief that the presence of a hard-of-hearing student in any class benefits his or her fellows, because modifications for the one student's special needs meet needs, perhaps unrecognized, of others as well. Any class will have considerably fewer students with hearing loss than with learning differences, who derive a similar benefit from being able to read as well as hear important comments, instructions, and information.

MEASURED RESULTS

The department of classical languages asks every student to evaluate the courses in which he or she is enrolled anonymously using a standard form. Fifteen specific questions ask for an evaluation on a scale of 1 (poor) to 5 (excellent), and for Latin 211, eight out of nine respondents chose 5 or 4 as the "general evaluation of the course." Students also had an opportunity for open-ended responses about strengths and weaknesses of the course, and in many ways, these answers are particularly valuable. To the question, "What appealed most to you about this course?" one of the eight respondents in 1998 offered, "the use of the computer as a teaching aid."

Lessons Learned

The application I used for this course in 1998, a web-based adaptation of Lotus Notes, was extremely unstable, with the result that students too frequently could not access their course materials. This semester, consequently, I have joined a group of faculty members who are pilot-testing the product CourseInfo, (http://www.wfu.edu/Library/ITC/training/cinfo/crse-info.htm), available from Blackboard, Inc. (http://www.blackboard.net). So far, students have not reported any difficulties with this application.

I have also added a new kind of supplementary material and made it available to my students. For the poems that the class is reading I create so-called GRASP texts (for Gradual Aggregative Syntactic Praxis), a method adapted for Latin texts by Claude Pavur of St. Louis University. It "presents the parts of sentences bit-by-bit, with variety and incremental complexity, to help learners attain the ability to grasp the original text in the order in which it was written, with immediate comprehension." Pavur explains their rationale and offers examples at his Latin Teaching Materials site (http://www.slu.edu/colleges/AS/languages/classical/latin/tchmat/pedagogy/grasp.html).

Because it is possible to distribute such ancillary materials with ease and speed electronically, I can develop these supplements for our assigned texts even at short notice.

Summary

For the purposes of Latin 211, electronic textbooks offer almost limitless flexibility in choices of texts and ancillary materials.

Contact Information

Mary Pendergraft, Associate Professor
    of Classical Languages
Wake Forest University
Winston-Salem, NC 27109-7343
Email: pender@wfu.edu

Vignette 31 | Computer-Enhanced Spanish 217: A Survey of Spanish Literature

Candelas S. Gala, Wake Forest University

Spanish 217 is the advanced course for students fulfilling the foreign language requirement and the introductory course to the Spanish major. It was designed to offer students an overview of Spanish literature and culture from its beginnings to the present. The incorporation of technology (multimedia, visual images, recordings of Spanish music and poetry, and hypertext) allowed me to expose students to the multifaceted reality of Spanish culture, thus fulfilling a major objective of our foreign language requirement.

The class met twice a week and used the course shell package CourseInfo. The 16 students had different computer resources, which created some problems. (This course was taught during the phasing-in of the computers-for-all-students plan.) Some materials had to be made available in printed form; the email systems of some students did not allow them to receive attachments; some lived off campus; and older students were much more reluctant to use this new technology than were the younger ones.

IDEAS BEHIND THE COURSE DESIGN

Spanish 217 may be the last course students will take in a foreign language, or it may be the gateway to more advanced study in Spanish. My objective was to provide students with a rich view of Spanish culture through literary texts, history, the plastic arts, music, and film. Integration of these ingredients was crucial; students should see the interconnectedness of literature with history and the other arts. By exposing them to a variety of media, I hoped to incite them to a critical analysis of the major ideas that have shaped Spain throughout history. From these goals emerged a set of educational principles.

1) Integrate language, literature, and culture

2) Provide motivating and authentic materials that allow the visualization and hearing of concepts

3) Provide timely feedback

4) Encourage comparative analysis

5) Encourage frequent dialogue between teacher and student

6) Provide equal and repeated access to materials

7) Maintain high expectations of student initiative to explore untraditional learning venues

8) Induce collaborative learning

COMPUTER-ENHANCED TECHNIQUES

I developed a number of computer tools that other colleagues and I might use in the future.

PowerPoint Presentations

To introduce each of the major cultural periods, I developed a series of PowerPoint presentations. These presentations include historical data, visuals of major artistic works and maps, and samples of music from the five major periods: Middle Ages, Spanish Golden Age (Renaissance and Baroque), Enlightenment (18th century), Romanticism and Realism (19th century), and the 20th century. I downloaded the presentations in CourseInfo to make them available to all students at all times. They were shown in class as a backdrop to the discussion of the particular period. As we moved on, these presentations became the centerpiece of discussions; students and I referred to them frequently in establishing connections among the different periods.

Web Pages

After the general introduction to each period using a PowerPoint presentation, I thought of ways to particularize the instruction of each period through the use of poetry. Poems concisely offer a rich array of literary devices that illustrate a variety of cultural, artistic, and historical concerns of the times. They can also be presented and discussed in one or two days at the most, a major issue in a survey course like Spanish 217. Having the material organized in web pages ahead of time freed class time for greater interaction among students and teacher.

Each web page consists of three sections:

1) A transcription of the poem with a recording of my voice reciting it

2) Background information about the type of poem (period in which it was written, author, themes, and images) and how it represents its particular period

3) A set of questions for students to further their understanding of the poem, how it illustrates the period in which it was written, and its possible connections with other poems, periods, and works of art

Each section was linked to the others as well as to other web sites related to the topic.

Email

Since CourseInfo makes it possible to email the entire class or individual students, the students and I exchanged frequent messages relating to assignments, class discussions, individual problems, questions, and concerns. I found email particularly helpful in communicating to my students strengths and weaknesses of the entire class, which became evident after a quiz or a test. By listing those findings, students learned collaboratively; no class time was wasted writing them on the board, and we could then move to a face-to-face discussion.

Internet Search

I have compiled a list of useful web sites as supplemental class materials. Students are encouraged to visit these sites and discover others in order to go beyond the prescribed course plan.

CourseInfo: Electronic Syllabus, Papers, Grades, Chats, Quizzes

I enrolled my class in CourseInfo, a pilot course shell and great course management tool. I highly recommend it for its variety of applications and easy use. The syllabus, PowerPoint presentations, web pages, links, grades, papers, brief quizzes, and other material may be stored in the same drawer. It makes all course materials available for all students at all times.

Personal Collections of Art Slides

I have been able to download images of artistic works by famous Spanish artists from museums all over the world into a PowerPoint presentation or web page or simply to show on a computer screen when teaching a particular cultural point. Thanks to technology, they are readily accessible to me and to other colleagues, a great move forward from the cumbersome old slide collections and projectors.

ASSESSED RESULTS

At the end of the semester, I administered the regular student evaluation used for all courses taught in the department. I did, however, ask students to comment specifically on the use of technology in the class. Leaving aside comments from seniors who, lacking the computer resources and expertise, understandably experienced frustration with the technology aspect of the course, the other responses were generally positive. Most students liked the accessibility of materials in the course shell and particularly enjoyed the visual and sound documents. They commented on the pedagogical value of the PowerPoint presentations. They did, however, feel somewhat overwhelmed by the number of links and web sites and complained about having to address unexpected discussion points in the chat room.

LESSONS LEARNED

Training Session on the Use of the Course Shell

The course shell is rather easy to use; I provided directions and the package provides a guide. Students felt apprehensive in dealing with a new tool. I recommend scheduling a special training session outside of regular class hours and taught by someone familiar with the material.

Links

It is necessary to explain to students the role links play in the course and what they are expected to do with them. Just as with bibliographical entries, students, particularly beginners, must understand the role that research plays in their overall education. They must be made aware that education is not just checking out clearly identified items on a list provided by the professor but, more importantly, venturing into other areas and establishing connections among apparently distant topics. Students failed to understand that these were resource materials to enrich their learning. Because they thought they would be tested and graded on the context of these links, they criticized me for overburdening them with work.

Chat Room Discussions

Students felt overwhelmed by chat topics that had not been indicated in the syllabus. It will be necessary in the future to explain the role of these exchanges as a means to further the discussion (at some point) outside of class time and to include in the syllabus a note about their occurrence throughout the semester. In an ideal world, students would engage freely in these exchanges and not view them as mere homework but rather as educational opportunities. However, since students expect a grade for everything they do that is related to the course, a good compromise may be to include this activity as part of the grade for class participation and to expect everyone to participate in the chats.

Electronic Papers

I favor turning in papers and returning them with comments electronically. If, however, the correcting is extensive, hard copy is better.

Computers in Class

I have seen the tremendous usefulness of computers for saving class time, organizing course materials, and enriching the educational experience. Class time, however, should be spent in face-to-face exchanges with the students. Even when I am showing a PowerPoint presentation, the screen is simply a backdrop to this interaction.

CONCLUSION

This computer-enhanced teaching and learning experience is the beginning of an ongoing process in my approach to teaching. I find myself rethinking the materials I will choose for my classes and the way I will present them to students. It is leading me into a complete revision of my teaching methodology. I realize that incorporating technology has increased tremendously the time I invest in preparing and planning and that college and university administrators should consider these new demands on faculty time. However, computer-enhanced learning proves very efficient in saving class time, in enriching the educational experience, and in promoting collaborative and interactive classes as well as an ongoing communication between professor and student outside of class.

ACKNOWLEDGMENTS

I would like to express my appreciation to Romance Languages' academic computer specialist, Bakhit Kourmanov and to the Wake Forest University STARS program, particularly to my STAR student, Erin Anderson, for facilitating the development of electronic tools for my classes.

CONTACT INFORMATION

Candelas S. Gala, Professor and Chair
Department of Romance Languages
Wake Forest University
Winston-Salem, NC 27109
Email: galacs@wfu.edu

Vignette 32 — Achieving Voice through Collaboration: Computers and Writing Communities in the Composition Classroom

Anne M. Boyle, Wake Forest University

Alexander, Shannon, and Jason:

This project is really difficult huh? It's hard to determine what the question specifically wants. I took some time to review and edit your rough draft. I hope I gave you some good ideas.

I think your group interpreted the question differently than my group. You have some good general ideas. A few suggestions: Don't use the word "you" if at all possible. Write in the third person.

Although you have some good ideas, they don't seem to be well supported or sometimes even logical. Like I said, you guys might have interpreted the prompt differently, but your writing doesn't seem to relate to information inhibiting critical thinking.

There also doesn't seem to be any organization. Don't get me wrong, I understand this is your rough draft, but it definitely needs work in the structure category. You need an introduction, conclusion, clear topic sentences, and nice transitions in your writing.

The style also seems choppy. Like I said, try not to use "you" and be more concise. Your sentences seem wordy at times. Sometimes, they don't really make sense. It might be that I'm misunderstanding your ideas, but that means that most readers might do the same thing. Just try to say what you want to say and don't beat around the bush.

It was nice reading your draft. I think this project is really interesting, but difficult. Adios.

These words, written by Ryan, a first-year student enrolled in my writing seminar, flashed from my computer's screen and lodged in my mind as I darted into class this morning. It is not yet midterm, and I had already begun to wonder what my students have learned about the writing process. Last night, I looked at my overloaded syllabus, the huge stack of student essays before me, and despaired. I have 14 weeks to teach them how to write clear, cogent, well-researched essays. After five weeks, they are in the midst of assignment #5.

Have I assigned so much reading and writing and so many new technological skills that they have little time to reflect, to question, to understand, and to improve their prose? Have I become a grading machine that checks off errors and endlessly drones on about the necessity to narrow that thesis, to generate more complex ideas, and to edit?

Then I listen to Ryan's humane yet critical voice. I wonder how he learned to respond so well to the text of Alexander, Shannon, and Jason, three students from Acadia University, whom he has never met and who are also working on assignment #5. I wonder how his response to his peers in Acadia will affect the collaborative essay he is writing with classmates Marissa, Carter, and Mike.

CREATING WRITING COMMUNITIES: EDUCATIONAL OBJECTIVES

For the past three years, Patricia Rigg, an English professor from Acadia University, and I have created writing communities in our composition classes. Working in small groups, our students collaborate on essays that will be edited and evaluated by their peers at the corresponding university. This year, Pat and I have chosen a highly theoretical assignment that will lead our students to conduct online research before they publish their essays on the World Wide Web.

We have four goals:

1) To introduce students to the collaborative writing process

2) To actively involve them in peer review

3) To teach them how to obtain and to evaluate information from online sources

4) To provide them with an audience outside the academy by having them publish their essays on the web

160   *Teaching with Technology*

Collaborative writing motivates students to understand different perspectives, to gain distance from their own prose, and to focus attention on the integrity of the text rather than on their own point of view (Bruffee, 1984; Duin & Hansen, 1994). The value of peer review has been well established in composition theory. To make students more conscious and critical of their own writing processes, writing teachers often set up peer review sessions. As readers, students are asked to locate the power and to point toward possible problems in development, coherence, and clarity in other students' essays. Peer review benefits readers by allowing them to exercise authority over the text and helps writers whose sense of purpose is enhanced by anticipation of a response from a supportive and interested audience (Elbow, 1973; Rodburg, 1992; Williams, 1998). By publishing their work on the web, students broaden their sense of audience, which enhances their sense of purpose (Bartholomae, 1995).

THE ASSIGNMENT

This year's assignment is divided into three parts.

Part 1

Students from Wake Forest and Acadia received the following essay prompt:

While there are many different ways of achieving postsecondary education, students at Acadia and Wake Forest have chosen to attend a liberal arts college. Although the college's mission statement is published in its bulletin, most students never fully understand the principles upon which a liberal arts education is founded. In the Victorian era, John Henry Newman defined many of them in The Idea of a University. Newman contrasts liberal learning with practical or useful learning: "Liberal knowledge does not benefit the body or the estate." The idea of a university is:

> *to open the mind, to correct it, to refine it, to enable it to know, and to digest, master, rule, and use its knowledge, to give it power over its own faculties, application, flexibility, method, critical exactness, sagacity, resource, address, eloquent expression... (Newman, 1972)*

Write about 500 words to explain your idea of a university and how you expect technology to contribute to—or work against—that idea.

Part 2

We established writing groups and gave each one the following questions. Students were asked to sharpen the focus of their individual essays and to draft a collaborative essay:

1) Is gaining knowledge the same thing as cultivating intellect?

2) Does easy access to information inhibit critical thinking? How can we assess the accuracy of information obtained through the web?

3) Does our notion of plagiarism have to change as we enter a world of shared information and collaborative communities? What ethical, political, and educational issues are involved in a new industry that allows students to buy research and research papers on the web?

4) How is technology changing our social interactions and student/professor relationships?

5) Can one achieve a liberal education through distance learning? Are traditional colleges soon to be replaced by distance education? Why or why not?

Part 3

After introductory exchanges, students posted drafts of their collaborative essays on the web for peer review. For the next three weeks, students will continue to research their topics, respond to the essays from their peers, and revise. In November, we have set aside one class period during which students will learn to design and publish their web pages.

TECHNOLOGICAL TOOLS

All students from Acadia and Wake Forest have ThinkPads and wired campuses. For campus collaborations, Acadia students use NortonTextra Connect and Wake Forest students have used both the Wake Forest Template, an electronic sharing environment built within Lotus Notes, and a commercial product, CourseInfo. During the first year of the project, Acadia students ventured into the Wake Forest environment through the web. Since then, Acadia has set up a web-based file-sharing system that Wake Forest students have used. Wake Forest students use the editing features of Microsoft Word.

LEARNING RESULTS AND PREDICTIONS

Pat and I assess our work each semester. Students use evaluation forms to provide us with feedback. During the last two years, we have found that, with few exceptions, groups have worked well together, with more apt writers and highly motivated students encouraging weaker students both emotionally and intellectually. In the single Wake Forest group out of ten that did not work well, the stronger students were frustrated and carried the weaker students. Students realized that true collaboration involves more than cutting and pasting different sections written by different students. They strove to understand different perspectives. Most of the Wake Forest teams met evenings, online and off, to integrate and to transform their material.

As Pat and I investigated the efficacy of peer review, we recognized how important it was to help students define their criteria. We also discovered that because students were forced to rely solely on the written word to establish a relationship and to communicate clearly, the help they offered and received was different than in the normal classroom; students seemed more focused on the text than on the writer. Some students used email for personal communication, but this did not diminish the critical quality of the peer review. It seemed to increase camaraderie and trust.

Students enjoyed publishing their work and sent the address to parents and friends. Although many Wake Forest students spent perhaps too much time designing their pages and not enough revising the content of their essays, they were extremely careful to edit errors and to try to personalize their essays.

In student evaluations, praise for the project outweighed criticisms by far. All rated it as a valuable assignment, and more than half described it as the most helpful assignment in terms of teaching them about the writing process. General criticisms included minor frustration at some technical glitches, the time spent on the project (close to six weeks), and concern that peer review would not be effective if standards differed at the two universities. Favorable comments indicated that students thought they were more motivated, obtained greater knowledge of grammar through group discussion, and better understanding of both the writing process and the uses of technology.

Readers are invited to view the essays published during the fall of 1998:

http://english.tribble.wfu.edu/courses/eng111-boyle-fa98/team1/coffeeshops.htm

http://english.tribble.wfu.edu/courses/eng111-boyle-fa98/team4/reynolda.htm

http://english.tribble.wfu.edu/courses/eng111-boyle-fa98/

OUR EXPECTATIONS FOR THIS YEAR'S PROJECT

As we made the assignment more complex, we anticipated two problems. The first is the recurrent feeling that we may be overloading our students. This assignment takes more than a month to complete and they write other essays on argumentation and literary analysis during the same period. The second concerns our more theoretical prompt. When students wrote about places in the community, meeting at a local coffee shop or museum, their bonding seemed more natural than it has been this year. As I write this, students are engaged in the second stage of the assignment, and, as we anticipated, forming writing communities around a theoretical issue rather than a physical place is more challenging, but we find they are intellectually stimulated and hope they will develop more sophisticated research skills.

Reviewing the entries in a journal Pat and I share, I find that we continue to be surprised at how motivated our students are; no group has reported problems, and all seem to work together well. Not all were able to post their essays during the first try, but all had posted them by the due date. The drafts have been very uneven; some groups have done a great deal of brainstorming and have lots of promising but incoherent ideas. Others wrote highly structured essays built on hasty generalizations. Most computer work at Wake Forest is done outside the classroom, and class time is spent on reading and writing skills. Students do ask questions in class about the information they obtain on the web.

While we are assessing the efficacy of writing communities and computers in the composition classroom, we are also investigating how best to balance our roles as guide and authority. We closely monitor the writings in the collaborative spaces, but we intervene only when asked or when students fall silent. We try to prod them in clear, but gentle and respectful ways. We can tell, at this point, that most students are, like Ryan, aware of the challenges of the assignment but also very excited. Thus far, their voices, like ours, have become prodding and clear, but they sound more human and familiar than ours do. As in past semesters, when given the freedom to write to one another about important issues, students do become motivated to use the electronic word to share ideas. As we encourage students to write to one another, we find that more students achieve the voice that Ryan has exhibited, the voice of the insightful, concerned, and authoritative reader and writer.

References

Bartholomae, D. (1995). Inventing the university. In R. Connors & C. Glenn (Eds.), *The Saint Martin's guide to teaching writing* (3rd ed.) (pp. 408-421). New York, NY: St. Martin's.

Bruffee, K. A. (1984). Collaborative learning and 'The Conversation of Mankind.' *College English, 46,* 635-652.

Bruffee, K. A. (1993). Writing, collaboration, and social construction. In K. Bruffee (Ed.), *A short course in writing: Composition, collaborative learning, and constructive reading* (4th ed.) (pp. 1-13). New York, NY: HarperCollins.

Duin, A. H., & Hansen, C. (1994). Reading and writing on computer networks as social construction and social interaction. In C. L. Selfe & S. Hilligoss (Eds.), *Literacy and computers: The complications of teaching and learning with technology* (pp. 89-112). New York, NY: MLA.

Elbow, P. (1973). *Writing without teachers.* New York, NY: Oxford University Press.

Newman, J. H. (1972). The idea of a university. In C. F. Harrold & W. D. Templeman (Eds.), *English prose of the Victorian age* (pp. 582-586). New York, NY: Oxford University Press.

Rodburg, M. (1992). Workshops in the teaching of writing. In N. Kline (Ed.), *How writers teach writing* (pp. 143-156). Englewood Cliffs, NJ: Prentice Hall.

Williams, J. D. (1998). The classroom as workshop. In J. D. Williams (Ed.), *Preparing to teach writing: Research, theory, and practice* (2nd ed.) (pp. 79-98). Hillsdale, NJ: Erlbaum.

Contact Information

Anne M. Boyle, Associate Professor of English
Wake Forest University
Winston-Salem, NC 27109
Email: boyle@wfu.edu
WWW: http://english.tribble.wfu.edu/courses/eng 111-boyle-fa99/

Nelson Hilton, University of Georgia

Three distinct courses incorporate my involvement with the renewal of English through computer-enhanced teaching and learning. The first concerns an introduction to the subject of English; the second, the traditional English subject of British Romanticism; and the third, Humanities Computing, the coming transfiguration of English as a traditional subject.

INTRODUCTION TO THE MAJOR

Rationale

ENGL3000 ("3K") is a lecture course for 150 prospective English majors offered every semester. The class meets en masse twice a week for lecture and once a week in teaching assistant (TA)-guided discussion sections of 25. The particular problems of presentation, communication, and interaction that accompany such a large class can be diminished through several computer mediations.

Technique

An extensive web site is used for the syllabus, assignments, examples of papers, web slide show versions of lecture presentations, and notes. Pages from this site are often projected during class as are PowerPoint presentations or lecture notes generated during the course of the meeting, creating a kind of electronic whiteboard. Each of the six discussion sections has its own WebCT bulletin board, monitored by its TA, to which students are required to post at least once a week; I oversee a seventh board provided for any additional questions or comments.

Perhaps more innovative are my attempts to enable collaborative possibilities with web-based wide-scale participation. For the final research project on a novel by James Joyce, for instance, the class was divided into groups of five, each of which was responsible for reading and annotating some selected criticism and then uploading the citation, annotation, and keywords to a collective class bibliography page using a form-based front-end. In this way, students were able to draw on a database of 30 detailed annotations to help decide what criticisms might be useful for their individual papers. A further refinement of such interaction will permit students to post examples from their own reading of the rhetorical figures studied in class. Here, students become teachers, and over the course of the semester, each rhetorical term is made vivid and concrete by more—and more relevant—examples than the instructor alone could hope to supply. While another 3K professor and I each produce new material for each class, we appropriate liberally from each other's past successes in a continual relay race toward an optimal site.

Outcomes

Large lecture courses can hardly aspire to be the most popular, but the electronic discussion groups did work to lessen some of the anonymity and to establish a comradeship among participants: one group posted over 650 messages. The few students who opted for the extra credit web portfolio of their work confirmed the viability of our intention to begin such dossiers for all majors.

Lessons Learned

Not all students arrive at 3K with even modest computer literacy, so provision must be made to assist those who have difficulties. The collaborative bibliography project would be even more useful if the articles in question could be accessed over the web.

ENGLISH ROMANTICISM

Rationale

The fundamental notion behind my course in English Romanticism is that "the spirit of its age" (itself a Romantic conceit) is multimodal or intratextual and exhibits itself in a variety of media, none of which are its definitive expression. One goal, therefore, is to make available for study (as opposed to a one-time demonstration in the classroom) a representative selection of visual and audio materials to accompany written text. A second leading idea is that the best teaching occurs live and unscripted. While I go into a class with a considered sense of what should be covered, I often have no specific notion past an opening gambit of how the session's goals will be reached. The wire, balancing pole, and safety net for proceeding in this manner are the multimedia library and the links I bring into the classroom so that material to address any tangent is readily available (very readily! lag-time is death). The desirability of peer review and ongoing out-of-class conversation also informs the course design.

Techniques

The digital library is the essential computer component of the course, and its content, a never-ending creation, is by far the most labor-intensive aspect of the course. My archive takes the form of a multimedia web site that I maintain on a local server and bring to the class via the ethernet, my laptop, and a projector that illuminates images and text so brightly that only the front row of classroom lights need be dimmed. With carpeting, moveable seats, the powerful projector, and a large ceiling-hung screen, the newly refurbished classroom inaugurated with this class provides a wonderful space for teaching. I sit with my back to the screen but can follow its content with the unobtrusive laptop. Important points or text can be entered and projected in a large font as the discussion unfolds and then saved to the class site at the end of the hour. In this setting, the technology becomes literally part of the background.

For peer review, I have set up a web page with cgi-script that enables students to upload their papers easily, after the small hump for some of getting their word-processing programs to convert the final draft to an html format. These papers are loaded onto other web pages generated for each peer review group of approximately five students. These pages, in turn, use frames, forms, and cgi-scripts to enable students to comment on each essay and on previous comments and to see each others' comments and the relevant essay at the same time. While papers and comments may be offered anonymously, the pages are login-protected, and all activity is archived to a private page for reference. I comment on the essays, of course, and occasionally on comments that have preceded mine, and as students may also visit the other peer review groups, the sum of all our responses to a given assignment is available to everyone; indeed, I try to set up cross-references. Class electronic discussion is carried out over the threaded bulletin board packaged with the WebCT site for the course, which I use for its student-tracking capabilities.

Outcomes

While specific outcomes are difficult to quantify, this class rated a 4.6 (of a possible 5) in an average of 17 student evaluations and received comments appreciative of how the electronic discussion "opened areas of discussion that would not have been possible in class" and how the technology was used not "as a crutch but merely to expand and elaborate on the issues in class."

HUMANITIES COMPUTING

Whatever one's conception of the discipline of English today, it no doubt continues to include writing, grammar, and literature as core elements. These concerns precipitate from the technological big-bang over two-and-a-half millennia back that abstracted the sounds of speech into letters—*grammata* in Greek, *litera* in Latin—to represent words. With that innovation came the *techné*, the art or skill of rhetoric which promised to teach *techni*ques for using the best or at least most persuasive words in the best or at least most persuasive order. Students and teachers of literature, grammar, and writing thus have a special interest in the new universe coming into being through the digitization of communication into bits. But what rhetoric, what literary and grammatical arts and skills can do justice to such technology?

Humanities Computing is one name often given to the attempt to grapple with the abcs, or elements, of digital inscription, but the new graduate course described here was instead denominated Literary Computing to forestall disciplinary anxieties in the department. The preeminent rationale for this course is the department's need for computer-literate graduate students to assist burgeoning commitments to online and other computer-assisted teaching. Having come to the realization that effective composition, that mainstay of the English department, will perforce include learning to compose different digitized media in new genres of document, we faced the immediate problem of finding teachers prepared to offer this instruction. As most of our composition instructors are our own students, we had also the opportunity of offering credit for such teachers to train on the spot.

Rationale

Several years ago, my colleague, Professor David Gants, and I began offering a group independent study that continued through two iterations, with more than 20 students altogether, as we experimented with various approaches and material before gaining approval for the course we now offer. While we have no definitive conclusions about either approaches or material, several assumptions persist.

Collaboration. It is difficult to imagine the course being taught by one person, given both the breadth of the material and the need in the class lab for someone to rotate among the stations to deal with the ongoing crises. Collaboration among the students is essential as well, not only in that they learn from each others' difficulties, but there are often one or two who are quite savvy in some particular technology.

Deprogramming or unlearning. Students often bring their own assumptions about the necessity for graphical interface (GUI) or what-you-see-is-what-you-get (WYSIWYG) word-processing, which need to be contextualized at the outset with a heavy dose of the command line interface.

Overview. While much of the class material could be presented in discrete training modules, faculty's crucial function is to provide some sense of the larger picture. Humanities students asking, "Why are we doing this?" must be shown how it will feed into later work with Perl and then pay off in creating mark-up. The necessity of hands-on training should go without saying.

Techniques

The class is offered in a 15-station lab won precisely for this purpose with an internal grant. Almost uniquely for a graduate class, it meets three days a week to facilitate comradeship and to permit difficulties to be dealt with quickly. Through attentive nurturing and prompting, the class bulletin board, also done through WebCT hums with an average of over four messages per student each week. There is no set text, but a de-tailed home page, designed also as a general university reference for Humanities Computing, provides annotated links to a wide variety of materials, including student projects. Students are given accounts on one of the servers and begin with a prolonged introduction to Unix; this command-line text-stream orientation continues through assimilation of the Emacs editor and basic programming in Perl, all of which are then combined into a consideration of mark-up (xml and that developed for literary work by the Text Encoding Initiative). Bots, optical character recognition, and the digitization and integration of graphics, sound, and video round out this introductory exercise.

OUTCOMES

Students of this course are among our most sought-after teaching assistants and graduates, and have, in several cases, suspended their academic pursuits for offers from the private sector.

LESSONS LEARNED

The class demands an inordinate contribution of time and resources and depends on the improbable combination of the instructors' faith in its future, their department's willing suspension of disbelief, and the strategic or foresighted benevolence of the university.

CONTACT INFORMATION

Nelson Hilton, Professor and Graduate Coordinator
Department of English
University of Georgia
Athens, GA 30602
Email: nhilton@english.uga.edu
WWW: http://www.english.uga.edu/nhilton
Phone: (706) 542-2197

Robin MacRorie, University of Notre Dame

Our required composition class acts as a bridge between the type of writing students did in high school and the academic inquiry in which we expect them to engage at the university level. Students learn different styles of argument and that analysis is not necessarily as difficult as finding meaning in a poem, which is their definition of analysis at the beginning of the semester. By the end of the semester, they have written an academic article themselves, often in the style of the discipline in which they want to study.

Eighteen of us meet three times a week in a 15-week semester. All students live in wired dorms and have access to multiple computer labs. Most have their own desktop computers. The class has a web page that includes a bulletin board electronic discussion group, the syllabus, and a listserv.

IDEAS BEHIND THE COURSE DESIGN

Remembering that the classes I enjoyed best were ones in which we changed activities and did some work in the classroom, I looked to see what was available to keep the students interested, while keeping them focused on improving their writing. I realized that I wanted to ensure the following:

1) Collaborative learning

2) Learning by doing

3) Frequent student/faculty dialog

4) Different strokes for different folks (encouraging those with different learning styles or levels of comfort)

5) More student time on task

6) Different = new

COURSE ACTIVITIES

Prewriting
Students generally dislike having their writing process taken apart in composition classes. To make it a little more enjoyable, I have students use Inspiration to work on their prewriting. This program allows them to show their cluster of ideas much more easily and neatly than had they drawn it out on paper. They can then use the computer to turn that cluster into an outline for their essay.

Email
We use email to ask each other questions, start conversations about the readings, ask about due dates, and so forth. Students can email a question to our entire listserv and reach everyone in the class, or they can email me privately.

Bulletin Board
Student read two assigned articles a week. They pick one of the two and post an analysis of it to the bulletin board. Students then reply to these analyses. This process serves two functions. First, students practice analyzing articles before they write formal analytical essays. Some of the pressure of learning to analyze is taken off the students, and they can experiment a bit. Second, students respond to other students' analyses and begin learning where arguments are strong and where they are weak. They learn by doing in a situation that holds less pressure than working on an essay. In fact, students often go beyond the required number of responses for the semester and continue their dialogs.

Electronic Syllabus
The ease of access to the syllabus and the course materials means that students cannot lose them and can even check on due dates or assignments from home during breaks.

Electronic Publication of Essays
Students submit an electronic copy of their essays, which goes onto the class web page. They are discussed in class as examples. We can discuss what rhetorical strategies worked and did not work as well. All students are aware of this publication from the first day of class.

Library Searches

The Notre Dame library catalog is completely online. Students learn how to search electronic databases and the Notre Dame catalog.

Workshop Critique of Essays

For the second draft of their essays, students look at electronic copies of each other's work. Using a program called CommonSpace, the students read an essay in one column of the screen and then use another column to comment on the essay. Because students do not have this program on their own machines, which have varying platforms, they print out the critique of the essay and hand it back to the author. Students tend to write much more and in more detail than when we have face-to-face critiques. Also, students have a ready-made record of what their group members think of their essays to take home and digest rather than a conversation they may not remember when they get ready to rewrite the draft.

ASSESSED OUTCOMES

At the beginning of the semester, many students ask, "Why are we using computers so much in an English class?" Most of the students wish to focus on only the subject matter at hand, not learning both composition and how to use computers. I discuss this with the students in class—they need to learn how to use computers regardless of the class or task at hand, no matter into what field they eventually go. By midsemester, students tend to come to me independently to tell me that they appreciate the time I spend helping them learn to work the computers. In fact, they often ask me about using computers in their other classes and how to accomplish certain goals or tasks. Also, many of the students continue using the prewriting program even after it is no longer required in class.

LESSONS LEARNED

First-year students, despite having grown up in a computer-based world, do not necessarily know how to use computers. Many are horribly uncomfortable with them and sure they will break them. I have had students attempt to put disks in upside-down and backwards, to hit return at the end of every line in a word processing document—and then hit return again to double-space the essay. I no longer assume that students have any computer skills when they walk into my classroom. Other lessons I have discovered include:

No Utopia

While holding asynchronous conversations is wonderful for students to practice analysis and argument, they need deadlines and requirements. Using some basic requirements—write an analysis every week, respond to at least five posts—gives students a jump-start. Once they get used to the bulletin board, they often exceed the required assignments, but without the deadline for responses, they are sluggish. Asynchronous conversations do not create an instant utopia for collaborative learning.

Learning New Programs

Handing out the instructions to a program the night before we use it for the first time is helpful but not enough. What I've found works best is to show the students a few steps of how to use a program, have them duplicate it on their computers, and then show them the next few steps. This keeps them involved, interested, and, above all, awake, despite dim lights.

CONCLUSION

Until that summer, I had never taught a class without computers. Those summer students had more questions on a day-to-day basis about assignments, expectations, and due dates than my regular semester students. Without the email to communicate, we were more distant from each other, and I hear less from them now that their semester is over than I do from students I had three or four years ago. Without the practice in workshopping and analysis that I normally do on the computer, the students did not develop as well in those areas as when I do use the computer. In short, I can no longer imagine as effective a class without computers. They give students a chance to respond differently than they do in other forms of assignments and work.

CONTACT INFORMATION

Robin MacRorie, Writing and Computer Consultant
University Writing Program
University of Notre Dame
Notre Dame, IN 46556
Email: macrorie.1@nd.edu
WWW: http://www.nd.edu/~rmacrori/syllabus
Phone: (219) 631-5578

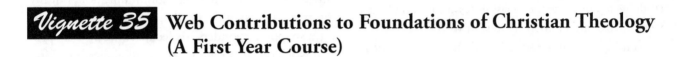

Vignette 35 Web Contributions to Foundations of Christian Theology
(A First Year Course)

Kern R. Trembath, University of Notre Dame

The University of Notre Dame requires that each undergraduate student take two courses in the department of theology. The first of these, called Foundations of Christian Theology, allocates roughly equal time to the history and texts of the Hebrew Bible, the New Testament, and the early Christian church. Because 25 to 30 sections of this course are offered each semester, each using a different, if large, number of textual and graphical resources, it is tailor-made to take advantage of the web. My class size is approximately 40 students per semester.

REDESIGN CONCEPTS

In revising my course to take full advantage of the web's distributive capabilities, I worked with the following assumptions:

- Students who are more interested in a course will learn more.

- Students who are spared the drudgery of taking notes are more likely to interact with the professor and their colleagues in class.

- Students who know exactly what they will be tested on will be more likely to remember it.

- Students want to participate in the learning process both with each other and with their professor.

- Students' eventual professions will depend upon collaborative adeptness, and, hence, any training along those lines now will pay them dividends later on.

- Any habits that simplify the professor's day are to be preferred.

ACTIVITIES

Here are the ways in which the web gradually helped me both to discover and to effect these values.

The first step was simply posting my classroom outlines on the web, freeing me from having to write them each day on the chalkboard. Soon afterward, I added graphics, expanding from five to six images through the entire semester to 20 to 30 on some days. Initially, it was disconcerting to see my students watching the screen rather than me, but I quickly learned that this expanded their interest and, hence, their learning.

Both the students and I appreciated this expansion, and so I next decided to augment my web offerings to include my complete lecture notes and student-written notes. When writing up the lecture notes, at the suggestion of students, I formatted them so that they printed on the left two-thirds of the page, leaving a wide right margin for students who wished to add or revise them, or simply doodle during classtime. I added my exam questions to the web as well, so that students could prepare at any point and at any pace. I paid two students to email me their class notes at the end of each week then shared a merged version with the class.

These developments allowed me to presuppose that students would have a greater familiarity with each day's lecture than could be expected otherwise. To put it bluntly, the students have my lecture notes before I begin to lecture. I tried to take advantage of this situation in two ways. First, I aggressively abbreviated various portions of the course and substituted group presentations, without decreasing student responsibility for the deleted materials. The group presentations may or may not be digital, as each group wishes, but they are possible precisely because of the changes wrought elsewhere in the semester by computers. Second, on occasion I will begin class by asking "OK, what did you think of the lecture that I would have delivered today? Any comments or questions?"

The next two components are simply fun. First, I continuously add open-ended links to sites that are deliberately not a direct part of the course (that is, they are not on the exam), but function instead as exploratory avenues for students whose interests were piqued by the topics and texts. Some of these links take users to textual, audio, and video files, while others bring them to encyclopedias, dictionaries, archives, geographical sites, and other open-ended resources. Not surprisingly, reflections on these links regularly show up in footnotes to papers and other creative ventures throughout the semester. The web also allows me to post anonymous best papers from previous semesters, an addition that many class members appreciate because, as first-year students, they are not yet comfortable with university-level writing.

The second fun element awaited the invention of chat software, which we used initially simply for exam preparation, usually three to four evenings before the exam itself. Evening usually means from 10 p.m. until midnight, which is when the greatest number of students are available. The transcripts from these sessions are saved and recycled as FAQs for subsequent semesters. On occasion, we chat about other topics, as either I or groups of students wish for more unstructured and spontaneous discussions.

Regular communication is accomplished by both email and listserv. I try to encourage the use of the former by never allowing more than 30 minutes between reception and response. By now, students are entirely accustomed to email communication, but my informal surveys indicate that professors are not always snappy responders, so feedback from their professors is crucial. In addition, email allows me to remain in contact with former students. It is a rare semester in which I am not contacted several times by Notre Dame graduates to request recommendations or advice or just to say hi and keep me up on their family developments.

OUTCOMES

I have not personally conducted quantitative pre- and post-web assessments of this course, relying instead on narrative feedback to guide further developments. Students regularly report in university-generated teacher/course evaluations that they appreciate this course well above the campus average. Almost uniformly, they specifically appreciate its digital nature. They like the closeness that email generates, the flexibility of preparing for exams at their own pace, the creative snooping that open-ended links allow them, and the relative intensity of visual presentations in a course they expected to be entirely lecture- and text-based. The relatively few students who are not as happy with the class's digital profile characteristically note their displeasure with all kinds of computer incursions into the classroom, especially in the humanities. By now, though, this course has acquired a campus reputation for using computers and the nondigerati tend to find their way into other sections.

Most professors and parents with whom I discuss these matters are surprised at my exam procedure, in particular the combination of class notes and exam questions. In all honesty, I was initially nervous about this feature myself, wondering whether it would contribute to artificial grade inflation. Here, though, results can be measured. After a surprising two to three semesters of zero growth, exam scores have risen by an average of 5% to 10%. More importantly, to my mind, student appreciation for taking tests has risen. Consistently, they report that they enjoy planning for, and taking, these exams. Since I began using chat discussions from previous classes as frequently-asked questions, their individual initiative in exam preparation has increased noticeably.

The most recent addition to my digital stable has been online grade distribution. Using FileMaker Pro and Claris Home Page, I easily constructed an interface between my class database and the web that allows the students to view relevant information. For authentication, the students create their own passwords, which thereafter only they and I can access. Overall simplification is accomplished by allowing them to enter their own chat session "buddy" names, which I then export to my chat client in preparation for group sessions—a far easier solution than copying and pasting from 40 emails to that same client.

LESSONS LEARNED

I was fortunate enough to be among the first professors at Notre Dame to use the web extensively in the classroom. I have tried to balance an aggressive appreciation for computer-based pedagogy with sensitivity to student feedback and immediate implementation of rea-

sonable suggestions. Some parts of a humanities course like mine resist digital conversion, however. I am not convinced, for instance, that final papers should be submitted digitally. Digital submission is perfectly appropriate for drafts, because the technology allows the professor and student to converse asynchronously, but it seems overkill to make the final submission on any medium but paper. Unless the student simply intends to delete it, s/he will most likely print it at some point anyway.

Likewise, while there are literally dozens of opportunities in the course to create video files for both current and future semesters, I am increasingly convinced that live lectures are best. Much learning is relational, and this is enhanced by as much personal presence and interaction as possible. Video vignettes are useful for syllabus pointers, brief comments on textual matters, and other, similar, by-the-way additions, but, in general, this type of humanities course is still best delivered in person.

CONCLUSION

The flexibility of the web provides the willing teacher with a wide array of instructional uses. In mulling over this variety, I have tried to keep the criterion of "relational pedagogy" as my ultimate compass point. Technology must serve the humane in physics as well as in theology, in the professions as well as in the university.

CONTACT INFORMATION

Kern R. Trembath, Assistant Chairman
Department of Theology
University of Notre Dame
Notre Dame, IN 46556
Email: ktrembat@nd.edu
WWW: http://www.nd.edu/~ktrembat/www-class/
    foundhome.html
Phone: (219) 631-4254

**Promoting Philosophical Discussion
with Computer-Mediated Communication**

Gary L. Hardcastle, University of Wisconsin, Stevens Point
Valerie Gray Hardcastle, Virginia Polytechnic Institute and State University

Student discussion is integral to a successful philosophy class. Intellectual transformation and the refinement of abstract ideas, the goals of philosophy, are products of dialectical exchange. Yet maintaining a philosophical dialog in a classroom presents no end of pedagogical problems. Students often find spontaneous, face-to-face discussion intimidating, and instructors must press them to ask questions or to offer comments. All too often a vocal few overshadow the quieter majority, and the philosophical ideal of nurturing an honest intellectual community moves out of reach. Varying levels of student readiness and the variety of learning styles compound the difficulty, and these problems grow with class size. In philosophy classes with more than a few students, fruitful discussion among all students is the exception, not the norm.

This vignette describes changes made in Knowledge and Reality, an introductory philosophy class taught at Virginia Tech. However, the techniques we use are applicable to any course that depends upon intellectual discussion.

EDUCATIONAL THEORIES

We reject the standard "credit for contact" model, which prizes the raw time teachers and students spend together in the same room, and emphasize the process of writing as a tool to promote active learning in our students. Our goal is not merely to provide our students with a better venue in which to have a philosophical discussion but to integrate the learning of difficult concepts, the challenging of fundamental ideas, and the construction of sound philosophical arguments.

COMPUTER-ENHANCED TECHNIQUES

We make extensive use of computer-mediated communication (CMC) to promote discussion in the philosophy classroom. We have, over the past five years, established a number of electronic venues within which philosophical discussion occurs.

WebChat

WebChat encompasses a variety of server applications, each of which allows participants to exchange text or images in real time. WebChats let participants jointly and continuously construct a web page containing written contributions from each, arranged in the order they are received. At the start of a WebChat session, the initiating participant browses the WebChat page and from it types a message, which WebChat then places at the top of that page with the date, time, and contributor's name. Others browse this page and respond similarly. Properly configured, a WebChat server will support as many as a hundred simultaneous participants.

From the web pages for our courses, students can initiate a WebChat session or join one already in progress. Alternatively, they can add to earlier WebChat sessions, which remain available. In this way, different WebChat sessions can serve as venues for impromptu discussion. We also arrange weekly 45-minute class meetings via WebChat. Every WebChat session produces a record of itself in the form of a web page, that is linked to the course homepage.

Running Commentaries

Running commentaries allow students to participate in a sophisticated version of an electronic bulletin board. Because these web-based environments organize comments in threads, they have an advantage over listservs: Students can view and review discussions that interest them without having to track other conversations. Running commentaries continue to exist as web pages, unlike the messages distributed on regular bulletin boards. In a running commentary, the instructor sets the topic and format of the discussion; this facility can be used to emphasize aspects of a text.

Over the course of the class, comments and their replies accumulate and compose a philosophical discussion. Here, specifically, we find our means to engage in a philosophical dialog, especially in larger classes: The students analyze the ideas of others critically and then, through an exchange with their instructors and their peers, revise and refine their own views.

Other Interactive Web Sites

WebChat and running commentaries are at the heart of our use of CMC in our philosophy courses, but they are not our only means of facilitating intellectual community and developing students' philosophical skills. Other efforts include Meet the Class web pages, interactive exercises on composing a philosophy paper, learning the basics of inductive and deductive logic, and online homework assignments in which student responses are converted to web pages and then linked, anonymously, to the homework question.

MEASURING THE IMPACT ON STUDENT LEARNING

Student surveys indicate that our students felt left out or left behind less often, were more inclined to ask the professor for help, believed they understood the content of the course better, and had greater access to the course materials than in traditional versions of the same course. Most tellingly, when papers from Valerie Hardcastle's introductory philosophy course were combined with papers from a traditional version of the same course and that set was submitted to external reviewers in a single-blind design, the papers from the CMC course scored better, by a statistically significant amount, on several of 17 criteria. Specifically, papers from the CMC course were judged to contain more arguments supporting the conclusion, fewer factual errors, greater sensitivity to counterarguments, and fewer errors in language use ($F < .05$).

LESSONS LEARNED

As might be expected, CMC changes the dynamic of philosophy classes. We have become active participants in our courses, guiding students through their ideas, rather than detached lecturers, impersonally dispensing our knowledge. Lectures now complement the electronic interactions, informing student discussion and setting the intellectual agenda, while at the same time allowing the students to take the initiative and pursue the avenues that interest them. A philosophical dialectic is integral to our courses; our students cannot succeed by taking, memorizing, and then regurgitating notes. They must participate, becoming responsible for their own progress and aiding in the advancement of their peers.

In addition, CMC strips away appearance, accent, ethnicity, gender, and background and thus promotes the identification of common interests and a sense of community. In larger classes, small discussion groups emerge around particular intellectual inquiries. Though every course contains a common core of material, CMC allows each student to participate in the class according to his or her interests and needs. Hence, even our large classes should satisfy more of our students.

CMC is not just a promising idea about how to engage in a philosophical dialog with students; it is a solution to the problem of promoting philosophical discussion in the classroom and ultimately meeting our instructional goals. Our students read more, write more, learn more, and, in the end, become better philosophers.

CONTACT INFORMATION

Valerie Gray Hardcastle
Department of Philosophy
Virginia Polytechnic Institute and State University
Blacksburg, VA 24061-0126
Email: valerie@vt.edu
WWW: http://mind.phil.vt.edu/
Phone: (540) 231-8491
Fax: (540) 231-6367

Gary Hardcastle
Department of Philosophy
University of Wisconsin, Stevens Point
Stevens Point, WI 54481-3897
Email: ghardcas@uwsp.edu
Phone: (715) 346-4625

Vignette 37 Motivating History Students to Inform Themselves

Daniel J. Pfeifer, Wake Forest University

For the study of history, reading is critical. From books, students gain information necessary for the exploration of historical themes and cultural traditions. When students do not read, the instructor is obliged to inform them in another way, generally through lecture.

When students do not retain important information, a well-planned discussion period can quickly deteriorate into individual recitation. Students simply cannot discuss the relationships of history if they do not know the data. While history, or any other discipline for that matter, is more than just data, Robert M. Gagne points out that, "The information is essential to [the event of instruction]. The learner must have such information available to learn a particular application" (Gagne, Briggs, & Wager, 1992). Students must know about people, places, events, and times in order to consider the larger historical questions.

In response to the problem of unprepared students, I determined to modify the textbook reading assignment, following the direction of Sidney L. Pressey. As Dr. Pressey states, "The average teacher is woefully burdened by such routine of drill and information-fixing" (1926). In the 1920s, he built a device to improve student learning by providing questions on important material and giving immediate feedback to student responses. While the industrial age gave Pressey's students a mechanical device, the information age has brought Wake Forest students the computer and the World Wide Web.

Using a password-protected web page, the professors distributed quizzes to their 19 world history students with the intent of "information fixing" through repetition and reinforcement. They recognized the potential for student displeasure over the additional workload and tried to make the quizzes motivational by providing immediate corrective feedback. Automatic scoring was preferable given the tight schedules of the instructors, and as a result, although the assignments meant more work for each student, the instructor workload would not be 19 times greater.

COMPUTER-ENHANCED TECHNIQUES

The online assignments consisted of 15 quizzes with 25 multiple-choice questions. The immediate feedback included passages from the textbook that helped students to answer the questions. To avoid plug-ins but to maintain interactivity, the quizzes were constructed with html forms and JavaScript. Each web page presented the students with five questions. If a student answered correctly, a JavaScript gave feedback, "You are Correct!" and posted the next question set. If a student answered incorrectly, a pop-up window appeared with the passages from the textbook. A Perl CGI recorded the student's work to a text file, which was then manually entered into an Excel gradebook.

The quizzes were due before the first of two class periods every week. Following each assignment, in-class discussion focused on questions relating various themes that the students learned from the textbook chapter and quiz. The other class period, in lecture format, focused on synthesizing new material with the information already learned.

ASSESSED OUTCOMES

First, the students showed little apprehension when informed of their reconditioned reading assignments. They seemed very comfortable with the technology. During the semester, they had no difficulty pointing and clicking through the quizzes.

Second, the best class discussions occurred at the beginning of the semester. Especially during the first class, the students were very willing to display knowledge they had gained from the textbook. Green observed this phenomenon 30 years ago when he wrote, "It is agreed that at first the student is motivated to work with the machine because he is fascinated by the gadgetry" (Green, 1962). However, the students continued to contribute to discussions to the end of the semester, albeit with less energy and on several occasions later in the semester, proving their familiarity with the textbook by quickly thumbing to appropriate pages to answer questions. The quizzes motivated several of the students to open their books and file away the location of the information.

At the end of the semester, the class filled out a survey to rate the effectiveness of the assignments. The quizzes were well received, although the students reported spending 60 to 90 minutes to complete each exercise. Fifteen of the 19 students expressed interest in "seeing similar textbook quizzes in their other history courses." On a scale of inconvenient (1) to helpful (10), the students rated the quizzes solidly on the helpful side (8.6 avg, 9 med). Apparently, the structure and feedback provided by the quizzes balanced the additional workload.

LESSONS LEARNED

Although humanists commonly scorn multiple-choice questions, their benefits were clear. The goal of the quizzes was information fixing, while class discussion was intended to teach critical thinking skills. The self-grading feature of the exercises was unavailable at the time for essays and short-answer responses, and some interpretation and analysis were required for the students simply to respond.

In spite of the successes indicated by the class survey, problems appeared in the assignment. As the semester wore on, the students were less prepared for class. The pass/fail nature of the textbook quizzes seemed to permit guessing. Curiosity apparently lessened as well, as it became more and more obvious that some of the students hastily checked boxes just to complete question sets.

The most important part of the assignment did not become apparent until the next semester, when the quizzes were used in a different class where the textbook information was much less integrated with class discussion. Because the students were not using the textbook readings and quiz information in class, they re-

sented the assignment and called it busy work—in spite of the fact that they reported spending 30 minutes less on each exercise than the satisfied class of the previous semester! The students stated emphatically and appropriately that the information must have utility.

The goal of motivating students to inform themselves on the subject of history was met with mild success. The quizzes obligated the students to become familiar with their textbook. By class time, they knew the information in a general way and were willing to share their knowledge with the class. Moreover, the students' responses to the survey showed that they value structure. The additional workload did not cause a class revolt but, on the contrary, gave students a positive weekly goal.

REFERENCES

Gagne, R. M., Briggs, L. J., & Wager, W. W. (1992). *Principles of instructional design* (4th ed.). Fort Worth, TX: Harcourt Brace.

Green, E. J. (1962). *The learning process and programmed instruction.* New York, NY: Holt, Rinehart, & Winston.

Pressey, S. L. (1926, March). A simple apparatus which gives tests and scores—and teaches. *School and Society, 23* (586), 374.

CONTACT INFORMATION

Daniel J. Pfeifer, Academic Computing Specialist
Wake Forest University
Winston-Salem, NC 27109
Email: pfeifedj@wfu.edu
WWW: http://www.wfu.edu/~pfeifedj,
    http://www.wfu.edu/Academic-departments/
    History/whistory
Phone: (336) 758-4850

ART AND MUSIC

Vignette 38   Student-Designed Online Art History References

Bernadine Barnes, Wake Forest University

Introduction to Art History is a course that puts great emphasis on "covering" the material, especially when the material ranges from prehistory to our own century and must be presented in one semester. While digital technology could be used to help students drill names and dates, I saw it as an antidote to the rapid survey—allowing students to experience how art historians work and to explore the breadth and depth of their artistic heritage. I wanted to stress that learning is a continuous process; we learn from others, and we pass on what we have discovered to those who come after us. Therefore, I developed plans for group projects that would be posted on the campus network so that future students could use them as well as revise them. The ideas behind these projects came from fifteen years of teaching: students learn best by doing; students write better when they are writing for a purpose and an audience; students making creative decisions, especially in a group, gain unique skills and value the strengths of others.

TECHNOLOGY

The projects take advantage of three valuable properties of digital publishing. First, publishing on the web entails gathering information and distributing it to an audience. The sense of an audience instills—one hopes—a responsibility to get it right, to say it well, to make it look good. Publication is a real outcome of research as opposed to presenting it for the approval of one authority figure, the professor. Second, a great advantage of html documents is the ease with which they can be changed. Additions, upgrades, and corrections are relatively easy and certainly less expensive than issuing new print editions. Third, images are easily incorporated into web pages, making them excellent tools for the study of art.

While these projects are ongoing—that is, I intend to have students add to and revise the work of pre-

vious semesters—two are relatively well developed. Each consists of small sections of text by individual students that are then assembled into a larger document. They differ in the level of group work involved in their construction as well as in structural complexity. The first project is a single web page with targets linked to images on the class's slide sheets; the second uses a series of pages, linked to each other and to the class pages in ways that allow students to explore ideas more freely. In both, moderately computer-savvy students find the technology easy to learn. We used a basic html editor; for most work, Netscape Composer was adequate but as projects became more sophisticated, we have also used Macromedia Dreamweaver. Images were acquired either by downloading them from the web, scanning photographs or slides, or taking new photographs with a digital camera. We used Adobe PhotoShop to adjust image quality and size, although a less complex photoediting program would have been sufficient. Wake Forest University provided training in web page construction for the students; staff assisted with scanning and image manipulation.

Projects and Philosophy

The first project is called "The Students' Guide to Iconography." Iconography—that is, the study of symbols and themes in works of art—is an essential part of any art history course, and I spend much of my lecture time explaining the stories depicted. But it would be impossible to cover every subject in Western art, and students vary widely in their backgrounds. This project was designed to teach students how to find out about traditional themes, to read the primary sources from which they derive, to find examples in various styles and periods, and to present the information in a manner that is useful to other students.

Students were asked to select a subject that was represented in one of the paintings or sculptures in a chapter of their textbook. Since the project began during the medieval and Renaissance part of my course, all subjects were Judeo-Christian although the range will be expanded in the future. Students were asked to submit the following information:

1) a one or two sentence description of the subject

2) quotations from the primary source(s) on the subject, with reference(s)

3) three examples of the subject, each dating at least a hundred years apart, with references

4) one paragraph descriptions of each work, explaining the differences between them

Although it was not required the first time, students were encouraged to submit their work as html-formatted pages. I provided a template to assist them in this process, which was moderately successful. In future semesters, I will require that they submit their work this way, with explicit instructions on formatting.

The second project focused on the architecture at Wake Forest University to help students understand and appreciate architectural styles, research, and analysis. The project was conceptualized during a summer session, with a class of only seven students. I thought of it as a stand-alone unit, that would supplement course lectures. I selected three aspects of the architectural environment for study: the campus plan; Wait Chapel (a building in the Georgian style that would introduce elements of classical architecture); and Scales Fine Arts Building (done in the modern style). Students decided on the tasks needed to fill out the project. One created a guide to architectural terms that would be activated when students clicked on an area of an image of a building. Another explored the microhistory of Wait Chapel, discovering plans (some never realized) in the university's archives; another did research on the modernist International style, and applied the concepts to the Fine Arts building.

It was important to me that these projects lead students to all types of research resources: archives, libraries, interviews, direct observation, and digital resources. Throughout, I emphasized the importance of critically assessing any resource and crediting others' work. Students were encouraged to ask questions about

the projects via email, and regular meetings were held outside class time with the students working on the architecture project.

RESULTS

Student responses to the projects were very favorable. The electronic component intimidated a few of them, especially at the beginning, but, in general, most students enjoyed learning how to create web pages. In course evaluations, most students felt the projects allowed them to be creative and taught them new skills. Although some complained that the projects took more time than they thought they should, others felt a sense of accomplishment that rarely follows ordinary term papers.

LESSONS LEARNED

For these projects to be successful, it is important to have students doing as much of the work as possible. Even simple tasks like reformatting text become very time-consuming if one person has to do it for the entire class. Usually, someone in the class has some interest in working with web pages; I would recommend planning group assignments so that each group has at least one. Pairing such students with others who have fewer technical skills promotes student-to-student learning. Projects should also be allowed enough time to develop fully. Critical discussion of the project's design and content is essential and most likely to lead to better projects and a better educational experience.

Please note: Because of copyright restrictions, these projects are accessible only to members of the Wake Forest community. Samples can be accessed through my home page (http://www.wfu.edu/~barnes).

CONTACT INFORMATION

Bernadine Barnes, Associate Professor
Art Department
Wake Forest University
Winston-Salem, NC 27109-7343
Email: barnes@wfu.edu
WWW: http://www.wfu.edu/~barnes/webpage-
    sample.html
    http://www.wfu.edu/~barnes/archunit.htm

Vignette 39 Portfolio Development: Multimedia Presentations for Designers

Marguerite L. Koepke, University of Georgia

A new design course, portfolio development, contained materials never before taught as a stand-alone subject. Its content focused on traditional presentation techniques professionals use to record, compile, and present design work. Photocopying, photography, cut-and-paste layout have been the standard methods of producing these documents for many years. Compiling projects that vary in subject, size, color, content, and dimension into a well-composed portable format, has always been challenging and technically difficult.

During course development, up-to-date hardware and software technologies were explored. It became clear that new, high-speed computers, digital imaging hardware, and a bounty of publishing software offered powerful tools for portfolio development. The possibilities were exciting! What would a portfolio look like if it were designed, developed, and delivered electronically? While course objectives relating to design and content remained aligned with traditional portfolio development practices, production techniques shifted to technology-based methods.

As the course evolved, so did the need to create a classroom to support it. The ideal classroom would be a multimedia presentation lab, including a variety of digitizing equipment, powerful computer workstations, storage and retrieval systems, and desktop publishing and web site design software. With support of the university through a learning technologies grant, the school established the lab, and the course is now a successful, growing part of the curriculum.

EDUCATIONAL THEORIES

During course planning and development, technology issues fell into two categories. Development of the new classroom focused on the ability of technology to affect the practice of the discipline. The structure and design of the course focused on the practice of teaching and would determine educational methods and strategies. The instructor was not a technology expert. She used the technology when developing the lab and the course but had never taught a computer-based class. Would tried-and-true teaching strategies, like hands-on learning and show-and-tell, work in the computer-enhanced learning environment? Would they work in this new classroom, and how could technology be used to promote a productive and dynamic environment? After much consideration, the following strategies were chosen to merge tried-and-true methods with the new, technology-based class.

1) **Teacher as facilitator:** places responsibility for learning on the student. The instructor facilitates learning by orchestrating course content, sequence, and activities and establishing professional standards.

2) **Student/teacher dialogue:** fosters the principle that when questions arise, the teacher appears. Students need time to develop rapport with their instructor.

3) **Expert/guest presenters:** add new dimensions to the classroom. They fill the technology gap, interject a broad range of opinions and expertise, stimulate a greater variety of ideas, and use varied formats like lectures and workshops to communicate information.

4) **Hands-on learning:** couples projects to specific types of skill development and is based on the principle of learning by doing.

5) **Show-and-tell:** features student work. Students explain their work to peers.

6) **Collaborative learning:** based on the principle that what you teach, you learn twice. This concept encourages students to share newfound techniques and to help one another solve problems.

7) **Establishing high expectations:** leads to exemplary results. Students anticipating innovative, useful outcomes are likely to perform to their expectations.

8) Timely evaluation of each subject and project: reveals how well the class understands the materials and where changes may be necessary. The teacher as facilitator uses a variety of tools and techniques to assess the class's progress.

METHODS

Now the challenge was to incorporate these strategies into specific class assignments and activities. Class met for three hours twice a week. Large blocks of time made it possible for students to get to know their instructor and classmates and to practice assignments. It also allowed time for collaboration, which was strongly encouraged. As students began to work together, to share ideas and techniques, learning became spontaneous and dynamic.

On the other hand, the instructor was concerned that the long class periods would become tedious. Periodic breaks were taken, and an attempt was made to schedule a variety of activities and presentations, like lectures, demonstrations, workshops, and even local field trips. Assignments and activities were varied and furnished as much information as possible to make each class period interesting and productive. These activities exemplify some of the strategies mentioned earlier.

Presentations by Professionals and Specialists

To produce a portfolio, students needed to know traditional practices and protocols. What work should be included, and how should it look and be organized? Guest professionals presented their ideas and offered examples. Technology specialists from campus presented on-site lectures and workshops on photography and a variety of software applications, including graphic design, page layout, and publications. Students valued the variety of ideas offered by guests, and during workshops were able to experiment and to apply new techniques immediately.

Student Presentations

Students were required to present all their projects. Some presentations were informal, much like a mid-project review and discussion group. Others were very formal. Explaining their projects had many advantages; it sharpened their presentation skills, demonstrated

their knowledge of the lab's technical equipment, such as LCD projectors, electronic pointer/mouse, and computers, and web site design and presentation software (PowerPoint and Front Page). Perhaps most importantly, they shared personal discoveries of techniques with the class.

Internet Searches

Students searched the Internet for resources relevant to their assignments. Searches broadened their knowledge of available information and public domain graphic materials and furnished good and poor examples of web site design. Students tended to share valuable discoveries and resources with their classmates.

Email

The instructor's email address was included with the office location and telephone number on the syllabus. Students compiled a list of their email addresses and posted it in the classroom. Students used addresses as needed to communicate with one another. They quickly learned that email was an efficient way to contact faculty outside office hours. Appointments were easily scheduled and uncomplicated questions and situations quickly resolved. Students were also able to contact each other with questions about assignments and collaborative work. Email strengthened communication and ties among class members.

Individual Projects

While all students worked on identical assignments, their projects were always individual. For example, an assignment might be to create a ten-frame PowerPoint presentation describing their design work. The presentations would all be on the same subject and of the same duration but contain very individual ideas and materials. Students observed each other during project development in the lab and always seemed to have open-handed suggestions for one another. Since all projects built on previous work, analyzing them continually improved their work and raised expectations.

Class Web Page

The course was, for all practical purposes, paperless. All course materials (such as syllabus, assignments, and supplemental information) were included on the web page. Since anyone could visit the web site, it became an open door to the classroom. It grew throughout the term and included pages on course background and development; the syllabus and all assignments; student projects; guest speakers, including pictures and profiles; and studio time, showing pictures of students engaged in class activities. The web site created a sense of community among class members, and since the location of the actual classroom was remote, it was a great way to inform and engage students across the curriculum in what this class was doing.

Projects were grouped into three sections. The first introduced the lab equipment and its potential applications. The second focused on developing a working knowledge of the software, and the third on finalizing work and putting it all together into a printed and electronic portfolio.

SECTION ONE PROJECTS

During the first two weeks, students learned how to operate imaging equipment, build a beginning library of their work, and best practices of storage and retrieval.

1) **Basic photography.** First, students learned basic principles and techniques of traditional studio photography using 35-millimeter cameras, specialized lighting, and films. Based on traditional techniques, they then experimented with digital photography to accomplish similar results.

2) **Creating digital images.** Students learned to operate slide and flatbed scanners and to digitize slides, photographs, and all two-dimensional work they planned to use in their portfolios.

3) **Managing files of digital images.** Digital images frequently generate very large files. Students were introduced to a variety of storage and retrieval options to help them manage their data.

SECTION TWO PROJECTS

The most exciting and interesting differences in producing a portfolio using technology rather than traditional techniques is the ease and speed of exploring a variety of design possibilities. Learning basic software applications enabled students to explore an endless number of ways to design and to communicate their work. The more ideas they generated, the more they

tended to employ different programs to produce them. Mastery of a program was not necessary before they started to use it. In fact, the more they used programs to achieve their design objectives, the more quickly they appeared to learn them. In other words, the learning objectives drove the use of the technology. The following software and projects were used sequentially to produce the portfolios.

1) **Adobe PhotoShop/CD cover.** This assignment introduced PhotoShop through the design of a CD cover to go with their next assignment, a PowerPoint version of their portfolio presentation.

2) **MS PowerPoint/design a portfolio presentation.** Students began this project just as they would any design problem: conducting research and employing hand-drawn, schematic diagrams, sketches, and drawings to explore ideas and to develop sequences and thematic content. Once resolved, students designed the entire presentation in PowerPoint. They designed all aspects of their presentations, including content, sequence, and connections between pages, text, and page layout. No templates were allowed. When completed, students used the pack-and-go feature of the software to produce a CD version of their portfolio.

3) **Front Page/web site design.** Based on their PowerPoint design, students created a web portfolio. Creating a portfolio for delivery over the Internet presented a new set of design challenges. They learned the relationship between file size and download time and that colors and fonts that can be sent and received are limited. Once they understood the major differences between the presentation programs, they redesigned those aspects of their portfolios that were most affected.

4) **Quark XPress/page layout and printed portfolios.** Creating a traditional portfolio (published copy) was an important aspect of the course. These manuscripts are portable, can be viewed anywhere, and are frequently the preferred format for viewing during interviews or by noncomputer users. A web page or PowerPoint presentation can be printed for this purpose. However, Quark XPress offers excellent design options for effective page layout and report formats. Students reworked their materials

using this program to produce a printable copy of their work.

As students progressed through these projects, they learned the benefits of each program and worked with several applications simultaneously. This increased their technical literacy and knowledge of what of each program does and does not do well. Working with and among applications also demonstrated that by learning a variety of programs and their interrelationships, students are better equipped to achieve maximum design potential.

SECTION THREE: FINAL PROJECT

With this strong working knowledge, students used the final two weeks of class to make changes and refinements to their final portfolio. They could produce as many portfolio formats as desired but were required to produce two versions, one printed and one electronic.

MEASURED RESULTS

Informal evaluations conducted throughout the term were helpful in making short-term adjustments to the schedule and assignments. However, the most informative assessments of the class came from outside reviewers attending the final presentation and student course evaluations. Outside reviewers were very complimentary about the quality of student work generated in this class and gave it high ratings for the use of technology to accomplish the course objectives. All students rated the class as high quality on all questions rating subject matter and methods of communication. Written comments strongly supported the incorporation of technology into the class and the curriculum. Students learned specific techniques and applications and, through class activities and projects, became proficient and comfortable integrating them.

LESSONS LEARNED

The entire process, beginning with course development and classroom design and continuing through teaching, was a remarkable learning experience. The instructor began as a basic user of the personal computer in her own work and ended up teaching high-tech applications in a state-of-the art, computer-enhanced classroom. A countless number of valuable lessons were learned along the way. Some that may translate across disciplines include:

1) **Do not abandon a good idea for a course because of technological uncertainties.** Today, technology will accommodate almost all tried-and-true teaching and learning techniques. Consult a forward-thinking technical support person and/or specialists on campus to learn what is current and ways to merge technology with course development.

2) **Create an environment that encourages collaboration among students.** Structure class time so students can move about, follow each other's work, and help one another. In this productive learning environment, students tend to form their own learning groups. Most of them enjoy teaching one another, and it reinforces their own understanding of the materials.

3) **Create an environment that encourages collaboration between instructor and students.** Since instructors are the subject experts but may not have the technical expertise, they can learn with and from students. An instructor's willingness to try new technology and learn new ways to express and explore the discipline is highly regarded. Inviting experts and specialists to present technologies or to join the class in learning them worked extremely well. Use the personal learning process to build bridges with the class.

4) **Expect greater output.** Because technology increases the ease of exploration and processing speed, students generated more design options than they would have with conventional techniques.

5) **When using technology, always have a back-up plan.** Some days, the equipment simply will not work. Networks, drives, and other connections are not always reliable, and outside users can often trip up the systems. When this happens, rely on those low-tech methods that have always worked in the past. Interject a history lesson or take a field trip. Students generally appreciate a day away from the monitors.

The course continues to improve and to evolve. Students who have been in the portfolio class or lab users during open-hours fully embrace the technology. Evaluations indicate that technology has become an integral part of the program and that there is growing need for expansion.

CONTACT INFORMATION:

Marguerite L. Koepke
Associate Professor of Landscape Architecture
School of Environmental Design
Caldwell Hall
University of Georgia
Athens, GA 30602
Email: mkoepke@arches.uga.edu
WWW: http://www.sed.uga/classes
      (go to LAND 4910-6910)

Vignette 40 Remediation before Matriculation: The Music Fundamentals Online Project

Eric J. Isaacson and William L. Findlay, Indiana University, Bloomington

INTRODUCTION

Music Fundamentals Online aims to provide pedagogically effective, low-cost remediation for high school students planning to major in music in college. Although the topics that fall under the term *music fundamentals* vary somewhat, they typically involve a combination of conceptual understanding and skills, including the ability to read fluently treble, bass, and alto clefs; to write and to recognize (both visually and, where appropriate, aurally) scales, key signatures, intervals, and chord types; and to know or to recognize basic aspects of rhythm and meter. A mastery of these music fundamentals ought to be prerequisite to the core music curriculum, which typically includes a four- or five-semester music theory sequence, a parallel sequence of aural skills courses, and a subsequent two- to four-semester sequence of music history.

Incoming students' mastery of these skills varies tremendously. Those who have studied piano or violin since age five, for example, are often better prepared than those who may have started studying a wind instrument at age 12, or singers who may never have studied an instrument and may have had no private music training until high school or perhaps none at all. To ensure success in the core curriculum, students deficient in music fundamentals must be identified and steps taken to address their deficiencies.

Some schools address the varied preparation of their students by including several weeks of music fundamentals at the beginning of their first course in the major—essentially subjecting all their students to remedial instruction. Besides the increased potential for boredom among well-prepared students, this approach steals time from the end of curriculum, when more advanced topics should be covered.

Most of the remaining schools determine mastery of music fundamentals through a placement exam, given either when a student auditions or during orientation. Students who do poorly are typically placed in a remedial music fundamentals course. In a 1998 survey of colleges, 15 out of 21 respondents reported that they provide such a course (see http://theory.music.indiana.edu/mfo/surveyresults.html). Unfortunately, it does not matter where students' deficiencies lie—whether they are weak in aural skills or conceptual skills, whether they need a little review or extensive instruction—they are simply identified as needing remediation.

This approach introduces scheduling problems as well. Running trailer sections for the students needing remediation requires additional faculty. Requiring the student to wait an entire year after completing the fundamentals course to start the core decreases the time available to complete the core from eight to six semesters. Shifting the entire core back one semester causes a similar squeeze for all students and also leaves those students not needing remediation without an academic music course in their first semester, a key time in their music studies. At Indiana University, this has forced us into perhaps the most bizarre solution of all—we place most students needing remediation into the music fundamentals course at the same time as they take the first course in the music theory core (Music Theory and Literature I). This is like putting the cart on top of the horse—yet it has proven the only practical solution to this problem in our setting.

In addition to the curricular problems associated with remediation, there are important cost considerations. Students pay from $350 to nearly $1,200 (in 1999-2000) to take the three-credit remedial course, depending on their residency status. For in-state students, the state must underwrite the difference, which comes to around $800 per student. The university must provide classroom space, which is in chronically short supply, and must hire graduate teaching assistants (3.5 positions), who get a stipend, tuition remission, and other benefits, Doing without these associate instructor positions would enable us to be even more selective in filling other AI positions in the department and to improve the overall quality of instruction provided by graduate students.

We concluded after extensive discussions that the best solution to both the curricular and cost issues involved in providing remediation would be to require

that students arrive on campus having already mastered music fundamentals. We recognized that the road from policy to practical implementation would be difficult, however. Students would not learn of their deficiency until after they took our diagnostic exam during their audition in the spring of their senior year. That would be too late to enroll in a high school course—if their school happened to offer one. A paper-and-pencil correspondence version of the course proved inadequate for many reasons. Simply telling students they had to learn these topics on their own seemed likely to scare them off to other schools. Many would not know where to look for help or would lack the motivation to do so.

LEARNING IDEAS

Unlike most material covered in music theory courses, music fundamentals consist largely of discrete information and skills for which computer-based instruction is well suited. We developed a proposal, subsequently funded by the Fund for the Improvement of Post Secondary Education (FIPSE) of the US Department of Education, to create a self-contained, web-based course in music fundamentals, in which instruction, skill development, and assessment would all be provided online. Students could access the course anytime from any web-equipped computer, and student progress could be tracked.

The course, called Music Fundamentals Online, goes online in the fall of 2000, in time for members of the incoming fall 2001 class to take it. The course is cross-platform and cross-browser compatible, runs on slower machines with 800×600 resolution and 28.8K modems, and requires only that the computer be sound-capable. A product called Pathware, which Lotus recently purchased from Macromedia, manages a database of students, courses and the lessons they contain, and enrollment information linking students to courses, and it provides a Java-based student front-end to the system.

The course will comprise roughly 50 distinct lessons in eight to nine topics. Because of this modularity, MFO can pretest students to determine which lessons they have already mastered. These will be marked as complete in Pathware which will save students time, because they will have to do only the lessons they need. It will also allow us to set a higher standard of mastery.

Instead of accepting a score of 70% on the diagnostic exam, we can now determine mastery on a topic or even lesson level and have the students work on only those lessons for which additional work is indicated.

TECHNIQUES USED

Each topic in MFO consists of alternating lesson and activity sections. The lesson sections (Figure 40.1) present a series of instructional screens with a consistent set of attributes: 1) minimal text, 2) a visual example that illustrates the point, and, where appropriate, 3) an audio example based on the visual example. In the instructional text, User-Triggered Animation Hyperlinks (UTAH), given the appearance of web-browser links, initiate animated visual examples to illustrate the instructional content. Because of bandwidth and copyright limitations, most audio examples are played as MIDI files. This connection of verbal, visual, and aural components, an important pedagogical strategy in general, is even more important in the absence of a hands-on instructor.

The activity sections serve multiple purposes (Figure 40.2). They provide an opportunity for the student to apply concepts introduced in the lesson sections, they help reinforce student understanding of the topic, they provide an opportunity to apply concepts to real musical situations, and they help develop speed on selected tasks. Activities are typically arranged in increasing levels of difficulty. The scope of the problem may be increased, complexity added, subskills combined, or response-time targets used. The activities are mastery-based—to pass a level, the student typically has to complete X of the last Y problems correctly.

Two types of feedback are employed: 1) scaled feedback, where the amount of feedback information increases for each wrong answer, leading students gradually to the correct answer, and 2) comparative feedback, which shows students their answer in direct comparison with the correct answer, which allows them to analyze their mistakes themselves. Students having trouble with an activity are directed back to the appropriate lesson section to review the concept.

FIGURE 40.1

SAMPLE LESSON SCREEN

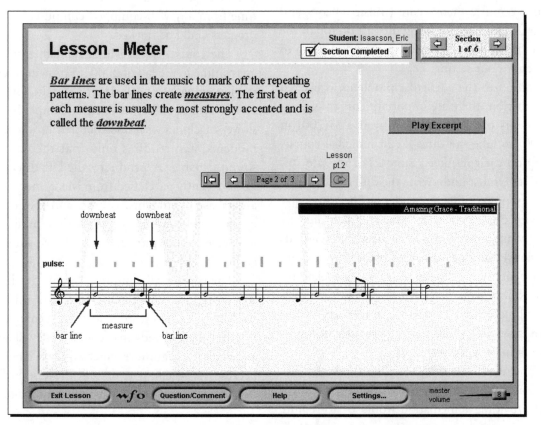

MEASURED RESULTS

Because the course is still under development, we have no formal evaluation results to report. During informal testing on lessons completed to date, student volunteers have reacted very positively. They found the user interface very effective. They thought the learning experience was more efficient than traditional instruction. They liked being challenged to remain on-task throughout the instruction; they couldn't tune out as they can in class. They liked the freedom to work at their own pace in their own setting. In the activities, they found the time goals and the gradual increase in difficulty effective motivators. Perhaps most importantly, they thought that students would be motivated to do the course before arriving on campus, knowing that it would save them from taking a course after they got there. The idea of computer-mediated remediation in this area has been positively received by many in the professional community as well.

LESSONS LEARNED

Since the course is still under development, most of the lessons we are likely to learn lie ahead. The courseware development has confirmed that it always takes longer than expected to develop high-quality, robust instructional software. It is likely that, despite our best intentions, we will not anticipate all the technical problems in access, initial software setup (the lessons require that certain browser plug-ins be installed), understanding of the interface, or ineffective instruction. We may also be underestimating the amount of administrative effort it will take to process student enrollments.

CONCLUSION

Music Fundamentals Online offers a new approach to the problem of remediation for college music majors. Many of its features set it apart from traditional classroom instruction, CD-ROM-based instruction, correspondence study, and instructor-based web courses. The course saves students time both by covering only as many topics as necessary and by keeping the student

FIGURE 40.2

SAMPLE ACTIVITY SCREEN

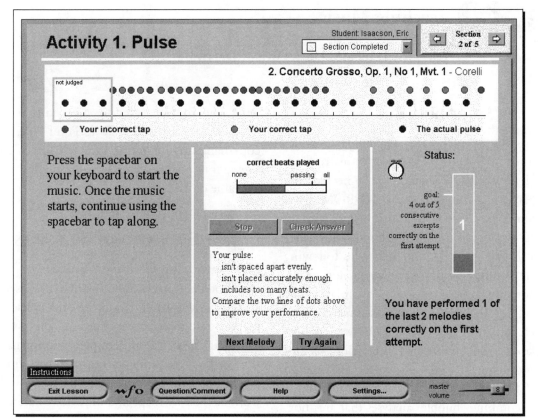

on task for more concentrated blocks of time. It provides flexibility in the time and location of instruction. It saves the student money. It is highly interactive and provides immediate feedback. (We do intend to have an instructor/administrator available for those times when questions arise.) Its server-based tracking will enable us to monitor student access, so we can follow up when a student is not making progress and also evaluate the effectiveness of the instruction.

Though initially conceived on a modest scale—only for those students planning to attend Indiana University—there is no reason (except server capacity) that it could not be used by any of the 34,000 students who begin music majors each year in the US, of whom perhaps half would benefit from some brush-up on these topics. Another important audience is students planning to take an advanced placement music theory course. It can be challenging for high schools to offer both a rudimentary music class and a college equivalency course. MFO would enable more high schools to offer advanced placement music theory or to increase enrollment in an existing course. Finally, although this type of instruction is not suitable for much of the music core curriculum, MFO-style lessons would be very effective for some topics.

CONTACT INFORMATION

Eric J. Isaacson, Associate Professor of Music Theory
William L. Findlay, Courseware Author
Indiana University School of Music
1201 East Third Street
Bloomington, IN 47405
Email: mfo@indiana.edu
WWW: http://theory.music.indiana.edu/mfo
Phone: (812) 855-0296

Vignette 41 Teaching Music

Larry W. Peterson, University of Delaware

INTRODUCTION

Using the computer and laserdisc technology provides me numerous opportunities to improve instruction. Basically, I use software, sometimes connected to a laserdisc player and sometimes to a CD-ROM drive, to teach four opera courses, two music history courses, and a long-distance music appreciation course. My experience began in 1981, and I use the following software: 1) ToolBook authorware to develop multimedia lessons that students use in a microlab in the music building; 2) SERF, an online course management developed at the University of Delaware to provide a syllabus, gradebook, email interaction, including a chatroom, for a long-distance music appreciation course; 3) CD TIME SKETCH, a software that allows students to combine "bubble" analyses that are "hot" with synchronized text that pops into a window as the piece is heard; and 4) PowerPoint slides plus hardcopy handouts for music history courses. I have designed four opera courses based upon opera repertory available on laserdisc.

EDUCATIONAL THEORIES

Demonstrating Creative Choices

ToolBook authorware allows me to use laserdiscs and CDs to isolate specific moments in a musical work to demonstrate the creative choices a composer made. I can chain three or four examples in immediate succession so that the students can compare different appearances of the same melodic material. Students can work at their own speed and review material at their discretion. My educational philosophy is to promote the exploration and comparison of fine details and to demonstrate creative choices more effectively. I have been using this software for over ten years in four courses a year.

Demonstrating Form and Details

CD TIME SKETCH, now published as Cap Media Tools, accomplishes two things. It allows students to demonstrate that they understand a musical work really well. They can demonstrate the form and indicate significant details as the piece is played. Also, the completed analyses give me an extensive library to use in my music literature, music appreciation, and music history courses. I have been using this software for over eight years.

Providing Ready Access

The online course management software allows students in any location in the world easy access to my long-distance course. At any time of the day, they may check the syllabus, their grade, or contact me or other students in the class via email. This software provides access to students outside a traditional classroom setting at any time of the day or night and allows me to interact with them. I have used this online course management software for five semesters.

Organizing Information

PowerPoint presentation software assists students in informational intensive courses to organize their notes and provides a guide for exam reviews. Further, it allows me to replace the chalkboard to indicate the spellings of terms and composers' names. Since music history and literature courses involve names and terms in French, German, Italian, and English, PowerPoint allows me to prepare my slides in advance, print them as handouts that students purchase when they purchase their textbooks, and use them again for review sessions. Since our classrooms are heavily booked, it used to require careful planning to get into the classroom in time to fill three chalkboards with the day's terms and names, erase them after the lecture, while trying to answer student questions, and then exit the classroom in a timely manner for the next instructor. Now I can prepare my slides before class, quickly load them after entering the classroom, and, after class, remove my diskette. Before using PowerPoint, I used

PODIUM, a presentation software developed at the University of Delaware. I have used presentation software for over five years.

COMPUTER-ENHANCED TECHNIQUES USED

ToolBook Lessons

The students go to a listening lab where they explore the lessons at their leisure. For opera, currently the students must complete three lessons, each requiring at least an hour of their time. The symphonic repertory requires about 30 minutes per work. The lessons are designed so that students have options: they can click *audio* buttons to hear an example, *video + audio* buttons to see excerpts through a video window that opens on the computer monitor while hearing the examples, or click an *audio + notation* button to see the printed music while hearing the example. Self-exams are provided for each lesson. The students may click a button to hear an example, then click and hold another button to view the correct answer. These lessons are designed to be interactive. The students may click a *notes* button to open word processing software, type notes, and save them to diskette or print them in the lab.

CD Time Sketch Lessons

The student views or creates these analyses while in a listening lab. Bubbles that are color-coded so that the same material (or bubble) receives the same color are "hot" which means that they play the corresponding portion of the musical work connected to that bubble. One field of text does not change and contains general information about the piece. Another field of text changes as the music plays. It may include the text in its original language plus an English translation, indicate what melodic material is being developed or what instrument or instruments are heard. This software was designed for my use in music literature and appreciation courses. The visual presentation is simple but very effective in communicating important aspects of a musical work. I now have a software analysis of almost every piece of music that I teach!

Online Course Management Software

What is unique about the use of this software is that 1) students are located in various states, not sitting in a classroom with me lecturing or performing for them; 2) they may access the information at any time; and 3) most of our interaction is via Internet. Students also submit logs where they discuss pieces of music by email, and I respond.

PowerPoint

Students have printed copies of my PowerPoint slides in their hands as I lecture. They may also use these handouts and accompanying notes for review for exams.

MEASURED RESULTS

A colleague in California and I completed a two-year evaluation of the use of laserdiscs. Also, over 150 students completed lengthy questionnaires about the use of my ToolBook opera lessons. The response has been overwhelmingly positive. Even when the students must come to the music building and spend over three hours per opera, only one student out of 150 complained. They were unanimous in their enthusiasm and, much to my amazement, suggested I create more lessons.

Regarding my use of PowerPoint and PODIUM, the students frequently express their appreciation on course evaluations about my use of the slides in class and for providing them printed copies. Their feedback has been informal. I have not evaluated the use of this software in any formal way.

LESSONS LEARNED

1) **ToolBook lessons.** This authorware is the most creative, vigorous, and long-term use I have made of new technologies. For this type of lesson, it is very important to learn a new type of writing. It is desirable to be specific, brief, clear, and to use language that is not unique to music, if possible. When musical terms are used, they are immediately explained. I have learned to rewrite often to achieve a succinct style that works. Also, it is important to be patient. This type of software has a steep learning curve. It required several years to master. Patience is important because software revisions are constant and sometimes frustrating. Learning manuals are often poorly written. What

helped me most was getting formal instruction in a classroom setting.

Patience is required to seek funding for software and hardware requirements. Page design was a new area of expertise. How to combine as little text as possible with colors to present a page that is both attractive, clear, and informative was a skill I had to learn. I learned from students in their questionnaires not to use multimedia lessons at the very beginning or at the very end of the semester. They work well in the middle of the course. Also, I was delighted with the success of these lessons. Students learn in more depth than I had ever achieved before, and they are general university students, not music majors. The improvement in content as well as student responses affirm the time, cost, and energy required to develop the lessons.

2) **CD Time Sketch.** I learned that this type of visual-aural presentation is very successful in conveying the details of a music work. Students like these lessons and even enjoy creating them. However, when the software does not work, or the computers are not functioning correctly, or, through some error, they lose their work, they become very frustrated and even angry.

3) **Online course management software.** I am still learning how to use this software effectively. I like it and the students seem to use it correctly. The benefits are obvious since the students are in a long-distance setting. I am exploring the use of a chat room presently. I have learned that student time management and motivation are disappointing in a long-distance format. They tend to put off assignments to the last minute and to suffer because of it. For example, the grades for these classes are the lowest in my 25 of college instruction. To improve their time management and motivation, I send out weekly email posts and have divided assignments into many small tasks to keep them involved. I joined a list devoted to long-distance learning and created an on-campus network of faculty using our online course management software to teach long-distance classes so that we could troubleshoot and share our experiences.

4) **PowerPoint.** Dark backgrounds are best, I have learned. I put all words in capital letters, so they are

more easily read in the back rows. I had to experiment to find a level of lighting that allows the students to see well enough to write yet low enough to minimize glare on the monitors or projection screen.

The slides are very useful for preparing exams. In general, I need only about an hour to prepare the slides for each class. Thus, my preparation time is almost identical to what it was before I started using PowerPoint. The only challenge is to have a semester's slides completed in time for the students to purchase with their books. I could put the slides on the web before each class for the students to download, but I do not. I also find using PowerPoint for guest lectures is incredibly useful for repeated use.

CONTACT INFORMATION

Larry W. Peterson, Professor of Music
Music Department
University of Delaware
Newark, DE 19716
Email: peterson@UDel.Edu
WWW: http://www.udel.edu/music/faculty/peterson/,
      http://www.udel.edu/present/best_practices/,
      http://www.udel.edu/serf/
Phone: (302) 831-8134
Fax: (302) 831-3589

BUSINESS, EDUCATION, AND SOCIAL SCIENCES

Vignette 42 — Double-Jeopardy Quizzing

Gordon E. McCray, Wake Forest University

INTRODUCTION AND BACKGROUND

I still recall the enlightenment I felt upon first reading Chickering and Gamson's (1987) recommended best practices in undergraduate education. Some of those guidelines validated philosophies and techniques I was already using, while others caused me immediately to think about some significant modifications to my teaching approach. Falling squarely into the former category was their recommendation that students be provided with immediate feedback. I always was diligent in providing copious written feedback on assignments submitted for grading and, further, encouraged extensive face-to-face and electronic interaction with students as they worked toward deliverables to be submitted for grading. This, I reasoned, minimized the amount of work students would perform while going down the wrong road. Of course, in some situations, allowing students to venture down this wrong road can be quite useful pedagogically, but that road is not taken here. I quickly concluded that the matter of rapid feedback had been addressed adequately.

Sometime later, however, I began using graded and timed online quizzing as an enticement to students to complete online multimedia lectures by a predetermined date and time (McCray, forthcoming). Students received their grades on the quiz immediately upon submitting it electronically. As a secondary benefit, I could identify prior to the next class meeting those areas that appeared problematic for a large proportion of students. Quite unexpectedly, however, large numbers of students began asking for clarification on why certain foils were incorrect or why the correct answer was, indeed, correct. Most often, there was a significant delay between the time the student took the quiz and my opportunity to field questions regarding its con-

tent. Students were thinking critically about the content and concepts captured in the quiz beyond its completion but decidedly *not* receiving rapid, useful feedback. Could information technology (IT) be used to enhance the learning experience?

THE DOUBLE-JEOPARDY QUIZ CONCEPT

Deciding to capitalize on student desire to explore further the content addressed in the online quizzes, I set about developing those quizzes into learning exercises as much as measurement activities. Online quizzes would consist of two distinct phases: exploration and commitment.

The Exploration Phase

When students first enter the quiz, they are presented with a series of apparently objective questions. Quiz items generally target the application of a core concept rather than testing mastery of lexicon or some lesser learning outcome and are of the true/false or multiple choice format. Under no time constraint, the student makes a selection and electronically submits that response for immediate evaluation.

Rather than provide a simple correct/incorrect response, however, the double-jeopardy quiz returns a probing question, insight, or conflicting perspective—so-called counterpoints—designed to force students to reconsider their original responses. Counterpoints are provided even if students responded correctly on the question as originally posed. Counterpoints for foils direct students' attention toward a concept that should prove useful in abandoning the incorrect response in favor of a correct response. The counterpoint for the correct initial response presents a compelling but incorrect argument against that response. Often these counterpoints reflect common misconceptions about the subject matter.

The Commitment Phase

Having been presented with a counterpoint to their original response, students now commit to a response. No time limit is imposed on this second phase of the quiz. Students are free to reference any resource in attempting to determine the correct answer. As in the exploration phase, students submit this final response for immediate evaluation. Having submitted an answer, they are presented with the correct answer to the question with an explanation of why this answer is correct.

PEDAGOGICAL JUSTIFICATION

The process described above differs from a traditional quiz only in the introduction of a counterpoint and second answer attempt. However, the potential learning dividend for this relatively simple change is significant. Double-jeopardy quizzes challenge students first, to arrive at an answer to a complex question only further challenged then on their initial response. To the extent that students become invested in this two-stage process, the rigor of thought brought to bear on the question leads to a more thorough appreciation of the richness of the question's context. By forcing students to address issues in an unexpected way, higher learning outcomes are achieved.

OUTCOMES

The double-jeopardy quizzing technique is in pilot testing within the context of a larger effort to use information technology to reengineer a required introductory management information systems course in the Wayne Calloway School of Business and Accountancy at Wake Forest University. A formal, empirical study has been underway for approximately one year to determine the efficacy of a number of IT-based teaching and learning innovations. Students in the study's group have demonstrated a deeper understanding of subject matter addressed in the course, although a follow-up study, currently under way, is required to tease out the impact of each of several innovations that have been introduced into the course.

At present, anecdotal evidence suggests that students view double-jeopardy quizzes most favorably. Based upon solicited feedback, students perceive that the quizzes lead them to a richer understanding of the topic and that they have a better appreciation of the complexity of the context within which various events or phenomena occur. As exams approach, students make particularly heavy use of the online quizzes to review.

LESSONS LEARNED

Several commercially available course management systems, or course shells, offer online quizzing functionality. None of these tools, however, offers double-jeopardy quizzing. Fortunately, if the instructor does not wish to grade the quiz, any simple html editor will suffice. The instructor simply creates a web page showing the original question with possible answers. Each answer is hyperlinked to a separate web page that presents a counterpoint for that answer, with another listing of possible answers to the question. Each of these answers is hyperlinked to a separate web page that presents the correct answer and a thorough explanation of why it is correct.

Should the instructor wish to impose a grading scheme on these quizzes, however, a multimedia authoring tool and the associated development skills may be called for. Furthermore, the instructor must define a grading scheme. Will only the final answer be graded, or will the grade on an item composite the first and second answers? What happens to the grade for the item if the student initially selects the correct response but is then convinced through a counterpoint to commit to an incorrect response? To date, I have elected not to grade double-jeopardy quizzes in the belief that any grading scheme will preoccupy the student's mind, effectively turning the quiz into a game rather than a learning exercise. I do, however, log student responses to the quiz items for the purpose of identifying areas that are consistently problematic and therefore may warrant further attention in a class meeting.

Finally, double-jeopardy quizzes require significant time to create. Not only must a correct response and multiple foils be created, but counterpoints for each must be constructed. These counterpoints typically are one to a few sentences long and reflect careful planning of their intended effect. Finally, a relatively extensive closing expository on which answer was correct and why must be constructed. Clearly, this process is more laborious than building a simple, objective quiz. Because of this, double-jeopardy quizzes should be constructed so that they can be used repeatedly across semesters. The investment of time required for their construction precludes a use-once-and-discard approach.

REFERENCES

Chickering, A. W., & Gamson, Z. F. (1987, March). Seven principles for good practice in undergraduate education. *AAHE Bulletin 39* (7), 3-7.

McCray, G. E. (forthcoming). The hybrid course: Merging online instruction and the traditional classroom. *Information Technology and Management.*

CONTACT INFORMATION

Gordon E. McCray
BellSouth Mobility Technology Faculty Fellow
The Wayne Calloway School of Business and
    Accountancy
Wake Forest University
Box 7285, Reynolda Station
Winston-Salem, NC 27109-7285
Email: gmccray@wfu.edu

Vignette 43 Computer-Mediated Learning Protocols for Enhancing Managerial Insight

Frederick H. deB. Harris, Wake Forest University

Many discussion-based applications of the computer in the classroom have exposed students to broader and deeper perspectives, using resources external to the university. The use of computer-mediated resources in a graduate school of business has a somewhat different objective. Management decision problems seldom have uniquely correct answers. Instead, complex possible solutions involving an integration of several functional areas of management must be weighed for their strengths, weaknesses, opportunities, and threats to the company's overall business plan. Management students are therefore taught to employ systems analytical frameworks that highlight the integrative nature of management processes and isolate controllable factors. Any recommendation for action then requires an analysis of the assumptions to which the decision is particularly sensitive. The ability to distinguish good, better, or best approaches to the analysis of the problem is what charac-

terizes the most valuable members of a management team. In this teaching environment, the student's acquisition of managerial insight is of prime importance.

Carefully designed practice in analytical thinking appears to best engender the requisite insight. Business school professors therefore root out wrong approaches and facilitate the acquisition of managerial insight by the use of fact situations (elaborate examples, applications, minicases, or full-blown cases) that provide context and motivation for the study of the topic. They also facilitate student cross-learning. To find out whether attainment of these objectives could be markedly enhanced by the use of web sites, intranets, and other computer-mediated discussion formats, the author undertook a developmental pilot project with the International Thompson Publishing Company. These efforts focused on a theory-in-business context approach to the required MBA-level course in managerial economics.

DISCUSSION DATABASES

Graduate management students bring an enormous variety of work histories and experiences to the classroom. These perspectives are a potentially enormous source of commentary and facilitate student learning of managerial insight. Learning from one another reinforces the team management concept. Rather than hoarding idiosyncratic knowledge, individual managers critique one another's ideas and contribute jointly to critical analysis and to the ultimate decision. Some of this cooperative effort characterizes preclassroom preparation by the four- and five-person teams. Much of the give-and-take occurs, however, within the structured dialog elicited by the classroom instructor. To extend the time during which this team-based learning happens, students were encouraged to post questions and commentary triggered by classroom issues on an intranet.

In a recent required MBA-level class in managerial economics, two teaching assistants monitored the threads twice a day and updated the professor on any issues that warranted response. The software employed was Cold Fusion. Each student could participate in the threaded discussions either as a questioner or as a respondent. In both cases, individuals were required to identify themselves to the professor and to the class. Each night before a class, the professor reviewed the issues under discussion and incorporated those matters in the next day's lesson plans.

Activity on the threaded discussion was of two types. Students with little prior exposure to managerial economics often posted queries confirming a straightforward interpretation of recent classroom analyses. Either one of the teaching assistants or the professor or occasionally another student would respond that the proposed connection between several concepts or the proposed analogous applications were indeed correct. For this type of student, the discussion database appears to reduce anxiety.

For other students, the discussion database served its intended purpose of extending the classroom interaction. For example, students from the telecommunications industry continued the classroom debate about the satellite communications challenge to the traditional cable TV companies. As hoped, this dialog took several directions at once: 1) the extraordinarily different scale economies in satellite as opposed to traditional cable, 2) the role of exclusive contracts and their subsequent challenge in the courts, 3) the desirability of sunset clauses on the natural monopoly protection from competitors, and 4) the installation of fiberoptic cable by phone companies desiring to compete directly in the TV and Internet access markets. In addition, some students went beyond the final exam and posted commentaries about the new signal compression technology that enables cable companies to transmit data and video over twisted pair copper wire. Both the breadth and depth of this discussion realized many of the ambitious objectives of the discussion database.

FULLY INTEGRATED COURSE-TEXT WEB SITE

The author/professor and textbook publisher of *Managerial Economics: Applications, Strategy, and Tactics,* (McGuigan, Moyer, & Harris, 1999) created an extensive web site to support the course. Students had Internet access to all their preparation questions and to the assigned reading from the text. The intent was to offer the text to students in a computer-mediated environment that mirrored the way professors use the material in a graduate business school classroom. Business students read applications that incorporate the learning issues and concepts from past sessions and raise questions motivating the next analytical topic. A learning protocol that could incorporate the role of motivating fact situations in management decision problems offers a new application of computer-mediated instruction.

Each session of the online syllabus was organized around "before class" and "in class" tabs. The former outlined the textbook material by section heading and served as a quick search index of the topics in the textbook. In addition, each preparation question was hotlinked to the relevant sections of the textbook. In this way, the reading assignment was ordered in accordance with the planned use of the reading material in the next class session. In preparation, the students could also examine the professor's session outline, which identified those tables and diagrams that would be referred to during the subsequent class. These materials were hotlinked from the session outline to the appropriate passages in the text.

Perhaps the greatest value-adding aspect of the web site was the creation of a new learning protocol. Upon accessing the in class tab, students were presented with the minicase that would open the class discussion session. These fact situations appear in the text sometimes as a chapter opening "Managerial Challenge" but at other times as one of 258 boxed applications embedded throughout the chapter. For students to know in advance what application was going to be used as a class-opening motivation for the new analysis allowed more focused preparation on the new material. Discussion in class could then proceed more quickly to sophisticated issues in the choice of analytical method and the execution of the analysis itself. Often, new analytical methods would be required to address the questions raised by the motivating minicase, and students were more curious and more eager to learn the new techniques or perspectives because of the demand for the topic built up by the web site minicase.

Since in class provided students access to the session outlines and hotlinks back into the assigned reading, some students would pursue the new analytical techniques in depth before class. Perhaps for this reason, questions in class were seldom about misunderstandings and requests for clarification. Instead, they were more typically about connections to analogous situations, perspectives on other knowledge acquired recently in other courses, or the fundamental insight of the new analysis. This web site-based learning protocol therefore achieved its objectives: enhancing the learning of theory in business context.

Why A "Theory-in-Context" Approach?

Along a continuum of pedagogical methods from abstract theory lecturing at one extreme to case teaching at the other, applications-based analysis fits squarely in the middle. Conceptual frameworks based on microeconomic theory provide the ever-present skeleton on which students should hang their new analytical skills and insights as they develop. However, in the natural progression in any microeconomics or managerial economics course from simpler to more complex theory, new theory is always motivated, first, by a context and then explained within a real-world business application. This theory-in-context approach brings theory to bear on relevant situations. The objective is to have the facts fit the theory on not merely one or two but five, eight, or even 12 dimensions. In this way, real-world applications come alive at the right moment to support the maximum learning.

Theory-in-context not only stimulates student interest at the inception of the learning process, but also promotes mastery of more challenging analytical tools. The students' understanding and critical reasoning skills are markedly enhanced when complex analytical tools are learned in an appropriate factual context. Best practices today require rigorous analysis but also sophisticated insight. Like case-based exercises, teaching analytical reasoning in a complex fact situation much facilitates the acquisition of student insight. To highlight the importance of analysis plus insight, the author often identifies for students fundamental insights of microeconomics. Finally and perhaps most importantly, the theory-in-context approach empowers students to spot analogous real-world situations and apply appropriate tools and insights outside of the classroom and beyond the final exam. When combined with professors as very active facilitators in the classroom and take-home assignments that challenge students to actually make a decision, this theory-in-context approach allows the coursework to progress further and reach the best practices that students and employers seek.

REFERENCE

McGuigan, J., Moyer, C. R., & Harris, F. H. deB. (1999). *Managerial economics* (8th ed.). Cincinnati, OH: International Thompson.

CONTACT INFORMATION

Frederick H. Harris, Professor
Babcock Graduate School of Management
Wake Forest University
P. O. Box 7659, Reynolda Station
Winston-Salem, NC 27109
Email: rickharris@mail.mba.wfu.edu

Vignette 44 The Studio Experience: Educational Reform in Instructional Technology

Lloyd P. Rieber, University of Georgia

INTRODUCTION

Our departmental faculty took advantage of a unique opportunity—the decision at the University of Georgia to convert from quarters to semesters in the fall of 1998—to reconceptualize our graduate curriculum in educational multimedia design in a way that we feel is more consistent with what we know about learning and closer to what our students will encounter upon graduation. We refer to our new curriculum as the "studio experience," because it borrows, at least metaphorically, from studio models historically found in schools of art and architecture. A brief overview of our studio experience is offered in this short vignette. More information as well as several detailed papers can be found at our web site (http://itech1.coe.uga.edu /studio).

IDEAS BEHIND OUR DESIGN

Two theoretical frameworks have guided our thinking and teaching. First, faculty in our department have generally held a constructivist perspective on teaching and learning. This perspective has philosophical and pedagogical implications beyond the scope of this vignette (see, for example, Jonassen, 1991) but, briefly, is based on several core ideas: 1) learning is an active and controllable process in which each individual constructs meaning, 2) learning is also a social activity founded on collaboration and respect for different viewpoints, and 3) learning is embedded in the building of works that are shared and critiqued by peers.

Second, we have been strongly influenced by the theory of situated cognition and its application in the cognitive apprenticeships and scaffolding (Brown, Collins, & Duguid, 1989). This point of view stresses that learning is best achieved through activities embedded in authentic and meaningful contexts. Scaffolding acknowledges that as individuals progress in their skill and experience, they require less structure and guidance. Just as a construction worker uses a scaf-

fold to support the building of a stone archway and then removes it once the arch can stand on its own, so a teacher provides additional support to learning in its early stages, gradually to remove the support as students gain expertise.

REDESIGN OF OUR CURRICULUM ACCORDING TO A STUDIO MODEL

The studio experience now comprises one-third of our students' coursework taken toward a master's degree. Under our team-taught studio approach, students at various levels of experience and skill with design techniques and tools collaborate and learn from each other in the context of authentic projects. Our students learn about design in general and instructional design while gaining more and more technical skills in authoring and multimedia software tools in a very social, both formal and informal setting. The most and least experienced students and faculty from all the studio courses meet and work together from day one. Mentoring is a big part of the studio, and we use all technological means to foster communication and collaboration, including email, the World Wide Web, and course tools, such as WebCT.

We refer to the first of our studio courses (EDIT 6190) as the "constructionist" course, based on the ideas of Seymour Papert (1991). Constructionism shares the philosophical goals of constructivism but under the assumption that learning is achieved through the building of works to be shared in a public forum. This approach can be summarized as "learning by building." Students read the professional design literature, learn a variety of authoring and multimedia tools, and design/develop a personally relevant and meaningful project. They complete one set of contracts to learn certain tools and another set of contracts for completing an independent project. A significant part of this course is reflection about design. Written reflections, tied to the literature, accompany the contracts.

We also strongly encourage design conversations and desktop critiques of developing projects. Students in this course propose the criteria for evaluating their independent projects and negotiate them with faculty. The second studio course (EDIT 6200) also involves an independent project, but it must meet instructional design criteria. The project must be web based and significantly interactive.

The final studio course (EDIT 6210) involves completion of a substantial educational multimedia team project.

LESSONS LEARNED

Coteaching is difficult. Each instructor must be open to different teaching styles, work habits, and management. One unexpected advantage of team teaching is that it becomes a means for faculty development. Faculty get the opportunity to see their colleagues in action and to pick up skills and knowledge.

We are just beginning to learn how to tap the most important mentoring resource—other students. There has been a natural and steady increase in students relying on other students for information and skill development. The studio experience seems to facilitate the informal mentoring that always happens, but we have been able to formalize it in various ways. For example, our students are required to provide at least ten hours of service to nonprofit groups. Some perform their service in schools or other community centers, but many choose to perform it in the studio. Experienced students are free to offer workshops and seminars and to lead online discussions of the studio readings, and they get service credit for doing so. We also now require experienced students to counsel students just starting the course. Also, as students take advantage of the opportunity to learn tools that they feel are most relevant to their needs, they, not the faculty, are becoming the studio experts. This has the positive result of decreasing the need for faculty to become jacks-of-all-trades.

It takes time for students to get accustomed to the studio model. There are clearly different expectations, roles, and responsibilities than they have previously experienced in their formal schooling. We all bring our own teaching and learning myths to an educational setting, and it is unsettling when we are asked to put many of our preconceived notions aside.

CONCLUSION

The studio experience as conceived and implemented at the University of Georgia is designed to practice what most professors of instructional technology preach. We are trying to prepare the next generation of multimedia designers, developers, and teachers by modeling an approach that is consistent with what we know about learning and performing in schools and the workplace. Admittedly, our approach is far from perfect, and we still must work within a system that best understands the one-course/one-instructor model. It would be presumptuous to think our efforts have turned the Titanic around, but we think we have at least nudged it toward warmer waters.

REFERENCES

Brown, J. S., Collins, A., & Duguid, P. (1989). Situated cognition and the culture of learning. *Educational Researcher, 18* (1), 32-42.

Jonassen, D. (1991). Objectivism versus constructivism: Do we need a new philosophical paradigm? *Educational Technology Research and Development, 39* (3), 5-14.

Papert, S. (1991). Situating constructionism. In I. Harel & S. Papert, (Eds.), *Constructionism*, (pp. 1-11). Norwood, NJ: Ablex.

CONTACT INFORMATION

Lloyd P. Rieber
604 Aderhold Hall
University of Georgia
Athens, GA 30602-7144
Email: lrieber@coe.uga.edu
WWW: http://itun1.coe.uga.edu/Fowlty/lprieber
    http://www.nowhereroad.com
Phone: (706) 542-3986
Fax: (706) 542-4032

Vignette 45 One Recipe for Success: Computers in Education

Don Lewicki, University of Pittsburgh

Teaching technology skills to students is much like teaching culinary skills. Students challenged to use technology often ask for an instruction sheet, the equivalent of a recipe. Similarly, there are many fine cooks in the world who can follow the recipe for any dish. Unfortunately, they are limited to cooking only the dishes they have in their recipe file. In terms of cooking, the ultimate is to be a great chef, like Julia Child. These chefs can create great dishes, because they understand the interactions of basic ingredients—how ingredients can be combined to create new and exotic flavors that are ever-pleasing to the palate. I have told my students that, at a minimum, they want to be technology cooks. They have to understand basic recipes to get work done. The ultimate goal, though, is to be a technology chef.

I relayed this analogy to my Computers in Education class—12 students preparing to become primary and secondary education teachers. Most were nontraditional students, and many were frightened by the prospect of coming face-to-face with the computer, including one student who had never been on the Internet. We met once a week for a three-hour session split into equal parts of classroom and computer lab time. In addition, we were pilot users of a new web-based software system called CourseInfo.

IDEAS BEHIND THE COURSE DESIGN

I prepared the course hoping to achieve the following general outcomes:

1) Students would obtain a basic, extendable set of technology skills (appetizer).

2) Students would be able to use technology effectively to enhance their own students' learning experience (entrée).

3) Students would be motivated to learn more about technology (dessert).

I decided to pursue a very immersive and collaborative learning environment. Assignments were defined in terms applicable to the students' future teaching as-signments and content areas. I felt that it was also imperative to convey basic technology concepts in a clear, concise manner and to make a concerted effort to avoid technobabble.

COURSE ACTIVITIES

Technology usage was intentionally overemphasized. Students were exposed to and used a variety of technologies during the course including:

Online Threaded Discussions

I used this facility in two ways. A general question topic was set up where students could ask questions relating to homework assignments, grading, test preparation, and so on. If one student had a general question, it was likely that others had the same one. I asked my students to check the general question topic first to see if their question was already answered before posting to that topic. A very nice side effect is that a Frequently Asked Questions (FAQ) document can be built. I also posted topics for discussion as an assignment on a regular basis. The discussions ended one week after they were posted, and students were encouraged to access the discussion more than once during the week.

Paperless Materials and Assignments

I placed all class materials, including the syllabus and PowerPoint lecture slides, in CourseInfo. Students could view them online and print out the materials when they had time or when they needed to reference them. I also required all written assignments to be completed in Microsoft Word. Students used the digital drop-box feature of CourseInfo to send me their assignments electronically. I then would read them into Word, imbed comments, grade them, and send them back in similar fashion.

Computerized Quizzes

I used CourseInfo's online quiz capability to administer lab quizzes to the students on a weekly basis. The quizzes were used to reinforce basic concepts and facts. I used a multiple-choice answer format that allowed CourseInfo to immediately grade the quiz. Feedback to the students was instantaneous. Students could then review incorrect answers as well as see their grade.

Recorded PowerPoint Presentations

Rather than just doing in-class presentations using PowerPoint, students worked on a group project that extended their skills beyond the basic composition of presentations. Students used the recorded narrative option within PowerPoint and composed a 20-minute presentation. After recording the narrative, a plug-in program was used to package the presentation, including narrative, for delivery and replay over the Internet. Not only did this reinforce and extend PowerPoint skills, but students also realized that this technique could be used to practice delivery of their own lessons to students. In addition, students found this exercise extremely helpful in understanding how audio and video could be transmitted over the Internet. Students also were given time in front of a web camera to do a visual self-evaluation of their presentation skills.

Web Scavenger Hunt

In order to reinforce web-searching skills, I put together a web scavenger hunt that was tailored to content areas suitable for teachers. Questions ranged from finding specific lesson plans to finding an interactive dissection of a frog. Students realized that the hunt could be adapted to their own teaching environment.

Student Web Pages

Although CourseInfo provided its own built-in web page capability, I did not use this function due to its limited support and primitive user interface. I taught the students Netscape Composer, a what-you-see-is-what-you-get (WYSIWYG) web page editor. Students' home pages included an online resume and a page of links that they found useful in their area of teaching, much of which was based on the results of the web scavenger hunt. Students also included links to the PowerPoint presentations that they posted to the Internet. The result of this exercise was a home page link that each student could include in his/her own resume. In essence, I made my students build a small-scale electronic portfolio, tying together much of what they learned in class.

Software Downloads

Students downloaded evaluation copies of educational software and were required to evaluate them.

Lesson Plans

The final project was to submit a set of five lesson plans that incorporated aspects of what they learned in the course. Many of these were quite creative.

MEASURED RESULTS

Student evaluations of the course exceeded my expectations. Over 70% of the students responded that they learned either "somewhat more" or "much more" than in other courses they have taken. The remainder answered "about the same." An even better response breakdown was noted to the question regarding the "amount of increased interest in the subject": over 80% answered "somewhat more" or "much more." The overall response to the question about "instructor's overall teaching effectiveness" was well above average. All students responded to the criteria "teacher interpreted difficult concepts clearly" with either "to a considerable degree" or "to a very high degree." I felt the responses to these questions as well as the positive written feedback supported the learning outcomes that I wished to achieve.

LESSONS LEARNED

Practice What You Preach

During the early part of the course, I repeatedly told the students to be prepared for technological failures. I did not listen to my own advice. The Internet did not cooperate at critical times, and hardware failures did occur. I was left scrambling to compensate in response to these problems. I also found that practicing lessons on my home computer was not the proper way to prepare for demonstrating technology in a public computer lab. Because machines were locked down in the lab, some software that worked properly on my own computer did not work properly in the lab. Virus software protection also played a key role in preventing some Internet-based demonstrations from properly working initially.

Read and Respond to Email Often

I found that email was most effective as a communication tool, if the time between a question and response was well within one day. If I did not respond in timely fashion, then students tended to move away from using email and instead began to track me down. I therefore checked my email faithfully at the start and end of each day with frequent checks in between.

Prodding Helps

Students initially used discussion boards as a single response mechanism to a specific topic. Students needed to be prodded into viewing the board often.

Use CourseInfo

Overall, students were happy with the CourseInfo tool. They liked the online quiz feature and immediate feedback that it provided. The least successful feature of CourseInfo was the drop-box feature. The students viewed the interface as clumsy. I also felt that the facility would be too awkward to use with large classes.

Stress the Visual

I constantly told students not to panic when trying to do something with software that they were not shown how to do. I repeatedly told them to look for visual cues—an icon, a button, or highlighted text. As we proceeded through the course, I tried to focus their ef-forts on the commonality of the software look and feel. This approach seemed to work. The students' Microsoft PowerPoint software skills were self-taught after they had learned the user interface of other Microsoft Office products.

CONCLUSION

Despite the fact that I burned dinner a few times, I felt that my students learned more than the basic recipes and gained insight on using technology effectively in their classrooms. In the end, my students combined basic ingredients and created their own menu of technological dishes to serve to their own students.

CONTACT INFORMATION

Don Lewicki
Assistant Professor of Business Management
University of Pittsburgh, Bradford
300 Campus Drive
Bradford, PA 16701
Email: lewicki@imap.pitt.edu
Phone: (814) 362-0988
Fax: (814) 362-7684

**Curtis J. Bonk, Robert B. Fischler, and Charles R. Graham,
Indiana University, Bloomington**

The SmartWeb is a web course developed over the past three years to teach introductory educational psychology to preservice teachers at Indiana University. Course enrollment has ranged from 20 to 30 students each semester (see SmartWeb homepage at http://www.indiana.edu/~SmartWeb). Undergraduate educational psychology covers theory, research, and applications related to human learning and development, cognition, motivation, classroom management, individual differences, instructional design, special education, and assessment and evaluation. Students in this class sign up for a three-credit class plus a corequisite two-credit early field experience and laboratory course. The web version of this course is typically taken by music majors, returning adult students, and students interested in integrating technology in their future teaching practices. Most are residential students, allowing some live meeting times at the start and end of the course.

SOCIOCULTURAL FRAMEWORK

In designing this course, we were curious how recent research on the sociocultural context of learning might affect student thinking and learning in a web environment. We were also drawn to research on how computer conferencing tools might raise student social interaction and dialog, meaning-making, and social construction of knowledge. After a series of research studies and classroom tests related to various conferencing tools (Bonk & King, 1998; Bonk, Malikowski, Angela, & East, 1998), it became important to experiment with teaching an entire course online, not just the discussion groups.

Six months prior to designing this course, the first author wrote a book chapter on web-based instruction that detailed ten potentially useful instructional techniques for each of the following three areas: creative thinking, critical thinking, and cooperative learning (Bonk & Reynolds, 1997). Most of the ideas described in that particular manuscript were eventually embedded in the SmartWeb. It was interesting that many

scholars at that time were debating how to best teach educational psychology, but few, if any, mentioned the role of technology. Nevertheless, computer conferencing and collaborative writing tools offered many opportunities for extending class discussion, structuring role play, linking preservice teachers to mentors, providing exam preparation, interacting with guest expert teachers, exploring personally meaningful topics with peers, and working on small group projects. Such activities paralleled ideas made by educational psychologists advocating constructivist and active learning frameworks (Anderson et al., 1995).

COURSE DESIGN FOCUS

We did not develop the SmartWeb without a plan. In fact, we embedded a set of specific learning principles in this course that were intended to create a thoughtful learning community. The focus on this course included the following 14 key principles.

1) **Writing as a medium for thinking.** All SmartWeb activities involve some form of writing. Students are involved in reflective writing, online debating, journaling, summary writing, chapter discussions, and freewriting.

2) **Social cognition and audience awareness.** A web class affords many possible authentic audiences beyond the class. In fact, peers, graduate students, and instructors from universities around the world often mentor SmartWeb students.

3) **Social interaction.** Since all learning must first take place on a social plane, the SmartWeb was designed with interactive commenting features.

4) **Mentoring and scaffolded learning.** The web offers the possibility for expert, peer, and instructor mentoring at any time and any place. Scaffolded support or guidance can be gradually removed as students acquire new competencies.

5) **Multiple perspectives.** Weekly role play, case debate activities, and international discussion forums are specifically designed to elicit different viewpoints during online discussions.

6) **Cognitive apprenticeship.** The web provides a vehicle for linking theory to classroom observations, thereby allowing students to see how classroom concepts and ideas are actually applied in the real world.

7) **Intersubjectivity and common ground.** In building a learning community, shared knowledge among participants is needed.

8) **Choice and variety.** Students have many types of SmartWeb tasks from which to demonstrate their competencies. Most of these tasks include alternative activities or choices.

9) **Guided exploration.** The web can be used as a tool for exploration and creative discovery. Though personal exploration is valued, students are also given starting points and tips on how to find useful web resources and information.

10) **Reflection.** Becoming a professional teacher requires constant reflection on instructional ideas and approaches.

11) **Generation of knowledge or creative thinking.** Brainstorming activities, case creations, metaphorical thinking tasks, role-play situations, and various top ten lists help students to generate knowledge for the class.

12) **Evaluation of knowledge and critical thinking.** Once knowledge is generated, the focus shifts to critical evaluation. Critical thinking techniques used here include ranking brainstormed ideas, listing pros and cons of teaching methods, comparing and contrasting field experiences to text-related concepts and ideas, evaluating web sites, completing and interpreting Venn diagrams, writing weekly chapter summaries, and discussing key points.

13) **Cooperative and collaborative learning.** As exhibited by learning team activities and email pals, a central focus within the SmartWeb is on how to facilitate student interaction and teamwork.

14) **Portfolio assessment.** Grading of student work is based on multiple tasks and cognitive dimensions as well as growth in the course.

SmartWeb Tools and Course Activities

Activities based on the above principles were specifically designed to foster learning in a sociocultural framework. At the most basic level, students are responsible for two types of activities (see Figure 46.1). First of all, student weekly SmartWeb chapter activities must be posted by 8 a.m. each Wednesday. This is the individual side of the class. Second, students must complete their chapter and field reflection discussions by 8 a.m. on Fridays, using the computer conferencing tool called COW (Conferencing on the Web) or, more recently, WebCrossing in the INSITE web site from Houghton Mifflin Company, discussed later. Computer conferencing represents the social side of the course. Some of the SmartWeb tools and activities are listed below.

Student Profiles
To promote community membership, students are asked to fill out their personal profile on the SmartWeb, which lists their major, email address, web home page, computer background, interests and hobbies, strengths and weaknesses, and hometown. Students can comment on each other's profiles, indicating what they have in common. There is also a digitized picture of the class taken during the initial live class meeting, in case students want to know what their classmates look like.

Student Portfolio
Student work from the weekly chapter assignments is appended to their individual portfolios. Since these portfolios are publicly viewable by instructors, peers, and SmartWeb guests, each student uses an avatar name (for example, Yoda or Spock) to secure confidentiality. Portfolios are dynamically updated as students complete their work. In addition, they may be reviewed or printed at any time during the semester.

Comment on a Portfolio

Peers, instructors, and outside guests can post a response in any student portfolio related to weekly SmartWeb chapter work. In fact, every student in the course has a designated email pal (or "critical friend") who provides weekly portfolio feedback, thereby lessening the workload on the instructor, while giving students fairly prompt feedback. Occasionally, graduate students respond to the undergraduates as part of their coursework.

Web Assignment Posting Chart

A complete listing of all student SmartWeb work and associated feedback is provided in the Web Assignment Posting Chart. This tool provides students and instructors with an overview of who have posted their work and received feedback on it. All work is hyperlinked to particular weeks and students.

Student Web Link Suggestions

Tools exist in the SmartWeb for students and the instructor to make web link suggestions that extend course resources. Importantly, students must provide justification for any web link that they recommend. To foster additional critical thinking and analyses, we recently added a rating and commenting option in the web link suggestions area.

Starter-Wrapper Chapter Discussions

Instead of using the web to post instructor lectures, a student, the designated starter, will read the chapter or set of articles prior to the rest of the class and summarize the content early in the week. Students then discuss the chapter as participants or within roles, for example, coach, devil's advocate, optimist, pessimist, or questioner. At the end of the week, a student acts as wrapper to summarize the discussion. The instructor serves as a second wrapper, who not only describes the key course issues brought up that week, but may also

FIGURE 46.1

SMARTWEB BASIC COMPONENTS

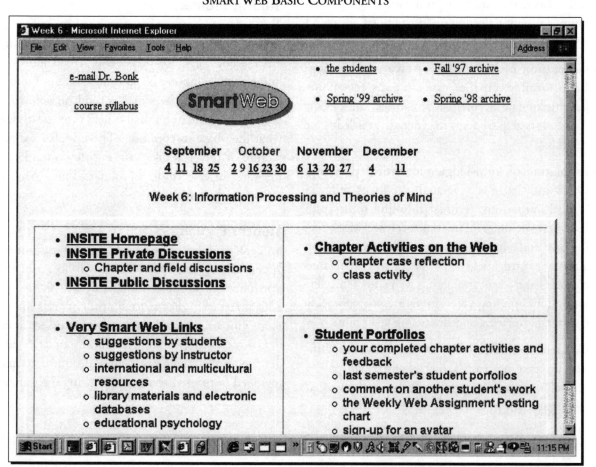

extend the discussion to key areas that the class failed to adequately address. In the past, we have used tools like COW, WebCrossing, and FirstClass for these starter-wrapper discussions.

Field Reflections

Instead of live meetings for students to practice teaching and to discuss their field observations, our students reflect on their teaching experiences in small groups on the web. For this assignment, the instructor provides the focusing questions or issues related to concepts from the week's readings. The students take those questions with them to the field. Students also must post web reflections for their volunteer or "service teaching" activities.

SmartWeb Small Group Activities

Working in small groups of four to five, students must electronically summarize Perkin's "Smart Schools" book. Each student is responsible for reading and summarizing different chapters. He or she must present his or her understanding of the concepts from this book and other self-selected readings during a final live presentation of their own Smarter School to the entire class.

Student Case Discussions

As part of their early field experience coursework, students reflect on their field observations by writing two case situations or problems on the web, leaving all school, teacher, and student names anonymous. They must also reply to the case posts of six to eight peers during the semester. Students and instructors from other universities and countries, such as Finland, Korea, and Peru, have also generated cases and replied to our students. We have relied on the free computer conferencing tool called COW for these posts.

The Caseweb

The Caseweb (http://www.indiana.edu/~caseweb) contains 40 cases in educational psychology that were originally generated by undergraduate students based on actual field experiences in Indiana schools. We rewrote these cases and then added introductions and questions before posting them to the web. All Caseweb cases are linked to an electronic bulletin board for discussion. These cases are currently used as quizzes and

discussion topics by instructors from various universities around the world.

The Café Latte

A café was created in our computer conference to help foster a sense of a learning community in the SmartWeb. Besides initial introductions, students can submit comments or raise issues in the café, while the instructor can post examples or summary lists of commendable student work or ideas.

Administrivia

The administrivia area is a preset topic in the computer conference for the instructor to post reminders to students about assignments, due dates, project team members, email pals, and weekly discussion starters and wrappers.

Based on our SmartWeb tools and activities, we recently worked with Houghton Mifflin to develop a more advanced web site called INSITE. INSITE is available for any educational psychology professor using the textbook *Psychology Applied to Teaching* (Snowman, Biehler, & Bonk, 2000) This web site contains sections related to 1) course resources, 2) field experiences, 3) class applications, and 4) sharing knowledge and experience. In INSITE, there are journal-reflection questions, class activities, semester projects, PowerPoint slides, self-test questions, field-observation questions, sample cases, technology citations and demonstrations, chapter themes, web links, sample lesson plans, debates, and other informational items and activities (see http://www.hmco.com/college/education/insite). Faculty and student development sections in INSITE list web links related to the further improvement of college teaching and student study skills.

What really makes INSITE unique is the opportunity for student and instructor sharing and collaboration. Most of the sharing takes place in the "Contributions Corner" of the instructor and student spaces. For instance, an instructor might become a contributor by posting a personal profile, listing the web location of his or her class syllabus, making a web link suggestion for a particular chapter, or posting stories relating how he or she teaches a certain section or chapter of the class. While INSITE is limited to educational psychology classrooms, in a new web environment, Courseshare.com, we are extending the collaboration and sharing tools to any higher education instructor or domain.

SOME RESULTS

We have conducted both qualitative and quantitative research related to this course. A few of our findings are listed below.

1) By using computer conferencing for chapter discussions and field reflections, students are required to read the comments of their peers in order to post relevant comments. As a result, many of our students claim that, unlike large-section college classes, they cannot sleep in a web class.

2) Student case quality and depth is increased as we add more participants from other countries to our discussions.

3) Undergraduate students need extensive task-structuring and rewards for task completion, such as points, or they will often fail to participate.

4) Students feel that the case discussions helped them connect real-life scenarios to concepts mentioned in the book, while providing multiple professional sources of feedback.

5) Students are attracted to familiar topics, controversial scenarios, interesting titles, and topics on which they have an opinion. While controversy spurs the most heated discussion, students are typically too nice to one another on the web. Returning adult students often are less afraid to state their perspectives and spark class discussion and debate.

6) Peer feedback is appreciated but usually not too deep, while mentor and instructor feedback is typically valued, pointed, motivating, and aimed at a higher level of discourse.

7) Direct instruction and modeling play a more limited role on the web, while feedback, social acknowledgment, task structuring, scaffolded advice, and questioning rise in importance in terms of useful online teaching approaches.

8) Students generally find conferencing tools like COW and WebCrossing easy to use. However, during the first few weeks of a web course, they are anxious and confused by the new types of tasks that they encounter on the web.

9) There is minimal off-task behavior in a web course; students are extremely task-focused. Ironically, to form a learning community, we may need technology tools that help pull students off-task once in a while.

10) Undergraduate student comments on the web too often lack justification and connections to their textbook. Specific instructions to link comments to concepts and pages from their text or other resources definitely help.

Adjustments Made

We have made numerous pedagogical and technological changes to the SmartWeb since August 1997. On the technological side, we added tools for increasing student social interaction on the web, including various commenting and rating features within student profiles, portfolios, and web suggestions. Equally important, we added the capability to notify students that their work was posted or feedback received. Along these same lines, email confirmation of student posts as well as posting indicators at the top of student portfolios, effectively lowers student anxiety. In addition, after various complaints from students who did not appreciate being given an avatar name (especially a young woman who, rightfully, did not want to be called Jaba by her classmates), our team created a simple tool for students to select their own avatar name from a list of 35 to 40 available names. We also created the summary Web Assignment Posting Chart, mentioned earlier, and made links to prior student work. Prior work is not only a useful classroom legacy and archive, it also provides numerous task examples and model answers for new students. In the future, we would like to explore links between video conferencing and web technologies, enhance case-based learning technologies, and develop new tools for role play and debate.

On the pedagogical side, we have continually tried to simplify the course tools and use different forms of assessment. We have moved away from collaborative, multiple-choice quizzes to using Caseweb cases as quizzes. Another important new course feature has involved allocating significant participation points during the first three weeks of the class. As a result, students receive early feedback from the instructor on how well they are doing, while having an incentive to test out all the required course features. In this way, students should recognize system or computer problems before getting too far behind in their coursework. As a means of reducing student dropouts in the course, which have ranged from 5% to 25%, students now have more choices on assignments and flexibility in due dates. The pedagogical future of the web is simultaneously bright and uncertain. To add some light, we would like to develop online mentoring guides, success stories, and additional vehicles for international online collaboration.

The SmartWeb has been an ideal forum for experimenting with new technology tools and pedagogical ideas for online learning. It has been both extremely fun and challenging. These are exciting times! While with each SmartWeb improvement, our team learns more about web-based teaching and learning, we also hope that our preservice teachers are getting smarter on the SmartWeb, too!

ACKNOWLEDGMENTS

We would like to thank Karen Hallett and the Instructional Technology Office in Educational Technology Services within the School of Education at Indiana University for their valuable help with development of the SmartWeb. We also want to thank Steve Malikowski for his assistance in using COW for class discussions. Along these same lines, we are grateful for help from Sun Myung Lee for enhancements to the SmartWeb (http://www.indiana.edu/~SmartWeb) and Noriko Hara for her creation of the Caseweb (http://www.indiana.edu/~caseweb). Finally, Brian Winchester, Director of the Center for Global Change at Indiana University, is recognized here for his support in obtaining an Instructional Technology Pilot Project grant to add international components to the SmartWeb (US Department of Education Grant 5-6264-4211151).

REFERENCES

Anderson, L. M., Blumenfeld, P., Pintrich, P. R., Clark, C. M., Marx, R. W., & Peterson, P. (1995). Educational psychology for teachers: Reforming our courses, rethinking our roles. *Educational Psychologist, 30* (3), 143-158.

Bonk, C. J., & King, K. S. (Eds.). (1998). *Electronic collaborators: Learner-centered technologies for literacy, apprenticeship, and discourse.* Hillsdale, NJ: Erlbaum.

Bonk, C. J., Malikowski, S., Angeli, C., & East, J. (1998). Web-based case conferencing for preservice teacher education: Electronic discourse from the field. *Journal of Educational Computing Research, 19* (3), 267-304.

Bonk, C. J., & Reynolds, T. H. (1997). Learner-centered web instruction for higher-order thinking, teamwork, and apprenticeship. In B. H. Khan (Ed.), *Web-based instruction.* Englewood Cliffs, NJ: Educational Technology Publications.

Perkins, D. (1992). *Smart schools: Better thinking and learning for every child.* New York, NY: Free Press.

Snowman, J., Bieler, R. F., & Bonk, C. H. (2000). *Psychology applied to teaching* (9th ed.). Boston, MA: Houghton Mifflin.

CONTACT INFORMATION

Curtis J. Bonk, Associate Professor
Department of Counseling and Educational Psychology
Indiana University
School of Education, Room 4022
Bloomington, IN 47405-1006
Email: cjbonk@indiana.edu
Home Page: http://php.indiana.edu/~cjbonk
Course URL: http://www.indiana.edu/~SmartWeb

Leah P. McCoy, Wake Forest University

The project described here is a capstone course requirement for all master's students in a graduate teacher education program. Each student carries out the individual reflective process of planning, producing, and presenting an electronic portfolio that represents his or her philosophy of teaching. This is an active, student-centered approach to technology use: Students are the technology users, and the instructor is a guide and facilitator. Since it was implemented four years ago, the project has been continuously evaluated and refined.

THEORETICAL FRAMEWORK

The goal of the portfolio project is to facilitate reflection in the students, who have recently completed student teaching experiences and are about to begin their first year of teaching. Based on a constructivist orientation, we want them to consider their experiences and their beliefs and to produce a portfolio that describes and illustrates their teaching philosophy in detail. This approach is in agreement with the definition of Lee Schulman (1998), a strong advocate of teacher portfolios, who calls the portfolio process a theory-building act. Lyons (1999) suggests that the portfolio may become a scaffold for new teacher professionalism. Portfolio assessment is recommended for all teacher education students (NCATE, 1997). The real value of this project is in the personal reflection and articulation process, and the product itself is a communication tool and a model for our authentic assessment of their success in our program.

The portfolio organization is based on the Interstate New Teacher Assessment and Support Consortium standards, INTASC (CCSSO, 1999). These ten core standards are used by several states in evaluating beginning teachers and provide a comprehensive yet flexible framework. We experimented with the National Board for Professional Teaching standards (NBPTS, 1999) but decided that they were more suited to experienced teachers. In brief, the ten IN-TASC standards address the following:

- Subject matter
- Learning and development
- Diverse learners
- Instructional strategies
- Motivation and behavior
- Communication
- Planning and curriculum
- Assessment
- Professional growth
- Relationships with colleagues, parents, and community

Students are required to produce a fully narrated CD-ROM that includes a section for each of the ten INTASC standards. They state their beliefs and present multimedia materials to support and to illustrate their implementation of these beliefs during their student teaching. They also include on the CD an electronic Artifact Folder that contains a resume and documents relating to each of the ten standards (see McCoy, 1999 for the complete online description and requirements). Students are encouraged to plan thoroughly and to select materials that represent their own interpretations and beliefs.

For example, INTASC Principle #3 states, "The teacher understands how students differ in their approaches to learning and creates instructional opportunities that are adapted to diverse learners." One student teacher of English included in this section his statement of his belief/interpretation, a video of a group presenting a project to write an advertisement for a new candy bar, several photos of students working in groups on the floor or alone at a desk, and photos of students watching movie versions of novels. He also included in the Artifact folder several lesson plans illustrating varied instructional methods and a scanned note from a parent thanking him for giving additional after school assistance to her son.

Another important component of the portfolio process is a public presentation. We require that each student present the portfolio in an exit interview to a committee of two department of education faculty and one local public school administrator. This format emphasizes the professional nature of the project and allows the committee of three to evaluate the product and to question the student further.

TECHNICAL CONSIDERATIONS

Our department computer lab has IBM computers, and two are equipped with video capture cards for converting videotape images to digital data. We also have scanners for capturing digital still pictures and two digital cameras that students can check out. All computers have microphones for sound recording. Our solution for storage of large amounts of video, audio, and graphic data during the production period was to obtain additional student space on our university LAN server. Students could access these files at any time from any lab computer, work on them, and then resave to the server account. When the project was complete, each student burned two CDs, one for department files and one for his or her personal use.

The project presentation used PowerPoint software, which allows the narration of the entire slide show. We manipulated the digital video with Adobe Premier and the graphic images with Paint Shop Pro. The Artifact folder was a separate file on the CD-ROM and was produced in html with Dreamweaver.

OUTCOMES

There are four major outcomes of this electronic portfolio process.

1) Students reflect on their beliefs and experiences and develop a comprehensive representation of their philosophy of education.

2) Students take away a product to share with prospective employers.

3) Students refine and develop their technology skills.

4) The department has a means of summative assessment in an authentic context.

While current evaluation data is only anecdotal, all of these outcomes appear to be successfully achieved. Student feedback is very positive, and they verify the value of the reflective process. Students and school administrators have reported that this portfolio was a key element in hiring decisions because of both the reflective content and the demonstration of technological skills.

LESSONS LEARNED

The technical process has gone through many changes over the past four years, as technology has advanced rapidly. We have tried and discarded a number of hardware and software options. We originally had students prepare a very brief PowerPoint presentation with only text and graphics so that it would fit on a floppy disk. They used this presentation as a visual aid as they presented their project in a speech. We decided that we would rather have a stand-alone product that could be viewed without the student presenting it. We experimented with web page format in html code, Netscape Composer, and Dreamweaver, and decided that PowerPoint was more appropriate, since the presentation was inherently linear. Once we added sound and video, we tried zip disks for storage, but found that their size severely limited the amount of video. The CD-ROM format provides enough storage space for a ten- to 15-minute presentation that includes narration and video clips. We have discussed using rewriteable CDs but have not changed to that medium because of our limited CD-ROM drives. We worried about having 30 students work on only two multimedia computers. This has not been a problem, as we have 16 other computers in the lab that can be used for everything except video and CD recording. The lab is always open, and students have taken advantage of this flexibility.

We have worked with Miro video capture cards, which have served our purposes well. Students are able to follow basic directions and manipulate the digitized video in Adobe Premier. We require that students tape at least four classes during their student teaching so that they will have a variety of situations from which to choose. We have had some problems with the quality of the original videos, particularly the audio in some classrooms. One solution has been to voice over the clip, explaining what is happening. We also have used auxiliary microphones with the camcorders to provide better quality audio.

Even though all students had completed a prerequisite educational technology course where they learned the basic skills required for this project, there were technical problems and questions. Five resources were available to help students solve these problems. First, handouts that were also duplicated on a web page gave them step-by-step instructions for basic multimedia operations. Second, a web page was set up in question-and-answer format so that the instructor could share information of common interest. Third, each student subscribed to a listserv and discussed problems and solutions there. Fourth, a lab assistant was trained and available to answer basic questions. Fifth, the instructor was always available, if all other resources failed.

The major lesson learned through experience with this project was that our students could become very capable at both professional reflection and multimedia production. The process was quite personal; after an initial orientation, students met with the instructor only on an individual basis to discuss philosophical questions or technical issues. Students were actively involved, even immersed, in the process, as the entire project was self-directed. It was common to see small groups of students working together on a technical issue or discussing points of educational philosophy. We have been very pleased by the responsibility and initiative of the students as well as the outcomes.

In conclusion, this course requires that each student prepare a multimedia electronic portfolio to illustrate his or her teaching philosophy. The key elements of the project are reflection and communication of the personal philosophy. Each student makes extensive use of multimedia technology to organize and to communicate his or her personal philosophy of education.

REFERENCES

Council of Chief State School Officers (CCSSO). (1999). *The interstate new teacher assessment and support consortium (INTASC)*. Washington, DC: Author. Available: http://www.ccsso.org/intasc.html. Accessed October 1, 1999.

Lyons, N. (1999). How portfolios can shape emerging practice. *Educational Leadership, 56*(8), 63-65.

McCoy, L. P. (1999). EDU 716: Professional development seminar. Winston-Salem, NC: Wake Forest University. Available: http://www.wfu.edu/~mccoy/EDU716/. Accessed October 1, 1999.

National Board for Professional Teaching Standards (NBPTS). (1999). *National board for professional teaching standards.* Southfield, MI: Author. Available: http://www.nbpts.org/. Accessed October 1, 1999.

National Council for the Accreditation of Teacher Education (NCATE), Task Force on Technology and Teacher Education. (1997). *Technology and the new professional teacher: Preparing for the 21st century classroom.* Washington, DC: Author. Available: http://www.ncate.org/projects/tech/TECH.HTM. Accessed July 22, 1999.

Schulman, L. (1998). Teacher portfolios. In N. Lyons (Ed.), *With portfolio in hand: Validating the new teacher professionalism.* New York, NY: Teachers College Press.

CONTACT INFORMATION

Leah P. McCoy, Associate Professor
Department of Education
Wake Forest University
P. O. Box 7266, Reynolda Station
Winston-Salem, NC 27109
Email: mccoy@wfu.edu

 **Introductory Psychology: Using Technology in a Large Lecture Course**

David W. Allbritton, University of Pittsburgh

Introductory Psychology at the University of Pittsburgh is both the gateway course for the psychology major and a popular course among nonmajors. As a result, it presents an instructor with the dual challenges of large enrollments and high variability in student interest levels and abilities. How can I make myself accessible to a class of 200 students? How can I support the learning of students who are struggling with the basic concepts, while at the same time keeping the most capable and motivated students interested and engaged? Although by no means a panacea, I have found that instructional technology can provide useful tools to help meet these challenges.

My section of the course had two lecture meetings plus one recitation meeting per week, with 25 students per recitation section. The recitations were led by graduate students. Most of the students were freshmen or sophomores using the course to fulfill a general education requirement in the natural sciences. Some were also considering psychology as a potential major, while a minority already planned to major in psychology and had a high level of interest and motivation. Many students in the class were still in the process of adjusting to college life and developing effective study skills.

Most of the students had access to the Internet from home, either through direct connections in their dorm rooms or via modem for those who lived off-campus. Those who did not own a computer relied on several public computing labs located throughout the campus. The course had a web site that included a threaded discussion board, a chat client, course materials such as lecture outlines, and a class roster that provided email addresses for all students. The site was managed through Blackboard Inc.'s CourseInfo software (see http://www.blackboard.com), which has been adopted by the University of Pittsburgh to present a consistent set of tools and a consistent look and feel for course web sites. In addition, a private, password-protected web site was maintained for the exclusive use of the TAs and the instructor. This site was implemented with the free Apache web server on a spare PC in my lab, but the same functionality could be achieved using various course management packages like CourseInfo or file-sharing tools available on most networks.

IDEAS AND OBJECTIVES MOTIVATING THE COURSE DESIGN

For most of my students, this course is their first official introduction to the field, but almost all have some preconceived notions about psychology that they have acquired from media, self-help books, and popular culture. Scientific inquiry and critical evaluation of evidence do not, in general, constitute the core of these preexisting ideas of what psychology is all about. Consequently, my primary instructional objective is for students to learn to think about psychological phenomena like scientists, using critical thinking to evaluate theoretical claims and to distinguish evidence from opinion. A second major goal is for students to appreciate the relevance of psychological science and to be able to apply it to their own experiences in the real world. These two course objectives, together with my own philosophy of teaching, led to the following specific goals and ideas that I wanted to implement in the course:

- Critical thinking and scientific reasoning

- Relevance to real-world applications and experiences

- Active learning

- Collaborative learning

- Mutual respect between instructors and students

- Being accessible to students

- Developing students' information-gathering skills (using both the Internet and traditional sources)

- Developing students' study skills and their ability to organize information

COMPUTER-ENHANCED COURSE ACTIVITIES AND ASSIGNMENTS

Syllabus and Lecture Outlines on the Web

The syllabus contained links to lecture outlines for each class meeting. Students were encouraged to print out each day's outline before class to facilitate note-taking during the lecture. The outlines served two major pedagogical purposes. First, they gave students a clear picture of each lecture's structure making it easier for them to understand the material during class and at the same time modeling the skill of organizing information into a logical outline form. Second, the outlines reduced the amount of class time and students' attention that had to be devoted to low-level transcription activities, allowing more time for thinking about and discussing the material.

While making lecture outlines available can help reduce the tendency to turn students into stenographers, I was conscious of the potential negative effects of providing extremely detailed notes over the web. Also to be avoided is a room of passive observers simply reading along in a script of the day's lecture or a room of empty chairs vacated by students who see no reason to attend class because the notes are provided on the web. By varying the level of detail in the outlines and consistently leaving some important details to be filled in during class, I attempted to avoid these pitfalls.

Study Aids and Tutorials

Study guides identifying key concepts and terms were provided for each of the exams along with sample questions from previous exams and from quizzes given in the recitations. A Java-based practice test, created by a student in the class during a previous semester, was also available. In addition, web-based tutorials, a combination of material I created for the course, and links to material on other sites, were provided for some topics with which students often have difficulty.

Sources for Further Exploration

Web links directed interested students to sites where they could further explore course topics on their own through interactive demonstrations and in-depth information on particular topics. Students were occasionally required to explore one or more of these sites

in connection with writing assignments in their recitation section

Group Projects

Students in groups of four collaborated throughout the semester on a research and writing project that used web-based resources extensively. Students had to select a topic related to psychology from a current news item, formulate a hypothesis on the topic, research information relevant to the hypothesis, gather input from their classmates, and then state their conclusions. Students used a web interface to the library's periodicals indexes and journal abstracts to identify relevant sources. To gather input from classmates, each group posted a question to the class discussion board that was designed to elicit data relevant to their hypothesis. Each student was also required to respond to at least one question posed by another group. Thus, each group had a thread in the discussion board consisting of its question and the responses to it. At the end of the term, each group turned in a paper summarizing its project and gave a brief oral presentation.

The group project was designed to serve both of the primary instructional goals I had for the course—relevance and critical scientific thinking. The process of formulating a hypothesis about an issue in the news and posing a question that would elicit data rather than just opinions was intended to lead students to begin to think like scientists, at least in an informal way. This task taught students to wrestle with the question of what should count as evidence when evaluating a hypothesis. The project also contributed to the instructional goals of promoting active and collaborative learning and developing students' information-gathering skills.

CourseInfo's threaded discussion tool was the key piece of technology that made this assignment possible. It provided a structured and convenient way for 200 students to communicate with one another, exchange ideas, and keep track of the results of those interactions.

Electronic Office Hours

My previous experiments using web-based chat clients for office hours revealed that students took advantage of such opportunities only when an exam was looming. For this course, therefore, I restricted my use of CourseInfo's chat tool to a single online review session before each exam. While conducting the review session, I created and updated a Frequently Asked Questions (FAQ) file on the course web site by cutting and pasting text from the chat window. This allowed students who arrived later in the session to see what they had missed, drastically reducing the need for retyping the same answers repeatedly. These review sessions were generally held between 9 p.m. and 11 p.m. a day or two prior to an exam.

Email

Students were encouraged to contact me or the TAs by email. This not only made instructors more accessible to students, it also reduced the number of phone calls and office visits students made for trivial questions that could easily be answered over email, such as, "What was my grade on the last exam?" I also relied on email to communicate regularly with the TAs.

Private Web Site for Instructor and Teaching Assistants

In addition to the group project and occasional writing assignments, recitation activities included graded quizzes, in-class group learning exercises, and hands-on demonstrations, all of which were carried out by the TAs. For each week's recitation meeting, I needed to give the TAs detailed instructions for executing activities, materials to be handed out or used in class, and quiz questions. A password-protected web site allowed TAs to download a file containing each week's materials and instructions, linked to the entry for that week in the online recitation schedule. They then edited the materials as needed and printed them out for use in class. The private web site was also used to supply TAs with students' exam scores.

MEASURED RESULTS

Evaluations of the course design's effectiveness came from two primary sources: 1) the standardized course evaluation administered by the university for all undergraduate classes, and 2) a survey I appended to the final exam that asked specifically about students' impressions of the group project.

Few questions on the standardized evaluation directly addressed the use of technology in the course, but the evaluation did indicate that students perceived the course as a whole to be effective. The instructor's overall effectiveness was rated as "very good" or "excellent" in 90% of the responses, and over 90% said they "probably" or "definitely" would recommend both the course and the instructor to other students. Most students also rated the amount learned in the course to be "somewhat" or "much more" than in other courses at the same level (50% of students' responses) or "about the same" (45%).

Two questions on the standardized evaluation did address specific issues related to technology use and the objectives I had for the course. One question asked whether students had skipped class because of the availability of notes on the web. Most (89%) said that they rarely did so (less than 20% of the time), and only one student reported that he did so "usually" or "almost always." Another question asked students to rate how accessible the instructor was. While the majority of responses indicated students thought the instructor was accessible "to a considerable" or "to a very high degree," that was only about average compared to all courses in the College of Arts and Sciences. However, given that the course was taught in a lecture hall on the opposite side of campus from my office and that the college average reflects students' experiences with smaller, upper-level courses as well as large lecture courses, perhaps this result should be viewed as a success rather than a failure.

In addition to the multiple-choice questions on the standardized survey, there were several open-ended questions. Students' responses to these questions were more informative about their perception of the effectiveness of instructional technology in the course than the previously discussed multiple-choice questions. By far the greatest number of positive comments was about the lecture outlines (21), study guides (7), or the web site in general (10). Only five students commented on ways they thought these aspects of the course should be improved, and most of them wanted more detailed lecture notes. Two students made positive comments about the online review sessions, although there was also one negative comment and several requests for an additional in-person review session. Two students also complained specifically about technical problems with the web site.

Although no one mentioned in their evaluations the instructor's accessibility through email, I received over 250 emails from students throughout the term. It is likely that email has now become such a common-place form of communication that it is, like the telephone, simply assumed and therefore not mentioned, even though it may have contributed significantly to students' perceptions of the instructor's availability.

The group project and discussion board elicited three positive comments in the course evaluations, including one student who reported the project "helped make friends" in the class, and four negative comments. The questionnaire given at the final exam, however, provided much more detail about students' evaluations of the group project. A total of 163 students completed this questionnaire out of 187 taking the final. Overall, reactions to the assignment were mixed. When asked how much they enjoyed the assignment, 31% indicated they enjoyed it or enjoyed it a lot, 24% disliked it, and 44% had no strong feelings either way. Similarly, when rating how much the group project contributed to their learning in the course, 65% chose the response "only a little," and only 25% selected either "significantly" or "a lot." Most of the negative comments made by students focused on problems related to working in groups, such as coordinating activities with others or dealing with members who did not do their share of the work. On the other hand, 62% reported that the assignment increased their interest in how psychologists do research either "a little" or "quite a bit," and 18% specifically commented that learning about doing research was one of the things they liked best about the assignment. Ninety-three percent reported that the project helped them to learn more about their topic, with 40% reporting "quite a bit" more. When asked specifically whether the discussion board was an effective way to communicate with other students when doing the project, 61% responded yes, 20% no, and 19% were not sure. Thus, the assignment seems to have been moderately successful in achieving its primary pedagogical purposes, and students generally found the discussion board to be a useful tool for carrying out the project.

LESSONS LEARNED

1) **Sometimes the simplest applications of technology can have the greatest impact.** The first observation to emerge from my experiences with tech-nology in this course is that for large classes, relatively simple and straightforward applications of technology can have a significant impact on student satisfaction and learning. For example, merely making lecture outlines available over the web was greatly appreciated by students. Also, encouraging students to contact me by email and promptly replying when they did so greatly increased the amount of contact between myself and students outside of the classroom.

2) **Use technology to serve a genuine purpose, rather than simply for the sake of using it.** A second lesson is that although students and faculty may initially enjoy using a new technology simply because of its novelty, they will quickly tire of the new toy if it does not serve some genuine purpose for doing their work in the course. This is a lesson that I learned the hard way with chat rooms and discussion boards for previous classes in which I simply invited students to "drop by and chat" at prescribed times or to "post a question to the discussion board you would like to talk about." When the chat specifically served the purpose of reviewing for an exam, however, students used and appreciated it. Similarly, when the discussion board served as a convenient way to gather information for the group project, students perceived it as an effective means of communication rather than merely something the instructor insisted they use.

3) **Be prepared for technology to fail.** A lesson that is probably already familiar to anyone who has been an early adopter of a new technology was dramatically reinforced when CourseInfo's chat server went down the evening we had scheduled the online review session for the first exam. By quickly posting an announcement on the course web site, I was able to explain the problem to students and meet with many of them through brief talk sessions instead, but it was still essentially a disaster. Several students mentioned the incident specifically in their course evaluations. For subsequent review sessions, I made sure that I had an alternate chat site available elsewhere and that students knew where to find it if our primary site was down. It is a good idea to have a back-up plan, particularly when the technology is young, or you have not had much experience with it.

CONCLUSION

This course demonstrated that some of the most easily implemented forms of instructional technology—web pages with lecture outlines and communication via email —can have a significant impact on the learning environment in a large class. Faculty need not master the latest and most exotic computer applications before putting technology to work to benefit both their students and themselves. It also showed that innovative applications of technology, such as the use of the discussion board in the group project, can make new learning experiences possible, in spite of inevitable shortcomings in execution. Although instructional technology was essential for successfully implementing the group project in this class, the activity also required a heavy investment of teaching assistants' time. The greatest challenge will be to design applications of technology for large classes that can deliver comparable learning experiences without the benefit of extensive TA support and discussion sections.

CONTACT INFORMATION

David W. Allbritton, Assistant Professor of Psychology
University of Pittsburgh
3939 O'Hara Street
Pittsburgh, PA 15260
Email: allbritt@pitt.edu
Phone: (412) 624-7083
Fax: (412) 624-9149

Vignette 49 Globalization (A Freshman Seminar): Using Technology to Enable Alumni and Outside Experts to Enrich a Class

Craig E. Runde, Wake Forest University

Wake Forest University chooses a theme for each academic year and offers a series of speakers, events, and activities centered on the topic. The theme for 1998–1999 was Globalization and Diversity, and Professor Hank Kennedy of the politics department and I offered a first-year seminar on the subject of globalization and the state.

Our ten students could take advantage of that year's on-campus programs, but we wanted to broaden the perspectives to which they were exposed. We sought the help of the Alumni Affairs office in recruiting former Wake Forest students in different countries to participate in the course using a web-based discussion forum. We also brought in guest experts by using video and teleconferences.

EDUCATIONAL PRINCIPLES

The first-year seminar presents a perfect opportunity to move students away from a passive learning model to one that engages them in more active roles. We wanted students be more interactive both orally in class and in written forms outside class. We also wanted students to interact beyond the two weekly in-class sessions.

Globalization is creating dramatic changes in the world. We felt our students should be able to analyze them from more than just an American perspective and be exposed to thoughts from people in different countries.

Computer-Enhanced Techniques Used in the Course

We tried several technology applications in the course.

Web Page

First, we created a web site for the course using a template created by the university where we posted a constantly updated version of the course syllabus and conducted our class discussion. By having the discussion on the web, alumni and guest participants from outside the university could readily access it.

Asynchronous Discussion Forum

We used our discussion forum for several purposes. Prior to class, the professors posted questions that students were required to answer. Later in the course, students began to comment on each other's answers. This discourse seemed to stimulate in-class discussion. As soon as class started, the professors could pick up where the discussion left off and delve more deeply into issues. The forum also permitted students to raise their own questions, both of the professors and each other. Our alumni participants, who came from Bolivia, England, the Czech Republic, Cameroon, and the United States, were able to access the discussion forum, read it, provide feedback on questions, and comment on student answers.

Videoconferences and Teleconferences

During the semester, we expanded on the idea of enabling student interaction with outside participants. We used videoconferences and teleconferences to expose students to leading experts in various subjects covered in the course. The experts provided an overview of the issues associated with their subjects and then interacted with the students via questions and answers. The students seemed particularly attentive during the videoconferences, especially when the guest called on them with questions.

Student Web Pages

Students were also expected to use technology as part of their class assignments. Their final project was to develop a web site that presented their impressions about where globalizing trends would lead over the next 25 years. At first, the students were a little reticent, because they had no experience building sites. After they finished, they seemed quite proud of the results.

Measured Results

Dr. Kennedy has been teaching at Wake Forest for 15 years, and he observed that these students participated more than any he had ever taught. Indeed, the in-class discussion seemed to pick up with the quality of the out-of-class forum. Student reviews at the end of the course also pointed to the interactive quality of the course as a plus.

Lessons Learned

Soliciting and Motivating outside Participants

We did not have a convenient way to solicit participation from alumni participants but received excellent assistance from University Advancement. To enable wider use of alumni, an easier method of contacting those interested in participating in particular fields would be necessary.

The faculty members teaching the course must also take extra steps to keep the alumni informed. The alumni do not have the benefit of attending the class and building a rapport with the students. Faculty must communicate effectively to keep alumni interested and to provide them with a better sense of how they can contribute.

Interaction Outside Class Contributed to In-Class Interaction

Proper use of the class discussion forum enabled students to think about the issues they would be reviewing in the next class. It also permitted the faculty members to see student perspectives in advance which helped shape in-class discussion. Students who were shy about speaking in class were given another forum where they could contribute.

Additional Benefits—Contacts and Networking

A significant unanticipated outcome was the opportunity for students to network with alumni and other experts. The alumni and experts themselves also interacted.

CONCLUSION

Technology can bring new and wider perspectives into the classroom. Alumni and outside experts can enrich interactions using relatively simple, cost-effective communications technologies.

CONTACT INFORMATION

Craig E. Runde, Director
International Center for Computer
    Enhanced Learning
Wake Forest University
Winston-Salem, NC 27109-7328
Email: runde@wfu.edu
WWW: http://www.wfu.edu/~runde (includes links to articles about the course)
Phone: (336) 758-4162

Vignette 50 Hyperlink to the Heart of the Matter: Internet and Society: A Senior Colloquium

David Blackmore, Lisa Fiorentino, and Tim Ziaukas, University of Pittsburgh

INTRODUCTION

In *Avatars of the Word: From Papyrus to Cyberspace* (O'Donnell, 1998), James J. O'Donnell argues that advances in "technologies of the word," for example, the introduction of the codex or the invention of the printing press, lead to cultural crises as new technologies challenge heretofore received traditions about the recording and dissemination of knowledge. Many scholars suspect that we are in the midst of another such cultural crisis as the electronic word overtakes and perhaps overwhelms the written word. The senior colloquium, Internet and Society, examines this transformation in the site where, we contend, it is played out with drama and urgency: the college classroom.

Internet and Society (I&S) is an interdisciplinary, team-taught opportunity for faculty and students to explore complex and timely subjects. For this colloquium, three faculty members—one from business, one from nursing, and another from public relations—met with 70 seniors in a traditional classroom setting once a week for two hours and 45 minutes.

The course raised a number of issues before a syllabus was developed. Our institution is a small regional campus—approximately 70 faculty members and 1,100 full-time students—and part of the University of Pittsburgh system. Despite our geographical isolation in rural Pennsylvania, we are attempting to address new questions, new technologies, and new pedagogies. Questions we were concerned with before teaching the course for the first time in spring term 1999 were: How do tradition-bound faculty, that is, teachers who tend to claim classroom authority for themselves, break with the past and engage a subject, the Internet, that by its nature decenters authority? How can we, with the limited resources of a rural college, serve a generally conservative student body and enact the potentially revolutionary theories we hope to describe? Indeed, some of the students were more proficient in navigating the technology than the instructors. How can we reconcile our received, traditional attitudes toward the written word with the radically democratic potential of the electronic word? It is a tricky pedagogical dilemma.

We used CourseInfo, a web-based software system, to communicate course documents, such as the syllabus and periodic assignments, student web pages, email, chat room, and threaded discussions.

THE IDEAS BEHIND THE COURSE

This course also attempted to situate the Internet in a historical context as well as to explore the technology's impact on society. We attempted to put all the learners in I&S, students and faculty alike, into a position to engage the subject of societal change through the topical focus of the Internet. The Internet itself was both the topic and the text for this course. We used this transformational technology, developing practical skills along the way, to investigate the rise of networked society. Specifically, we investigated the Internet's historical context and how it compares with other communication revolutions. In addition, through traditional lecture and discussion, we investigated the Internet's impact on topics like law, ethics, commerce, medicine, education and politics, among others. As an interactive course, I&S was designed both to show and to tell.

COURSE ACTIVITIES AND ASSIGNMENTS

Web Page Presentations

Students developed their own web pages, complete with photos and links to their favorite sites. At the opening of each class, six or seven students were randomly selected to present their web pages, discuss their design, and bring up their links. Repeat links were discouraged, making it important to see other students' presentations, many of which grew more elaborate and interesting as the term wore on.

RESEARCH PAPERS

Eight- to ten-page research papers were investigated as one aspect of the impact of networked society as it related to the students' majors. The students were required to develop a researchable topic and turn in a proposal on that topic by the third week of class.

Group Presentations

While papers were major-specific, group presentations were interdisciplinary and further underscored the "society" part of the course. Here, students were assigned to groups of seven or eight, representing as many different majors as possible. Each group developed a topic and made a 30-minute PowerPoint presentation. Topics included cyberstalking, Internet law, e-commerce, and Internet2. Nonpresenting students emailed a 100-word peer review to instructors within 36 hours of each presentation.

Online Chat

Over the course of the term, students participated in a virtual community of learners. Each student spoke through a character, or avatar, which was revealed during the last class. Students generally spent one hour a week engaged in virtual chat. Regularly scheduled chat times, complete with assignments, were posted on the course site. Nine assignments were posted over the term, frequently paralleling the topic of class discussion for that week. Topics included opinions on virtual communities, research on the web, and regulations

Threaded Discussion

Assignments for the discussion board paralleled those assignments for virtual chat. Students were expected to reflect on the assignment and post their ideas on the discussion board, creating threaded discussion. Students also on occasion generated their own topics and threaded discussions; one on Y2K was particularly lively.

Book Review

Students chose a book from more than a dozen selections and, after submitting their drafts to instructors, posted their reviews at the Amazon.com web page for their selection.

MEASURED RESULTS

The students completed quantitative and qualitative course evaluations. Formal quantitative evaluations were completed through the university's office of measurement and evaluation. Qualitative evaluations were completed by the students through an instructor-designed tool that elicited data specifically related to this course. Quantitative student evaluations revealed ratings in the average to above-average range on all criteria, especially in areas rating "presented course in an organized manner," "stimulated my thinking," and "maintained a good learning environment." Qualitative evaluations revealed positive comments with respect to CourseInfo. Students reported that it nicely complemented the course and was easy and convenient to use. Students liked having the ability to contact the instructors easily and to communicate between weekly class periods. Interestingly, some students reported that they would have liked to have had more interaction of this type and greater use of CourseInfo throughout their college career.

Many students seemed genuinely interested in studying the idea of the Internet as well as having the opportunity to become more technically facile while exploring new aspects of this technology.

LESSONS LEARNED

Like the subject, this colloquium was a challenging mix of tradition and innovation, conventional pedagogy (lectures, papers, but no tests) and unique opportunities offered by the Internet. While some things worked, other devices needed further development or elimination.

What Worked

1) **Threaded discussions.** Students enjoyed and seemed to connect in new and exciting ways through this tool.

2) **Web page presentations.** These presentations were fun and often hinted at the extent of the Internet through students' favorite links. This proved among the more popular aspects of the course.

3) **Research papers and presentations.** Students used PowerPoint to build enlightening, entertaining, even provocative presentations.

What Didn't Work

1) **The textbook.** We used Victor Vitanza's *CyberReader* (Vitanza, 1999). A fine anthology, the text seemed to chug along behind the class. Because we didn't go over essays in any explicit way but intended them to act as background, students found the text superfluous.

2) **Attendance tools.** The peer review was viewed as a traditional attendance-taking device wrapped in new technology.

3) **Chat room.** Most students reported that they did not like the virtual chat designed for the course. They said that it was difficult to chat because of the uneven participation; often no one else was there. Some students suggested exploring and participating in real chat rooms on the Internet as opposed to one created for this course.

CONCLUSION

This course dramatized a transitional period at our institution between conventional pedagogy and a new teaching paradigm. While holding on to some of the relationships (and relics) of traditional teaching, Internet & Society attempted to begin to build on new relationships between students and instructors by using technology to level a field of discovery.

REFERENCES

O'Donnell, J. J. (1998). *Avatars of the word: From papyrus to cyberspace.* Cambridge, MA: Harvard University Press.

Vitanza, V. (1999). *CyberReader* (2nd ed.). Boston, MA: Allyn & Bacon.

CONTACT INFORMATION

Lisa Fiorentino, Assistant Professor of Nursing
University of Pittsburgh, Bradford
205 Swarts Hall
Bradford, PA 16701
Phone: (814) 362-7640
Fax: (814) 362-0919

**Nancy J. Pelaez, California State University, Fullerton
(formerly at Indiana University-Purdue University Indianapolis)**

As a graduate student at Indiana University School of Medicine, I was a part-time instructor of biology in the Weekend and Community College. My students ranged from 18 to 70 years of age. Most worked full-time and many were full-time mothers who were making sacrifices to build in new directions. Sadly, my commuter students were only marginally connected to our community of learners. My goal was to open a whole new world of current science research so that they could make better choices for themselves and those who depend on them. I expected my students to discover the value of science research and to vote to increase future funding for science and research endeavors. One problem I encountered was that my students performed poorly. I was in a lab, and my students worked, so I could not communicate well enough to prevent them from conceiving a dislike of science—until the Oncourse Internet resource was made available. Oncourse enabled us to establish a community of learners where the science issues addressed were the real issues of students in our own community. Case studies that grew out of concerns expressed by the students enrolled in the course were used to reinforce each topic.

COURSE DESIGN

The design of the Internet-enriched Biology of Women course was to address clearly defined basic biology objectives within a context defined by the students. The Internet changed the way we worked, and my students mastered more demanding science. Commuter and part-time student attendance was more of a problem than student motivation. Jobs required travel, and children got sick. With Oncourse, handouts and assignments were available at the students' convenience. The Internet allowed students to work together and to help each other.

Course activities did not change drastically with the introduction of the Oncourse Internet resource.

Assignments were still organized around reading and homework. However, with the Internet, student answers were posted instead of graded, and student email discussions grew around the questions posted. Equal access to discussions included students who could barely make it to class. Internet access was available at the Marion County Public Library, the Community College Learning Center of our Glendale Shopping Mall, and the university library. Our community invested in these learners, and they responded.

Students got excited about sharing Internet resources. An assignment to research a topic of personal interest developed into a source of material for collaborative learning. As the instructor, I became more of a coach than an expert, because the students provided the resources to optimize learning. They could help each other by communicating, providing valuable links with answers, and they developed a camaraderie that grew into close ties. For example, we studied food groups and the food pyramid. An Internet program converted record of foods consumed during 24 hours into a personalized list of actual nutrients consumed. This had more impact than looking at a food pyramid diagram. Gelatin became inferior to egg protein when students discovered that it lacks some essential amino acids. Concerns about a diabetic classmate grew.

Knowing that a member of our classroom community could be a case study motivated students to do rigorous science and to tackle complex issues that require real knowledge. Some of the older treatments for diseases like diabetes were quite different than those suggested today, and students grew to value modern research institutions when they had to make recommendations to a classmate who was considering converting to a new, genetically engineered insulin, Humalog. Students used the course objectives to address their own concerns. In the unit on hormones, we learned that some breast cancer treatments cause premature menopause. That became an important context for tracing the complex hormonal changes over time. Our students will not forget the importance of this problem and the impact menopause can have on a newlywed couple.

Another treasure on the Internet came in the form of visual aids. Clear diagrams—for example, animations of protein synthesis and links to download free software to view 3-D molecular models—changed the way students learned complex topics. Real pathology slides, Pap tests, images of cancer and skin diseases converted learning into participation within a medical community.

RESULTS

Results can be measured in terms of the student failure rate that declined from more than 35% before using the internet to a 10% with Oncourse. Even more outstanding is the number of students who elected to serve as mentors and guides to subsequent classes. With the Internet, it was easy to maintain contact with former students, who continued to provide useful information resources and to urge new students to work hard and to master the concepts with the promise that they would deepen their understanding of crucial science research events that would make a difference.

LESSONS LEARNED

The Internet did not save us time. We got carried away. Oncourse changed the way we worked together, and it made communication more efficient, and it made my students better students. We had more fun. But the fun did not come without problems, and I would be remiss if I did not mention them. Introducing the Internet required time and some real patience. The first obstacle was solved by a field trip to the computer lab. My initial flexibility had allowed students to communicate via fax rather than Internet, but those students who chose not to become computer literate became isolated from our community. One lesson learned was to require that all students become Internet participants and then to rely on instructional technology experts to help those in need of additional assistance. Another requirement is a campus that believes in technology enough to invest in the technical support demanded by new equip-

ment. The result may turn out to be cheaper since part-time instructors like graduate students don't cost much. By providing the technology, the campus made it possible for a graduate student instructor to do a good job. I will not forget my excitement the day I learned I could use the Internet to support my classroom instruction. The result was that I worked harder. Educational technology taught me to scan documents and to find other resources to help students achieve more. It seems to me that technology that allows part-time faculty and students to work together better is a wise investment.

CONCLUSION

In conclusion, we must learn to live with some frustration and to provide the structure required to seek answers, if we want commuter and weekend students' hard work to grow into motivation and compassion into action. Oncourse grew in response to my own efforts and my students' efforts. Science research became a relevant topic, and students connected with it in a way that will keep them interested in future advances. Institutional and community investment in the teachers and learners may be an expense that is cost effective. Much of the Internet-enriched Biology of Women course (without student answers or copyright-protected resources) can be accessed via the URL http://oncourse.iupui.edu/ Select IUPUI, and then use the "Advanced Search" link with the following selections: Campus–Indianapolis, Semster–Spring 1998–1999, Course–n200, Biology of Women, Nancy Pelaez, instructor.

In this most recent online section of Biology of Women, the following lessons were built around student case studies:

- Gynecological problems
- Sexuality and contraception
- Pregnancy, labor, and delivery
- Pain, drugs, menopause, and aging

Additional examples discussed were selected from previous semesters.

CONTACT INFORMATION

Nancy J. Pelaez
Assistant Professor of Biological Sciences
California State University
P. O. Box 6850
Fullerton, CA 92834-6850
Email: npelaez@fullerton.edu
Phone: (714) 278-7260
Fax: (714) 278-3426
WWW: http://biology.fullerton.edu/people/faculty
/nancy-pelaez/index.html

 **Computer-Mediated Communication and Face-to-Face Instruction: An Integrative Perspective for a Changing Society Using a Case Study Approach**

Ananda Mitra, Connie Chesner, Jennifer Berg, and Matthew Ferebee, Wake Forest University

This essay describes the conditions under which an instructor at Wake Forest University chose to include an online component. The experience offers several directions, prescriptions, and implications and raises fundamental questions about the enterprise of teaching and ethos of a university.

Since the initiation of the computerization component of the Plan for the Class of 2000 in the fall of 1996, the Wake Forest University community has discussed the various ways in which the new technology could be best used for teaching. In brief, the plan distributed standardized portable computers to all students by the fall of 1999 and established a robust and reliable local area network (LAN) that afforded high-speed connections to the Internet from dorm rooms, classrooms, the library, and most public places on campus.

Studies related to the evaluation of the computerization component demonstrated a remarkable increase in the use of electronic mail between students and between students and teachers (Mitra & Steffensmeier, in press; Mitra, Steffensmeier, Lenzmeier, & Massoni, in press; Mitra & Hazen, 1999; Mitra, Hazen, LaFrance, & Rogan, 1999; Mitra, 1998). There was also evidence of the increasing use of other standard computer programs for creating presentations and composing written assignments. However, the key area in facilitating student/student and student/teacher interactions was computer-mediated communication (CMC), operating primarily at the asynchronous level with the use of email, listservs, and specific groupware.

It should also be noted that while there was a remarkable increase in the amount and variety of CMC interactions, neither the faculty nor the students sensed any reduction in the face-to-face (FTF) interactions. In every way, asynchronous CMC (henceforth referred to as A-CMC) supplemented, complemented, and enhanced ongoing FTF instructional practice.

We argue that there were several reasons for this tendency to supplement FTF with CMC as opposed to replacing it. First, students and faculty had minimal acquaintance with the process of recreating real-time instructional scenarios that could replace the FTF format. Second, only in fall 1999 were portable computers diffused among almost 100% of the undergraduates. Third, the standard software installed on each computer did not offer any tool that would allow experimentation with S-CMC.

Finally, and most critically, there was no reason to replace FTF teaching with the S-CMC model, because Wake Forest does not have a substantial distance-learning program. Indeed, transformation to S-CMC could be considered exactly counter to the pedagogy fundamental to a university that prides itself on close FTF contact between students and teachers. Within the ethos, any attempt to replace the traditional teaching method could be perceived as unnecessary and artificial—a classic manifestation of the "technological determinism" described by Arnold Pacey in his seminal book, *The Culture of Technology* (1993).

In the fall of 1999, nearly all undergraduate students gained access to a standardized portable computer. Yet, a complete dismantling of the FTF teaching system was still unwelcome. Now, however, some FTF meetings could be replaced by S-CMC without taking apart the general and overall instructional style and the traditions of the university. In teaching a class called Communication and Technology, this opportunity was seized by both teacher and students. It was mutually agreed that the substance of the course was uniquely suited to replacing some FTF sessions with S-CMC meetings. The class was designed so that an S-CMC technology would replace FTF instruction every two weeks.

TECHNOLOGY AT WORK

Replacing some segments of FTF education with CMC was first attempted in the fall of 1998, when nearly 75% of undergraduates had standardized portable computers. Based on the lessons of the 1998 trial, the fortnightly S-CMC classes were incorporated into the fall 1999 syllabus. It was agreed that S-CMC would be mobilized as follows:

- All the students in the class would register to a web-based chat room that could be accessed from any computer connected to the Internet.

- All students would arrive in the chat room at the scheduled class time.

- The teacher would act as a moderator, guiding the discussion with a specific question that would be used as a kernel for the 50-minute class.

- Students could be geographically dispersed, as long as they were able to attend the class through a reliable Internet connection.

- The teacher would minimally control the discussion once the participants began to interact.

- All students were expected to participate in the discussion.

- No policies were stated about grading standards in the evaluation of the quality and quantity of discussions in the chat classroom.

These basic principles were used to organize the S-CMC classroom. While adherence to most was accomplished, the level of moderation in the chat classroom had to be modified. After a few sessions, it became evident that the online structure had to incorporate some of the traditional moderation formats of the FTF class. For example, students would have to acknowledge the presence of the teacher and follow his/her specific instructions. This need for authority demonstrates how real-life power structures can easily bleed into cyberspace—a place often presented as having flattened hierarchies and power structures that are unrelated to individuals' real-life status. Specific moderation rules included simple strategies, such as the teacher posting to the chat room in all capital letters; the use of specific symbols (for example, "!" and "?" to indicate that a statement is a comment or a question, respectively), and the teacher retaining the power to terminate a discussion and initiate new ones. Once these rules were adopted, the class proceeded.

The technology allowed some unique conditions to develop, such as:

- The presence of a guest student from India in one of the class sessions

- Students attending the class from different geographic locations (for example, Charlotte, NC; Kernersville, NC)

- The teacher moderating the class from different geographic locations (for example, Rome, Italy; Nashville, TN)

- An S-CMC class with students in the geographic classroom, allowing FTF interactions in tandem with S-CMC relations

- Specialists entering the chat classroom (for example, a retired school teacher)

Based on the experience of conducting this class, we have developed a set of provisional findings about the burdens and benefits of attempting to replace some segments of a FTF class with S-CMC.

LESSONS LEARNED

Our experience reinforces the research that has shown that, "although electronic group mail reduces the amount of meeting time needed for coordination activities, it doesn't eliminate the need for face-to-face meetings. Face-to-face meetings are particularly important in getting a group started, in negotiating issues, and in problem solving" (Sproull & Kiesler, 1991).

FTF communication will strengthen as CMC is implemented. Students in this class have a distinct advantage over their distance-learning peers who only meet online. Their face-to-face interaction opportunities add to their CMC relationships. Distance learning develops based on the knowledge that "an electronic tie combined with an organizational tie is sufficient to allow the flow of information between people who may never have met face-to-face" (Garton, Haythornthwaite, & Wellman, 1999). Through the incorporation of FTF contact and CMC, the relations between students become more layered. "Social network analysts have found that multiplex ties are more intimate, voluntary, supportive, and durable" (Garton,

Haythornthwaite, & Wellman, 1999). CMC contact affords students the opportunity to strengthen social ties to their peers.

Our case study shows the strengthening of FTF relationships after CMC. CMC was first implemented in synchronous time with FTF relations, and then an asynchronous pattern of alternation was established. Students could respond either electronically or verbally. Students who normally did not speak in class would respond through the online chat.

Later, when purely FTF meetings and CMC were implemented, relations among class members were stronger. CMC interaction, whether through asynchronous (listserv) or synchronous (chat room) means, usually spurred dialog that carried over into the classroom. As a result, more FTF interaction occurred in the classroom, and the students who did not speak in the classroom voiced a feeling of inclusion based on the online discussion opportunities.

Participant Confusion of Message-Sender Identity and Medium of Communication

As the relationships become increasingly multifaceted, participants may have trouble associating online identities and communication with FTF identities and incorporating the dual messages from each class member into a coherent sphere of information. Evidence of this confusion has been observed in our case study, and several causal factors have been identified through discussion and analysis.

A few of these factors include:

- An online chat already poses the difficulty of participants following rapidly scrolling text; to expect the connection of each comment to the real-life face of the person who is posting is asking for a level and speed of mental capacity that many students voiced as difficult, if not impossible, in initial meetings.

- In our case study, users selected a random screen name upon entry into the online chatting community. This name often varied from the user name shown at the start of their listserv email address and, in all but one case, from the person's real name. This multiname aspect of online and real-life interaction increased confusion among class members as to who was posting what messages and where and how those messages connected with other messages from that classmate.

- Online class meetings conducted in a chat room often posted a number of topic threads simultaneously; this made following any one discussion difficult for many.

- The real-life classroom was structured in stationary, stadium seating. Students faced the professor and/or the backs of other students' heads. This seating arrangement prevented student association of faces with names.

Kinesthetic Interaction Will Enhance the Level of Comprehension and Retention among Class Members

"Constructivist instructional principles...dictate that students who are actively involved in the learning process will achieve higher levels of learning" (McCray, McCoy, Hoppe, Greenwood, & Ganzert, 1999). The incorporation of Internet class meetings with FTF class meetings alters the communication channels and opportunities for active involvement that are available to both the students and instructor in an educational setting. An increase in the comprehension level of participants is likely when members are provided not only verbal and paper interaction, but also information in a cyber environment. The increase in interaction availability better serves the various learning styles of students attending the class.

Incorporating the Internet into the classroom allows students to post questions at any time and to receive feedback from the group when outside the geographical classroom setting. "List servers have a widely recognized reputation for providing a communication arena particularly fostering debate and discussion" (McCray, McCoy, Hoppe, Greenwood, & Ganzert, 1999). Listserv participants can read over and refer back to logs of Internet texts for clarification on the content of discussions and then utilize the geographical classroom meetings to confirm their perceptions in interactions. "Because electronic mail [and other electronic communications] can archive the complete text of every message, the same group memory is available to every member" (Sproull & Kiesler, 1991) in referencing discussion content objectively and retrospectively.

Improvement in Participant Relationships and Interaction Levels

"The composition of a relation or a tie is derived from the social attributes of both participants...CMC tends to underplay the social cues of participants by focusing on the content of messages rather than on the attributes of senders and receivers" (Garton, Haythornthwaite, & Wellman, 1999). In our class interaction increased among class members and the instructor without regard for the status barriers that often affect interaction in the geographical classroom.

"Computer-based communication lets groups improve their coordination by having members simultaneously linked with and buffered from one another" (Sproull & Keisler, 1991). Several students in the case study voiced a preference for online communication due to its facelessness. A few students later increased their level of interaction within the geographical classroom *after* interacting in the online setting. Studies have also shown that "many students who are reticent in class prove themselves fonts of knowledge and insight when afforded the opportunity to communicate in an electronic forum" (McCray, McCoy, Hoppe, Greenwood, & Ganzert, 1999).

Interactions between the instructor and students also improve. Email messages and postings to the listserv may occur at any time of day and from any location. Just as status barriers are often ignored during peer interactions online, so are the status barriers between students and the instructor. In the first few online class meetings for our case study, students would often ignore or overlook requests posted by the instructor to stop the posting process or refocus on a key question. This disregard for a traditional authority figure was observed in both the synchronous online/FTF class meeting and the strictly online meetings but was not evident in the strictly FTF class meetings. In response to concerns voiced over such interaction patterns, rules of communication for the online meetings were established, and later meetings and reactions of students to instructor postings conformed more to typical student/teacher hierarchies.

CONCLUSION

While this paper principally discussed the pragmatic benefits and burdens of online teaching, some very fundamental questions about teaching arise out of this technological experimentation. Indeed, what is at stake here is precisely the ethos of the university, where online instruction calls into question what teachers, teaching, and classrooms are all about. When is the use of the technology ethical? In other words, how radically does the ethos of a university alter when technology is deployed to enhance the traditional form of teaching? The lesson here is concerned with much more than how to use technology. "Our highest obligation to society and to ourselves is to work within the context of change to ensure that it follows a trajectory of maximum benefit to society" (Hooker, 1997). As a society, we have a shared responsibility to acknowledge the extraordinarily high stakes associated with altering the dwelling place—the ethos—of a university, and we must initiate a dialog regarding what is on the line when classrooms go online.

REFERENCES

Garton, L., Haythornthwaite, C., & Wellman, B. (1999). Studying online social networks. In S. Jones (Ed.), *Doing Internet research: Critical issues and methods for examining the Net.* Thousand Oaks, CA: Sage.

Hooker, M. (1997). The transformation of higher education. In D. Oblinger & S. Rush (Eds.), *The learning revolution: The challenge of information technology in the academy.* Bolton, MA: Anker.

McCray, G. E., McCoy, L., Hoppe, B., Greenwood, T., & Ganzert, R. (1999). The pedagogical merit of information technology: Teaching and learning outcomes in a ubiquitous computing environment. In D. Brown (Ed.), *Electronically enhanced education: A case study of Wake Forest University.* Winston-Salem, NC: Wake Forest University Press, Scientific Division.

Mitra, A. (1998). Categories of computer use and their relationships with attitudes towards computers. *Journal of Research on Computing in Education, 30* (3).

Mitra, A., & Hazen, M. (1999). Longitudinal assessment of computer enhancement at Wake Forest University. In D. Brown (Ed.), *Electronically enhanced education: A case study of Wake Forest University.* Winston-Salem, NC: Wake Forest University Press, Scientific Division.

Mitra, A., Hazen, M., LaFrance, B., & Rogan, R. (1999). Faculty use and non-use of electronic mail: Attitudes, expectations and profiles. *Journal of Computer Mediated Communication, 4* (3).

Mitra, A., & Stefensmeier, T. (in press). Changes in student attitudes and student computer use in a computer enriched environment. *Journal of Research on Computing in Education.*

Mitra, A., Stefensmeier, T., Lenzmeier, S., & Massoni, A. (in press). Institutional implications of changes in attitudes towards computers and use of computers by faculty. *Journal of Research on Computing in Education.*

Pacey, A. (1993). *The culture of technology.* Cambridge, MA: MIT Press.

Sproull, L., & Kiesler, S. (1991). *Connections: New ways of working in the networked organization.* Cambridge, MA: MIT Press.

ABOUT THE STUDENTS

Connie Chesner, Jennifer Berg, and Matthew Ferebee are first-year master's-level communication students at Wake Forest University in Winston-Salem, North Carolina. They have been working to develop an in-depth examination of the implications of CMC and FTF integration on dialog in the classroom.

CONTACT INFORMATION

Ananda Mitra, Assistant Professor
Department of Communication
Wake Forest University
P. O. Box 7347, Reynolda Station
Winston-Salem, NC 27109
Email: ananda@wfu.edu

BIBLIOGRAPHY

Alcohol 101, available from http://www.century council.org/

American Association for Higher Education. (1996, April). What research says about improving undergraduate education: Twelve attributes of good practice. *AAHE Bulletin.*

Anderson, L. M., Blumenfeld, P., Pintrich, P. R., Clark, C. M., Marx, R. W., & Peterson, P. (1995). Educational psychology for teachers: Reforming our courses, rethinking our roles. *Educational Psychologist, 30* (3), 143-158.

Anderson-Harper, H., Kavookjia, J., & Munden, C. D. (1998, Fall). Teaching students to develop a web site as a tool for marketing pharmaceutical care services. *American Journal of Pharmaceutical Education, 62* (3), 284-289.

Angelo, T. A. (1993, April 1). A teacher's dozen. *AAHE Bulletin,* 3-13.

Arons, A. B. (1997). *Teaching introductory physics.* New York, NY: John Wiley.

Authorware 5 Attain. (1999). Macromedia, Inc.

Baddeley, A. (1992). Working memory. *Science, 255,* 559.

Barr, R., & Tagg, J. (1995, November/December). From teaching to learning: A new paradigm for undergraduate education. *Change,* 13-25.

Bartholomae, D. (1995). Inventing the university. In R. Connors & C. Glenn (Eds.), *The Saint Martin's guide to teaching writing* (3rd ed.) (pp. 408-421). New York, NY: St. Martin's.

Bass, R. (1999, October). *Exemplary models for web-based learning.* PBS live satellite downlink.

Beichner, R. J. (1993, June). A multimedia editing environment promoting science learning in a unique setting—A case study. *Proceedings of the Educational-Media 93, World Conference on Educational Multimedia and Hypermedia,* Orlando, FL.

Bonk, C. J., & King, K. S. (Eds.). (1998). *Electronic collaborators: Learner-centered technologies for literacy, apprenticeship, and discourse.* Hillsdale, NJ: Erlbaum.

Bonk, C. J., Malikowski, S., Angeli, C., & East, J. (1998). Web-based case conferencing for preservice teacher education: Electronic discourse from the field. *Journal of Educational Computing Research, 19* (3), 267-304.

Bonk, C. J., & Reynolds, T. H. (1997). Learner-centered web instruction for higher-order thinking, teamwork, and apprenticeship. In B. H. Khan (Ed.), *Web-based instruction.* Englewood Cliffs, NJ: Educational Technology Publications.

Bringuier, J. C. (1980). *Conversations with Jean Piaget.* Chicago, IL: University of Chicago Press.

Brown, D. G. (Ed.). (2000). *Interactive learning: Vignettes from America's most wired campuses.* Bolton, MA: Anker.

Brown, D. G., & Elson, F. S. (1999, Winter). Faculty development. *Multiversity,* 17-20.

Brown, J. S., Collins, A., & Duguid, P. (1989). Situated cognition and the culture of learning. *Educational Researcher, 18* (1), 32-42.

Bruffee, K. A. (1984). Collaborative learning and 'The Conversation of Mankind.' *College English, 46,* 635-652.

Bruffee, K. A. (1993). Writing, collaboration, and social construction. In K. Bruffee (Ed.), *A short course in writing: Composition, collaborative learning, and constructive reading* (4th ed.) (pp. 1-13). New York, NY: HarperCollins.

Carbone, E. (1998). *Teaching large classes: Tools and strategies.* Thousand Oaks, CA: Sage.

Carlucci, D. (1999, March 8). Building clinical computer competency. *ADVANCE for Speech-Language Pathologists,* 7-9.

Chandra, A., & Holt, G. (Fall, 1996). Need to enhance computer skills of pharmacy students. *American Journal of Pharmaceutical Education, 60,* 297-303.

Chickering, A. W., & Gamson, Z. F. (1987, March). Seven principles for good practice in undergraduate education. *AAHE Bulletin, 39* (7), 3-7.

Chickering A. W., & Gamson, Z. F. (1991). *Applying the seven principles for good practice in undergraduate education.* San Francisco, CA: Jossey-Bass.

Christian, W., & Titus, A. (1998). Developing web-based curricula using Java Applets. *Computers in Physics, 12,* 227-232.

Cochran, P. S., Masterson, J. J., Long, S., Katz, R., Seaton, W. H., Wynne, M., Lieberth, A., & Martin, D. (1993, September). Computing competencies for clinicians. *ASHA,* 48-49.

Cohen, S. S., Mason, D. J., Kovner, C., Leavitt, J. K., Pulcini, J., & Sochalski, J. (1996). Stages of nursing's political development: Where we've been and where we ought to go. *Nursing Outlook, 44,* 259-266.

Collins, A. (1991, September). The role of computer technology in restructuring schools. *Phi Delta Kappan.*

Cope, R., & Hannah, W. (1975). *Revolving college door: The causes and consequences of dropping out and transferring.* New York, NY: John Wiley.

Council of Chief State School Officers (CCSSO). (1999). *The interstate new teacher assessment and support consortium (INTASC).* Washington, DC: Author. Available: http://www.ccsso.org/intasc.html. Accessed October 1, 1999.

Cross, K. P. (1991, October). Effective college teaching. *Prism.* ASEE. Available: http://www.ccsso.org/intasc.html. Accessed October 1, 1999.

Cyrs, T. E. (1997). *Teaching at a distance with the merging technologies.* Las Cruces, NM: Center for Educational Development, New Mexico State University.

Draves, W. A. (1997). *How to teach adults* (2nd ed.). Manhattan, KS: The Learning Resources Network (LERN).

Duin, A. H., & Hansen, C. (1994). Reading and writing on computer networks as social construction and social interaction. In C. L. Selfe & S. Hilligoss (Eds.), *Literacy and computers: The complications of teaching and learning with technology* (pp. 89-112). New York, NY: MLA.

Ehrmann, S. C. (1995, March/April). Asking the right questions: What does research tell us about technology and higher education? *Change.*

Ehrmann, S. C., & Zuniga, R. E. (1997). *The Flashlight™ evaluation handbook.* Washington, DC: AAHE.

Elbow, P. (1973). *Writing without teachers.* New York, NY: Oxford University Press.

Ercolano, V. (1994, November). Learning through cooperation. *Prism.* ASEE.

Farquhar, J. D., & Surrey, D. W. (1995). Reducing impositions on working memory through instructional strategies. *Performance and Instruction, 34* (8), 4-7.

Gagne, R. M., Briggs, L. J., & Wager, W. W. (1992). *Principles of instructional design* (4th ed.). Fort Worth, TX: Harcourt Brace.

Gardner, H. (1999). *Intelligence reframed: Multiple intelligences for the 21st century.* New York, NY: Basic Books.

Garton, L., Haythornthwaite, C., & Wellman, B. (1999). Studying online social networks. In S. Jones (Ed.), *Doing Internet research: Critical issues and methods for examining the Net.* Thousand Oaks, CA: Sage.

Gillet, D., Franklin, G. F., Longchamp, R., & Bonvin, D. (1994, August). *Introduction to automatic control via an integrated instruction approach.* The 3rd IFAC Symposium on Advances in Control Education, Tokyo, Japan.

Green, E. J. (1962). *The learning process and programmed instruction.* New York, NY: Holt, Rinehart, & Winston.

Hake, R. R. (1998). Interactive-engagement versus traditional methods: A six-thousand-student survey of mechanics test data for introductory physics courses. *American Journal of Physics, 66* (1), 64-74.

Hall, D. W. (1996a). Creating computer-based instructional animations. *NACTA Journal, 40,* 8-11.

Hall, D. W. (1996b). Multimedia in the entomology classroom. *American Entomologist, 42,* 92-98.

Halloun, H. (1985). Force Concept Inventory (FCI). *American Journal of Physics, 53,* 1043-1055.

Harasim, L. (1999). A framework for online learning: The virtual-U. *IEEE Computer, 32,* 44-49.

Hofstetter, F. (1998, October). *Three waves of the SERF web-based teaching and learning environment.* PBS Online. <http://www.udel.edu/fth serf/serf1-3.html>

Holzer, S. M. (1994, Spring). From constructivism to active learning. *The Innovator, 2.*

Holzer S. M., & Andruet, R. H. (2000). Experiential learning in mechanics with multimedia. *International Journal of Engineering Education.*

Hooker, M. (1997). The transformation of higher education. In D. Oblinger & S. Rush (Eds.), *The learning revolution: The challenge of information technology in the academy.* Bolton, MA: Anker.

Iskowitz, M. (1999, March 8). What can technology do to improve your practice? *ADVANCE for Speech-Language Pathologists,* 10-11.

Johnson, D. W., Johnson, R. T., & Smith, K. A. (1991). *Active learning: Cooperation in the classroom.* Edina, MN: Interaction Book.

Jonassen, D. (1991). Objectivism versus constructivism: Do we need a new philosophical paradigm? *Educational Technology Research and Development, 39* (3), 5-14.

Kagan, S. (1990, January). The structural approach to cooperative learning. *Educational Leadership.*

Kolb, D. (1984). *Experiential learning.* Englewood Cliffs, NJ: Prentice Hall.

Kozma, R. B., & Johnston, J. (1991, January/February). The technological revolution comes to the classroom. *Change, 23* (1).

Landis, C. R. et al. (1998). The new traditions consortium: Shifting from a faculty-centered paradigm to a student-centered paradigm. *Journal of Chemical Education, 75.*

Laws, P. (1991, July/August). Workshop physics: Learning introductory physics by doing it. *Change, 23* (4).

Lee, J. L., & Van Patten, B. (1995). *Making communicative language teaching happen.* New York, NY: McGraw-Hill.

Lemke, J. L. (1990). *Talking science: Language, learning, and values.* Norwood, NJ: Ablex.

Lieux, E. M., & Luoto, P. K. (2000). *Exploring quantity food production and service through problems.* Upper Saddle River, NJ: Prentice Hall.

Light, R. J. (1990). *The Harvard assessment seminars, 1st Report.* Cambridge, MA: Harvard University.

Lochhead, J. (1987). Teaching analytical reasoning through thinking aloud pair problem solving. In J. E. Stice (Ed.), *Teaching thinking through problem solving.* New Directions for Teaching and Learning, No. 30. San Francisco, CA: Jossey-Bass.

Lyman, F. (1987). Think-pair-share: An expanding teaching technique. MAACIE, *Cooperative News, 1* (1).

Lial, M. L., Hornsby, E. J., & Schneider, D. I. (1997). *College algebra and trigonometry.* Reading, MA: Addison-Wesley.

Lyons, N. (1999). How portfolios can shape emerging practice. *Educational Leadership, 56* (8), 63-65.

Mason, D., & Leavitt, J. K. (Eds.). (1998). *Policy and politics in nursing and health care* (3rd ed.). Philadelphia, PA: WB Saunders.

Masterson, J. J., Wynne, M. K., Kuster, J., & Stierwalt, J. A. G. (1999, May/June). New and emerging technologies: Going where we've never gone before. *ASHA, 41,* 16-20.

Mazur, E. (1987). *Peer instruction.* Upper Saddle River, NJ: Prentice Hall.

McCoy, L. P. (1999). EDU 716: Professional Development Seminar. Winston-Salem, NC: Wake Forest University. Available: http://www.wfu.edu/~mccoy/EDU716/. Accessed October 1, 1999.

McCray, G. E. (forthcoming). The hybrid course: Merging online instruction and the traditional classroom. *Information Technology and Management.*

McCray, G. E., McCoy, L., Hoppe, B., Greenwood, T., & Ganzert, R. (1999). The pedagogical merit of information technology: Teaching and learning outcomes in a ubiquitous computing environment. In D. Brown (Ed.), *Electronically enhanced education: A case study of Wake Forest University.* Winston-Salem, NC: Wake Forest University Press, Scientific Division.

Mitra, A. (1998). Categories of computer use and their relationships with attitudes towards computers. *Journal of Research on Computing in Education, 30* (3).

Mitra, A., & Hazen, M. (1999). Longitudinal assessment of computer enhancement at Wake Forest University. In D. Brown (Ed.), *Electronically enhanced education: A case study of Wake Forest University.* Winston-Salem, NC: Wake Forest University Press, Scientific Division.

Mitra, A., Hazen, M., LaFrance, B., & Rogan, R. (1999). Faculty use and non-use of electronic mail: Attitudes, expectations and profiles. *Journal of Computer Mediated Communication, 4* (3).

Mitra, A., & Stefensmeier, T. (in press). Changes in student attitudes and student computer use in a computer enriched environment. *Journal of Research on Computing in Education.*

McGuigan, J., Moyer, C. R., & Harris, F. H. deB. (1999). *Managerial economics* (8th ed.). Cincinnati, OH: International Thompson.

Mitra, A., Stefensmeier, T., Lenzmeier, S., & Massoni, A. (in press). Institutional implications of changes in attitudes towards computers and use of computers by faculty. *Journal of Research on Computing in Education.*

Mormer, E. (1999). Personal communication.

Mormer, E., & Palmer, C. (1998, June). A guide to using the Internet: It could change the way you work. *The Hearing Journal, 51* (6), 29-30.

Nagata, C. (1999, September 29). University of Hawaii at Manoa, Educational Technology Department [personal email].

National Board for Professional Teaching Standards (NBPTS). (1999). *National board for professional teaching standards.* Southfield, MI: Author. Available: http://www.nbpts.org/. Accessed October 1, 1999.

National Council for the Accreditation of Teacher Education (NCATE), Task Force on Technology and Teacher Education. (1997). *Technology and the new professional teacher: Preparing for the 21st century classroom.* Washington, DC: Author. Available: http://www.ncate.org/projects/tech/TECH.HTM. Accessed July 22, 1999.

Newman, J. H. (1972). The idea of a university. In C. F. Harrold & W. D. Templeman (Eds.), *English prose of the Victorian age* (pp. 582-586). New York, NY: Oxford University Press.

Novak, G. M., Patterson, E. T., Garvin, A. D., & Christian, W. (1999). *Just-in-time teaching: Blending active learning with web technology.* Upper Saddle River, NJ: Prentice Hall.

O'Donnell, J. J. (1998). *Avatars of the word: From papyrus to cyberspace.* Cambridge, MA: Harvard University Press.

Pacey, A. (1993). *The culture of technology.* Cambridge, MA: MIT Press.

Papert, S. (1991). Situating constructionism. In I. Harel & S. Papert (Eds.), *Constructionism,* (pp. 1-11). Norwood, NJ: Ablex.

Papert, S. & Harel, I. (Eds.). (1991). *Constructionism.* Norwood, NJ: Ablex.

Perkins, D. (1992). *Smart schools: Better thinking and learning for every child.* New York, NY: Free Press.

Peters, P. C. (1982). Even honors students have conceptual difficulties with physics. *American Journal of Physics, 50* (6), 501-508.

Pfundt, H., & Duit, R. (1991). *Students' alternative frameworks and science education.* Kiel, Germany: Institut fur die Paedagogik der Naturwissenschaften.

Piaget, J. (1954). *The construction of reality in the child.* New York, NY: Basic Books.

Pressey, S. L. (1926, March). A simple apparatus which gives tests and scores—and teaches. *School and Society, 23* (586), 374.

Pyramid Film & Video. *A private universe: An insightful lesson on how we learn.* (1988). Santa Monica, CA: Pyramid Film & Video.

Redish, E. F. (1994). Implications of cognitive studies for teaching physics. *American Journal of Physics, 62* (9), 796-803.

Rodburg, M. (1992). Workshops in the teaching of writing. In N. Kline (Ed.), *How writers teach writing* (pp. 143-156). Englewood Cliffs, NJ: Prentice Hall.

Schulman, L. (1998). Teacher portfolios. In N. Lyons (Ed.), *With portfolio in hand: Validating the new teacher professionalism.* New York, NY: Teachers College Press.

Schumacher, K., Brodnik, M., Sachs, L., & Schiller, M. R. (1997, Fall). Therapists' anxiety and attitudes toward computerized documentation in the clinical setting. *Journal of Allied Health,* 151-158.

Sept, J. (1997). *Investigating Olduvai. Archaeology of human origins CD-ROM.* Bloomington, IN: Indiana University Press.

Simon, H. A. (1974). How big is a chunk? *Science, 183,* 482-488.

Snowman, J., Bieler, R. F., & Bonk, C. H. (2000). *Psychology applied to teaching* (9th ed.). Boston, MA: Houghton Mifflin.

Sproull, L., & Kiesler, S. (1991). *Connections: New ways of working in the networked organization.* Cambridge, MA: MIT Press.

Stice, J. E. (1987, February). Using Kolb's learning cycle to improve student learning. *Engineering Education, 77* (5).

Sylvester, R. R. (1997, Spring). Incorporation of Internet databases into pharmacotherapy coursework. *American Journal of Pharmaceutical Education, 61,* 50-55.

Terenzini, P. T., & Pascarella, E. T. (1994, January/February). Living with myths: Undergraduate education in America. *Change.*

Tissue, B. M., Earp, R. L., & Yip, C. W. (1996). Design and student use of World Wide Web-based prelab exercises. *Chemical Educator, S1430-4171* (96), 01010-2.

Tobias, S. (1990). *They're not dumb, they're different: Stalking the second tier.* Tucson, AZ: Research Corporation.

Tobias, S. (1992*). Revitalizing undergraduate science: Why some things work and most don't.* Tucson, AZ: Research Corporation.

University of Hawaii Technology Intensive Standards. (1997, July 1; last modified 2/22/99). *What should our graduates know?* <http:www.Hawaii.edu/ti/TIC/te_in st.tm> (9/29/99).

Vitanza, V. (1999). *CyberReader* (2nd. ed.). Boston, MA: Allyn & Bacon.

Vouk, M. A., Bitzer, D. L., & Klevans, R. L. (1999). Workflow and end-user quality of service issues in web-based education. *IEEE Transactions on Knowledge and Data Engineering, 11* (4), 673-687.

Vygotsky, L. S. (1962). *Thought and language.* Cambridge, MA: MIT Press.

Williams, J. D. (1998). The classroom as workshop. In J. D. Williams (Ed.), *Preparing to teach writing: Research, theory, and practice* (2nd ed.) (pp. 79-98). Hillsdale, NJ: Erlbaum.

Winter, M. K., & Lockhart, J. S. (1997, September/October). From motivation to action: Understanding nurses' political involvement. *Nursing and Health Care Perspectives, 18*, 244-250.

Wong, Y. L., & King, A. G. (1999). Application of interactive web tools in teaching redox Chemistry. *Interactive Multimedia Electronic Journal, 1* (1). (http://www.wfu.edu/IMEJ).

Wynne, M. K., Seaton, W. H., & Allen, R. (1993, September). Integration into office management. *ASHA,* 50-51.

URLs

These are web site addresses (URLs) for commercial products mentioned in the book:

Adobe Premiere: http://www.adobe.com/products/premiere/

Apache Web Server: http://www.apache.org

CD-Time Sketch (now called CapMedia Tools):
http://www.capmedia.com

CommonSpace: http://www.sixthfloor.com/CSQA.html

CourseInfo: http://www.blackboard.com

Daedalus: http://www.daedalus.com/

Dreamweaver: http://www.macromedia.com/

Inspiration: http://www.inspiration.com/

Jamba: http://www.jamba.com

Microsoft Frontpage: http://www.microsoft.com/frontpage

PaintShop Pro: http://www.jasc.com/

PowerPoint: www.microsoft.com/office/powerpoint/

ToolBook: http://www.Asymetrix.com/

Virtual Flylab: http://www.biology.com

WebCT: http://www.webct.com/

INDEXES

Sept, Jeanne, 113
Shaw, J. Scott, 66

Trembath, Kern R., 169

Watson, George, 63
Wittlich, Gary E., 25
Wong, Yue-Ling, 86

Yip, C. W., 51

Ziaukas, Tim, 215

COLLEGE/UNIVERSITY INDEX

COMPUTER TOOLS AND TECHNIQUES INDEX

(Bold Type indicates that the chapter author regards this as one of the most significant elements of the course.)

DISCIPLINE INDEX

EDUCATIONAL BELIEFS INDEX

(Bold Type indicates that the chapter author regards this as one of the most significant elements of the course.)

REFERENCES INDEX